THE MIKE OLDFIELD
CHRONOLOGY

The Recording & Release History

Second Edition

by Patrick Lemieux

Published by
Across The Board Books™
Toronto, Ontario, Canada

The Mike Oldfield Chronology. Copyright © 2018 by Patrick Lemieux. All Rights Reserved. This book may not be used or reproduced, in whole or in part, without written permission from the copyright holder(s) except in the case of limited Fair Dealing or Fair Use (or similar with respect to territorial legislation) excerpts for critical articles and reviews. For information address Across The Board Books at: contact@acrosstheboardbooks.ca

Visit us at: www.acrosstheboardbooks.ca

The right of Patrick Lemieux to be identified as Author of this Work has been asserted by him in accordance with the Copyright Act of Canada, 1997.

ISBN: 978-1-926462-13-4

First Edition: April, 2014

Second Edition: May, 2018

Cover Artwork:
"Tubular World"
Acrylic on canvas
16" x 20"
Copyright © 2018, Patrick Lemieux

Last page artwork
"Maestro"
Acrylic on canvas
10" x 14"
Copyright © 2014, Patrick Lemieux

To John M. Sheridan,
Friend, Teacher
And the man who introduced me to Mike Oldfield's music.

Table Of Contents

The Sallyangie	1
The Whole World	6
Opus One	14
The Manor	19
Tubular Bells	22
Hergest Ridge	26
Ommadawn	34
Boxed	42
Cuckoo Song	49
Incantations	55
Platinum	58
QE2	69
Wonderland	78
Five Miles Out	85
Crises	96
Discovery	103
Pictures In The Dark	113
Shine	120
Islands	124
The Wind Chimes	130
Earth Moving	133
Amarok	140
Heaven's Open	146
Tubular Bells II	150
Elements	157
The Songs Of Distant Earth	165
Variations On A Rhythm	169
Voyager	174
XXV	178
Tubular Bells III	181
Guitars & The Millennium Bell	186
Music Virtual Reality	198
The Best Of Tubular Bells	201
Tr3s Lunas	204
Tubular Bells 2003	213
Maestro	217
Light + Shade	219
The Platinum Collection	223
Song For Survival	226
Music Of The Spheres	229
Tubular Bells Revisited	231
Hergest Ridge & Ommadawn Revisited	234
Incantations Revisited	237
Islanders	241
Tubular Beats	248
Man On The Rocks	256
Zombies	261
The 1984 Suite	264
Return To Ommadawn	270

WHAT IS THE MIKE OLDFIELD CHRONOLOGY?

The Chronology tracks the known recording and release dates of Mike Oldfield, including his albums, singles, projects, collaborations and guest appearances, with the additional aim to account for every known version of songs and music he worked on.

What you will find in this book is a chronological list of dates compiled from many sources. These dates range from exact days, to months, to seasons and to years, based on how specific the source material was. It is presented here in the most linear fashion for ease of reference and simplicity. Some entries are marked Date Unknown, because, despite exhaustive research, the date could not be found. These entries are placed where they seemed mostly like to have occurred, given what is known at the time of print.

You will also find descriptions of every known song version, including demos, out-takes, edits, remixes, extended versions and released live versions. Each such description is presented in the following way:

- Demos and Out-takes, both released and unreleased and with a few exceptions, appear with the date the sessions were recorded.

- Single Versions, Edits, Remixes, Non-album tracks, etc., appear with their original release dates.

- Live tracks released as singles or otherwise individually are listed with the concert where they were recorded. One exception to this is the *Exposed* live album, as the date of this concert has not been released to the public by the record company for contractual reasons. The tracks from this release are noted with the album's release.

The intention of including the descriptions of these alternate versions is to expand upon the information in the Chronology by illustrating what makes the version of the track unique compared to the album version.

The releases noted are primarily those of the UK, Europe and North America, a result of the fact that these territories had this information more readily available and consistently recorded. Not all known single or album releases and album formats (8-track, cassette, etc.) are included in this Chronology. More complete listings of releases and their variants can be found online.

The various collections and singles sometimes list different names for the same song version, so generally that version will be listed throughout the book with the name by which it was originally called on its first release, even if it contradicts the later release's sleeve or label. This is done to clarify the actual content of the release over what is listed.

In the descriptions of the tracks, the Chronology is not noting the listed runtime from the sleeve or label, but rather that of runtime of the file lifted from the original vinyl or CD source, so there may be a margin of difference of several seconds.

Guest appearances were sometimes harder to track when it came to releases, so not every individual release or re-issue that features Mike Oldfield is noted.

I did my best to avoid mistakes or inaccuracies, and to be as transparent as possible. Should a mistake be found, it is hoped that the discrepancy is viewed as appearing despite my efforts to the contrary.

Lastly, thanks go out to everyone whose work prior to this release formed the foundation on which the Chronology could be built. As complete a list as possible of the research material of the Chronology appears in the Bibliography section.

Patrick Lemieux
April, 2018

The Sallyangie

1953

-May 15-
Michael Gordon Oldfield is born to Dr. Raymond Oldfield and Maureen Oldfield, at Battle Hospital, Reading, Berkshire, England.

-May 19-
Michael Oldfield's birth certificate is registered.

1960

-Date Unknown-
Michael Oldfield composes the following at his family home, Reading, Berkshire, England:
"The Dying Swan" – A simple piano piece **Oldfield** came up with on the family's grand piano.

1962

-Date Unknown-
Around this time, **Michael Oldfield** begins visiting folk clubs with his sister, Sally Oldfield, and her friend Marianne Faithfull.

1963

-Dates Unknown-
According to his autobiography, *Changeling*, around the age of nine or ten, **Michael Oldfield** was composing what he called "little tunes" on his father's acoustic guitar.

-Date Unknown-
Michael Oldfield plays live for the first time at a village hall, Reading, Berkshire, England, organized by a fellow young musician, Eddie Moss. **Oldfield** plays two songs.

This starts **Oldfield** playing local clubs with folk musicians. Around this time, **Michael** begins composing and performing his own pieces.

1965

-Date Unknown-
During his club days, **Michael Oldfield** writes the following:
"Caveman" - In a 1998 article in *Mojo* magazine, **Oldfield** says he wrote this piece first with the chords then adding "teenage angst lyrics" which he later didn't like.

1966

-Date Unknown-
The Oldfield family moves to Harold Wood, Greater London, England.

1967

-Date Unknown-
Sally and **Michael Oldfield** periodically visit Marianne Faithfull in London, England, at the flat Faithfull shares with Mick Jagger. **Michael** meets Jagger, Keith Richards and Anita Pellenberg during these visits.

-Date Unknown-
Sally and **Michael Oldfield** begin playing clubs in and around Harold Wood, Greater London, England, with Sally on vocals and **Michael** on guitar.

-Date Unknown-
Mick Jagger arranges a demo session for Sally and **Michael Oldfield** at Sound Techniques, London, England, with Gus Dudgeon as tape operator. Jagger is on hand for the recording, as well as a tabla player named Rafiq. **Oldfield** notes in his autobiography *Changeling* that he does not know what happened to the tapes. These are **Oldfield**'s first studio recordings.

1968

-Date Unknown-
Sally Oldfield meets John Renbourn at the Troubadour Folk Club in Bristol, England. He gives his recommendation to Transatlantic Records that Sally record an album of her songs. Sally recruits **Michael** to record with her.

-May 15-
Michael Oldfield drops out of school on his 15th birthday to pursue a career in music.

-Dates Unknown-
Sally and **Michael Oldfield** audition for Nat Joseph at Transatlantic Records, London, England, and are signed to record an album. Joseph suggests the name **The Sallyangie**, after Sally's name and the name of a Davey Graham instrumental.

-August-
The Sallyangie record their debut album at Sound Techniques, London, England (*Children Of The Sun* sessions). The album is produced by Nat Joseph. After the **Oldfields** record their parts, Joseph brings in session musicians Terry Cox (percussion) and Ray Warleigh (flute) to add to the recording, along with orchestral arrangements by David Palmer.
Additional tracks worked on include:
"Twilight Song"
"Song Of The Healer"

>"Twilight Song" 2:35
>Written by Sally Oldfield
>Appears on: Children Of The Sun (2002, 2003, 2011 & 2017 Re-issues)
>An upbeat number from the duo here, with a curious error in Sally's vocal track, where she cuts out around the 1:23 mark, as she sings "when the twilight comes." Her vocal track is still present for the rest of the song and the music is unaffected, so who knows what happened there? The end of the song sees Sally really trying to reach that high note.

>"Song Of The Healer" 3:03
>Written by Sally Oldfield
>Appears on: Children Of The Sun (2002, 2003, 2011 & 2017 Re-issues)
>Like in some of their other songs, Sally employs the folk technique of singing in such a way in places as to be almost speaking in clipped syllables (called staccato, for those musically inclined), whereas other parts on the same verse or line are sung without that effect. Other times, she employs a tremolo technique, that vibrating vocal sound, and alternates between the three in this

song so frequently that the unaccustomed ear may find it distracting. Despite that, she really does have an excellent voice.

-November-
Transatlantic Records releases **The Sallyangie**'s album *Children Of The Sun* (TRA 176) in the UK and Europe on LP. Track listing as follows:

"Strangers"
"Lady Mary"
"Children Of The Sun"
"A Lover For All Seasons"
"River Song"
"Banquet On The Water"
"Balloons"
"Midsummer Night's Happening"
"Love In Ice Crystals"
"Changing Colours"
"Chameleon"
"Milk Bottle"
"Murder Of The Children Of San Francisco"
"Strangers (Reprise)" – listed in the sleeve as "Strangers".

Note: **Michael** is credited by his full name, **Michael Oldfield**, on the sleeve credits, but as **"Mike Oldfield"** on LP label.

-Date Unknown-
The Sallyangie begins a UK tour of colleges and clubs which last about a year. Their brother, Terry Oldfield, is their driver. The tour is arranged by their new agent, Roy Guest.

-December 24-
Apollo 8 orbits the moon and astronauts Frank Borman, Jim Lovell and Bill Anders broadcast via NASA their reading of the Bible's Book of Genesis. **Mike Oldfield** would use an excerpt of this broadcast in 1993/1994 for his album *The Songs Of Distant Earth*.

1969

-Early 1969-
Warner Bros. releases **The Sallyangie**'s album *Children Of The Sun* (WS-1783) in North America on their Seven Arts Records on LP. Track listing as follows:

"Strangers"
"Lady Mary"
"Children Of The Sun"
"A Lover For All Seasons"
"River Song"
"Banquet On The Water"
"Balloons"
"Midsummer Night's Happening"
"Love In Ice Crystals"
"Changing Colours"
"Chameleon"
"Milk Bottle"
"Murder Of The Children Of San Francisco"
"Strangers (Reprise)" – listed in the sleeve as "Strangers".

Note: **Michael** is credited by his full name, **Michael Oldfield**, on the sleeve credits, but as **"Mike Oldfield"** on LP label.

The Sallyangie finish their UK tour.

The Sallyangie begin recording their second album, likely at Sound Techniques, London, England. The recordings feature additional production and orchestrations, possibly by the same musicians as *Children Of The Sun*. Tracks recorded include:
"Mrs Moon And The Thatched Shop"
"Branches"
"A Sad Song For Rosie"
"Colours Of The World" - **Mike** may not be on this track, no one is quite certain. Produced by Shel Talmy.
"Two Ships" – written by Carole Bayer and Toni Wine, previously recorded in 1968 by Maria Dallas. It may or may not feature **Mike**. Produced by Shel Talmy.
"Child Of Allah" - This could have **Mike** on it. Or not.
"Lady Go Lightly" – same as above.

> "Mrs Moon And The Thatched Shop" 6:18
> Written by Michael Oldfield
> Appears: Children Of The Sun (2002, 2003 & 2011 Re-Issues)
> This is a guitar improv piece with Mike on solo acoustic guitar, a dynamic piece that starts gently before alternating between dark, moody sections and ending with a truly maniacal rendition of "Three Blind Mice." Mike thrashes the guitar so intensely at some points, it sounds almost like an electric guitar. It's highly recommended that serious Oldfield fans seek out one of the *Children Of The Sun* CD re-issues to hear this material!
>
> "Branches" 6:45
> Written by Michael Oldfield
> Appears on: Children Of The Sun (2002, 2003 & 2011 Re-Issues)
> Here's another fantastic acoustic guitar improv piece from Mike. Keen-eared fans will recognize a melody which later appears on Amarok (the "Mad Bit" which starts at 15:00). The piece ends with some "Bah Bah Black Sheep."
>
> "A Sad Song For Rosie" 2:14
> Written by Michael Oldfield
> Appears on: Children Of The Sun (2002, 2003 & 2011 Re-Issues)
> Mike, apparently not being one to let a good idea go to waste, would re-record this piece with Paddy Moloney's bagpipes on *Ommadawn* (Part Two, Band 2, 5:20 to 10:04).

-March-
Michael Oldfield leaves **The Sallyangie** to pursue more rock-oriented music. The duo's second album remains unfinished and unreleased, though tracks from it appear on later re-issues of *Children Of The Sun*.

-August 8-
Transatlantic Records releases **Sallyangie**'s 7" single "Two Ships" in the UK on their sub-label Big T.

UK 7" single (Big 126):
"Two Ships" – a cover of the 1968 Maria Dallas song.
"Colours Of The World"

UK 7" single (Big 126) promo:
"Two Ships" – a cover of the 1968 Maria Dallas song.
"Colours Of The World"

"Two Ships" 3:17
Written by Wine/Bayer
Appears on: 7" single; Children Of The Sun (1996, 2002, 2003, 2011 & 2017 Re-Issues)
The original full title of this song is "Two Ships Passing In The Night" and it was previously recorded by Maria Dallas in 1968. The Sallyangie version is simply "Two Ships." The song is by the writing team of Carole Bayer and Toni Wine. It's unclear whether Mike appears on this track. The single misspells Toni Wine's last name as "Wie".

"Colours Of The World" 2:30
Written by The Sallyangie
Appears on: 7" single; Children Of The Sun (1996, 2002, 2003, 2011, 2017 Re-Issues)
Some lush backing accompanies this track, with Sally on vocals. It's unclear whether Mike appears on this track, as Sally did continue with Transatlantic after he left.

Note: The release date may actually be either July 29th or August 28th, reports differ. A date stamp on one release notes the "8-8-69," hence its listing here.

-Date Unknown-
Mike Oldfield auditions for the band Family as bass player and meets Roger Chapman. **Oldfield** doesn't get the job.

-Date Unknown-
Michael and Terry Oldfield form **Barefoot**, with Terry Oldfield on bass, **Michael** on lead guitar and with an unnamed drummer, possibly from Long John Baldry's band. Details are scarce. The band played only a reported three or four gigs around London, England, playing "heavy blues" according to Terry. Some claims have the "Piltdown Man" grunting vocal style first appearing during this time. **Barefoot**'s management is taken over by Roy Guest's assistant, Julie Creasy. In 2012, Terry would describe in the liner notes of the album *Journey Into Space* a song **Barefoot** used to play, which started and ended in a similar way as a track the two recorded years later for that album.

The Whole World

1970

-Date Unknown-
Julie Creasy joins Blackhill Enterprises, London, England, taking **Barefoot** with her to the new management company.

-March-
Michael Oldfield auditions for the job of bass player for Kevin Ayers' new backing band The Whole World, at the EMI offices, London, England. The band is needed for Ayers' upcoming tour in support of his debut solo album *Joy Of A Toy*. In addition to Ayers, the audition features avante garde composer/keyboardist David Bedford and sax player Lol Coxhill, both members of The Whole World. **Michael Oldfield** gets the bass player job with Kevin Ayers And The Whole World, which also includes Mick Fincher on drums.

-March 14-
Kevin Ayers And The Whole World debut at the Atomic Sunrise Festival, at the Roundhouse Club, London, England. The festival runs from March 9th to 15th and features David Bowie, Genesis, Hawkwind and many other acts. This starts the group's series of concert dates around the UK and mainland Europe.

-March 22-
Kevin Ayers And The Whole World perform at the Roundhouse Club, London, England, as part of the Implosion Festival.

-March 28-
Kevin Ayers And The Whole World perform at Le Bourget Airport, Paris, France, part of the Paris Festival. Also performing at the Festival is Pink Floyd, Bridget St. John and others.

-March 31-
Kevin Ayers And The Whole World perform at Tavern de l'Olympia, Paris, France. Bridget St. John is also on the bill. The show is filmed for *Pop 2*.

-April-
Kevin Ayers And The Whole World begin recording material for an album at Abbey Road Studios, London England. Sessions are produced by Kevin Ayers and Peter Jenner, and last until September 1970. **Michael Oldfield** uses the time to come into the studio early to experiment and learn both the instruments and gear.

-April 9-
Kevin Ayers And The Whole World perform at the Hampstead Country Club, Hampstead, England. Some sources list this concert on April 16th, it's unclear which is correct.

-April 12-
Kevin Ayers And The Whole World perform at Mothers, Birmingham, England.

-April 25-
Kevin Ayers And The Whole World perform at the Van Dyke Club, Plymouth, England.

-May 2-
Kevin Ayers And The Whole World perform at Kingston Polytechnic, London, England.

-May 3-
Kevin Ayers And The Whole World perform at the Esmeralda's, Bletchley, Milton Keynes, Buckinghamshire, England.

-May 7-
Kevin Ayers And The Whole World record a session for John Peel's radio show, at Paris Cinema, London, England:
"Love Is (Peel Session 05/07/70)"
"We Did It Again (Peel Session 05/07/70)" - Previously a Soft Machine song.

-May 9-
Kevin Ayers And The Whole World perform at Imperial College, London, England.

-May 10-
Kevin Ayers And The Whole World perform at The Marquee Club, London, England.

-May 20-
Kevin Ayers And The Whole World work on the following at Abbey Road Studios, London, England:
"Hat" - Bridget St. John provides guest vocals on this track. Ayers also previously recorded the track on February 20th for the BBC Radio show *Top Gear*, before **Michael** had joined the band.

> "Hat" 5:27
> Written by Kevin Ayers
> Appears on: Shooting At The Moon (2003 Re-Issue)
> A very zany, sometimes utterly manic piece on which Mike plays bass and likely provides backing vocals. Of interest to Oldfield fans is the brief reference to the song "Don Alfonso," which Mike would record with David Bedford a few years later. You can also clearly hear Bridget St. John's backing vocals throughout. According to the 2003 album liner notes, this is Take 4 of the track. The recording was mixed in 2003 for the re-issue.

Kevin Ayers And The Whole World records the following at BBC Studios, London, England, for the Alan Black Show. This session would later be released in 2005.
"Gemini Child (Alan Black session 05/20/70)"
"Lady Rachel (Alan Black session 05/20/70)"
"Shooting At The Moon (Alan Black session 05/20/70)"

> "Gemini Child (Alan Black session 05/20/70)" 3:13
> Written by Kevin Ayers
> Appears on: Kevin Ayers - The BBC Sessions 1970 - 1976
> A good version of the song that precedes the recording for the *Shooting At The Moon* album. This version is a bit rougher around the edges, but is pretty close to the final version.

> "Lady Rachel (Alan Black session 05/20/70)" 6:15
> Written by Kevin Ayers
> Appears on: Kevin Ayers - The BBC Sessions 1970 - 1976
> This song appears on Ayers' *Joy Of A Toy* album, so it's only natural that he'd record it with The Whole World. And a good version it is, too, worth tracking down by Mike Oldfield fans.

> "Shooting At The Moon (Alan Black session 05/20/70)" 2:57
> Written by Kevin Ayers
> Appears on: Kevin Ayers - The BBC Sessions 1970 - 1976
> This version is shorter than the album recording almost by half, basically making it a teaser version for the forthcoming LP.

-May 23-
Kevin Ayers And The Whole World perform at the 1832 Club, Windsor, England.

-May 30-
Kevin Ayers And The Whole World perform at Liverpool Stadium, Liverpool, England.

-May 31-
Kevin Ayers And The Whole World perform at the Farx Club, Potters Bar, Southall, England.

-Date Unknown-
Michael Oldfield adds the following to his live guitar repertoire with **Kevin Ayers And The Whole World**: "The Sailor's Hornpipe"

-June-
Kevin Ayers And The Whole World record the following at Abbey Road Studios, London, England:
"Gemini Child"
"Puis-Je?" – This track would be used as a non-album B-side.

> "Gemini Child" 3:16
> Written by Kevin Ayers
> Appears on: Odd Ditties; Shooting At The Moon (2003 Re-Issue)
> This unused track from the *Shooting At The Moon* sessions is excellent, with the band in fine form. Definitely a treat on the CD re-issue of the album; highly recommended. This track could easily have been a single instead of being left in the vault.

-June 6-
Kevin Ayers And The Whole World perform at Clitheroe Castle, Lancashire, England, during a free open air concert.

-June 7-
Kevin Ayers And The Whole World perform at the Locarno Ballroom, New Entertainment Centre, Bristol, England.

-June 9-
Kevin Ayers And The Whole World record tracks for BBC Radio's *Top Gear*. This session would later be released in 2005. Peter Jenner produced this sessions (as noted by the group pointing him out in the [many] dedications at the start of "We Did It Again."
"Derby Day (Top Gear 06/09/70)"
"The Interview (Top Gear 06/09/70)"
"We Did It Again/Murder In The Air (Top Gear 06/09/70)" – "We Did It Again" is another recording of the Soft Machine song. Also, **Mike Oldfield** has cited the repetitive nature of the song as being a big influence on his work later on "Tubular Bells" and beyond.

> "Derby Day (Top Gear 06/09/70)" 3:07
> Written by Kevin Ayers
> Appears on: Kevin Ayers – The BBC Sessions 1970 – 1976
> A waltz-timed bit of silliness here, bordering on being a novelty song. It's not hard to see the influence Kevin had on Mike, particularly when Oldfield came to recording off-beat ditties like "Don Alfonso," "Speak (Thou You Only Say Farewell)" and "Rite Of Man" in the years following. All the same, it's a fun number and worth finding.

> "The Interview (Top Gear 06/09/70)" 0:59
> Written by Kevin Ayers
> Appears on: Kevin Ayers – The BBC Sessions 1970 - 1976

Here's short track, with just Kevin and an electric guitar, and no Mike; noted here only because it was part of the session that day.

"We Did It Again/Murder In The Air (Top Gear 06/09/70)" 11:41
Written by Kevin Ayers
Appears on: Kevin Ayers - The BBC Sessions 1970 - 1976
"We Did It Again" was a song in the group's live repertoire that varied length every time they played it. Reportedly, some versions reached as much as 45 minutes in length (!). Clearly, they enjoyed playing it and experimenting throughout each performance. "Murder In The Air" takes over at the end of an intense jam session in the form of something like a radio sketch. Really, making sense of what's going on in this performance is futile, just enjoy.

-June 11-
Kevin Ayers And The Whole World perform at St. Michael's Hall, Oxford, England.

-June 19-
Kevin Ayers And The Whole World perform at Sophia Gardens, Cardiff, England.

-June 22-
Kevin Ayers And The Whole World perform at the Mercury Theatre, London, England.

-July 10-
Kevin Ayers And The Whole World perform at the Star, Croydon, England.

-July 11-
Kevin Ayers And The Whole World perform at the Aachen Open Air Pop Festival, Aachen, West Germany. The Festival runs from July 10th to 12th. The band's scheduled Euro-Pop '70 AZ Musikfest concert in Munich is cancelled, they perform at Aachen instead.

-July 12-
Lol Coxhill starts working on his album *Ear Of The Beholder*. He employs present and future members of **The Whole World** to contribute, including Kevin Ayers, David Bedford, **Mike Oldfield**, Dave Dufort and Robert Wyatt.

-Mid-July-
Kevin Ayers replaces drummer Mick Fincher with Robert Wyatt in **The Whole World**.

-July 18-
Lol Coxhill finishes his album *Ear Of The Beholder*, featuring **Mike Oldfield** on the tracks "Vorblifa - Exit" and "A Collective Improvisation."

Kevin Ayers And The Whole World perform at Queen Elizabeth's Grammar School for Boys, London, England.

Kevin Ayers And The Whole World perform at Hyde Park, London, England.

-July 19-
Kevin Ayers And The Whole World perform at the Implosion Festival, the Roundhouse Club, London, England.

-July 25-
Kevin Ayers And The Whole World perform at the Phun City Festival, Patching Ecclesden Common, Sussex, England. The Festival runs from July 24th to 26th.

-July 30-
Kevin Ayers And The Whole World perform at the VPRO Piknik, Gemeendecentrum, The Netherlands. Bridget St. John is also on the bill. The concert is filmed.

-August 1-
Kevin Ayers And The Whole World perform at Vondelpark, Amsterdam, The Netherlands.

-August 5-
Kevin Ayers And The Whole World perform at the Nice Jazz Festival, Nice, France. This concert is absent from some concert listings of the band.

-August 7-
Kevin Ayers And The Whole World perform at the Sussex Lewes Festival, Sussex, England.

-August 8-
Kevin Ayers And The Whole World performs at the Paradiso, Amsterdam, The Netherlands.

-August 9-
Kevin Ayers And The Whole World perform at the Pop Festival, Stade Municipal, Saint-Raphaël, France. Like the August 5th date, it's unclear if this show went on or was cancelled.

-August 21-
Kevin Ayers And The Whole World perform at the Lyceum Ballroom, London, England.

-September-
Kevin Ayers And The Whole World record the following at Abbey Road Studios, London, England:
"Butterfly Dance" – **Mike Oldfield** plays bass and guitar and The Ladybirds sing backing vocals on this track.

-September 4-
Kevin Ayers And The Whole World perform at the Lyceum Ballroom, London, England.

-Mid-September-
Robert Wyatt is replaced on drums by Dave Dufort in **The Whole World**.

Kevin Ayers And The Whole World record the following at Abbey Road Studios, London, England:
"Stars"[1] – **Mike** plays bass and The Ladybirds sing backing vocals on this track. *Odd Ditties* (1976) lists "September 1970" as the recording date. It also lists Dave Dufort as drummer (placing it here at the earliest, as he'd just joined the group). The 2003 re-issue of *Whatevershebringswesing* lists the recording date as "July 1971," which would have it recorded around the same time as it's eventual A-side track, "Stranger In Blue Suede Shoes."

Kevin Ayers And The Whole World complete their album *Shooting At The Moon* this month. The sessions ran from April to September.

-September 13-
Kevin Ayers And The Whole World perform at the Roundhouse Club, London, England.

-September 22-
Kevin Ayers And The Whole World are scheduled to perform at the Liverpool Philharmonic Hall, Liverpool, England, but the show is cancelled.

-September 23-
Kevin Ayers And The Whole World perform at the Newcastle City Hall, Newcastle, England.

-September 26-
Kevin Ayers And The Whole World perform at the Queen Elizabeth Hall, London, England. The London Sinfonietta accompanies the group for David Bedford's composition "The Garden Of Love," which is recorded by BBC Radio 3 for an October 20th broadcast. This recording is released in 1997.

"The Garden Of Love" 21:07
Written by William Blake (words) / David Bedford (music)
Appears on: The Garden Of Love
Mike plays bass on this piece, an avant garde work by Bedford. There are interesting melodic and musical passages and there are the expected moments of utter strangeness. I can only imagine what radio listeners tuning in thought of what they were hearing.

-October-
Kevin Ayers And The Whole World release their album *Shooting At The Moon* in the UK (Harvest SHSP 4005). **Michael** is credited as *Mike* Oldfield. He does not appear on the tracks "The Oyster And The Flying Fish" (which features Bridget St. John) and "Underwater." Track listing as follows:

Side 1:
1 a) "May I?"
1 b) "Rheinhardt & Geraldine"
1 c) "Colores Para Dolores"
2 a) "Lunatics Lament"
2 b) "Pisser Dans un Violon"

Side 2:
1 a) "The Oyster And The Flying Fish"
1 b) "Underwater"
1 c) "Clarence In Wonderland"
1 d) "Red Green And You Blue"
2 "Shooting At The Moon"

-October 9-
Kevin Ayers releases the 7" single "Butterfly Dance" on Harvest Records in the UK. The sleeve lists it only as a Kevin Ayers single, but the label credits **Kevin Ayers And The Whole World**.

UK 7" single (HAR 5027):
"Butterfly Dance"
"Puis-Je?"

UK 7" single (HAR 5027) promo:
"Butterfly Dance"
"Puis-Je?"

"Butterfly Dance" 3:45
Written by Kevin Ayers
Appears on: 7" single; Shooting At The Moon (2003 Re-Issue)
The lead single from the *Shooting At The Moon* sessions, despite not actually appearing on the original album. It would be included as a bonus track in 2003. The song starts with a gentle mood before picking up the pace into psychedelic, almost prog, rock. Mike plays bass in the first part and guitar in the second. A great track!

"Puis Je?" 3:41
Written by Kevin Ayers
Appears on: Butterfly Dance; 7" single; Shooting At The Moon (2003 Re-Issue)
A French re-recording of their track "May I?," which doesn't feature the truck intro heard on the English album version. That shaves 20 seconds off the run time. Mike plays bass.

-October 10-
Kevin Ayers And The Whole World perform at Central London Polytechnic, London, England.

-October 16-
Kevin Ayers And The Whole World perform at Falmer House, University of Sussex, Brighton, England.

-October 19-
Kevin Ayers And The Whole World cancel a show at Audimax, Hamburg, Germany.

Kevin Ayers And The Whole World perform at the Letchworth Youth Centre, Letchworth, England.

-October 26-
Kevin Ayers And The Whole World perform at the Dorothy Ballroom, Cambridge, England.

-October 30-
Kevin Ayers And The Whole World perform at Waltham Hall, Wolverhampton, England.

-October 31-
Kevin Ayers And The Whole World perform at Free Trade Hall, Manchester, England.

-November 6-
Kevin Ayers And The Whole World perform at Hatfield College of Technology, Hatfield, Hertfordshire, England.

-November 12-
Kevin Ayers And The Whole World perform at the Lyceum Ballroom, London, England. Bridget St. John is also on the bill.

-November 13-
Kevin Ayers And The Whole World perform at the All Night Rave at Thames Polytechnic, London, England.

-November 28-
Kevin Ayers And The Whole World perform at Liverpool Stadium, Liverpool, England.

-December 12-
Kevin Ayers And The Whole World perform in Nijmegen, The Netherlands.

-December 14-
Kevin Ayers And The Whole World perform at the Benefit For South American Political Prisoners, Salle de la Mutualité, Paris, France. A French TV station films the band both on and off stage for a feature on them and the concert.

-December 15-
Kevin Ayers And The Whole World perform at Verblifa-Hal, Dordecht, The Netherlands.

-December 16-
Kevin Ayers And The Whole World perform at Eksit, Rotterdam, The Netherlands.

-December 18-
Kevin Ayers And The Whole World perform at Rasa, Utrecht, The Netherlands.

-December 19-
Kevin Ayers And The Whole World perform at the Paradiso, Amsterdam, The Netherlands.

-December 20-
Kevin Ayers And The Whole World perform at Don Quichotte, Sittard, The Netherlands.

-Late December-
Mike Oldfield returns to England after suffering panic attacks and leaves **The Whole World**. While staying with his parents, he starts writing his own instrumental music:
"Opus One" – **Mike**'s compositions during his break from **The Whole World** which would eventually evolve into "Tubular Bells."

Opus One

1971

-January-
After a few weeks, Kevin Ayers asks **Mike Oldfield** to rejoin **The Whole World**. **Mike** agrees, on the conditions that he have a greater say in arrangements, take over lead guitar, bring in a new drummer and the group does more instrumental and progressive material.

Around this time, Ayers sets himself and **The Whole World** up in a rented house in Westbourne Gardens, Tottenham, London, England. While living there, **Mike Oldfield** would continue to compose his own music.

-January 9-
Kevin Ayers And The Whole World perform at Ewell Technical College, Ewell, Surrey, England, supported by Genesis and Queen.

-January 14-
Kevin Ayers And The Whole World perform at Arnolfini Gallery, Bristol, England, with the BBC Training Orchestra for Bedford's "The Garden Of Love."

-January 16-
Kevin Ayers And The Whole World perform at the Student Union, University of Manchester, Manchester, England.

-January 29-
Kevin Ayers And The Whole World perform at The Temple, London, England.

-January 31-
Kevin Ayers And The Whole World perform at Palais de Sports, Paris, France.

-February 6-
Kevin Ayers And The Whole World perform at Van Dyke Club, Plymouth, England.

-February 7-
Kevin Ayers And The Whole World perform at the Roundhouse Club, London, England, part of the Release Benefit.

-February 13-
Kevin Ayers And The Whole World perform at Théâtre des Amandiers, Nanterre, Paris, France.

-February 14-
Kevin Ayers And The Whole World perform at Le Piblokto, Dourges, France.

-February 20-
Kevin Ayers And The Whole World perform at Old Shire Hall, University of Durham, Durham, England.

-Date Unknown-
As per **Mike Oldfield**'s request, auditions are held for a new drummer and bass player for **The Whole World**.

-Date Unknown-
Lol Coxhill releases his album *Ear Of The Beholder* in the UK (Dandelion Records - DSD 8008) and North America (Ampex Records - C-10132), featuring **Mike Oldfield** on the tracks "Vorblifa - Exit" and "A Collective Improvisation."

> "Vorblifa - Exit" 6:35
> Written by Lol Coxhill
> Appears on: Ear Of The Beholder
> After some lengthy saxophone noodling by Lol, the track goes into a groovy jazz number with Mike on bass, before ending on some keyboard fiddling. If you like your music straightforward and uncomplicated, this is not for you.

> "A Collective Improvisation" 2:45
> Written by Lol Coxhill
> Appears on: Ear Of The Beholder
> Mike on bass again. This is a pretty free form performance here, with the group variously playing their instruments and making noise, without structure or collective rhythm. Not for the faint of heart.

-Late March-
Kevin Ayers records the following at Abbey Road Studios, London, England:
"There Is Loving" - written by Ayers, with arrangements by David Bedford. **Mike Oldfield** plays bass on this track.
"Among Us" - Written by David Bedford. **Mike Oldfield** plays bass on this track.

-March 27-
Kevin Ayers And The Whole World perform at Isleworth Polytechnic, London, England.

-April-
Kevin Ayers and **Mike Oldfield** re-organize **The Whole World** line-up, which now consists of David Bedford (keyboards and arrangements), **Oldfield** (lead guitar), William Murray (drums) and Andy Robertson (bass).

-April 15-
Kevin Ayers And The Whole World perform at the Marquee Club, London, England. Also on the bill is Bridget St. John.

-April 29-
Kevin Ayers And The Whole World perform at the Glen Ballroom, Llanelli, Dyfed, Wales.

-April 30 or May 1-
Kevin Ayers And The Whole World perform at Mid-Essex Technical College, Chelmsford, England. The exact date is unclear.

-May 15-
Kevin Ayers And The Whole World perform at the Implosion Festival, the Roundhouse Club, London, England.

-June-
Kevin Ayers starts recording his next album, employing some **Whole World** band members, including **Mike Oldfield** (lead guitar and bass), David Bedford (keyboards), Dave Dufort (drums), along with other artists and session musicians. The sessions occur at Abbey Road Studios, London, England, produced by Kevin Ayers and Andrew King, and last until August.
"Song From The Bottom Of A Well" - An early track recorded during these sessions, according to the 2003 *Whatevershebringswesing* CD re-issue liner notes.

-June 19-
Kevin Ayers And The Whole World perform at Kingham Hall, Watford, England.

-June 20-
Kevin Ayers And The Whole World are scheduled to play at Auvers-sur-Oise, France, but the festival is cancelled.

-June 23-
Kevin Ayers And The Whole World perform at City University London, London, England.

-Date Unknown-
Mike Oldfield records the following at Abbey Road Studios, London, England:
"Champagne Cowboy Blues" – Though not called this until later, **Oldfield** actually recorded much of the backing track himself while waiting for Kevin Ayers to arrive at the studio. **Mike** also had different lyrics sung by the studio staff. Ayers was apparently annoyed at first when he arrived, but then rewrote the lyrics and used **Mike**'s backing track as the foundation for the finished album version.

-July 3-
Kevin Ayers And The Whole World perform at Market Hall, Carlisle, England.

-July 4-
Kevin Ayers And The Whole World perform at Windsor Hall, Blackburn, England, at the Festival Of Contemporary Music.

-July 9-
Kevin Ayers records the following at Abbey Road Studios, London, England:
"Stranger In Blue Suede Shoes" – According to the Kevin Ayers *Odd Ditties* collection liner notes, **Mike Oldfield** does not appear on this track, though it is noted here because it is part of the album sessions.

-July 10-
Kevin Ayers And The Whole World perform at The Temple, London, England, during All Nighter.

-July 12-
Kevin Ayers And The Whole World perform at De Doelen, Rotterdam, The Netherlands, as part of a festival.

-July 21-
Kevin Ayers And The Whole World perform at Gamages, London, England.

-Late July-
Kevin Ayers breaks up **The Whole World**. Accounts from **Mike Oldfield** and others agree that the group had become unmanageable and were playing poorly for a variety of reasons (such as personality conflicts and heavy drinking).

-August 27-
Kevin Ayers releases his 7" single of "Stranger In Blue Suede Shoes" on Harvest Records in the UK. **Mike Oldfield** appears on the B-side "Stars."

UK 7" single (HAR 5042):	UK 7" single (HAR 5042) promo:
"Stranger In Blue Suede Shoes"	"Stranger In Blue Suede Shoes"
"Stars"	"Stars"

"Stars" 3:32
Written by Kevin Ayers
Appears on: Stranger In Blue Suede Shoes 7" single; Odd Ditties; Whatevershebringswesing (2003 CD Re-Issue)
As straightforward a rock track as you'll hear from Kevin Ayers, with some quiet parts and some heavier moments. Mike Oldfield plays guitar. Worth tracking down.

-Late August-
Kevin Ayers lends Mike **Oldfield** his two track tape machine with which to record his demos. **Oldfield** modifies Kevin Ayers' tape recorder to better allow him to record multiple tracks for his demos and sets to work recording the following at the former-**Whole World** band house, Westbourne Gardens, Tottenham, London, England. The sessions last several months, by all accounts from the point where Ayers left to tour with Gong (which went from late August '71 to January 2, '72) to **Mike** playing his "Opus One" demo for Ayers, David Bedford, Peter Jenner and others at Abby Road in January, 1972. At some point during this time, **Oldfield** returns to Harold Wood, Greater London, England, and continues writing and recording there.
"Tubular Bells (Long)" - the working title is "Opus One."
"Caveman Lead-In"
"Caveman"
"Peace Demo A"
"Peace Demo B"
"Hoover" - according to Tom Newman, **Oldfield** had a demo segment that featured a vacuum cleaner (a "Hoover," if you're English). Newman says he was fond of this piece, but was disappointed it didn't get used on the album. This demo has yet to be released.

"Tubular Bells (Long)" 22:54
Written by Mike Oldfield
Appears on: Tubular Bells 2003 DVD-A; Tubular Bells (2009 Ultimate Edition)
Well, here it is, Mike Oldfield's original demo recording of what would become "Tubular Bells (Part One)." All the movements are more or less worked out and much has been written about his process of writing each one. The recording is presented in its untouched state, complete with drop-outs and tape wear. It's a fascinating recording.

"Caveman Lead-In" 2:45
Written by Mike Oldfield
Appears on: Tubular Bells 2003 DVD-A; Tubular Bells (2009 Ultimate Edition)
This demo is what would become the "Bagpipe Guitars" section of "Tubular Bells (Part Two)." The guitars don't sound quite as bagpipe-like here, but are still heavy and grinding. As with all the 1971 demos, it's well worth checking out!

"Caveman" 5:05
Written by Mike Oldfield
Appears on: Tubular Bells 2003 DVD-A; Tubular Bells (2009 Ultimate Edition)
No Piltdown Man vocal, which Mike apparently would only later decide to add because he felt the piece needed something. Otherwise, it's pretty familiar and still just as fun as the album version.

"Peace Demo A" 7:00
Written by Mike Oldfield
Appears on: Tubular Bells 2003 DVD-A; Tubular Bells (2009 Ultimate Edition)
Here's one of two demos of what would become the second movement of "Tubular Bells (Part Two)," titled on the 2003 re-record as "Peace." Unlike the album version, this piece is longer, repeating the theme instead of building to the bridge which leads into "Bagpipe Guitar." After the repeat, there is a bit of music not reworked into "Tubular Bells."

"Peace Demo B" 4:21
Written by Mike Oldfield
Appears on: Tubular Bells 2003 DVD-A; Tubular Bells (2009 Ultimate Edition)
This a reworking of the "Peace" melody, only now including what would become the bridge into "Bagpipe Guitars," though after the bridge it repeats on a variation of the melody. Clearly, many of the pieces for "Tubular Bells (Part Two)" were written by this point, evidenced in these demos, awaiting their final arrangement on the album.

-Dates Unknown-
Mike Oldfield is offered a job by Alex Harvey, to join Harvey's band as guitarist. Harvey also asks **Mike Oldfield** to take over as replacement bass player (when Harvey is performing with the band Tear Gas) for the production of the musical *Hair*, Shaftsbury Theatre, London, England. **Mike** works the production for "about six months."

-Autumn – Winter-
Kevin Ayers finishes the *Whatevershebringswesing* sessions, at Abbey Road Studios, London, England. **Mike Oldfield** is a part these sessions.
"Opus One" – **Oldfield** plays his demo for Kevin Ayers, David Bedford, Peter Jenner and others during this time at Abbey Road. Bedford gives him positive feedback. The others reportedly "don't get it." **Mike** decides to shop the demo around to record companies.

-Late 1971-
Mike Oldfield losses the bass player job at *Hair* and is offered a bass player job with Arthur Louis. Louis begins recording demos at The Manor, Shipton-on-Cherwell, Oxfordshire, England. There, **Oldfield** meets Simon Heyworth and Tom Newman. A roadie drives **Oldfield** back to his mother's house to retrieve his "Opus One" demos, as **Mike** wants to play them to Heyworth and Newman, who are impressed and say they'll talk to owner Richard Branson. The Arthur Louis rehearsals last a week to ten days.

Note: According to the book *The Making of Mike Oldfield's Tubular Bells*, Arthur Louis and his group (including **Mike**) are the first band in at The Manor, followed by The Bonzo Dog Doo Dah Band. The Bonzo Dogs record there in November 1971, as noted on their album sleeve for *Let's Make Up And Be Friendly*. Both sessions are reportedly plagued by technical problems and delays due to The Manor still being under construction. **Oldfield** notes in his biography that construction work at The Manor was still going on during his first visit.

The Manor

1972

-January-
Kevin Ayers releases *Whatevershebringswesing* on Harvest Records in the UK (SHVL 800). **Mike Oldfield** does not appear on the tracks "Margaret," "Stranger In Blue Suede Shoes" and "Lullabye." Track listing as follows:

"There Is Loving/Among Us/There Is Loving (Reprise)"
"Margaret"
"Oh My"
"Song From The Bottom Of A Well"
"Whatevershebringswesing"
"Stranger In Blue Suede Shoes"
"Champagne Cowboy Blues"
"Lullabye"

-January 6-
Kevin Ayers, David Bedford, **Mike Oldfield**, Lol Coxhill, Dave Dufort, and The Ladybirds perform at the Paris Theatre, London, England, for *BBC In Concert*. The concert would later be released in 1992 and again in 2010. Set list as follows:

"Lady Rachel"
"May I?"
"Clarence In Wonderland"
"Whatevershebringswesing"
"There Is Loving"
"Margaret"
"Colores Para Dolores"
"All This Crazy Gift Of Time"
"Why Are We Sleeping?" - **Mike** essentially plays the "Ambient Guitars" movement of *Tubular Bells* during his solo here.

-February-
Kevin Ayers, David Bedford, **Mike Oldfield**, Dave Dufort and The Ladybirds record the following at Abbey Road Studios, London, England:
"Lady Rachel" - a Kevin Ayers song previously recorded for his solo *Joy Of A Toy* album. *Odd Ditties* notes this new recording was planned as a single, which goes unreleased. **Oldfield** plays bass.

> "Lady Rachel" 4:51
> Written by Kevin Ayers
> Appears on: Odd Ditties
> Vastly more polished than the earlier Alan Black session recording. The Ladybirds and Bedford's orchestrations elevate the song considerably, taking the song from good to great, yet retaining all the mood and ambience of earlier versions.

-April 4-
Kevin Ayers, David Bedford, **Mike Oldfield**, Lol Coxhill, Dave Dufort and Johnny Van Derek tape their appearance on *The Old Grey Whistle Test* TV show, London, England, performing "Oh My" and "May I?"

-Date Unknown-
Mike Oldfield records bass guitar for "Nurses Song With Elephants," the title track of David Bedford's album. Sessions take place at Marquee Studios, London, England.

-Date Unknown-
David Bedford releases his album *Nurses Song With Elephants* in the UK on Dandelion Records (2310 165). **Mike Oldfield** plays bass on the title track. Kevin Ayers also appears on the album.

> "Nurses Song With Elephants" 15:50
> Written by David Bedford (music)/William Blake (words)
> Appears on: Nurses Song With Elephants
> This track demonstrates just how avant garde David Bedford could get. At nearly 16 minutes long, the track varies between almost nonsensical instrument playing, cleverly evocative audio imagery and manic dissonance. This is art rock and prog rock combined and is certainly not everyone's cup of tea. It will definitely challenge the casual listener for the first 12 minutes, before becoming a more traditional song, setting William Blake's poem "Nurse's Song" to music. Mike's bass work can be easily heard in the last 3 and a half minutes.

-Late 1972-
Simon Draper of Caroline Records (later known as Virgin Records) invites **Mike Oldfield** to join him and Richard Branson for dinner on Branson's houseboat in London, England, to discuss recording "Opus One." Branson agrees to give **Oldfield** a week at The Manor to record it. **Oldfield** gives Draper and Branson a list of the instruments he'll need to record with.

Branson also signs **Mike Oldfield** to a contract for six albums, with an option for four more.

-September 8-
Virgin Records rents from Maurice Placquet Ltd the instruments needed by **Mike Oldfield** to record "Opus One." The date comes from the rental invoice. The Farsisa organ sent was apparently broken and some JBL gear did not show up.

-September 20-
Maurice Placquet Ltd issues an invoice to Virgin Records for the gear rented for the recording of **Mike Oldfield**'s "Opus One."

-November-
Mike Oldfield records the following at The Manor, Shipton-on-Cherwell, Oxfordshire, England, with producers Tom Newman and Simon Heyworth (this date is given in **Oldfield**'s autobiography):
"Opus One" - Most of this 25+ minute piece is recorded in a week. By all accounts, the Bonzo Dog Doo Dah Band was scheduled to use the studio immediately afterwards, so were around late in the week as **Oldfield** worked, inspiring him to use Vivian Stanshall to introduce the instruments, similar to the Bonzo Dog song "The Intro & The Outro." An early mix is sent to Simon Draper, who gives his approval.

Note: The album or project for which the Bonzo Dogs were recording is a bit unclear. It could not have been for their *Let's Make Up And Be Friendly* album (their last release together until 2007) as that was completed a year before (November 1971).

After finishing his week of recording, **Mike Oldfield** is allowed to stay at The Manor. He starts work on the second half, now planning an album with the record label's support. **Oldfield** records material during downtime at the studio, first finishing the end of "Opus One (Part One)," with Sally Oldfield providing backing vocals.

-December 1-
Mercury Records (Philips) releases **Sally Angie**'s "Child Of Allah" 7" singles in the UK and US (as a promo).

UK 7" single (6006 259):
"Child Of Allah"
"Lady Go Lightly"

US 7" single (40718):
"Sweet Child Of Allah"
"Lady Go Lightly"

US 7" single (40718) promo:
"Sweet Child Of Allah"
"Lady Go Lightly"

> "Child Of Allah" AKA "Sweet Child Of Allah" 2:56
> Written by S. Angie (AKA Sally Oldfield)
> Appears on: UK 7" single; US Promo 7" single; Children Of The Sun (2011 Re-Issue)
> The US releases title it "Sweet Child Of Allah." It's unknown of Mike appears on this track.
>
> "Lady Go Lightly" 3:02
> Written by S. Angie (AKA Sally Oldfield)
> Appears on: UK Child Of Allah 7" single; US promo Sweet Child Of Allah 7" single; Children Of The Sun (2011 Re-Issue)
> More laid back than its A-side, but still jaunty, but it's unclear if Mike is on this track either. If someone gets a chance, cold you please ask him. Thanks in advance.

-Late December-
Around Christmas, **Mike Oldfield** returns to Harold Wood, Greater London, England.

Tubular Bells

1973

-February-
Mike Oldfield returns to The Manor, Shipton-on-Cherwell, Oxfordshire, England, to finish recording his album (*Opus One* sessions). These sessions last until April.

-Spring-
Mike Oldfield works on the following at The Manor, Shipton-on-Cherwell, Oxfordshire, England.

> "Tubular Bells (Part One) (Scrapped Early Mix)" 25:12
> Written by Mike Oldfield
> Appears on: Tubular Bells (2009 Ultimate Edition)
> This rejected mix features a variety of differences compared to the standard album version. Though familiar as being the same recording used for the finished album mix, this version changes the presence of the various instruments throughout. It's a wonderful reminder that albums require a great deal of care and attention in the mixing process in order to get them sounding the way the artist wants. Compared to the standard album version, this mix is downright noisy in places.

-April-
Mike Oldfield completes his *Opus One* album sessions, including mixing and mastering. The date is noted in an April 2013 interview with *Sound On Sound*. Since February, tracks worked on include:
"The Sailor's Hornpipe" - A drunken monologue by Vivian Stanshall is recorded, but not included on the standard album version.

Richard Branson suggests *Breakfast In Bed* to replace the working title *Opus One*. **Mike** soon suggests *Tubular Bells*, based on both the wrecked bells from the recording sessions and Viv Stanshall's delivery of "...plus tubular bells!" on the recording. Trevor Key designs the cover art.

Test pressings done on recycled vinyl (standard for rock LPs at the time) are rejected by **Oldfield** and Branson has the album pressed on new vinyl, a process normally done only for classical releases.

Branson also insists that **Oldfield** launch the album with a live performance. Though **Mike** is reluctant, he agrees. **Mike** then starts orchestrating *Tubular Bells*, to be played by an ensemble.

-Date Unknown-
Tom Newman begins work on his first album, *Fine Old Tom*, at The Manor, Shipton-on-Cherwell, Oxfordshire, England. The sessions run until 1975 and feature **Mike Oldfield** on several tracks. Neil Innes (of The Bonzo Dog Doo Dah Band) and Lol Coxhill work on the album.

-May – June-
Mike Oldfield engineers the first session for the album *The Henry Cow Legend*, by Henry Cow, including part of the track "Nirvana For Mice." The sessions take place at The Manor, Shipton-on-Cherwell, Oxfordshire, England. **Oldfield** did this because engineer Tom Newman (who recorded the rest of the sessions) was indisposed that day.

-May 25-
Mike Oldfield releases *Tubular Bells* on Virgin Records (their debut release) in the UK (V2001) and North America (VR 13 105). Track listing as follows:

"Tubular Bells (Part One)"
"Tubular Bells (Part Two)" – contains "The Sailor's Hornpipe"

As excerpts from the album are used in many later releases, for clarity this book will refer to each movement in Parts One and Two by the individual titles given on the *Tubular Bells 2003* release. As follows:

Tubular Bells (Part One)
    "Introduction"
    "Fast Guitars"
    "Basses"
    "Latin"
    "A Minor Tune"
    "Blues"
    "Thrash"
    "Jazz"
    "Ghost Bells"
    "Russian"
    "Finale"

Tubular Bells (Part Two)
    "Harmonics"
    "Peace"
    "Bagpipe Guitars"
    "Caveman"
    "Ambient Guitars"
    "The Sailor's Hornpipe"

In the US, a unique 7" EP single is included in some radio promo LPs, titled *Tubular Bells - Excerpts from Virgin LP 13-105*.

Tubular Bells - Excerpts from Virgin LP 13-105
US 7" single (PR 196) promo:
"Excerpt 1A" - 2:44
"Excerpt 1B" - 1:40
"Excerpt 1C" - 5:36
"Excerpt 2A" - 2:35
"Excerpt 2B" - 2:40
"Excerpt 2C" - 1:30 - "The Sailor's Hornpipe (Single Version)"

    "Excerpt 1A" 2:44
    Written by Mike Oldfield
    Appears on: *Tubular Bells - Excerpts from Virgin LP 13-105* Promo 7" single
    This Excerpt starts with a much edited version of the "Introduction" movement before jumping to equally abbreviated "Fast Guitars" and "Basses" before ending on a snippet of "Latin," then fading out. This Excerpt is similar to, but even harder on the ears than, the later "Now The Original..." single versions. It also demonstrates just how unique and foreign the idea of *Tubular Bells* was in 1973, as Virgin scrambled to figure out how to promote the music to a listening audience used to much shorter pieces of music.

    "Excerpt 1B" 1:40
    Written by Mike Oldfield
    Appears on: *Tubular Bells - Excerpts from Virgin LP 13-105* Promo 7" single
    Starting with an edited ending of "Blues," this Excerpt then jumps to "Thrash" (skipping the opening bit), moves normally to "Jazz" (which jumps to the end) before proceeding normally into "Ghost Bells". Like with "Excerpt 1A," this is hard to listen to.

"Excerpt 1C" 5:36
Written by Mike Oldfield
Appears on: *Tubular Bells - Excerpts from Virgin LP 13-105* Promo 7" single
Following from the previous Excerpt, we pick up with "Russian" in its entirety before moving into the "Finale." The "Finale" is edited, jumping to Vivian Stanshall's introduction of the "grand piano." The track proceeds normally through the rest of the instruments, but after "plus...tubular bells!," it all falls apart with more really terrible edits before crashing to a sudden close. This was almost a halfway decent excerpt. Almost.

"Excerpt 2A" 1:40
Written by Mike Oldfield
Appears on: *Tubular Bells - Excerpts from Virgin LP 13-105* Promo 7" single
Here we start with "Peace," which gets trimmed down so we can stumble into "Bagpipe Guitars." Don't get comfortable, though, because no sooner do we arrive at the start of "Bagpipe Guitars" then we skip ahead to the end. The track fades out on the opening drum beats of "Caveman."

"Excerpt 2B" 2:40
Written by Mike Oldfield
Appears on: *Tubular Bells - Excerpts from Virgin LP 13-105* Promo 7" single
This Excerpt is a heavily edited version of "Caveman," ending on a fade out. Needless to say, the track suffers from all the cuts.

"Excerpt 3B" 1:30; AKA "The Sailor's Hornpipe (Single Version)" 1:34
Written by: Unknown (trad., arr. Oldfield)
Appears on: *Tubular Bells - Excerpts from Virgin LP 13-105* Promo 7" single; Take 4 EP; Impressions; Elements boxed set; The Best of Tubular Bells; The Platinum Collection
This cut is identical to its appearance on the original *Tubular Bells* album, but like "On Horseback" it's handy to have a stand-alone version of the track.

-Dates Unknown-
Mike Oldfield auditions and assembles his group for the upcoming *Tubular Bells* launch concert. The ensemble consists of:

Sally Oldfield	Terry Oldfield	David Bedford	Kevin Ayers
Viv Stanshall	Tom Newman	John Greaves	John Leig
Fred Frith	Tim Hodgekinson	Mick Taylor	Steve Hillage
Pierre Moerlen	Steve Broughton	Jon Field	Mundy Ellis
Ted Speight	Vulpy	Nick Haley	Ashley Mason
Simon Ingram Hill	Janet Townley		

Rehearsals take place over a few weeks.

-June 25-
Mike Oldfield and his ensemble perform *Tubular Bells* at Queen Elizabeth Hall, London, England. Mick Jagger is on hand (as his Rolling Stone bandmate, Mick Taylor, is playing electric guitar) and visits **Oldfield** in the dressing room to offer his support.

"Tubular Bells (Parts One + Two) (Live at Queen Elizabeth Hall)" 57:35
Witten by Mike Oldfield ("The Sailor's Hornpipe" trad. arr. Oldfield)
Appears on: Unreleased
A bootleg recording of this performance has surfaced and to hear the first live version is a real treat. Mike has said repeatedly that he was disappointed with this concert, that there were problems galore with it. Well, you can indeed hear some of them. The timing of the players is off in places (such as the end of the "Introduction," and the introduction of the instruments in the "Finale" is cringe-worthy, as you hear Viv Stanshall call in the wrong ones and the audience

chuckles). At certain points, it sounds like there's about to be a train wreck, wherein two players or sections trip over each other, but being professionals they pull it out, simply repeating bars until they all get back in synch. Overall, though, the performance is pretty good for a first time, given the complexity of the piece.

-August-
Henry Cow releases their album *The Henry Cow Legend* on Virgin Records, featuring **Mike Oldfield**'s engineering work on the track "Nirvana For Mice."

-Date Unknown-
Mike Oldfield assembles a new group for the forthcoming TV broadcast of "Tubular Bells (Part One)." The group consisted of Terry Oldfield, Steve Hillage, Pierre Moerlen, Mike Ratledge, Karl Jenkins, John Field, Mick Taylor, Fred Firth, John Greaves, Tim Hodgkinson and Geoff Leigh. **Oldfield** later says this period after the release of the album is a bit of a blur.

-Date Unknown-
Richard Branson informs **Mike Oldfield** that *Tubular Bells* is being used in the forthcoming film *The Exorcist*. **Oldfield** later says the phone call lasts only about ten seconds.

-Date Unknown-
Also released by Virgin Records is a picture disc edition of **Mike Oldfield**'s album *Tubular Bells* (VP2001).

-November 30-
Mike Oldfield and his ensemble perform "Tubular Bells (Part One)" for BBC 2's TV series *2nd House*, BBC Studios, Shepherd's Bush, London. This recording would be used on several releases in later years, such the *Elements* VHS and DVD, and both *Tubular Bells* Deluxe and Ultimate Editions.

> "Tubular Bells (2nd House Performance)" 24:36
> Written by Mike Oldfield
> Appears on: Elements DVD; Tubular Bells (2009 Deluxe Edition & Ultimate Edition)
> A fascinating alternative to the album version, the 2nd House live performance shows the group doing a pretty good job recreating Part One. It's an important recording, made only months after the release of the album, when Mike was barely able to do interviews and definitely not a tour. Being the second proper live rendition of the piece (after the Queen Elizabeth Hall show) and the first video recording, it's a great archive of a time when *Tubular Bells* was still taking the world by storm and when a good many people still hadn't heard it.

-Date Unknown-
Mike Oldfield moves to The Beacon, near Hergest Ridge, Herefordshire, England. He begins work setting up a home studio there.

-December 26-
The Exorcist film is released in North America. It uses passages from *Tubular Bells* throughout.

Hergest Ridge

1974

-Early 1974-
Mike Oldfield writes and records demos for his second album at his home, The Beacon, Herefordshire, England.
"Hergest Ridge (Part One) (1974 Demo)"
"Hergest Ridge (Part Two) (1974 Demo)"
"Chinese Tune" – Not much is known of this piece apart from its description in the March 16, 1974, issue of *Melody Maker*. It may have been rewritten into a part of what became *Hergest Ridge* or was an unused idea.

> "Hergest Ridge (Part One) (1974 Demo)" 20:19
> Written by Mike Oldfield
> Appears on: Hergest Ridge (2010 Deluxe Edition)
> It's pretty much all here, the various movements and structure of what would appear on the album. Of course, being a demo, it's a bit rough, but it shows Oldfield organizing his new ideas. Some of the parts are played by different instruments than would be on the album.

> "Hergest Ridge (Part Two) (1974 Demo)" 18:10
> Written by Mike Oldfield
> Appears on: Hergest Ridge (2010 Deluxe Edition)
> Like the Part One demo, this also shows Mike having assembled the parts of the piece into a cohesive whole, thus giving him a detailed map for the actual album sessions.

-February 3-
Atlantic Records releases the singles "Tubular Bells" in North America. The label advertises "Now the Original Theme from 'The Exorcist'."

US 7" single (VR-5510):
"Tubular Bells (Now the Original Theme from 'The Exorcist' - Version 1)"
"Tubular Bells (Part One - Finale Edit)"

US 7" single (VR-55100) promo:
"Tubular Bells (Now the Original Theme from 'The Exorcist' - Version 1)" (Mono)
"Tubular Bells (Now the Original Theme from 'The Exorcist' - Version 1)" (Stereo)

Canada 7" single (VR 5510):
"Tubular Bells (Now the Original Theme from 'The Exorcist' - Version 1)"
"Tubular Bells (Part One - Finale Edit)"

New Zealand 7" single (VS 101):
"Tubular Bells (Now the Original Theme from 'The Exorcist' - Version 1)"
"Tubular Bells (Part One - Finale Edit)"

Chile 7" single (V 96S):
"Tubular Bells (Now the Original Theme from 'The Exorcist' - Version 1)"
"Tubular Bells (Part One - Finale Edit)"

France 7" single (640 034):
"Tubular Bells (Now the Original Theme from 'The Exorcist' - Version 2)"
"Tubular Bells (Part One - Finale Edit)"

"Tubular Bells (Now the Original Theme from 'The Exorcist' - Version 1)" 3:18
Written by Mike Oldfield
Appears on: North American 7" singles; New Zealand 7" single; Chile 7" single; Japan 7" single; Tubular Bells - Original And Best; Icon; Lo Mejor De... Mike Oldfield
Until recently, it was believed that there was only one original 1974 version of the "Now..." single edit. Yannick Dély's independent research, after years of collecting, has uncovered multiple versions of this edit appearing on different 1974 singles. The most common of this infamous edit appeared in North America that year, released as a single to promote *The Exorcist* film, without approval from Mike. As such, Oldfield fans try to ignore it (it's rarely listed on collector websites, even very detailed ones). Disowned as it is by fans and Oldfield himself, it does exist and did do a good deal to help promote the album. The edit itself is pretty brutal. The "Introduction" portion is truncated before it jumps ahead to "Fast Guitars," then "Basses," then the "Introduction" starts over before fading out. Not the best representation of the album, by far.

"Tubular Bells (Now the Original Theme from 'The Exorcist' - Version 2)" 3:24
Written by Mike Oldfield
Appears on: France 7" single
Exclusive to France (so far, at least, it hasn't popped up anywhere else), this version edits the "Introduction" segments differently, with fewer cuts compared to Version 1. The "Fast Guitars" and "Basses" use the same segments as Version 1. At the end, the "Introduction" comes back and runs for 30 second before fading out.

"Tubular Bells (Part One - Finale Edit)" 4:39
Written by Mike Oldfield
Appears on: North American 7" single; North American 7" Promo
The B-side to the single is a more straightforward edit of the "Finale" section, starting just before the "grand piano" announcement and ending with a fade out after "...plus tubular bells!"

-February – March-
Kevin Ayers records his album *The Confessions of Dr. Dream and Other Stories* at Air Studios and Ramport Studios, London, England. **Mike Oldfield** records a guitar solo for "Everybody's Sometime And Some People's All The Time Blues."

-Date Unknown-
Warner Brothers releases *Music Excerpts from The Exorcist* soundtrack LP in North America (W 2774) and the UK (K56071), featuring two edits of "Tubular Bells (Part One)."

"Georgetown/Tubular Bells" 5:27
Written by Mike Oldfield
Appears on: Music Excerpts from The Exorcist
The version starts with audio from the film as the character Chris MacNeil leaves her home in Georgetown, segueing into the familiar "Introduction," which starts so quietly as to be nearly inaudible as it very slowly fades in. As it reaches the end, it fades into a segue of itself starting over, before fading out again.

"Tubular Bells (Short Soundtrack Excerpt)" 0:27
Written by Mike Oldfield
Appears on: Music Excerpts from The Exorcist
This is a very short clip of the "Introduction," which cuts off abruptly (because of the next track jumping in). Pointless as a standalone piece, but it works on the album as a whole.

-Spring-
Mike Oldfield starts recording his second album at Basing Street Studios, London, England (early *Hergest Ridge* sessions). These sessions go poorly as **Oldfield** dislikes the environment.

Mike Oldfield tries to work at a new studio (possibly Chipping Norton Studios, Oxfordshire, England), on *Hergest Ridge*, but does not use the booked time at all.

Mike Oldfield begins work anew on *Hergest Ridge*, now at The Manor, Shipton-on-Cherwell, Oxfordshire, England. Tracks worked on include:
"Theme From Tubular Bells" – this is a re-recording of the "Bagpipe Guitars" movement from "Tubular Bells (Part Two)." The new arrangement was an idea from George Martin (producer of The Beatles).
"Froggy Went A-Courting" – two versions of the song are recorded, using the same backing track. Both are duets between **Mike** and Vanessa Branson.

-April – May-
Robert Wyatt, formerly of **The Whole World**, works on his album *Rock Bottom*, at The Manor, Shipton-on-Cherwell, Oxfordshire, England. **Mike Oldfield** records guitar for the track "Little Red Robin Hood Hit The Road."

-May-
Mike Oldfield finishes recording *Hergest Ridge* at The Manor, Shipton-on-Cherwell, Oxfordshire, England. Sally and Terry Oldfield appear on the album, as does William Murray (formerly of **The Whole World**) and Clodagh Simonds.

A white label *Hergest Ridge* 7" test pressing is made by EMI Records for Virgin for a planned single that is not released.

UK *Hergest Ridge* 7" single (VS 112) white label test pressing:
"Spanish Tune (Original Version)" – unlisted
Note: Side B is a test tone

> "Spanish Tune (Original Version)" 3:10
> Written by Mike Oldfield
> Appears on: UK 7" single white label test pressing
> The existence of this single was long the stuff of legends, appearing in the discography of the Oldfield biography *10*. Little else was known at the time until collectors tracked down the white label test pressing and shared their findings online. This excerpt comes from the 1st movement of "Hergest Ridge (Part Two)," from 2:36 to 5:46 and starts at full volume. The later 2010 Hergest Ridge Deluxe Edition explains the single was planned but never issued (it also incorrectly says the excerpt comes from the finale of Part Two). The 2010 Deluxe Edition features a slightly different version from the original test pressing, as well (see the 2010 entry for more details).

Kevin Ayers releases his album *The Confessions of Dr. Dream and Other Stories* (Island Records) in the UK and North America on LP (ILPS 9263), featuring **Mike Oldfield** on the track "Everybody's Sometime And Some People's All The Time Blues."

> "Everybody's Sometime And Some People's All The Time Blues" 5:06
> Written by Kevin Ayers
> Appears on: The Confessions of Dr. Dream and Other Stories
> A laid back bit of blues that chugs along nicely. It features a good solo by Mike Oldfield and definitely worth the effort to hunt this down.

-June 1-
Kevin Ayers, John Cale, Brian Eno and Nice perform at the Rainbow Theatre, London, England. Among the guest artists is **Mike Oldfield**.

> "Everybody's Sometime And Some People's All The Time Blues (June 1, 1974)" 5:06
> Written by Kevin Ayers
> Appears on: June 1, 1974

This live version of the song is pretty much like the album version. Mike plays electric guitar and Kevin introduced him as he goes into his solo.

"Two Goes Into Four (June 1, 1974)" 2:37
Written by Kevin Ayers
Appears on: June 1, 1974
This is a pretty faithful version to the album cut, only with Mike on acoustic guitar. This is a great live album in itself, even the tracks Mike doesn't play on.

-June 28-
Mike Oldfield releases *Mike Oldfield's Single* in the UK and Europe.

UK 7" single (VS.101):
"Theme From Tubular Bells"
"Froggy Went A-Courting (UK Version)"

UK 7" single (VS.101) promo:
"Theme From Tubular Bells"
"Froggy Went A-Courting (UK Version)"

Germany 7" single (13 245 AT):
"Theme From Tubular Bells"
"Froggy Went A-Courting (German Version)"

Australia 7" AA-side single (K-5515):
Side A "Tubular Bells (Now the Original Theme from 'The Exorcist' – Version 3)"
Side AA "Froggy Went A-Courting (German Version)"

Netherlands 7" AA-side single (13 245 AT):
Side A "Tubular Bells (Now the Original Theme from 'The Exorcist' – Version 3)"
Side AA "Froggy Went A-Courting (German Version)"
Note: Side A is listed as "Extract From 'Tubular Bells."

Holland 7" AA-side single (13 245 AT):
Side A "Tubular Bells (Now the Original Theme from 'The Exorcist' – Version 3)"
Side AA "Froggy Went A-Courting (German Version)"
Note: Side A is listed as "Extract From 'Tubular Bells."

South Africa 7" AA-side single (PD 9990):
Side A "Tubular Bells (Now the Original Theme from 'The Exorcist' – Version 3)"
Side AA "Froggy Went A-Courting (German Version)"
Note: Side A is listed as "Extract From 'Tubular Bells."

Italy 7" single (VIN 45001):
"Tubular Bells (Introduction – Italian Edit)"
"Froggy Went A-Courting (German Version)"

"Theme From Tubular Bells" 3:55
Written by Mike Oldfield
Appears on: UK 7" single; Tubular Bells (2009 Stereo Mix Edition, Deluxe Edition & Ultimate Edition), The Collection
This is a gentler version of the "Bagpipe Guitars" part of *Tubular Bells*, with a brand new arrangement and a few of the additional musicians from the *Hergest Ridge* sessions, when it was recorded. It used to be something of a rarity, but re-issues have made it much easier to get a hold of. There's no excuse for serious Oldfield fans to not have this.

"Froggy Went A-Courting (UK Version)" 4:26
Written by: Unknown (16th Century trad., arr. Oldfield)
Appears on: UK Tubular Bells 7" single
Unlike the A-side, this recording of the traditional English folk song has been left off releases like the *Elements* boxed set and the 2009 Editions of *Tubular Bells*, making the only released formats the vinyl singles. Thus, it's part of a group of Mike Oldfield tracks many yearn to see both remastered and released digitally. The song itself is unlike other modern recordings of it made by rock/pop stars. Mike does away with the olde time "uh-huh" in each line and sings it in a less quaint way. The backing track, though, is as beautifully arranged as anything Mike was doing at the time and is the real reason to seek this track out. Listen closely to just how much is going on in there.

"Froggy Went A-Courting (German Version)" 4:26
Written by: Unknown (16th Century trad., arr. Oldfield)
Appears on: German Tubular Bells 7" single; Australia Tubular Bells 7" single; Italy Tubular Bells 7" single; Holland Tubular Bells 7" single
This version, found on the German single (and other territories, such as Australia), features a different vocal take each from Mike and Vanessa. It may even have been an earlier take, as it's less polished (Branson actually seems to start giggling after her lines near the end). The most noticeable difference is that Mike sings one of her verses instead of her ("The owls did hoot..." bit).

"Tubular Bells (Now the Original Theme from 'The Exorcist' - Version 3)" 4:00
Written by Mike Oldfield, Edited by Ad Bouman
Appears on: Australia 7" single; Holland 7" single; Netherlands 7" single; South Africa 7" single
This version starts with about the first 30 seconds of the "Introduction," before jumping to "Blues" (which is edited down), then "Thrash," followed by "Jazz" and closing with a segment of the "Finale," from right after the "...plus tubular bells!" part, fading out over the choral vocals. Not as chopped as Version 1, but not much better.

"Tubular Bells (Introduction - Italian Edit)" 4:35
Written by Mike Oldfield
Appears on: Italy 7" single
Unlike the earlier "Now..." Versions of "Tubular Bells (Part One)," this unique edit is entirely the "Introduction" movement, though it cuts down the first 5:50 of Part One to 4:35 by removing bits throughout.

Kevin Ayers, John Cale, Brian Eno and Nico release their live album *June 1, 1974*, in the UK on LP (Island Records ILPS 9291) featuring **Mike Oldfield** on two tracks.

-Date Unknown-
Virgin Records, via Atlantic Records, issues a promo 7" single for **Mike Oldfield**'s album *Tubular Bells* in North America.

US 7" single (E.P.-PR-199):	Canada 7" single (E.P.-PR-199):
"Tubular Bells (Part One - Finale Edit)"	"Tubular Bells (Part One - Finale Edit)"
"Tubular Bells (Part One - Finale Long Edit)"	"Tubular Bells (Part One - Finale Long Edit)"

"Tubular Bells (Part One - Finale Long Edit)" 7:40
Written by Mike Oldfield
Appears on: North American 7" Promo
Where the A-side of the promo single features the earlier edit that backed the US "Now..." *Exorcist* version, this is a more complete cut of the "Finale" of Part One. It removes much of the repeating bit before the introduction of the instruments by Vivian Stanshall. Not bad if you want a stand-alone version of the "Finale."

-July 24-
Robert Wyatt releases his album *Rock Bottom* on Virgin Records in the UK (V2017), featuring **Mike Oldfield** on the track "Little Red Robin Hood Hits The Road."

> "Little Red Robin Hood Hits The Road" 6:08
> Written by Robert Wyatt
> Appears on: Rock Bottom
> Mike's contribution to this track is limited to the first half, where his layered, repeating guitars create a hypnotic atmosphere under Wyatt's mellow, almost Pink Floyd-esque vocals (which may not be a coincidence, as Floyd's Nick Mason produced the album). The second half of the song (which doesn't feature Oldfield) is an odd, droning piece with curiously atonal spoken-word lyrics.

-July 31-
Virgin Records issues a test pressing of **Mike Oldfield**'s forthcoming album *Hergest Ridge* on LP (VR13-109) in the UK. The sleeve lists him as "Michael Oldfield."

-August-
David Bedford records his album *Star's End* with the Royal Philharmonic Orchestra via Manor Mobile at Barking Town Hall, Barking, Essex, England. **Mike Oldfield** co-produces the album with Bedford and records guitar on it. The score is conducted by Vernon Handley.

-August 28-
Mike Oldfield releases his album *Hergest Ridge* on LP in the UK (V2013), Europe and North America (VR 13-109). Track listing as follows:

"Hergest Ridge (Part One)"
"Hergest Ridge (Part Two)"

Also released by Virgin Records in the US is a promo LP edition of *Hergest Ridge* (VR 13-109), which features a breakdown of Parts One and Two on each side with the relative track lengths of each movement, as noted:

"Hergest Ridge (Part One)"
> Part I - 8:25
> Part II - 5:00
> Part III - 4:17
> Part IV - 3:31

"Hergest Ridge (Part Two)"
> Part I - 5:36 - contains "Spanish Tune."
> Part II - 3:03
> Part III- 7:03
> Part IV - 3:08

Note: the lengths of each part listed on the labels are arguably a little off by anywhere from 5 to 10 seconds or more, even accounting for the uninterrupted flow of music and judging by ear where one part starts and another ends. However, the times do provide a good general idea of the different movements.

Around this time, Virgin Records releases "Hergest Ridge" promo singles in the US and Australia.

US 7" single (PR-223) promo:
"Hergest Ridge (FM Version)"
"Hergest Ridge (AM Version)"

Australia 7" single (DJ-20) promo:
"Hergest Ridge (AM Version)" – listed as "Special Radio Cut."
"Hergest Ridge (AM Version)" – listed as "Special Radio Cut."

> "Hergest Ridge (FM Version)" 5:25
> Written by Mike Oldfield
> Appears on: US 7" Promo single
> Taking a similar approach as the "Now…" versions of "Tubular Bells (Part One)," this edit condenses "Hergest Ridge (Part Two)" via numerous cuts jumping from movement to movement.
>
> "Hergest Ridge (AM Version)" AKA "(Special Radio Cut)" 2:55
> Written by Mike Oldfield
> Appears on: US 7" Promo single; Australia 7" single
> The same segment as "Spanish Tune (Original Version)," this excerpt comes from the 1st movement of Part Two. It differs from the version heard on the test pressing by fading out a little earlier.

-September-
The Royal Philharmonic Orchestra performs *The Orchestral Tubular Bells* and *The Orchestral Hergest Ridge* at the Royal Albert Hall, London, England. They are arranged and conducted by David Bedford and recorded by Manor Mobile. *The Orchestral Hergest Ridge* was, like *The Orchestral Tubular Bells*, planned for an album release, but was never issued.

-September 1-
Virgin Records releases **Mike Oldfield**'s "Tubular Bells" single in Japan.

Japan 7" single (LL-2638-VR):
"Tubular Bells (Now the Original Theme from 'The Exorcist' - Version 1)"
"Tubular Bells (Part One - Finale Edit)"

-September 8-
Mike Oldfield performs with Robert Wyatt at Wyatt's concert at Theatre Royal Drury Lane, London, England.

-Date Unknown-
Mike Oldfield overdubs his guitar parts for *The Orchestral Tubular Bells* at Worcester Cathedral, Worcestershire, England, recorded by Manor Mobile.

-Date Unknown-
The Orchestral Tubular Bells is mixed at The Manor, Shipton-on-Cherwell, Oxfordshire, England.

-Date Unknown-
David Bedford releases his album *Star's End* on Virgin Records in the UK (V 2020), US (VR 13-114) and Europe on LP, co-produced by and featuring **Mike Oldfield** on guitar. Track listing as follows:

"Star's End (Part One)"
"Star's End (Part Two)"

> "Star's End (Part One)" 23:45
> "Star's End (Part Two)" 22:51
> Written by David Bedford
> Appears on: Star's End
> This is a fine example of avante garde classical music. The closest traditional work you could compare it to would be Holst's *The Planets*, only Bedford plays with the form by slipping in jarring (but not unpleasant) moments to surprise and enthral the listener. Throughout, a story of drama and excitement unfolds in the majestic vastness of space. Mike's guitar work is interwoven with the

orchestra and fits naturally into place, even as it sometimes rips through the passages like a blade. Oldfield seems to have been very involved in this work, more so than simply being a guest and playing a solo or two (he co-produced it, after all). An excerpt of Part One would later appear on *Boxed*, so that should give fans a taste of what to expect if they're interested in exploring this album (and they should, they won't regret it!).

-October-
Mike Oldfield records the following at The Manor, Shipton-on-Cherwell, Oxfordshire, England:
"Don Alfonso" – Written by Ted Waite. David Bedford sings and Kevin Ayers plays wine bottles (!). Bedford had previously recorded the song with Lol Coxhill for Coxhill's album *Ear Of The Beholder*.

-November-
Mike Oldfield begins writing his third album at The Beacon, Herefordshire, England. At one point, a working title for this third album is apparently *Pickles On My Glockenspiel*. He also records the following tracks there:
"Speak (Tho' You Only Say Farewell)" – A version of the old 1926 show tune by Ray Morello & Horatio Nicholls. David Bedford sings and plays piano, **Oldfield** sings backing vocals.
"In Dulci Jubilo (For Maureen) – A version of the traditional Christmas carol. It's likely the dedication to his mother was added in January.

Ommadawn

1975

-January-
Mike Oldfield begins recording his third album at The Beacon, Herefordshire, England (*Ommadawn* sessions). The sessions last until September.

-January 17-
Virgin Records releases *The Orchestral Tubular Bells* on LP in the UK (V 2026) and North America (VR 13-115) composed by **Mike Oldfield**, arranged and conducted by David Bedford, performed by the Royal Philharmonic Orchestra and **Mike Oldfield**.

A US promo edition of *The Orchestral Tubular Bells* LP (VR 13-115) is issued, which features a breakdown of Parts One and Two on each side with the relative track lengths of each movement, as noted:

"The Orchestral Tubular Bells (Part One)"
       Part One – 4:33
       Part Two – 3:41
       Part Three – 3:58
       Part Four – 4:30
       Part Five – 9:27

"The Orchestral Tubular Bells (Part Two)"
       Part One – 5:26
       Part Two – 7:02
       Part Three – 5:46
       Part Four – 4:25
       Part Five – 1:38

Note: this edition is also banded, with noticeable spaces between the grooves on both sides to visibly separate listed parts for ease of playback. The music on each side is uninterrupted.

Note: some sources list the release date as February 8th.

Around this time, Virgin Records releases a UK and Australia promo 7" single supporting *The Orchestral Tubular Bells*, featuring extracts from the album.

UK 7" single (VDJ-1) promo:
"Extract from the Orchestral Tubular Bells (Extract A)"
"Extract from the Orchestral Tubular Bells (Extract B)"

Australia 7" single (K-5840) promo:
"Extract from the Orchestral Tubular Bells (Extract A)"
"Extract from the Orchestral Tubular Bells (Extract B)"

       "Extract from the Orchestral Tubular Bells (Extract A)" 5:50
       Written by Mike Oldfield, arr. David Bedford
       Appears on: UK Promo 7" Single
       I have not heard this Extract, so cannot say what movement it represents.

"Extract from the Orchestral Tubular Bells (Extract B)" 6:00
Written by Mike Oldfield, arr. David Bedford
Appears on: UK Promo 7" Single
I have not heard this Extract, so cannot say what movement it represents.

-Mid-January-
Sally Oldfield calls **Mike** at The Beacon, Herefordshire, England, to inform him their mother, Maureen Oldfield, has died that day. A 2017 article published in *Music Radar* claims her death is a suicide.

-February 21-
Mike Oldfield releases his single "Don Alfonso" in the UK, Europe and Australia on Virgin Records.

UK 7" single (VS.117):
"Don Alfonso"
"In Dulci Jubilo (For Maureen)"

Germany 7" single (13 880 AT):
"Don Alfonso"
"In Dulci Jubilo (For Maureen)"

Australia 7" single (K 5856):
"Don Alfonso"
"In Dulci Jubilo (For Maureen)"

Germany 7" single (13 927 AT):
"Don Alfonso (German Version)"
"In Dulci Jubilo (For Maureen)"

"Don Alfonso" 4:12
Written by Ted Waite
Appear on: 7" single; The Platinum Collection
This is a bit of a goofy song, but don't be surprised if it grows on you a bit. It's one of the "abandoned" tracks, left off the *Elements* boxed set and even the *Hergest Ridge* Deluxe Edition, which featured its B-side, "In Dulci Jubilo (For Maureen)." It did see new life on *The Platinum Collection*, where it appears to be remastered. The video appears on both the *Elements* VHS and DVD.

"Don Alfonso (German Version)" 4:12
Written by Ted Waite
Appear on: German 7" single
As if Oldfield's back catalogue wasn't filled with enough strangeness, there's this. Credited only as "Paul" (AKA Roland Paulick) this person sings the song in German. That would be fine, except for the fact that he's simply singing over the English version, complete with David Bedford's vocals audible underneath. Why this exists is a question that may better be left unexplored. Exactly how official this version is is debatable (I'm guessing not very) and I can't really suggest anyone seek it out, unless oddball releases are your thing.

"In Dulci Jubilo (For Maureen)" 2:46
Written by: Unknown (Trad. arr. Oldfield, based on Pearsall)
Appears on: Don Alfonso 7" single; Hergest Ridge (Deluxe Edition)
Most Oldfield fans are familiar with Mike's 1975 hit of the same name, but some may not realize he previously recorded the piece a year earlier, handily adding the dedication to his mother, making it easier to differentiate the two. This is that earlier recording, featuring a sparser arrangement. Worth tracking down and most easily found on the 2010 *Hergest Ridge* Deluxe Edition CD.

-February 28-
Monty Python member Michael Palin is asked by Richard Branson to play the title role in the promo film for **Mike Oldfield**'s single "Don Alfonso," Palin declines as he is too busy.

-Early 1975-
Lea Nicholson records the following with **Mike Oldfield** (*The Concertina Record* sessions):
"Kopya!" - a traditional folk dance. This recording would later appear on the album in 1980, whereas the other tracks from this session remain unreleased. It's said Nicholson himself doesn't even have copies.

"Nancy"
"The Redesail Hornpipe" or "The Boys Of Bluehill" – Lea says he doesn't remember which of these he and **Mike** recorded.
"Jesu, Joy Of Man's Desiring" – written by Johann Sebastian Bach.

-Date Unknown-
Tom Newman finishes his album *Fine Old Tom*. The sessions since 1973 feature **Mike Oldfield** on several tracks. The following do not appear on the original album:
"Superman (Demo)" – **Mike** plays piano on the demo, but not the album version.
"Day Of The Percherons (Demo) – **Mike** plays guitar on the demo, but not the album version.
"Sweet 16"
"Have Mercy On My Eyes"

> "Superman (Demo)" 3:56
> Written by Ned Callan
> Appears on: Fine Old Tom (1995 CD Re-Issue); Faerie Symphony And Other Stories; Variations On A Rhythm Of Mike Oldfield
> This is a very Jamaican-influenced track with Mike on piano. Not as finicky as the album cut (that doesn't feature Oldfield), which arguably suffers from over production. Honestly, this is the better of two versions, because what it may lack in polish it more than makes up for in simplicity and fun.

> "Day Of The Percherons (Demo)" 2:29
> Written by Tom Newman
> Appears on: Faerie Symphony And Other Stories; Variations On A Rhythm Of Mike Oldfield
> This is a simple piece, with a repeating melody on which instruments are layered, including Mike on guitar. Curiously, this demo was released as 1999 bonus track on for Newman's Faerie Symphony album (and not Fine Old Tom, the album it would belong to) and David Bedford's Variations album in 1995. So, it's out there, just not where you'd expect to find it.

> "Sweet 16" 2:28
> Written by Tom Newman
> Appears on: Fine Old Tom (1995 CD Re-Issue)
> An acoustic country ditty, "Sweet 16" is a short foot-stompin', beer swillin' good time! Mike plays electric guitar.

> "Have Mercy On My Eyes" 4:40
> Written by Tom Newman
> Appears on: Fine Old Tom (1995 CD Re-Issue); Variations On A Rhythm Of Mike Oldfield
> Some good old blues rock, complete with piano and harmonica, on a song that could well have been on the album. Mike plays bass.

-Spring-
A rough mix of the following is copied and sent to Virgin Records. It's eventually stored in their archives and is forgotten.
"Ommadawn" – this is **Mike Oldfield**'s original recording of Part One.

> "Ommadawn (Lost Version)" 17:107
> Written by Mike Oldfield
> Appears on: Ommadawn (2010 Deluxe Edition)
> Mike spent months writing and recording this material and the oft-told story is that the tape stock he was using turned out to be of poor quality, leading to the tape wearing out or disintegrating after the many overdubs he'd done, rendering it unusable. The result was Mike having to re-record that material all over again. The re-recorded version is what appears on the album as Part One. I guess everyone involved forgot a copy had been made at some point in the spring and thus the

original recording was considered lost to the ages until 2010, when that copy was found, much to fans' delight.

The differences are noticeable throughout. It's still recognizable as "Ommadawn (Part One)," but there are some unique arrangements not used on the re-recorded version. The most obvious difference comes in around the 12:39 mark, where what sounds like a drunken bar conversation between two men comes in. It's amusing, but it really does throw off the mood of the piece and it's probably a good thing it was not included in the re-recording.

At some point after the copy is sent to Virgin, **Oldfield** discovers the problem with the tape stock and is forced to record "Part One" over again at Beacon, Herefordshire, England.

"Ommadawn" - **Mike** notes that the sessions for "Part One" lasted several months, where as "Part Two" was recorded in about a week.

"On Horseback" - written by **Mike Oldfield** (words and music) and William Murray (words).

"A Sad Song For Rosie" - This **Sallyangie** guitar improvisation is re-recorded by **Mike** with bagpiper Herbie (and later Paddy Moloney) and appears on "Part Two." (In a January 23, 1976, interview with Disco Express, **Mike** says two acoustic pieces of his were developed into *Ommadawn*. "A Sad Song For Rosie" would seem to be one of those pieces.

"Ask Me No Questions" - written by Bridget St. John and previously recorded by her, it was recorded one day during the *Ommadawn* sessions and remains unreleased by mutual agreement between the two, despite being an apparently excellent recording.

-June-

Mike Oldfield records his guitar parts for David Bedford's album *The Rime Of The Ancient Mariner*, at The Beacon, Herefordshire, England.

-July 28-

Virgin Records releases a quadraphonic version of **Mike Oldfield**'s album *Tubular Bells* in the UK. This first quad mix is not a true 4 channel mix, but a modified stereo mix with phasing. The first 40,000 pressings feature this mix, until a proper 4 channel mix is released with the same catalogue number (VQ2001).

> "Tubular Bells (Part Two) (1975 Quad Mix)" 23:30
> Witten by Mike Oldfield ("The Sailor's Hornpipe" trad. arr. Oldfield)
> Appears on: Tubular Bells (1975 Quadrophonic Remix)
> The quad mix features the sound of a model airplane which travels from speaker to speaker, to showcase the 4 channels. It comes in after "The Sailor's Hornpipe and is not really part of piece. However, Oldfield and Tom Newman did like playing with model airplanes while working, so there is that connection.

-August-

The Edgar Broughton Band mixes their album *Bandages* with **Mike Oldfield** at The Beacon, Herefordshire, England. **Oldfield** also performs on the tracks "Speak Down The Wires," "The Whale" and "Frühling Flowers (For Claudia)."

-Date Unknown-

Tom Newman releases his album *Fine Old Tom* in the UK (Virgin V2022), Europe and the US (Antilles AN 7042), featuring **Mike Oldfield** on "Sad Sing," "Suzie" and "Ma Song."

> "Sad Sing" 2:24
> Written by Tom Newman
> Appears on: Fine Old Tom; V; Faerie Symphony And Other Stories
> This is a bouncy folk song and well worth tracking down. Mike's guitar work stands out wonderfully.

> "Suzie" 3:34
> Written by Tom Newman
> Appears on: Fine Old Tom

Written in waltz time, with Mike on guitar, finds Tom recreating the '50s-style love song like you'd hear at a high school dance.

"Ma Song" 2:06
Written by Tom Newman
Appears on: Fine Old Tom
Employing a classic blues rhythm evoking dusty railroad tracks to forgotten towns, this is a short but sweet number. Mike has a guitar solo.

-Date Unknown-
Virgin Records releases a 2xLP sampler, titled *V*, of its artists' music, including **Mike Oldfield**'s "Don Alfonso (Long Version)." It also includes "Sad Sing" by Tom Newman, featuring **Mike Oldfield**.

UK *V* Sampler 2xLP (VD 2502)
Spain *Las Cosas Del "Virgin Sound"* - *V* Sampler 2xLP (88588-XH)
France *V* Sampler 2xLP (940.801)
Germany *V* Sampler 2xLP (88 588 XBT)
Yugoslavia *V* Sampler 2xLP (VD 2502)
Italy *V* Sampler 2xLP (AVIL 2502)
1979 Italy *V* Sampler 2xLP Re-issue (ORL 8309/8310)

"Don Alfonso (Long Version)" 6:05
Written by Ted Waite
Appear on: V
The more well-known Oldfield recording of the song is actually an edit of this version, removing an instrumental part, a chorus and a verse which can be heard here.

-Date Unknown-
David Bedford releases his album *The Rime Of The Ancient Mariner* in the UK (V 2038), featuring **Mike Oldfield** on guitar.

"The Rime Of The Ancient Mariner (Part Two)" 20:32
"The Rime Of The Ancient Mariner (Part Two)" 20:38
Written by Samuel Taylor Coleridge (words), Susato (music, arr. Bedford), Traditional (arr. Bedford), David Bedford (music)
Appears on: The Rime Of The Ancient Mariner
The entire album is the poem of the same name, by Coleridge, set to music by Bedford, and Mike plays guitar throughout the album. Most notable is his variations on melodies that he wrote for *Hergest Ridge*, so don't be surprised if some of his playing sounds very familiar. He also appears on the traditional sea shanty "The Rio Grande," which appears in "Part Two." If you like David Bedford's other work, this is worth exploring. A remixed excerpt of "Part Two" appears on the Oldfield boxed set, *Boxed*, in 1976.

-September-
Mike Oldfield finishes recording and mixing *Ommadawn*. Sessions between January and September take place at The Beacon, Herefordshire, England, for most of the album and at The Manor, Shipton-on-Cherwell, Oxfordshire, England, for the Jabula percussion parts. Among the other artists to appear on the album are: Terry Oldfield, Sally Oldfield, Bridget St. John, Clodagh Simonds, William Murray, Leslie Penning, Pierre Moerlen and Paddy Moloney. During these last sessions, engineer Phil Newell works on the album with **Mike**, including the following parts:
"Sad Song For Rosie" - Paddy Moloney records his uilleann bagpipe parts for this section after the rest of "Part Two" was complete.
"Ommadawn (Part One) 5th movement" - Newell is present for **Oldfield**'s recording of the guitar parts of this movement and the subsequent mixing of the album.

Note: Newell also later says that he is uncredited because the sleeve was printed before both his involvement and the completion of the album. He says there was a delay in finishing the album, resulting in the sleeves being printed before the album was done.

-October-
Mike Oldfield records the following at The Manor, Shipton-on-Cherwell, Oxfordshire, England:
"In Dulci Jubilo" - **Mike** recycles some of the backing track of the 1974 recording, in addition to recording new parts.

-October 15-
Virgin Records makes a test pressing at Columbia Recording Studios, New York, New York, US, of **Mike Oldfield**'s forthcoming album *Ommadawn*.

-October 28-
Mike Oldfield releases his album *Ommadawn* in the UK (V 2043), Europe and North America (PZ 33913) on LP on Virgin Records. This date is noted in the 2010 *Ommadawn* Deluxe Edition liner notes. Track listing as follows:

"Ommadawn (Part One)"
"Ommadawn (Part Two)" - contains "On Horseback."

Note: "On Horseback" is not listed as a separate track and is only referred to in passing in the original liner notes as "the horse song."

Note: Some sources list the release date as October 21st.

The standard Canadian LP and US promo LP pressings (both PZ 33913) feature noticeable bands in the grooves of the vinyl which visibly separate the different movements/sections of music. Each band is noted on the label with its length. As the US promo LPs notes "The music on this album is uninterrupted and the banding is a visual device for the convenience of radio programmers."
The bands listed are as follows:

"Ommadawn (Part One)"
    Band 1 - 4:07
    Band 2 - 4:07
    Band 3 - 3:39
    Band 4 - 4:25
    Band 5 - 2:56

"Ommadawn (Part Two)"
    Band 1 - 5:21
    Band 2 - 4:46 - from "A Sad Song For Rosie."
    Band 3 - 3:38
    Band 4 - 3:22 - "On Horseback," unlisted as such.

-Autumn-
Mike Oldfield moves out of The Beacon, Herefordshire, England, to Througham Slad, Gloucestershire, England, and starts renovations to turn it into a home studio.

-November 14-
Mike Oldfield releases his "In Dulci Jubilo" 7" single in the UK, Europe and Australia.

UK 7" single (VS 131):
"In Dulci Jubilo"
"On Horseback (Single Version)"

Germany 7" single (16 655 AT):
"In Dulci Jubilo"
"On Horseback (Single Version)"

Italy 7" single (VIN 45004):
"In Dulci Jubilo"
"On Horseback (Single Version)"

Spain 7" single (VIN 45004):
"In Dulci Jubilo"
"On Horseback (Single Version)"

Australia 7" single (K-6214):
"On Horseback (Single Version)"
"In Dulci Jubilo"

New Zealand 7" single (VS 131):
"In Dulci Jubilo"
"On Horseback (Single Version)"

On or around this date, a "Theme From Ommadawn" promo 7" single is released in North America.

US 7" single (ZS8 9505):
"Theme From Ommadawn"
"On Horseback (Single Version)"

US 7" single (ZS8 9505) promo:
"Theme From Ommadawn" (Mono)
"Theme From Ommadawn" (Stereo)

Canada 7" single (ZS8 9505) promo:
"Theme From Ommadawn"
"On Horseback (Single Version)"

On or around this date, "An Extract From Ommadawn" promo 12" single is released in the UK.

UK 12" single (VDJ. 9) promo:
"An Extract From Ommadawn – Part I"
"An Extract From Ommadawn – Part II"

"In Dulci Jubilo" 2:52
Written by: Unknown (Trad. Arr. Oldfield, based on Pearsall)
Appears on: 7" single; France Ommadawn LP; Boxed; Netherlands Ommadawn LP; Take Four single; Impressions; Mike Oldfield's Wonderland; Music Wonderland; The Complete Mike Oldfield; The Complete Mike Oldfield 7" Promo single; The Mike Oldfield Christmas EP; Elements: The Best Of Mike Oldfield; Elements boxed set; Collection; The Mike Oldfield – The Collection; The Platinum Collection; Ommadawn (2010 Deluxe Edition); Icon; Moonlight Shadow – The Collection; 2013 UK Record Store Day Single; 2016 Collaborations LP
Similar to the "For Maureen" recording (and in fact it uses parts of that version's backing track), but by comparison this version sounds fuller and more complete. I guess Mike felt he could improve upon the first version and the result is one of his most popular hits. This track has become one of his most widely used pieces for collections of his work, so it's pretty easy to get a hold of as far as non-album tracks go.

"On Horseback (Single Version)" 3:23
Written by Mike Oldfield (words & music) & William Murray (words)
Appears on: In Dulci Jubilo 7" single; Theme From Ommadawn 7" single; Impressions; 1986 Ommadawn Picture Disc CD; 1986 Canada Ommadawn CD Re-issue; 1991 US Ommadawn CD Re-issue; Elements boxed set
There's no difference between the track that appears on the single and on the album, but it is nice to have a stand-alone version.

"Theme From Ommadawn" 3:32
Written by Mike Oldfield
Appears on: US 7" single; Canada 7" single; US 7" single promo; France 7" single
This remix condenses the 4th and 5th movements of Part One and does so extremely well. As brilliant as the original is, this shortened version gets right to the point and loses none of the thrilling momentum of the album version. Find it and play it loud!

"An Extract From Ommadawn – Part I" 7:18
Written by Mike Oldfield
Appears on: UK 12" single promo
I have not heard this extract, but the runtime suggests it might be the 4th and 5th movements from Part One, similar or identical to the excerpt that appeared on later collects starting with *Episodes*. Or it could be the closing 7+ minutes of the album, similar to the excerpt later used on *Mike Oldfield's Wonderland*.

"An Extract From Ommadawn – Part II" 3:25
Written by Mike Oldfield
Appears on: UK 12" single promo
I have not heard this extract, but the runtime suggests it might be "On Horseback."

-Date Unknown-
Virgin Records in France re-issues **Mike Oldfield**'s album *Ommadawn (Featuring In Dulci Jubilo)* as a gatefold LP (940 529). Track listing as follows:

"Ommadawn (Part One)"
"Ommadawn (Part Two – Edit)"
"In Dulci Jubilo"

"Ommadawn (Part Two – Edit)" 13:47
Written by Mike Oldfield
Appears on: Ommadawn (Featuring In Dulci Jubilo); 1986 Ommadawn Picture Disc CD; 1986 Canada Ommadawn CD Re-issue; 1991 US Ommadawn CD Re-issue
Because this French edition of the album removes "On Horseback" and replaces it with "In Dulci Jubilo" as a separate track, "Ommadawn (Part Two)" is shorter, ending at the point where "On Horseback" would come in. One wonders why "On Horseback" was taken off, since the standard Part Two only has a runtime of 17:17. Adding "In Dulci Jubilo" would only put side two at around 20:09 (50+ seconds longer than side one). The Netherlands 1976 *Ommadawn* release would do exactly that with no problem. This version of Part Two without "On Horseback" would reappear on some CD re-issues where "On Horseback" was made its own track.

Boxed

1976

-January
Mike Oldfield records the following at Througham Slad, Gloucestershire, England.
"Argiers" – The traditional folk tune, with Les Penning on recorder.
"Portsmouth" – The traditional folk tune, also with Penning on recorder.

Virgin Records releases **Mike Oldfield**'s album *Ommadawn* as a quadraphonic mix in the UK on their V2 label (QV 2043).

-February-
Kevin Ayers releases a rarities compilation *Odd Ditties* LP (SHSM 2005) and cassette (TC-SHSM 2005) on Harvest in the UK. **Mike Oldfield** appears on several of the tracks. Track listing as follows:

"Soon, Soon, Soon"
"Singing A Song In The Morning"
"Gemini Child" – features **Mike Oldfeld**.
"Puis Je?" – features **Mike Oldfeld**.
"Butterfly Dance" – features **Mike Oldfeld**.
"Stars" – features **Mike Oldfeld**.
"Stranger In Blue Suede Shoes"
"Jolie Madame"
"Lady Rachel" – features **Mike Oldfeld**.
"Connie On A Rubber Band"
"Fake Mexican Tourist Blues"
"Don't Sing No More Sad Songs"
"Take Me To Tahiti"
"Caribbean Moon"

-March-
Virgin Records releases the **Mike Oldfield** album *The QS Quadrophonic Ommadawn* LP in the UK on their V2 label (QVQS 2043).

Note: it's unclear if this LP was issued commercially or only as a promo (*The Virgin Discography: The 1970s*).

-Date Unknown-
With a boxed set planned of **Mike Oldfield**'s three studio albums, non-album tracks and collaborations, remixing begins on the following:
Hergest Ridge – remixed by **Mike Oldfield**
Ommadawn - remixed by **Mike Oldfield** and Phil Newell

-Date Unknown-
Tom Newman recruits **Mike Oldfield** to record on his follow-up album, at The Argonaut Studio, London, England, on the track "Just For Old Times." The album and this track are not released until 1995, due to Newman parting ways with Virgin Records.

"Just For Old Times" 4:35
Written by Tom Newman
Appears on: Live At The Argonaut
This slow waltz country number has some good Mike guitar and is worth tracking down. Good stuff.

-Date Unknown-
Director Tony Palmer films **Mike Oldfield** for his documentary *All You Need Is Love: The History of Popular Music*. **Mike** is interviewed and recorded performing excerpts from compositions, at Througham Slad, Gloucestershire, England.

-July-
Mike Oldfield records guitar parts for the tracks "The Phaeacian Games" and "The Sirens" for David Bedford's album *The Odyssey*, at Througham Slad, Gloucestershire, England. Bedford engineers the session.

The Edgar Broughton Band releases their album *Bandages* in the UK on LP (NEMS NEL 6005), featuring **Mike Oldfield** on the tracks "Speak Down The Wires," "The Whale" and "Frühling Flowers (For Claudia)."

> "Speak Down The Wires" 3:15
> Written by Robert Edgar Broughton
> Appears on: Bandages
> Mike plays dulcimer on this track.
>
> "The Whale" 5:34
> Written by Robert Edgar Broughton
> Appears on: Bandages
> Mike plays steel guitar in this track, but his work doesn't stand out very much
>
> "Frühling Flowers (For Claudia)" 5:03
> Written by Robert Edgar Broughton
> Appears on: Bandages
> Mike plays both harp and ARP (an early keyboard synth instrument). Like the other two Bandage tracks, it's hard to pick him out in the piece. Normally in his collaborations his work is distinctive, but these three tracks sort of leave me wondering. Mike has said working with other artists tended to either find him taking over or being buried in background, so maybe the latter is happening here.

-August-
Mike Oldfield and David Bedford write and record the following at Througham Slad, Gloucestershire, England.
"First Excursion"

David Bedford releases his album *The Odyssey* on Virgin Records in the UK & North America (V 2070), and Europe, featuring **Mike Oldfield** on "The Phaeacian Games" and "The Sirens."

> "The Phaeacian Games" 3:59
> Written by David Bedford
> Appears on: The Odyssey; Boxed; 2016 Collaborations LP
> A bright and almost triumphant piece demonstrating just how well Bedford and Oldfield worked together. It's really no wonder they kept appearing on each other's releases. Mike's guitar soars and compliments Bedford's arrangements.
>
> "Sirens" 10:17
> Written by David Bedford
> Appears on: The Odyssey
> This is a long, haunting piece that invokes the dangerous loneliness of the sea and the temptation of the Sirens' call. Mike's guitar comes in at the end, as our hero passes into safety, having been tied to the mast of the ship to prevent him following the creatures to his doom.

-Date Unknown-
For the forthcoming **Mike Oldfield** *Boxed* set project, the following is worked on:
Tubular Bells – remixed by Phil Newell and Alan Perkins, this was the last remix to be done. It was undertaken by Newell primarily as **Oldfield** wanted to move onto other projects. Phil later presents his work to **Mike**, who approves it. At the time, several elements of the multitrack are missing or erased, so have to be replaced, recorded by Manor Mobile with Alan Perkins.

-October 29-
Mike Oldfield releases his 4xLP boxed set, *Boxed*, in the UK (VBOX1) and Europe. It collects his three studio albums (now remixed) and features an addition LP of non-album tracks and collaborations. The 3 albums are new quadraphonic remixes which are also stereo compatible.

LP 1: *Tubular Bells* (1976 Boxed Edition)
"Tubular Bells (Part One – Boxed Remix)"
"Tubular Bells (Part Two – Boxed Remix)"

Note: some editions of the Spanish *Boxed* (28009-XF) do not include "The Sailor's Hornpipe".

LP 2: *Hergest Ridge* (1976 Boxed Edition)
"Hergest Ridge (Part One – Boxed Remix)"
"Hergest Ridge (Part Two – Boxed Remix)"

LP 3: *Ommadawn* (1976 Boxed Edition)
"Ommadawn (Part One – Boxed Remix)"
"Ommadawn (Part Two – Boxed Remix)"

LP 4: *Collaborations*
"The Phaeacian Games" David Bedford
"An Extract from 'Star's End'" David Bedford
"The Rio Grande (Boxed Version)" David Bedford
"First Excursion"
"Argiers"
"Portsmouth"
"In Dulci Jubilo"
"Speak (Tho' You Only Say Farewell)" – a version 1926 Ray Morello & Horatio Nicholls song.

Note: The above *Collaborations* are listed with the title artist of the original track release, where applicable. "Argiers" and "Portsmouth" were released on Mike Oldfield singles, *Star's End*, *The Rime Of The Ancient Mariner* and *The Odyssey* are David Bedford albums, etc.

"Tubular Bells (Part One – Boxed Remix)" 25:47
Written by Mike Oldfield
Appears on: Boxed
There are noticeable mixing differences throughout, but the biggest being the reed and pipe organ parts were re-recorded for the *Boxed* version, as were the tubular bells. During the "Finale" movement the reed and pipe organ sound much softer and the tubular bells don't have the same sparkle. It gives the end of Part One a bit different sonic texture.

"Tubular Bells (Part Two – Boxed Remix)" 25:45
Witten by Mike Oldfield ("The Sailor's Hornpipe" trad. arr. Oldfield)
Appears on: Boxed
The finale here has been changed also, with the inclusion of the original monologue recorded by Vivian Stanshall, **Oldfield** and the others that drunken evening as Viv toured The Manor. The original release cut the monologue portion out and only used the fast "Sailor's Hornpipe" performance which follows the monologue. Here is the complete track. The later released version

on *Tubular Bells'* 2009 Deluxe Edition uses a different, newer remix of the piece, despite claiming to be the "original" "Sailor's Hornpipe."

"Tubular Bells (Part Two – Spanish Boxed Remix Edit)" 21:55
Witten by Mike Oldfield
Appears on: Boxed (Spanish Edition)
In an unusual move, the Spanish edition of the boxed set does not feature "The Sailor's Hornpipe" at all, either the standard album version or the monologue version. The track ends after the "Ambient Guitars" movement.

"Hergest Ridge (Part One – Boxed Remix)" 21:29
"Hergest Ridge (Part Two – Boxed Remix)" 18:43
Written by Mike Oldfield
Appears on: Boxed; Hergest Ridge (1976 LP to 2010 CD releases)
Mike did a full remix of the *Hergest Ridge* album for *Boxed* and the result is an almost entirely new version of the album. Among the changes is the removal of the lead guitar parts and layered vocals in places, giving this new mix a much lighter, mellow feel. Mike apparently preferred this mix to the original for a long time, declaring it the default mix for future releases, such as CD remasters. That changed in 2010 with the release of the *Hergest Ridge* Deluxe Edition, which uses the original mix, even as the basis for the updated 2010 Stereo Mix. Owning both versions has its rewards, as each offers a different perspective on the same music, as well as insight into the perfectionist nature of Mike Oldfield towards his work.

"Ommadawn (Part One – Boxed Remix)" 19:18
"Ommadawn (Part Two – Boxed Remix)" 17:20
Written by Mike Oldfield, "On Horseback" written by Mike Oldfield (words & music) & William Murray (words)
Appears on: Boxed;
Actually more of a remaster than a remix, as the tracks sound a bit clearer on this version. Changes to the mix are minor and rather subtle. Mike's on record saying he was extremely happy with how *Ommadawn* turned out, so it's unlikely he felt there was much work to do a year after the original album came out.

"An Extract from 'Star's End'" 7:33
Written by David Bedford
Appears on: Boxed; 2016 Collaborations LP
This extract is the last 7 and a half minutes from Part One, highlighting some of Mike's most dynamic playing on the album. It's a good representation of *Star's End* as a whole and if you like this piece, you might want to track down the entire album.

"The Rio Grande (Boxed Version)" 6:34
Written by: Unknown (Trad. Arr. Bedford)
Appears on: Boxed; 2016 Collaborations LP
This version of the song is a bit different from the one which appears on *The Rime Of The Ancient Mariner*. The album mix has some organ work playing throughout it, carrying over from the previous movement. The organ part is not present on here. The *Boxed* version is also a mix of two separate pieces from Part Two: "The Rio Grande" song itself and a guitar solo by Mike, which on the original album features narration spoken over it. On the *Boxed* Version, this closing solo is absent the narration. As an extract from the album, it holds up well and is a beautiful song and arrangement in its own right.

"First Excursion" 5:54
Written by Mike Oldfield & David Bedford
Appears on: Boxed; William Tell Overture 7" single; Elements boxed set; Ommadawn (2010 Deluxe Edition); Moonlight Shadow – The Collection; 2016 Collaborations LP

Of all the Oldfield/Bedford collaborations, this is the only piece genuinely co-written by both men together, where previously one appeared as a guest on the other's work. This dark, almost brooding instrumental features Mike on guitar and David on piano, both playing around discordant melodies they seem to sort of throw back and forth at each other. The end result is a very dramatic, powerful track.

"Argiers" 3:59
Written by: Unknown (Trad. Arr. Oldfield)
Appears on: Boxed, European Portsmouth 7" single; William Tell Overture 7" single; Elements boxed set; Ommadawn (2010 Deluxe Edition); 2016 Collaborations LP
Mike arranges this traditional folk tune by transposing the notes down a key, whereby the previously upbeat melody (in a major key) becomes mysterious and haunting, almost lonely (in a minor key). The process is called diatonic transposition and it should come as no surprise to Oldfield fans that he'd play around with a quaint melody and turn it into something unexpectedly riveting. For comparison, if you're not familiar with the traditional arrangement of "Argiers," it tends to normally sound something like "Portsmouth." Neat, huh?

"Portsmouth" 2:00
Written by: Unknown (Trad. Arr. Oldfield)
Appears on: Boxed; Portsmouth 7" single; 1977 Russia William Tell Overture 7" single; Impressions; Mike Oldfield's Wonderland; Music Wonderland; Episodes; The Complete Mike Oldfield; The Complete Mike Oldfield 7" Promo single; The Best Of Mike Oldfield: Elements; Elements boxed set; The Mike Oldfield Christmas EP; XXV: The Essential Mike Oldfield; Collection; The Platinum Collection; Ommadawn (2010 Stereo Mix & Deluxe Editions); Mike Oldfield - The Collection; Icon; Lo Mejor De... Mike Oldfield; 2016 Collaborations LP
This traditional English folk tune dates back at least as far as the 16th Century. The single release would reach number 3 in the UK charts. Like "In Dulci Jubilo," it's incredibly easy to find, having appeared on practically every Mike Oldfield collection.

"Speak (Tho' You Only Say Farewell)" 2:53
Written by Ray Morello & Horatio Nicholls (AKA Lawrence Wright)
Appears on: Boxed; Portsmouth UK 7" single; 2016 Collaborations LP
This old dance hall waltz was previously recorded by such artists as the New Princes Toronto Band and Dora Vayne & Gerald Adams, whose recordings both date from 1926. Oldfield and Bedford perform it as intended: a duet with staggered, repeating vocals. Straight out of the Roaring Twenties, it's a song which may sound very earnest and weird to modern listeners, but its utter lack of irony is part of the charm. Mike later said in 1999, when asked what the worst record he ever made was, he cites this. Oh well. That probably explains why it never saw a re-issue after this year apart from the 1989 CD re-issue of *Boxed*. It disappeared again until 2016 with the standalone LP release of *Collaborations*.

Also on this date, **Mike Oldfield** releases his "Portsmouth" 7" singles in the UK, Europe and North America to support *Boxed*.

UK 7" single (VS 163):
"Portsmouth"
"Speak (Tho' You Only Say Farewell)" – a version
1926 Ray Morello & Horatio Nicholls song.

UK 7" single (VS 163) promo:
"Portsmouth"
"Speak (Tho' You Only Say Farewell)" – a version
1926 Ray Morello & Horatio Nicholls song.

Ireland 7" single (VS 163):
"Portsmouth"
"Speak (Tho' You Only Say Farewell)" – a version
1926 Ray Morello & Horatio Nicholls song.

Spain 7" single (17.422-A):
"Portsmouth"
"Argiers"

Italy 7" single (VIN 45008):
"Portsmouth"
"Argiers"

Germany 7" single (17.422-A):
"Portsmouth"
"Argiers"

Netherlands 7" single (17 422-AT):
"Portsmouth"
"Argiers"

US 7" single (ZS8 9510):
"Portsmouth"
"Argiers"

US 7" single (ZS8 9510):
"Portsmouth" (Mono)
"Portsmouth" (Stereo)

Canada 7" single (ZS8 9510):
"Portsmouth"
"Argiers"

Australia 7" single (K-6582):
"Portsmouth"
"Argiers"

Note: Some sources list the release date as November 29th.

-Late 1976-
Mike Oldfield records the following at Througham Slad, Gloucestershire, England:
"The Path"
"Vivaldi Concerto In C" - written by Antonio Vivaldi, as "Concerto Com Molti Stromenti C Major, RV 558, Allegro".
"William Tell Overture" - written by Gioachinio Rossini.
"Woodhenge"

Note: It's been said that **Oldfield** recorded other Vivaldi and/or other classical works during these sessions, though no other tracks have surfaced.

> "The Path" 3:31
> Written by Mike Oldfield
> Appears on: Shine 7" & 12" singles; Elements boxed set
> "The Path" was recorded in 1976 (part of it can be heard in the documentary *Reflection* in 1977), but wasn't released until it appeared on the "Shine" single ten years later. A gentle composition, with acoustic guitar, glockenspiel and synth strings, it is a great instrumental!

> "Vivaldi Concerto In C" 3:52
> Written by Antonio Vivaldi
> Appears on: Elements boxed set; The Mike Oldfield Christmas EP
> This is a pretty faithful adaptation, even accounting for the change in instrumentation. The recording went unreleased until 1993, when it appeared on the *Elements* boxed set.

-November 22-
Pekka Pohjola works on his album *Keesojen Lehto* (English title: *The Mathematician's Air Display*) at Througham Slad, Gloucestershire, England. Prior to this, Pohjola had recorded the basic tracks for two pieces at Marcus Music, Stockholm, Sweden. **Mike Oldfield** is heavily involved with this project, co-producing, engineering, mixing and performing throughout the album. The sessions last two weeks, and Sally Oldfield and Pierre Moerlen are also involved.

-December 5-
Pekka Pohjola finishes recording and mixing his album *Keesojen Lehto* at Througham Slad, Gloucestershire, England. Tracks worked on with **Mike Oldfield** include:
"Hands Straighten The Water" - **Mike** plays acoustic and electric guitars, and mixes this track with Paul Lindsay. Sally Oldfield sings on this track.
"The Mathematician's Air Display" - **Mike** plays guitar and mixes this track. Pierre Moerlen plays drums.

"The Consequence Of Head Bending, Part One: The Pain Left Melting" – **Mike** plays guitar and mixes this track with Paul Lindsay. Pierre Moerlen plays percussion.
"The Consequence Of Head Bending, Part Two: The Plot Thickens" – **Mike** plays guitar and percussion. Pierre Moerlen plays glockenspiel.
"False Start From The Shadows" – **Mike** plays whistle and mandolin, and mixes this track with Paul Lindsay. Sally sings on this track and Pierre plays drums.

The album is later mastered at Utopia Studios, London, England.

Cuckoo Song

1977

-January 25-
David Bedford and an ensemble of musicians, including **Mike Oldfield** on guitar, perform his album *The Odyssey* live at the Royal Albert Hall, London, England. The show is recorded by the BBC and later released in 2011.

-February 11-
Mike Oldfield releases his "William Tell Overture" 7" single in the UK, Europe and South Africa.

UK 7" single (VS 167):
"William Tell Overture"
"Argiers"

South Africa 7" single (PD 1467):
"William Tell Overture"
"Argiers"

Ireland 7" single (VS. 167):
"William Tell Overture" – listed as "The William Tell Overture."
"First Excursion"

Germany 7" single (17 480 AT):
"William Tell Overture" – listed as "The William Tell Overture."
"First Excursion"

Netherlands 7" single (17 480 AT):
"William Tell Overture" – listed as "William Tell."
"First Excursion"

Italy 7" single (VIN 45010):
"William Tell Overture"
"First Excursion"

Russia 7" single (6079 201):
"William Tell Overture" – listed as "The William Tell Overture."
"Portsmouth"

"William Tell Overture" 3:56
Written by Gioachinio Rossini, arr. Oldfield
Appears on: 7" single, The Complete Mike Oldfield, The Complete Mike Oldfield Promo 12" single, Elements boxed set, The Mike Oldfield Christmas EP, The Platinum Collection, Mike Oldfield – The Collection
This famous overture from the opera *William Tell* is probably better known to most people as *The Lone Ranger* theme and a piece used ironically for any fast paced movie or TV show scene these days. So, unsurprisingly, Mike's version has a much lighter feel while retaining the same energy as the original. There's still a lot going on, many little musical details that may require several listens to fully appreciate.

-February 14-
David Bedford and an ensemble of musicians, including **Mike Oldfield** on guitar, perform his album *The Rime Of The Ancient Mariner* at Queen Elizabeth Hall, London, England. The show is recorded by the BBC.

-March-
Pekka Pohjola releases his album *Keesojen Lehto* (aka *The Mathematician's Air Display*) in Finland (LRLP 219) and the UK (V 2084). The album features **Mike Oldfield**.

Note: Because of the different releases featuring different album titles, track titles and track indexing points, this Chronology will use the 2010 UK re-issue by Esoteric Records.
Track listing as follows:

"The Perceived Journey – Lantern / The Sighted Light"
"Hands Straighten The Water"
"The Mathematicians Air Display"
"The Consequences Of Head Bending
      Part One: The Pain Is Melting
      Part Two: The Plot Thickens"
"False Start Of The Shadows"

"Hands Straighten The Water" 4:33
Written by Pekka Pohjola
Appears on: The Mathematician's Air Display
Some releases list this at "Hands Calming The Water," which makes a bit more literal sense. The first part of track is almost classical, with a slow, steady arrangement that gradually builds up layers of synth strings and guitar (by Mike) without overpowering the piece. The second part is much lighter, with Pekka's piano accompanied by Sally's vocals, which also gradually layer. Mike's guitar comes back in and the track builds to a crescendo.

"The Mathematician's Air Display" 6:42
Written by Pekka Pohjola
Appears on: The Mathematician's Air Display
Part of the melody sounds suspiciously like Bizet's *Carmen*. Otherwise an interesting track, building on top of repeated patterns; and whether this was Mike's influence or not, the piece does end up sounding a lot like his approach.

"The Consequences Of Head Bending" 15:14
Written by Pekka Pohjola
Appears on: The Mathematician's Air Display
Some releases list this as "The Consequences Of Indecisions" and it's sometimes two separate tracks, "Part One: The Pain Is Melting" and "Part Two: The Plot Thickens." Mike plays guitar on both. "Part One" is a darker, guitar driven piece and "Part Two" (which starts at 4:20) is less dramatic, more rhythmic and keyboard driven in places, and longer (almost 12 minutes). Very good stuff!

"False Start Of The Shadows" 1:50
Written by Pekka Pohjola
Appears on: The Mathematician's Air Display
This is a frenetic piece, with Pekka, Mike, Sally and Pierre having a lot of fun on it. The main repeating melody gets downright silly at points and that only adds to it.

Note: The album seems to have presented the various release territories with something of a poser, resulting in the different companies deciding to market it in different ways. Pekka's native Finland released the album as *Keesojen Lehto* (translated as *The Grove Of Keesos*), credited (correctly) to Pekka himself, whereas Germany (Happy Bird 90 096) and The Netherlands (Happy Bird 90133 Picture Disc) released it (misleadingly) as a **Mike Oldfield** album titled *The Consequence Of Indecisions* in 1981. Also in 1981, the North American release couldn't seem to decide whose album it was and released it untitled, credited to **Mike Oldfield, Sally Oldfield, Pekka Pohjula** (US-101). Similarly, the 1982 German re-issue (Bellaphon BID 11002) credits it untitled to **Mike & Sally Oldfield / Pekka Pohjula.** As noted earlier, **Oldfield** himself performs on all but one track, co-produced the album with Pekka, and mixed and engineered various tracks, as well as most of it having been recorded at his Througham Slad studio, Gloucestershire, England. Despite that, it's still Pekka's album and **Mike** has never said otherwise or tried himself to tie it to his own releases (such as never using tracks from it on his own collections). All that being said, it's definitely an album that **Oldfield** fans should investigate.

-Spring-
Mike Oldfield begins early work on his *Incantations* album. He composes about 20 minutes of mostly string music (conducted by David Bedford) and plays it to Richard Branson and various Virgin Records executives. Virgin Records is unimpressed.

"Incantations (Early Version)" - This piece would become "Incantations (Part Four)" and some of "Part Three" after some further refining.

"Piano Improvisation"

"Northumberian"

> "Incantations (Early Version)" 20:00(?)
> Written by: Mike Oldfield (Words & Music), Kathleen Raine ("A Spell for Creation")
> Appears on: Unreleased
> It's entirely possible the (approximately) 20 minutes of music Mike composed by this point was not one full track, but instead several shorter sections. What appears in the film *Reflection*, which is most likely this music, is recognizably most of "Part Four" and a piece of what would become "Part Three".
> Mike records Raine's "A Spell for Creation" in keeping with the spirit of the original idea of invoking actual pagan incantations and spells in the music. "A Spell for Creation" would appear in the soundtrack to *The Space Movie*. It's heard as part of what would become "Incantations (Part Four)," around the 8:07 mark (after the "Canon For Two Vibraphones" movement). It's possible Mike kept the backing track and replaced the "Spell For Creation" vocals with more guitar (it's hard to tell from the muddy mix of the piece in *The Space Movie*).
> Apparently, the removal of "A Spell For Creation" prompted Mike to record Jonson's "Ode To Cynthia." As heard in the film *Reflection* later this year, the rhythmic section that immediately precedes "Ode To Cynthia" already existed by this point, with some "Woodhenge"-sounding guitar here and there, not heard on the album ("Woodhenge" also appears in *Reflection* and the similarities in orchestrations suggest perhaps the two were at one point both a part of "Incantations" at an early stage. Thematically, "Woodhenge" would seem to be in keeping with planned concept of the album.
> Another part of the music is the "song" known as "Making Way," which would also form a movement of "Part Four," the biggest difference of which is the inclusion of sung/chanted lyrics not heard in the album version.
>
> "Piano Improvisation (2011 Stereo Mix)" 5:38
> Written by Mike Oldfield
> Appears on: Incantation (2011 Deluxe Edition)
> This is Mike playing a solo piano and doing what the title describes: improvising. This piece is heard in *Reflection*, indicating it was recorded around the time of the early Incantations sessions (rather than the December 1977 sessions onward). Part of the melody near the end is strikingly similar to "Platinum (Part Two)," which is probably not a coincidence. Mike later mixed this track for release in 2011.
>
> "Northumbrian (2011 Stereo Mix)" 2:56
> Written by Mike Oldfield
> Appears on: Incantation (2011 Deluxe Edition)
> Mike plays a gentle tune here with Northumbrian bagpipes layered over acoustic guitar. This piece does not seem to have made it onto *Incantations* or any later Oldfield work (so far, anyway). Mike later mixed this track for release in 2011.

-May 18-
Virgin Records signs the Sex Pistols, marking the company's shift in focus from **Mike Oldfield**'s work and that of his rock and prog contemporaries to focus on punk artists and bands. Work on *Incantations* would seem to stop until December.

-Date Unknown-
Mike Oldfield (possibly) records guitar work for Tom Newman's forthcoming album *Faerie Symphony*, on the track "Dance Of The Daoine Sidhe."

-Date Unknown-
Virgin Records releases a 7" single for **Mike Oldfield**'s "In Dulci Jubilo" in France.

France 7" single (2097 930):
"Theme From Ommadawn" – listed as "Ommadawn"
"In Dulci Jubilo"

-June 4-
The BBC documentary series *All You Need Is Love: The Story Of Popular Music - Episode 17: "Imagine: New Directions"* is broadcast in the UK, highlighting **Mike Oldfield**.

-Summer – Autumn-
Mike Oldfield records the following at Througham Slad, Gloucestershire, England.
"Cuckoo Song" – written by Michael Praetorius. Features Les Penning.
"Pipe Tune"
"Wreckorder Wrondo" – an arrangement of Susato's "Rondo," from his Third Book of Music, *All Sorts of Dances* (1551).

-Date Unknown-
Vortex Productions uses some of **Mike Oldfield**'s music in their film *Reflection*.

Note: Details are scarce about this film's production. **Oldfield** does not mention it at all in his autobiography and his level of direct involvement is unknown. The film has since appeared on YouTube, but before that it was fairly obscure (and still is for many fans). Its relative importance stems from the fact that it contains some alternate versions of **Mike**'s recordings. The music may have been provided by Virgin with or without **Mike**'s approval, evidenced by the appearance of the "Ommadawn (Lost Version)" (which was said to have been forgotten in the Virgin vault).
The film contains the following:
"The Path"
"First Excursion"
"Ommadawn (Lost Version)"
"Piano Improvisation"
"Incantations (Early Version)"
"Woodhenge"
"Portsmouth"

-Date Unknown-
David Bedford records "Instructions For Angels," what would be title track for his next album, live with **Mike Oldfield** on guitar at Worcester Cathedral, Worcester, England. The track is later mixed at Througham Slad, Gloucestershire, England.

-Date Unknown-
Tom Newman releases his album *Faerie Symphony* in the UK on Decca Records (TXS 123). It (probably) features **Mike Oldfield** on the track "Dance Of The Daoine Sidhe." **Oldfield** is (apparently) uncredited on the album.

"Dance Of The Daoine Sidhe" 3:22
Written by Tom Newman
Appears on: Faerie Symphony; 7" single
The single helpfully renders the title phonetically as "Dance Of The Theena Shee (Daoine Sidhe)" (the Gaelic "daoine sidhe" being pronounced "theena shee") The daoine sidhe in Gaelic mythology

are elf/fairy-like creatures who live in mounds under the earth. None of the album releases or re-issues list Mike on this track. Fans pretty much agree that this track features his distinctive guitar playing. Coupled with his friendship with Tom and additional appearances on other Newman releases, that's enough to convince a lot of people. The song is a folk-rock-prog piece, starting dark and eerie, before erupting in a medieval-sounding dance number. Recommended.

-October 28-
Also released by Tom Newman is the "Dance Of The Daoine Sidhe" 7" single.

UK 7" single (F 13735) promo:
"Dance Of The Theena Shee (Daoine Sidhe)"
"The Unseelie Court"

-Date Unknown-
David Bedford releases his album *Instructions For Angels* on Virgin Records in the UK (V2090), featuring **Mike Oldfield** on the title track. The album presents each track as a variation on the "Theme" that is track 1. A quadrophonic mix is also released on LP in the UK (V2090, Matrix H).

> Variation 6: "Instructions For Angels" 6:04
> Written by David Bedford
> Appears on: Instructions For Angels
> David Bedford plays the cathedral's organ and Mike wails on guitar for six minutes, creating a heavy, dramatic combination. All I can say is that it must have been pretty satisfying to let the guitar rip like that in a church!

-November 25-
Mike Oldfield with Les Penning release their "Cuckoo Song" 7" single in the UK, Europe and Australia.

UK 7" single (VS 198):
"Cuckoo Song" Mike Oldfield with Les Penning
"Pipe Tune" Mike Oldfield

Germany 7" single (11 779 AT):
"Cuckoo Song" Mike Oldfield with Les Penning
"Pipe Tune" Mike Oldfield

Italy 7" single (VIN 45015):
"Cuckoo Song" Mike Oldfield with Les Penning
"Pipe Tune" Mike Oldfield

France 7" single (2097 935):
"Cuckoo Song" Mike Oldfield with Les Penning
"Pipe Tune" Mike Oldfield

Australia 7" single (K-6995):
"Cuckoo Song" Mike Oldfield with Les Penning
"Pipe Tune" Mike Oldfield

> "Cuckoo Song" 3:23
> Written by Michael Praetorius
> Appears on: 7" single; Impressions; The Complete Mike Oldfield; The Platinum Collection; Incantations (2011 Deluxe Edition)
> This tune dates back to around the 16th or 17th Century. It's a playful piece, full of childlike wonder.

> "Pipe Tune" 3:28
> Written by Mike Oldfield
> Appears on: Cuckoo Song 7" single; Impressions; Incantations (2011 Deluxe Edition)
> This piece bears some similarities to *Incantations* and serves as sort of a teaser for the eventual album. Given Mike's propensity for naming pieces of music "[...] Tune" (such as "Spanish Tune" and "Chinese Tune"), it's likely this was Mike working out ideas he'd revisit for the album or was a piece at one time a contender for the album. This and "Guilty" make for interesting bookends to *Incantations*.

-December-
Mike Oldfield returns to work on *Incantations*, at Througham Slad, Gloucestershire, England. The sessions last until September 1978.

-Date Unknown-
The Arts Council of Great Britain releases the film *Reflection*, which uses released and unreleased music by **Mike Oldfield**.

Incantations

1978

-Early 1978-
Mike Oldfield continues work on *Incantations*, at Througham Slad, Gloucestershire, England. **Mike** has said work on the album during this time was slow.

-Date Unknown-
Mike Oldfield mixes the following at Througham Slad, Gloucestershire, England:
"Star Clusters, Nebulae & Places In Devon" - a David Bedford composition, dating from 1971, likely recorded this year.
"The Song Of The White Horse" - written in 1971, with the performance commissioned this year by the BBC TV series *Omnibus*.

These two tracks would be revisited by **Oldfield** and Bedford in 1983.

-June-
Mike Oldfield attends a 3 day Exegesis seminar, seeking help with his mental and emotional health. He gains some ability to cope with his problems by doing so.

-June - September-
Pierre Moerlen's Gong records their album *Downwind*. The sessions for the title track take place at Througham Slad, Gloucestershire, England. **Mike Oldfield** co-produces the track with Moerlen and plays guitar, some bass ("centre section only") and Irish drum. Terry Oldfield plays flute and Steve Winwood play synths.

-Date Unknown-
Transatlantic Records re-releases **The Sallyangie** album *Children Of The Sun* in Netherlands (5C 038-62631) and Germany (811 924-1) on LP. The album is credited to **Mike & Sally Oldfield** and titled *The Sally Angie* in Belgium (TRA 3544).

-Summer-
Following the Exegesis seminar, **Mike Oldfield** spends two weeks doing as many interviews as he can.

-Date Unknown-
Mike Oldfield marries Diana D'Aubigny, sister of Robert D'Aubigny (founder of Exegesis). The marriage lasts only a few weeks.

-September-
Mike Oldfield completes his album *Incantations* at Througham Slad, Gloucestershire, England. The mix down of the album takes place at The Town House, London, England, with Phil Newell (again uncredited because the sleeves were printed before his involvement). Newell also confirms that a quad mix of the album exists at this point. Among the guest artists for the sessions between December 1977 and September 1978 are Sally Oldfield, Terry Oldfield, David Bedford (as choir conductor), Jabula, Pierre Moerlen and Maddy Prior. **Oldfield** incorporates Henry Wadsworth Longfellow's poem "The Song of Hiawatha" into "Part Two." He also removes the "Spell for Creation" movement and incorporates Ben Jonson's "Ode To Cynthia" in "Part Four."

Following the completion of the album, **Mike Oldfield** begins preparations for a concert tour to promote *Incantations*.

-Early Autumn-
Tony Palmer and Richard Branson visit **Mike Oldfield** at Througham Slad, Gloucestershire, England, to discuss **Oldfield** scoring *The Space Move* documentary. An angry **Mike** gets into a drunken fight with Richard and sends them away.

-October-
Two weeks after their initial visit, **Mike Oldfield** has Tony Palmer and Richard Branson back to at Througham Slad, Gloucestershire, England, to discuss *The Space Movie*. **Oldfield** agrees to do it and starts writing material soon after.

-Date Unknown-
Mike Oldfield assembles a group of musicians and singers for his upcoming Tour Of Europe 1979. With him this ensemble performs at every show on the tour and consists of:

David Bedford	Nico Ramsden	Phil Beer	Pierre Moerlen
Benoit Moerlen	Mike Frye	Ringo McDonough	Pete Lemmer
Tim Cross	Maddy Prior	Ray Gay	Ralph Izon
Simo Salminen	Colin Moore	Sebastian Bell	Chris Nicholls
Dick Studt	Ben Cruft	Jane Price	Liz Edwards
Nicola Hurton	Jonathan Kahan	Don McVay	Pauline Mack
Danny Daggers	Melinda Daggers	Liz Bulter	Ross Cohen
Nigel Warren Green	Vanessa Park	David Bucknell	Jessica Ford
Nick Worters	Joes Kirby	Debra Bronstein	Marigo Acheson
Emma Frued	Diana Coulson	Mary Elliot	Mary Creed
Cecily Hazell	Wendy Lampitt	Clara Harris	Emma Smith
Catherine Loewe	Pekka Pohjola		

-November 1978 to January 1979-
Bram Tchaikovsky records his album *Strange Man, Changed Man* at Pebble Beach Studios, Worthing, and Basing Street Studios, London, England. **Mike Oldfield** records tubular bells on the track "Girl Of My Dreams."

-November 24-
Mike Oldfield releases his double 2xLP album *Incantations* in the UK (VDT 101) and Europe on Virgin Records. Track listing as follows:

LP 1:
"Incantations (Part One)" - includes "Hymn To Diana"
"Incantations (Part Two)" - includes "Hymn To Diana (Reprise)" and "The Song Of Hiawatha"

LP 2:
"Incantations (Part Three)"
"Incantations (Part Four)" - includes "Canon For Two Vibraphones" and "Ode To Cynthia"

-November 25-
An article about **Mike Oldfield** written by Karl Dallas **is** published in *Melody Maker* on this date. **Oldfield** says he plans to return to the studio following the tour.

-December-
Some sources note that **Mike Oldfield** begins his *Platinum* album sessions this month, likely at Througham Slad, Gloucestershire, England. It's been said that the working album title was *Airborne*. He also works at The Manor, Shipton-on-Cherwell, Oxfordshire, England.

-December 1-
Mike Oldfield releases his EP single *Take 4* singles in the UK and Australia.

Take 4 UK 7" single (VS 238):
"Portsmouth"
"In Dulci Jubilo"
"Wreckorder Wrondo"
"The Sailor's Hornpipe (Single Version)"

Take 4 UK 12" single (VS23812) white vinyl:
"Portsmouth"
"In Dulci Jubilo"
"Wreckorder Wrondo"
"The Sailor's Hornpipe (Single Version)"

Take Four Australia 7" single (X-11, 815):
"Portsmouth"
"In Dulci Jubilo"
"Wreckorder Wrondo"
"The Sailor's Hornpipe (Single Version)"

Take Four New Zealand 7" single (VS 238):
"Portsmouth"
"In Dulci Jubilo"
"Wreckorder Wrondo"
"The Sailor's Hornpipe (Single Version)"

> "Wreckorder Wrondo" 2:36
> Written by Teilman Susato (arr. Mike Oldfield & Richard Harvey)
> Appear on: Take 4 EP; Incantations (2011 Deluxe Edition)
> Mike was going through a period in the mid- to late '70s where he was listening to a lot of classical music, which helped with his stress and personal demons (this was before his Exegesis experience). Tracks like this, the "William Tell Overture," Cuckoo Song" and "Vivaldi Concert In C" were the result. Like those others, here Mike recreates the classical form literally with a mixture of modern and traditional instruments. This piece, known originally as "Rondo," is a standard piece taught to young woodwind players even today.

Virgin Records re-issues **Mike Oldfield**'s album *Tubular Bells* as picture disc LPs in the UK (VP 2001). Two versions are issued with the same catalogue number. Track listing as follows:

UK 12" Picture disc (VP 2001) Version 1:
"Tubular Bells (Part One - Boxed Remix)"
"Tubular Bells (Part Two - Boxed Remix - Picture Disc Version 1)"

UK 12" Picture disc (VP 2001) Version 2:
"Tubular Bells (Part One - Boxed Remix)"
"Tubular Bells (Part Two - Boxed Remix - Picture Disc Version 2)"

> "Tubular Bells (Part Two - Boxed Remix - Picture Disc Version 1)" 23:26
> Written by Mike Oldfield ("The Sailor's Hornpipe" trad. arr. Oldfield)
> Appears on: Tubular Bells Picture Disc (Version 1)
> The first version of Part Two that appears on the picture disc is the *Boxed* remix up until "The Sailor's Hornpipe" comes in. Instead of featuring the full monologue by Vivian Stanshall that appeared on the boxed set, the original album version (no monologue) is used.

> "Tubular Bells (Part Two - Boxed Remix - Picture Disc Version 2)" 24:28
> Written by Mike Oldfield ("The Sailor's Hornpipe" trad. arr. Oldfield)
> Appears on: Tubular Bells Picture Disc (Version 2)
> The second version of Part Two that appears on the picture is identical to Version 1, a mix of the *Boxed* remix and the original version of "The Sailor's Hornpipe," but also includes the quadraphonic airplane demo after a few seconds of silence.

Platinum

1979

-Early 1979-
Mike Oldfield records the following at Electric Lady Studios, New York City, New York, US.
"Guilty" – Steve Winwood plays organ on the track.
"Tubular Bells (Disco Version)" – Mike reportedly records this disco arrangement of *Tubular Bells* during these sessions. If so, it's never been released.

-January – February-
Mike Oldfield and his tour ensemble rehearse in Germany for the Tour Of Europe.

-February 9-
Pierre Moerlen's Gong releases its album *Downwind* on LP in the UK (SPART 1080), Europe and North America (AB 4219). **Mike Oldfield** co-produced the title track (recorded at Througham Slad) and plays on it.

> "Downwind" 12:31
> Written by Pierre Moerlen
> Appears on: Downwind
> Mike wasn't doing as many guest appearances when he worked on this track, so busy he was with his own recording, but having worked with Moerlen for years, it was a natural fit he'd work on his friend's own album. This is a percussion extravaganza! Mike's guitar appears throughout and Terry's flute is easily spotted. This is definitely a track Oldfield fans should pick up, as it has all his hallmarks in production.

-February 14-
David Bedford performs his album *The Rime Of The Ancient Mariner* live at Queen Elizabeth Hall, London, England. **Mike Oldfield** plays guitar.

-Date Unknown-
Transatlantic Records re-releases **The Sallyangie** album *Children Of The Sun* in Spain (GS-11041) and Italy (ORL 8366) on LP.

-March 11-
Mike Oldfield performs with Gong at their show at The Venue, London, England.

-March 31-
Mike Oldfield begins his Tour Of Europe 1979 at Palacio Municipal de los Deportes, Barcelona, Spain, with two performances. The tour consists of the ensemble group **Mike** put together.

-April 1-
Mike Oldfield performs at Palacio Municipal de los Deportes, Barcelona, Spain.

-April 2-
Mike Oldfield performs at Pabellón Deportivo del Real, Madrid, Spain.

-April 4-
Mike Oldfield performs at Pavillon Baltard, Nogent-sur-Marne, Paris, France.

-April 5-
Mike Oldfield performs at Phillipshalle, Düsseldorf, Germany.

-April 6-
Mike Oldfield releases his "Guilty" singles in the UK, Europe, Australia and Japan.

UK 7" single (VS245):
"Guilty"
"Excerpt from Incantations"

UK 12" single (VS24512):
"Guilty"
"Guilty (Long Version)"

UK 12" single (VS24512) blue vinyl:
"Guilty"
"Guilty (Long Version)"

France 7" single (2097983):
"Guilty"
"Excerpt from Incantations"

Netherlands 7" single (100.439):
"Guilty"
"Excerpt from Incantations"

Netherlands 7" single (101.009):
"Guilty"
"The Sailor's Hornpipe (Single Version)"

Italy 7" single (VIN 45022):
"Guilty"
"Excerpt from Incantations"

German 7" single (100 439):
"Guilty" – listed as "I'm Guilty."
"Excerpt from Incantations" – listed as "Excerpts From Incantations."

Spain 7" single (100439A):
"Guilty"
"Excerpt from Incantations"

Portugal 7" single (VV45002ES):
"Guilty"
"Excerpt from Incantations"

Portugal 7" single (VV45002ES) yellow vinyl:
"Guilty"
"Excerpt from Incantations"

Japan 7" single (VIP-2749):
"Guilty"
"Excerpt from Incantations"

Australia 12" single (X 13025):
"Guilty (Long Version)"
"Guilty"

"Guilty" 4:00
Written by Mike Oldfield
Appears on: 7" & 12" single; Canada 1980 Platinum LP; Impressions; The Complete Mike Oldfield; Elements boxed set
Building on musical themes explored on the *Incantations* album, Mike created this disco-sounding track in New York, during his first recording sessions outside England. Many agree that "Guilty" refers to the ideology imparted during his Exegesis experience, the belief that the individual is solely responsible for things which happen in their life, rather than "blaming" others. Therefore, Mike is taking ownership of his guilt over the problems he felt he created.

"Guilty (Long Version)" 6:46
Written by Mike Oldfield
Appears on: 7" & 12" single; The Platinum Collection; Mike Oldfield – The Collection
An extended version of the track, with some longer breakdowns and repeated sections, this original single cut is well worth getting.

"Excerpt from Incantations" 4:10
Written by Mike Oldfield
Appears on: Guilty 7" single
This excerpt comes from "Part Four," the movement from 8:07 to 12:17, ending just before the "Ode To Cynthia" movement.

-April 7-
Mike Oldfield performs at Eissporthalle, Berlin, Germany.

-April 9-
Mike Oldfield performs at Forest National, Brussels, Belgium.

-April 10-
Mike Oldfield performs at De Doelen, Rotterdam, The Netherlands

-April 12-
Mike Oldfield performs at Falkoner, Kobenhavn, Denmark.

-April 14-
Mike Oldfield performs at Stadhalle, Bremen, Germany.

-April 15-
Mike Oldfield performs at CCH, Hamburg, Germany.

-April 17-
Mike Oldfield performs at Saal des Deutschen Museums, München, Germany.

-April 18-
Mike Oldfield performs at Jarhunderthalle, Frankfurt, Germany.

-April 21-
Mike Oldfield performs twice at Royal Festival Hall, London, England.

-April 25 & 26-
Mike Oldfield performs at Wembley Conference Centre, London, England. These shows are recorded and one (or both edited) is released in 2005 as the *Exposed* DVD. A BBC Transcription Service 2xLP radio promo set of the concert is also released later this year, *In Concert featuring Mike Oldfield*.

-April 28, 29 & May 2-
Mike Oldfield performs at Wembley Arena, London, England.

-May 3-
Mike Oldfield performs "Guilty" on the BBC TV series *Top Of The Pops*, London, England.

Mike Oldfield performs at the Odeon, Birmingham, England.

-May 4-
Mike Oldfield performs at Kings Hall, Belle Vue, Manchester, England.

-May 5-
Mike Oldfield appears on the BBC kids TV series *Tiswas*.

-May 6-
Mike Oldfield performs at National Exhibition Center, Birmingham, England. The Tour Of Europe 1979 ends. This performance is recorded and later appears on the North American LP *Airborn*.

> "Tubular Bells (Part One) (Live, Tour Of Europe 1979)" 23:40
> Written by Mike Oldfield
> Appear on: Airborn (2xLP Edition)
> The exact date is not listed on the sleeve, but reliable sources and evidence point to this day. If so, this recording is of the last show of the tour. Regardless, it's an excellent live version and worth tracking down!

-June-
By this point, according a 2007 interview with Tony Palmer, **Mike Oldfield** had an approximately 4:30-long piece of music written and recorded for *The Space Movie*, which he played for Palmer and Richard Branson at Througham Slad, Gloucestershire, England. Without enough music for the film, **Oldfield** agrees that using his existing work is the best solution to scoring the film, which is due for completion by July. Virgin Films, the production company branch of Virgin Records, provides Palmer with recordings of *Tubular Bells*, *Hergest Ridge*, *The Orchestral Tubular Bells*, *The Orchestral Hergest Ridge*, *Ommadawn*, *Incantations* and "Portsmouth."

Note: Curiously, part (or all) of the "Incantations (Early Version)" was sent to Palmer along with the other albums, as "A Spell for Creation" appears in the finished documentary. This causes confusion later, as the assumption became that the original work **Mike** did for *The Space Movie* later evolved into *Incantations*. That assumption is not supported by the timeline of either the film's production or *Incantations*' recording sessions (as the album was done, or nearly done, when Palmer approached **Oldfield**).

-Mid-1979-
Mike Oldfield works with Phil Beer on the following, venue unknown:
"Sit You Down" - this track would later be released by Phil Beer himself, part of his Official Bootleg series.
"Passed You By" - written by Phil Beer, this track would be released in 1986, on the compilation *Where Would You Rather Be Tonight?*

> "Sit You Down" 4:01
> Written by Phil Beer
> Appear on: Official Bootleg, Vol. 1
> A slow track, with Beer on acoustic guitar and vocal, backed by Oldfield, whose work doesn't really leap out at you, but you can tell it's him by the woodwind and synth string arrangement.

Around this time, **Mike Oldfield** also records the following for the BBC TV series *Blue Peter*. The recording process is filmed for a segment of the show.
"Blue Peter (TV Version)" - This theme is basically the traditional sea shanty known as "Barnacle Bill," written by Herbert Ashworth-Hope.

-Summer-
Mike Oldfield sells Througham Slad and buys a house in Denham, Buckinghamshire, England. He sets up a studio and records part of his next album there (*Platinum/Airborne* sessions).

Mike Oldfield moves his album sessions to Electric Lady and Blue Rock Studios, New York City, New York, US. Tracks worked on during this period include:
"Platinum"

> "Platinum (Live Studio Session)" 5:11
> Written by Mike Oldfield
> Appears on: Platinum (2012 Deluxe Edition)
> This is Mike and his group running through what would become "Part Two: Platinum." Not radically different from the album recording, just in its early stages and you can hear them working out ideas and having fun. The track starts and ends with some studio chatter.

-July 17-
Mike Oldfield releases his 2xLP live album *Exposed* in the UK (VD2511), Europe and Australia, as a stereo compatible quadraphonic mix. It is a collection of tracks from various tour dates between March and April. Due to the contract with the Musicians Union, the specific dates used cannot be listed by Virgin Records, because they would have to pay the musicians their recording fees (not just the performance rates). Several tracks from this concert compilation have been released individually over the years.

"Extract From Tubular Bells (Live - Exposed)" 4:05
Written by Mike Oldfield
Appears on: Germany 7" & 12" single; In Concert - Germany 1980 EP
This is the first 4:05 of Part One, "Introduction," from *Exposed*. It ends on a fade out.

"Tubular Bells (Part One - 'Blues + Thrash') (Exposed - Edit)" 3:20
Written by Mike Oldfield
Appears on: The Best Of Tubular Bells
This excerpt from the live album starts and ends with no fading, which works alright in the context of The Best Of... collection.

"Tubular Bells (Part One) (Live - Exposed CD Edit)" 28:21
Written by Mike Oldfield
Appears on: Exposed CD Editions
For the CD releases, rather than having the track fade out over the crowd, which was what appeared on the original LP, much of the audience noise was removed, as was the fade out at the end. Instead, after a few seconds the track ends at full volume with crowd before "Part Two comes in. Not a really significant change, but it's there.

"Tubular Bells (Part Two) (Live - Exposed CD Edit)" 11:05
Written by Mike Oldfield
Appears on: Exposed CD Editions
The opening fade in from the LP is removed here and the track starts at full volume immediately with the music.

"Tubular Bells (Part Two - 'Ambient Guitars') (Exposed - Edit)" 4:15
Written by Mike Oldfield
Appears on: The Best Of Tubular Bells
This live version of the "Ambient Guitars" section of the album is a much more aggressive arrangement, very different from the studio album throughout most of the performance. This edit fades out at the end.

"Guilty (Live - Exposed)" 3:41
Written by Mike Oldfield
Appears on: Germany 7" & 12" single; In Concert - Germany 1980 EP
Starting with the music, no crowd noise, this cut from the live album is identical up to about the 2:50 mark, at which point it goes into the closing part of the track, the reprise of "Tubular Bells (Part One): Finale."

"Guilty (Exposed - Wonderland Edit)" 4:05
Written by Mike Oldfield
Appears on: Mike Oldfield's Wonderland
This is a straight edit of the live Exposed version, removing about 2 minutes from the track it's a well done edit and not noticeable on casual listening. It differs from earlier German single edit, retaining more of "Guilty" (in the form of Mike's wailing guitar solo) before going into the "Finale."

"Guilty (Exposed - Music Wonderland Edit)" 3:56
Written by Mike Oldfield
Appears on: Episodes; Music Wonderland
A different edit of "Guilty" from *Exposed*, this is re-cut in several places.

Note: Some sources list the release date as July 27th.

-July 24-
Virgin Records releases the **Mike Oldfield** live "Guilty" singles in Germany and Portugal.

Germany 7" single (100 932):
"Guilty (Live - Exposed)"
"Extract From Tubular Bells (Live – Exposed)"

Germany 12" single (600 115):
"Extract From Tubular Bells (Live - Exposed)" - incorrectly listed as "Tabular Bells,"
"Guilty (Live - Exposed)"

Portugal 7" single (VV-45.022ES):
"Guilty (Live - Exposed)"
"Extract From Tubular Bells (Live – Exposed)"

-August 24-
Bram Tchaikovsky releases his single "Girl Of My Dreams" on Radar Records, from his *Strange Man, Changed Man* album, featuring **Mike Oldfield**.

UK 7" single (ADA 28):
"Girl Of My Dreams"
"Come Back"

> "Girl Of My Dreams" 4:10
> Written by Bram Tchaikovsky
> Appears on: 7" single, Strange Man Changed Man
> A good song, but difficult to pick out of any of Mike's bell work here, though he's credited on the song, so I guess he's in there somewhere. I suspect that's him around the 2:20 mark. Maybe?

-August/September-
Wendy Roberts recalls she recorded her vocal parts for **Mike Oldfield**'s forthcoming album (*Platinum* sessions) at Denham, Buckinghamshire, England, around this time.
"I Got Rhythm" - a version of the 1930 Gershwin song.
"Into Wonderland" - Wendy Roberts recalls in 1995 that "Into Wonderland" was titled "Sally" when she recorded it and was unaware of the original "Sally."
"All Right Now" - a cover of the 1970 Free song, recorded for the Tyne Tees Television program "Alright Now."

-September 3-
BBC Transcription Services release the 2xLP *In Concert Featuring Mike Oldfield*, parts 206 & 207 of their *In Concert* promo series. The recording comes from **Mike Oldfield**'s April 25/26, 1979, concerts at the Wembley Conference Centre. Track listing as follows:

In Concert Featuring Mike Oldfield Radio Promo 2xLP (CN 3393/S)
LP 1:
Side 1:
"Brian Matthew Intro 1"
"Incantations (Parts One & Two) (BBC In Concert, April 1979)"
LP 2:
Side 1:
"Incantations (Parts Three & Four) (BBC In Concert, April 1979)"
LP 1:
Side 2:
"Brian Matthew Intro 1"
"Tubular Bells (Part One) (BBC In Concert, April 1979)"

LP 2:
Side 2:
"Guilty (BBC In Concert, April 1979)"
"Tubular Bells (Part Two) (BBC In Concert, April 1979)"
"Guilty (Reprise) (BBC In Concert, April 1979)"

Note: Because this was a radio promo release, designed to played by stations as a full programme, using two turntables in the studio for ease of crossfading, the tracks are arranged on the LPs so the DJ plays both Side 1s first, then flip the LPs to play both Side 2s. These weren't meant to be played the traditional way of simply flipping the LP over when it reached the end of the side of the record.

Note: Some sources list this concert recording as from May 2nd, 1979, at the Wembley Conference Centre, which is wrong. The audio is the same as on the *Exposed* DVD and **Mike** didn't perform at the Conference Centre on May 2nd. Instead, he played at Wembley Arena. The transcription track sheets don't appear to list May 2nd anywhere, so I can only guess as how that date came to be associated with this release.

-Late Summer or Autumn-
Mike Oldfield completes work on his new album. The title is decided upon as *Platinum*. Guest artists include Sally Cooper, Peter Lemmer, Pierre Moerlen, Morris Pert, Nico Ramsden, Wendy Roberts and David Bedford (vocal arrangements). Tom Newman produced the album. During the sessions between late-1978 and this date, **Mike** records the following:
"Blue Peter" - **Mike** re-records the track with a more polished arrangement and also adds a few other bits and pieces in (like "Drums and Fife" and "The Sailor's Hornpipe") to round it out. Several mixes are made which later appear on different releases.

-November 10-
Mike Oldfield performs "Guilty" and "Tubular Bells (Part One): Finale" on the German TV show *Rockpop* (the performances are mimed to the *Exposed* versions). Sally Oldfield also performs (mimes) her song "The Sun In My Eyes" between **Mike**'s sets.

-November 23-
Mike Oldfield releases his album *Platinum* in the UK (V 2141, matrix B-1) and Europe. Track listing as follows:

"Platinum (Part One): Airborne"
"Platinum (Part Two): Platinum"
"Platinum (Part Three): Charleston"
"Platinum (Part Four): North Star/Platinum Finale"
"Woodhenge"
"Sally"
"Punkadiddle (Original Version)"
"I Got Rhythm" - a version of the 1930 Gershwin song.

>"Sally" 5:00
>Written By Mike Oldfield & Nico Ramsden
>Appears on: Platinum LP (1st & 2nd Pressings); Platinum cassette (1st Pressing - TCV 2141)
>This song, written for Mike's then-girlfriend Sally Cooper, was removed from the album by the time of the 3rd pressing and has not been officially re-issued, despite several opportunities over the years. Because of that, it has become one of the most sought after collectors' items for Oldfield fans. In a lot of thematic ways, the album suffers from its removal. Various musical phrases interspersed throughout the rest of the album all intersect at "Sally," making it something of a lynch pin for the entire work. Without it, those phrases have nothing to connect to. The track itself may seem a bit silly, with the "gorilla" lyrics, but give it time and it may grow on you.

"Punkadiddle (Original Version)" 4:56
Written By Mike Oldfield
Appears on: Platform (1st to 4th LP Pressings); *In Concert - Germany 1980* 7" EP Promo single; Impressions; Episodes; Music Wonderland; 1989 Japan Platinum CD
Noted here because the track "Punkadiddle" was originally not meant to start with the outro "bridge" from "Sally." This is borne out by the LP label times, with "Sally" at 5:00 and "Punkadiddle" at 4:56. The later *Platinum* CD re-issues have "Punkadiddle" with a time of 5:46, as it was given the leftover ending to the original "Sally" when "Sally" was replaced by "Into Wonderland." Since the 3rd LP Pressing of *Platinum*, including the later CD releases, the version of "Punkadiddle" with the "Sally" ending at the start has become the Standard Version.

Note: The LP matrix suffix B-1 on side two is the first pressing of *Platinum*. The later LP matrix B-2 is the second pressing of *Platinum*. Both matrixes B-1 & B-2 both contain the track "Sally" and its contents are described above.

-Date Unknown-
A blue, one-sided flexidisc single of **Mike Oldfield** recording of "All Right Now" is (apparently) released in the UK by Virgin Records.

UK 1-track 7" single (TT 362) blue flexidisc promo:
"All Right Now" - a cover of the 1970 Free song.

"All Right Now" 3:19
Written by Andy Fraser & Paul Rodgers
Appears on: Flexidisc 7" single
Next to "Sally," this might be the most sought-after Mike Oldfield release. Bootlegs copies are out there of varying quality. There have been several great opportunities to re-issue this track properly, such as the *Elements* boxed set or the 2012 *Platinum* Deluxe Edition. This cover of the Free song is screaming for a good remastering when all most fans have is low-quality copy. Wendy Roberts' vocals are quite good and Pierre Moerlen's vibraphone work is excellent, along with Mike's guitar playing. If anyone out there has this flexidisc in good condition, I beg of you to make a high quality recording and share it with the rest of us!

Note: Different stories circulate about the source of this recording, which *does* exist (appearing on bootlegs and even with some video footage available on YouTube). Some claim the blue flexidisc was included with a music magazine, while others say it was given to Virgin executives. In recent years, the very existence of the blue flexidisc (or any single containing the track) has been called into question by some fans, based on the fact that no image of it seems to exist online, no collector is known to verifiably own a copy or to have even seen one in recent memory, if at all. Attempts to backtrack details such as the catalogue number lead to dead ends of merely the same scant information. The authenticity of the catalogue number itself has been questioned.

-November 30-
Molly Oldfield is born to **Mike Oldfield** and Sally Cooper.

Mike Oldfield releases his "Blue Peter" singles in the UK, Europe and Australia.

UK 7" single (VS 317) [Standard]:
"Blue Peter" - a cover of the 1958 TV show theme.
"Woodhenge (Single Version)"

UK 7" single (VS 317) [Alternate]:
"Blue Peter (Refined Ending)" - a cover of the 1958 TV show theme.
"Woodhenge (Single Version)"

France 7" single (2097 820):
"Blue Peter" - a cover of the 1958 TV show theme.
"Woodhenge (Single Version)"

Scandinavia 7" single (VS-317):
"Blue Peter" - a cover of the 1958 TV show theme.
"Woodhenge (Single Version)"

Sweden 7" single (VS317) [Standard]:
"Blue Peter" - a cover of the 1958 TV show theme.
"Woodhenge (Single Version)"

Sweden 7" single (VS317) (Alternate]:
"Blue Peter (Dutch Mix)" - a cover of the 1958 TV show theme.
"Woodhenge (Single Version)"

Australia 7" single (K-7744):
"Blue Peter" - a cover of the 1958 TV show theme.
"Woodhenge (Single Version)"

New Zealand 7" single (VS 317):
"Blue Peter" - a cover of the 1958 TV show theme.
"Woodhenge (Single Version)"

"Blue Peter" 2:08
Written by Unknown (trad. arr. Oldfield), W. Burns ("Drums and Fife"), Ashworth-Hope ("Barnacle Bill")
Appears on: UK 7" single [Standard]; New Zealand 7" single; In Concert - Germany 1980 EP; Music Wonderland; The Complete Mike Oldfield; Elements boxed set; The Platinum Collection; Mike Oldfield - The Collection; Platinum (2012 Deluxe Edition)
This is Mike's more complete rendition of "Blue Peter," which appeared on most, but not all, single releases. It's not too hard to find, having been used on a few collections and remastered for the *Platinum* album Deluxe Edition. This standard version contains an edit at the end, where the layered guitars, percussion, etc, build to the finish, but are cut off and replaced with the intro synth recorder/flute part, the exact same recording that starts the piece.

"Blue Peter (Refined Ending)" 2:08
Written by Unknown (trad. arr. Oldfield), W. Burns ("Drums and Fife"), Ashworth-Hope ("Barnacle Bill")
Appears on: UK 7" single [Alternate];
This version is unedited, with the finale complete, giving it a grander ending.

"Blue Peter (Dutch Mix)" 2:08
Written by Unknown (trad. arr. Oldfield), W. Burns ("Drums and Fife"), Ashworth-Hope ("Barnacle Bill")
Appears on: Sweden 7" single [Alternate]; Mike Oldfield's Wonderland
This version is very similar to the Refined Ending version, with the only difference being that the electric guitars come in earlier. The complete Refined Ending is also present. If you want your "Blue Peter" theme a bit heavier than the standard single version, hunt this mix down! It is called the Dutch Mix because it was first observed by collectors as appearing on the 1981 collection *Mike Oldfield's Wonderland* in The Netherlands.

"Woodhenge (Single Version)" 4:07
Written by Mike Oldfield
Appears on: Blue Peter 7" single, Elements boxed set, The Platinum Collection
Identical to the album version, the single cut fades out at the very end, before the segue into "Sally" or "Into Wonderland" (depending on which edition of the album you're listening to).

-Date Unknown-
As the story goes, Richard Branson and/or Virgin Records takes a dislike to the *Platinum* track "Sally" and **Mike Oldfield** removes it from the album, replacing it with "Into Wonderland."

UK *Platinum* LP (V 2141, matrix B-3)
UK *Platinum* LP (V 2141, matrix B-4)
New Zealand *Platinum* LP (V 2141)
Finland 1980 *Platinum* LP (201 206)

"Platinum (Part One): Airborne"
"Platinum (Part Two): Platinum"
"Platinum (Part Three): Charleston"
"Platinum (Part Four): North Star/Platinum Finale"
"Woodhenge"
"Into Wonderland (with "Sally" Outro)" – listed as "Sally."
"Punkadiddle (Original Version)"
"I Got Rhythm" – a version of the 1930 Gershwin song.

> "Into Wonderland (with "Sally Outro)" 4:36
> Written by Mike Oldfield
> Appears on: Platinum (3rd & 4th UK LP Pressing); European LP releases; 1989 Japan Platinum CD
> When it was decided to replace "Sally" with this track, it was not done cleanly. Because "Sally" was designed to fit into that position on the album, what ended up happening with the switch was that the beginning and end of "Sally" remained in place and "Into Wonderland" was spliced into that spot. On the first edition of the updated album, visible by the bands in the groove of the vinyl and the listed track times, "Into Wonderland" includes the outro to "Sally."

Note: It's possible the argument over "Sally" between **Oldfield** and Virgin began before the album was released and **Mike** recorded "Into Wonderland" as a fallback in case it was decided to nix "Sally" (or it was recorded anyway and **Mike** knew he had a back-up plan). It might then be that it was only after the 2nd album pressing that Virgin put their foot down and enforced the switch.

The following are examples of LP releases which correctly list "Into Wonderland" on the sleeve and label, and where the track includes the "Sally" outro music:

Italy *Platinum* LP (VIL 12141)
Germany *Platinum* LP (201 206)
Austria *Platinum* LP (201 206)
France *Platinum* LP (201206)
Scandinavia *Platinum* LP (V 2141)
Australia *Platinum* LP (L 37150)
Netherlands *Platinum* LP (201 206)

"Platinum (Part One): Airborne"
"Platinum (Part Two): Platinum"
"Platinum (Part Three): Charleston"
"Platinum (Part Four): North Star/Platinum Finale"
"Woodhenge"
"Into Wonderland (with "Sally Intro")"
"Punkadiddle (Original Version)"
"I Got Rhythm" – a version of the 1930 Gershwin song.

Note: This would appear to be the most common LP edition from 1979 in Europe. It forms the basis for early CD re-issues of the album.

And the final version, which ultimately became the standard edition for later CD re-issues, is the one which shifted the "Sally" outro to the start of "Punkadiddle."

UK *Platinum* LP (V 2141, matrix B-5)
"Platinum (Part One): Airborne"
"Platinum (Part Two): Platinum"
"Platinum (Part Three): Charleston"
"Platinum (Part Four): North Star/Platinum Finale"
"Woodhenge"
"Into Wonderland"
"Punkadiddle" – includes "Sally" outro.
"I Got Rhythm" – a version of the 1930 Gershwin song.

"Into Wonderland" 3:46
Written by Mike Oldfield
Appears on: Platinum
After a time, it was decided for whatever reason to shift the "Sally" outro from the end of "Into Wonderland" to the start of "Punkadiddle." This allows for a more standalone version of "Into Wonderland," though the opening few notes of "Sally" still remain after the segue from "Woodhenge." Here the track ends on the final vocal.

"Punkadiddle" 5:46
Written by Mike Oldfield
Appears on: Platinum (UK 5th LP Pressing); 2000 Platinum CD Edition; 2012 Platinum Deluxe Edition
Alas, another ripple effect came when "Into Wonderland" replaced "Sally." On the fifth pressing of *Platinum*, "Into Wonderland" lost the "Sally" outro and it was given to "Punkadiddle" as an extended opening. Musically, nothing changed on the album after the 3rd UK printing, all that happened on the 5th UK printing was a change in the LP's groove banding and listed track time. "Punkadiddle" became longer by gaining the "Sally" outro and "Into Wonderland" got shorter. This arrangement would later become the digital standard for CD and online releases.

QE2

1980

-Early 1980-
The ITV cartoon series *Aubrey* airs in the UK and (possibly) features opening and closing theme music by **Mike Oldfield.**

> "Aubrey – Opening Theme" :30
> "Aubrey – Closing Theme" :30
> Written by Mike Oldfield (possibly)
> Appears on: N/A
> It's possible this is Mike, being a quirky little theme, which is something he's good at. Also, he was doing things like "Blue Peter" at the time. On the other hand, it could be just about any goofy cartoon theme. I've only read one source that cites Mike as the composer, but says the series is from 1989, which seems incorrect, unless there was a later series by the same name, though I can't find a listing for such. Some fans have suggested that it sounds similar to "False Start Of The Shadows" from *The Mathematician's Air Display*. All in all, the evidence seems pretty thin. If you're ever talking to Mike, maybe ask him about it.

-Date Unknown-
Virgin Records release the **Mike Oldfield** 7" single "North Star / Platinum Finale" in Spain.

Spain 7" single (A-101.468):
"Platinum (Part Four): North Star/Platinum Finale" - listed as "North Star / Platinum Finale"
"Into Wonderland" - listed as "Into The Wonderland"

-Date Unknown-
Virgin Records Canada releases **Mike Oldfield**'s album *Platinum* on LP (V 2141) in Canada. Track listing as follows:

"Platinum (Part One): Airborne"
"Platinum (Part Two): Platinum"
"Platinum (Part Three): Charleston"
"Platinum (Part Four): North Star/Platinum Finale"
"Guilty"
"Into Wonderland (Airborn Version)"
"Punkadiddle"
"I Got Rhythm" - a version of the 1930 Gershwin song.

-February-
Virgin Records releases the **Mike Oldfield** compilation album *Airborn* in North America. Two editions are issued, track listings as follows:

US *Airborn* 2xLP Edition (VA 13143)
LP 1:
Side 1:
"Platinum (Part One): Airborne"
"Platinum (Part Two): Platinum (Airborn Edit)"
"Platinum (Part Three): Charleston"
"Platinum (Part Four): North Star/Platinum Finale"

Side 2:
"Guilty (Airborn Version)"
"Into Wonderland (Airborn Version)"
"Punkadiddle"
"I Got Rhythm" – a version of the 1930 Gershwin song.

LP 2:
Side 3:
"Tubular Bells (Part One) (Live, Tour Of Europe 1979)"

Side 4:
"Incantations (Studio And Live)"

Canada *Airborn* 2xLP Edition (V2153/2)
LP 1:
Side 1:
"Platinum (Part One): Airborne"
"Platinum (Part Two): Platinum (Airborn Edit)"
"Platinum (Part Three): Charleston"
"Platinum (Part Four): North Star/Platinum Finale"

Side 2:
"Guilty (Airborn Version)"
"Into Wonderland (Airborn Version)"
"Punkadiddle"
"I Got Rhythm" – a version of the 1930 Gershwin song.

LP 2:
Side 3:
"Incantations (Studio And Live)"

Side 4:
"Tubular Bells (Part One) (Live, Tour Of Europe 1979)"

Canadian *Airborn* LP (V2153)
"Platinum (Part One): Airborne"
"Platinum (Part Two): Platinum (Airborn Edit)"
"Platinum (Part Three): Charleston"
"Platinum (Part Four): North Star/Platinum Finale"
"Guilty (Airborn Version)"
"Into Wonderland (Airborn Version)"
"Punkadiddle"
"I Got Rhythm" – a version of the 1930 Gershwin song.

Note: the Canadian pressing of *Airborn* appears to be mastered overall at an ever-so-slightly faster speed than the US pressing and the original *Platinum* album tracks.

Canadian *Airborn* cassette (TCV 2153)
"Platinum (Part One): Airborne"
"Platinum (Part Two): Platinum (Airborn Edit)"
"Platinum (Part Three): Charleston"
"Platinum (Part Four): North Star/Platinum Finale"
"Guilty (Airborn Version)"
"Into Wonderland (Airborn Version)"
"Punkadiddle"

"I Got Rhythm" – a version of the 1930 Gershwin song.

Virgin Records issues a promo 10" single of "Guilty" with US promo copies of *Airborn*.

US 10" single (PR 361):
"Guilty (Airborn Version)"
"Platinum (Part Four): North Star/Platinum Finale" – listed as "North Star / Platinum Finale."

> "Platinum (Part Two): Platinum (Airborn Edit)" 4:57
> Written by Mike Oldfield
> Appears on: Airborn
> Just over a minute's worth of music is edited out on the *Airborn* version of this track, from about 2:40 – 3:43 of the original. It's a clean edit and you may not notice it unless you know the track very well. The label still incorrectly lists the full 6:03 runtime.
>
> "Guilty (Airborn Version)" 3:50
> Written by Mike Oldfield
> Appears on: Airborn; 1980 Guilty US 10" single
> This version of "Guilty" is both double-tracked and plays too fast. It pretty much races along and is immediately noticeable The label gives the incorrect run time of 4:00 (the length of the correct speed).
>
> "Into Wonderland (Airborn Version)" 3:41
> Written by Mike Oldfield
> Appears on: Airborn
> This is actually the proper standalone version, featuring neither the intro nor outro music left over from "Sally," which appears on the various *Platinum* editions.
>
> "Incantations (Studio And Live)" 19:50
> Written by Mike Oldfield
> Appears on: US & Canada Airborn 2xLP
> The track starts with the album version of "Incantations (Part One)" and segues to the same track from *Exposed* (the "Hymn To Diana" movement), before fading out and jumping into the "Canon For Two Vibraphones" opening movement of "Part Four" it then segues into the *Exposed* live versions of "Tubular Bells (Part Two)" (specifically "Ambient Guitars" and "The Sailor's Hornpipe"). It would seem that the 2xLP edition of *Airborn* was in part designed to cover the North American gap in Mike's recording career since the release of *Ommadawn*, as the albums *Incantations*, *Exposed* and *Platinum* (in the US), as well as the single "Guilty," were not issued in that territory.

-Date Unknown-
Mike Oldfield assembles a new, smaller group with which to tour. They begin rehearsals at Shepperton Studios, Shepperton, Surrey, England. The group is:

Pierre Moerlen	Benoit Moerlen	Hansford Rowe	Tim Cross
Pete Lemer	Pete Acock	Mike Frye	Wendy Roberts
Maggie Reilly	Nico Ramsden		

Tour Note: the In Concert 1980 Tour dates listed here are mostly correct, though several early dates (pre-April 17th) are in question, as different sources cite or exclude various dates. I've attempted to reconcile the conflicting accounts by listing them all with the caveat that some may be incorrect.

-Date Unknown-
Lea Nicholson releases his album *The Concertina Record* on Kicking Mule Records (SNKF165) in the UK, featuring **Mike Oldfield** on the track "Kopya."

"Kopya" 1:27
Written by Traditional, arr. Nicholson/Oldfield
Appears on: The Concertina Record
This short folk piece finds Mike on guitar, bodhrán and sleigh bells, with Nicholson on the titular concertina (the little accordion-like free-reed instrument). The piece is a fun number with lots of flavour.

-April-
Transatlantic Records re-releases **The Sallyangie** album *Children Of The Sun* in Japan (YS-7020-LA) on LP.

-April 9-
Mike Oldfield performs at Loughborough University, Loughborough, England, beginning the In Concert 1980 Tour.

-April 11-
Mike Oldfield performs at Lancaster University, Lancaster, England.

-April 12-
Mike Oldfield performs at Strathclyde University, Glasgow, Scotland.

-April 13-
Mike Oldfield performs at University of Dundee, Dundee, Scotland.

-April 17-
Mike Oldfield performs at Falkoner, Kobenhavn, Denmark.

-April 18-
Mike Oldfield performs at Ostseehalle, Keil, Germany.

Around this time, in support of the German leg of the In Concert tour, Virgin Records issues a 7" promo EP single in Germany, titled *In Concert - Germany 1980*.

In Concert - Germany 1980 EP
Germany 7" issue (696 009-00) promo:
"Punkadiddle (Original Version)"
"Extract from Tubular Bells (Live - Exposed)"
"Guilty (Live - Exposed)"
"Blue Peter"

-April 19-
Mike Oldfield performs at ICC, Berlin, Germany.

-April 21-
Mike Oldfield performs at Phillipshalle, Düsseldorf, Germany.

-April 22-
Mike Oldfield performs at Halle Münsterland, Münster, Germany.

-April 23-
Mike Oldfield performs at Jahrhunderthalle, Frankfurt, Germany.

-April 24-
Mike Oldfield performs at Sporthalle, Köln, Germany.

-April 25-
Mike Oldfield performs at Stadhalle, Bremen, Germany.

-April 26-
Mike Oldfield performs at Eilenriedhalle, Hannover, Germany.

-April 28-
Mike Oldfield performs at Stadhalle, Vienna, Austria. This show is recorded and the following track is released:

> "Polka (Live in Vienna, 1980)" 3:38
> Written by: Unknown ("42 Pound Checque" & "John Ryan's Polka" trad., arr. Mike Oldfield)
> Appears on: Arrival 7" single; Elements boxed set; Platinum (2012 Deluxe Edition)
> This Irish polka is a combination of two tunes, "42 Pound Checque" and "John Ryan's Polka." Mike never strayed far from his folk music roots and this piece served as a fun interlude during his concerts. The group was in fine form that evening!

-April 29-
Mike Oldfield performs at Olympiahalle, München, Germany.

-April 30-
Mike Oldfield performs at Sporthalle Eppelheim, Heidelberg, Germany.

-May 4-
Mike Oldfield performs at Gaumont, Ipswich, England.

-May 5-
Mike Oldfield performs at Fairfieldhall, Croydon, England.

-May 6-
Mike Oldfield performs at the Winter Gardens, Bournemouth, England.

-May 7-
Mike Oldfield performs at the Apollo, Manchester, England.

-May 8-
Mike Oldfield performs at Guildhall, Portsmouth, England.

-May 9-
Mike Oldfield performs at Leisure Centre, Gloucester, England.

-May 10 & 11-
Mike Oldfield performs at the New Theatre, Oxford, England.

-May 13-
Mike Oldfield performs at the Brighton Centre, Brighton, England.

-May 14-
Mike Oldfield performs at Bingley, Stafford, England.

-May 15-
Mike Oldfield performs at the Apollo, Manchester, England.

-May 17 & 18-
Mike Oldfield performs at the Edinburgh Playhouse, Edinburgh, Scotland.

-May 19 & 20-
Mike Oldfield performs at the Apollo, Glasgow, Scotland.

-May 22-
Mike Oldfield performs at Newcastle City Hall, Newcastle, England.

-May 23-
Mike Oldfield performs at Guild Hall, Preston, England.

-May 24-
Mike Oldfield performs at Sheffield City Hall, Sheffield, England.

-May 25-
Mike Oldfield performs at Colston Hall, Bristol, England.

-May 26-
Mike Oldfield performs at the Gaumont Theatre, Southhampton, England. This show is recorded and the following track is released individually:

> "I Got Rhythm (Live at Gaumont Theatre, 1980)" 4:47
> Written by George Gershwin (music) & Ira Gershwin (lyrics)
> Appears on: Impressions
> In a 2001 interview, Phil Newell confirmed that this version of "I Got Rhythm" is in fact a live recording, mixed by him and planned for a single release. The single was shelved, but the Newell mix of this track would appear on the compilation *Impressions*. Unlike most live releases, this recording doesn't feature any audience noise, having been mixed out, likely to make for a cleaner sounding single. This previously led to the belief that this version was a studio recording, but we now know that isn't the case. It's a great live performance and it's actually quite nice to hear it without the audience, compared to the later released version from the Wembley concert on the 2012 *Platinum* Deluxe Edition (which is also excellent).

-May 27-
Mike Oldfield performs at the Art Centre, Poole, England.

-May 28 & 29-
Mike Oldfield performs at Wembley Arena, London, England. The May 28th concert is later released on the *Platinum* Deluxe Edition.

-May 31-
Mike Oldfield performs at Royal Dublin Society Hall, Dublin, Ireland.

-June-
Mike Oldfield performs at the following venues, with specific dates unknown:
De Doelen, Rotterdam, The Netherlands
Forest National, Bruxelles, Belgium
Paris, France

-June 17-
Mike Oldfield performs at either Konserthuset, Stockholm, Sweden, or at Carlyon Bay, Cornwall, England.

-June 18-
Mike Oldfield performs at Sophia Gardens, Cardiff, England

-June 21-
Mike Oldfield performs at the Knebworth Festival, Stevenage, Herefordshire, England. The Beach Boys and Santana are also in the bill. The show is recorded and released later this year as *The Essential Mike Oldfield* VHS

-June 28-
Mike Oldfield performs at Dundonald, County Down, Ireland.

-June 29-
Mike Oldfield performs at the McCroom Castle Festival, Cork, Ireland. Van Morrison and The Chieftains are also on the bill.

-Summer-
Mike Oldfield works on his next album at his home studio, Denham, Buckinghamshire, England. This home studio is designed by Eddie Veale. He says in a 1980 interview with Tim Oakes for *International Musician And Recording World* magazine that he plans to start right after the tour, possibly early August. Working titles for the album are reportedly *Mirage* and *Carnival*. **Oldfield** considers the title *Titanic* before deciding on (the less superstitious) *QE2*. Tracks worked on include:
"Arrival" - a cover of the 1976 ABBA instrumental.

-September 12-
Mike Oldfield releases his "Arrival" 7" single in the UK and Europe.

UK 7" single (VS 374):
"Arrival" - a cover of the 1976 ABBA instrumental.
"Polka (Live in Vienna, 1980)"

Spain 7" single (A-102389):
"Arrival" - a cover of the 1976 ABBA instrumental.
"Polka (Live in Vienna, 1980)"

France 7" single (102389):
"Arrival" - a cover of the 1976 ABBA instrumental.
"Polka (Live in Vienna, 1980)"

Netherlands 7" single (102.389):
"Arrival" - a cover of the 1976 ABBA instrumental.
"Polka (Live in Vienna, 1980)"

Germany 7" single (102 389):
"Arrival" - a cover of the 1976 ABBA instrumental.
"Polka (Live in Vienna, 1980)"

Portugal 7" single (VV 45.033ES):
"Arrival" - a cover of the 1976 ABBA instrumental.
"Polka (Live in Vienna, 1980)"

7" single:
"Arrival" - a cover of the 1976 ABBA instrumental.
"Polka (Live in Vienna, 1980)"

-Mid-September-
Mike Oldfield completes work on his album *QE2*. Exact recording dates are unknown, though given his tour dates and the album and singles' release dates, this seems the most likely period. Guest artists include Phil Collins, Maggie Reilly, Tim Cross, Mike Frye and Morris Pert. Tracks worked on since the summer include:
"Wonderful Land" - a cover of The Shadows' 1962 instrumental.
"Taurus" - named after **Mike**'s astrological sign.
"Molly" - named after **Mike**'s daughter.

-September 19-
Mike Oldfield performs at Plaza España, Barcelona, Spain. For this leg of the tour, **Mike** reportedly reduces his touring group to a 10-piece band.

-September 20-
Mike Oldfield and his group fly from Barcelona to San Sebastián, Spain, on a charter plane over the Pyrenees Mountains. They fly through a thunderstorm and this event serves as the inspiration for the song "Five Miles Out."

That evening, the group performs at Velódromo de Anoeta, San Sebastián, Spain.

-September 21-
Mike Oldfield performs at the PCE Festival, Alicante, Spain.

-September 23-
Mike Oldfield performs at Pabellón Deportivo del Real Madrid, Madrid, Spain.

-September 25-
Mike Oldfield performs at Festical de Cascais, Lisbon, Portugal.

-September 26-
Mike Oldfield performs at the Pavilhão Infante Sagres, Oporto, Portugal.

-September 27-
Mike Oldfield performs at the Venice Festival, Venice, Italy.

-September 28-
Mike Oldfield performs at the Pontevedra, Spain.

-October-
Tellydisc releases a 2xLP compilation in the UK of **Mike Oldfield**'s work via mail-order, titled *Impressions* (TELLY 4) The collection is mastered at The Town House Studios, London, England. Also released is a cassette edition (MC TEL4).

LP 1:
"Tubular Bells (Part One) (Live – Exposed – LP Version)"
"Ommadawn (Part One)"

LP 2:
"Platinum (Part One): Airborne"
"Platinum (Part Two): Platinum"
"Platinum (Part Three): Charleston"
"Punkadiddle (Original Version)"
"I Got Rhythm (Live at Gaumont Theatre, 1980)" – a version of the 1930 Gershwin song.
"Guilty"
"Pipe Tune"
"In Dulci Jubilo"
"Wreckorder Wrondo"
"Cuckoo Song" Mike Oldfield with Les Penning
"On Horseback (Single Version)"
"Portsmouth"
"The Sailor's Hornpipe (Single Version)"

-October 31-
Mike Oldfield releases his album *QE2* on LP in the UK (V2181), Europe and Canada (VL4-2216) on Virgin Records and in the US on Epic Records (FE 37358). Track listing as follows:

"Taurus 1"
"Sheba"
"Conflict"
"Arrival" – a cover of the 1976 ABBA instrumental.
"Wonderful Land" – a cover of The Shadows' 1962 instrumental.
"Mirage"

"QE2/QE2 Finale"
"Celt"
"Molly"

Note: the LP lists "QE2" and QE2 Finale" as separate tracks, but with a shared total run time. CD re-issues tend to simply combine them as "QE2," one track. Make of that what you will.

-Date Unknown-
Virgin Records releases the concert/interview VHS *The Essential Mike Oldfield*, which contain clips from his June 21, 1980, Knebworth concert and interview segments.

-November 28-
Mike Oldfield releases his "Sheba" and "Wonderful Land" 7" single in the UK and Europe. This release is a bit curious, as the label lists "Sheba" as the A-side and "Wonderful Land" as the B-side, however the sleeve advertises it as the "Wonderful Land" single and that track got a music video and not "Sheba."

UK 7" single (VS 387):
"Sheba"
"Wonderful Land (Single Version)" – a cover of The Shadows' 1962 instrumental.

Ireland 7" single (VS 387):
"Sheba"
"Wonderful Land (Single Version)" – a cover of The Shadows' 1962 instrumental.

Australia 7" single (VS 387):
"Sheba"
"Wonderful Land (Single Version)" – a cover of The Shadows' 1962 instrumental.

Portugal 7" single (VV-45.056ES):
"Sheba"
"Wonderful Land (Single Version)" – a cover of The Shadows' 1962 instrumental.

Germany 7" single (VS 387):
"Sheba"
"Wonderful Land (Single Version)" – a cover of The Shadows' 1962 instrumental.

> "Wonderful Land (Single Version)" 2:53
> Written by Jerry Lordan
> Appears on: Sheba/Wonderful Land 7" single; Mike Oldfield's Wonderland; Elements boxed set, The Mike Oldfield Christmas EP
> The track was originally recorded by The Shadows. With the removal of about 45 seconds of the opening, the single version tightens up the track and loses none of its power.

-December-
Mike Oldfield performs at the Gateway Theatre, Edinburgh, Scotland. The show is recorded and broadcast in Scottish TV.

-December 8-
John Lennon is shot and killed, New York City, New York, US. **Mike Oldfield** notes later in his autobiography that he is in New York when this event takes place.

-December 20-
Mike Oldfield performs at Rock Pop In Concert, Westfalenhalle, Dortmund, Germany.

Wonderland

1981

-Early 1981-
Mike Oldfield assembles a new touring group, consisting of Maggie Reilly, Rick Fenn, Tim Cross, Morris Pert and Mike Frye.

-March-
Ariola Benelux B.V. releases a compilation LP of **Mike Oldfield** tracks in The Netherlands, titled *Mike Oldfield's Wonderland* (203.550). This release coincides with the German dates of the tour. Track listing as follows:

"In Dulci Jubilo"
"Excerpt from Tubular Bells (Part One)"
"Portsmouth"
"Excerpt from Hergest Ridge (Part One – Boxed Remix)"
"Platinum (Part Four): North Star/Platinum Finale"
"Blue Peter (Dutch Mix)" – a cover of the 1958 TV show theme.
"Excerpt from Ommadawn (Part Two)"
"Wonderful Land (Single Version)" – a cover of The Shadows' 1962 instrumental.
"Excerpt from Incantations (Part Two – 'The Song Of Hiawatha')"
"Guilty (Exposed – Wonderland Edit)"

>"Excerpt from Tubular Bells (Part One)" 9:35
>Written by Mike Oldfield
>Appears on: Mike Oldfield's Wonderland
>This edit starts at "Russian" and continues into "Finale" before ending "Part One" normally.
>
>"Excerpt from Hergest Ridge (Part One – Boxed Remix)" 7:55
>Written by Mike Oldfield
>Appears on: Mike Oldfield's Wonderland
>This is the 3rd and 4th movements of "Part One."
>
>"Excerpt from Ommadawn (Part Two)" 7:10
>Written by Mike Oldfield
>Appears on: Mike Oldfield's Wonderland
>This unique excerpt is the 3rd and 4th movements of Part Two (the 4th movement being "On Horseback").
>
>"Excerpt from Incantations (Part Two – 'The Song Of Hiawatha')" 8:40
>Written by Longfellow (words, arr. Oldfield), Mike Oldfield (music)
>Appears on: Mike Oldfield's Wonderland
>This is the "The Song Of Hiawatha" movement from "Part Two."

-March 9 & 10-
Mike Oldfield performs at Stadthalle, Offenbach, Germany, starting The European Adventure Tour.

-March 11-
Mike Oldfield performs at Heidelberg, Rhein-Neckar-Halle, Germany.

-March 12-
Mike Oldfield performs at Rheingoldhalle, Mainz, Germany.

-March 14-
Mike Oldfield performs at Tauberfrankenhalle, Würzburg, Germany.

-March 15-
Mike Oldfield performs at Hemmerleinhalle, Nürnberg, Germany.

-March 16-
Mike Oldfield performs at Rudi-Sedelmayer-Halle, München, Germany.

-March 17-
Mike Oldfield performs at Oberschwarzwaldhalle, Karlsruhe, Germany.

-March 18-
Mike Oldfield performs at Sporthalle, Köhn, Germany.

-March 21-
Mike Oldfield performs at Congress Center Hamburg, Hamburg, Germany.

-March 22-
Mike Oldfield performs at Ostseehalle, Kiel, Germany.

-March 23-
Mike Oldfield performs at Stadhalle, Bremerhaven, Germany.

-March 25-
Mike Oldfield performs at Eilenriedehalle, Hannover, Germany.

-March 26-
Mike Oldfield performs at Stadhalle, Bremen, Germany.

-March 27-
Mike Oldfield performs at Deutschlandhalle, Berlin, Germany.

-March 29-
Mike Oldfield performs at Phillipshalle, Düsseldorf, Germany.

-March 30-
Mike Oldfield performs at Halle Münsterland, Münster, Germany.

-March 31-
Mike Oldfield performs two shows at Siegerlandhalle, Siegen, Germany.

-April 1-
Mike Oldfield performs at Grugahalle, Essen, Germany. This show is recorded and an edited version is released on the 2012 *QE2* Deluxe Edition. Also, the following tracks are released individually:

> "Sheba (Live At Essen, 1981)" 3:30
> "Mirage" (Live At Essen, 1981)" 5:12
> Written by Mike Oldfield
> Appears on: The Complete Mike Oldfield
> On CD releases of *The Complete* compilation, these pieces are a single track, as they were played back to back in the actual concert. They were later made available with the nearly full concert release on the *QE2* Deluxe Edition concert disc, which features this show. The mix by Dirk Hohmeyer heard on The Complete Mike Oldfield runs a little slower than the *QE2* Deluxe Edition.

"Platinum (Live At Essen, 1981)" 14:28
Written by Mike Oldfield ("North Star" by Philip Glass, arr. Mike Oldfield)
Appears on: The Complete Mike Oldfield
This live version of "Platinum" (Parts One to Four) should be of great interest to Oldfield fans, as it was left off the later release of the Essen concert that appears on the *QE2* Deluxe Edition. Its removal was probably done for two reasons: firstly, to keep the concert to a single disc, and secondly, because a live performance of "Platinum" appears on the 2012 *Platinum* Deluxe Edition. Right or wrong, editing it out would serve to not to seem to repeat content. So, if you actually want the more complete Essen 1981 concert, get your hands on this release of "Platinum" and place it between "Mirage" and "Conflict." "Tubular Bells (Part Two)" was played after "Platinum," but that piece hasn't been officially released yet.

"Live Punkadiddle" 5:37
Written by Mike Oldfield
Appears on: Five Miles Out 7" single; Elements boxed set; Lo Mejor De... Mike Oldfield
Though awkwardly named, this is indeed "Punkadiddle" live. It's the same performance as appears on the *QE2* Deluxe Edition concert disc, though here it is nicely faded in and out, making for a good standalone version. It's a good performance of the track. Interestingly, the sleeve credits this track to The Mike Oldfield Group.

-April 2-
Mike Oldfield performs at Hannover, Eilenriedehalle, Germany.

-April 3-
Mike Oldfield performs at De Doelen, Rotterdam, The Netherlands.

-Date Unknown-
Love Records releases Pekka Pohjola's album *Keesojen Lehto* (AKA *Mathemetician's Air Display*) untitled, credited to **Mike Oldfield, Sally Oldfield, Pekka Pohjola** in North America on LP (US-101).

-June 15-
Mike Oldfield performs in Helsinki, Finland.

-June 17-
Mike Oldfield performs at Grönalund, Stockholm, Sweden.

-June 18-
Mike Oldfield performs at Falkoner Teatret, Kobenhaven, Denmark.

-June 19-
Mike Oldfield performs in Oslo, Norway.

-June 21-
Mike Oldfield performs at Forest National, Brussels, Belgium.

-June 22-
Mike Oldfield performs in Nijmegen, The Netherlands.

-June 23-
Mike Oldfield performs at De Doelen, Rotterdam, The Netherlands.

-Date Unknown-
Virgin Records releases the LP compilation of **Mike Oldfield** material titled *Episodes* (70065 / 203.803), in France. It appears to coincide with the French tour dates. Track listing as follows

"Excerpt from Ommadawn (Part One)" – listed as "Ommadawn (Extrait)."
"Tubular Bells (Part One – Boxed Remix) (Episodes Extract)"
"Incantations (Part One) (Episodes Extract)"
"Incantations (Part Four) ('Ode To Cynthia')"
"Hergest Ridge (Part Two – Boxed Remix) (Episodes Extract)"
"Platinum (Part One): Airborn (Episodes Edit)"
"Punkadiddle (Original Version)"
"Sheba"
"Arrival" – a cover of the 1976 ABBA instrumental.
"Celt"
"Portsmouth"

Note: this collection is later re-issued in France on CD (30025).

"Ommadawn (Part One) (Episodes Extract)" 7:10
Written by Mike Oldfield
Appears on: Episodes, Music Wonderland, The Complete Mike Oldfield, The Complete Mike Oldfield Promo 12" single, XXV: The Essential Mike Oldfield, The Platinum Collection, Mike Oldfield – The Collection
This is the 4th and 5th movements, the closing seven minutes of "Part One." It goes by the name "Ommadawn (Extrait)" on the French collection *Episodes*, and appears again on various other collections.

"Tubular Bells (Part One – Boxed Remix) (Episodes Extract)" 8:32
Written by Mike Oldfield
Appears on: Episodes, Music Wonderland
This is both the "Russian" and "Finale" movements from the Boxed Remix of "Part One."

"Incantations (Part One) (Episodes Extract)" 5:41
Written by Mike Oldfield
Appears on: Episodes
This is the opening movement of "Incantations (Part One)," fading out early.

"Incantations (Part Four) ('Ode To Cynthia')" 4:40
Written by Mike Oldfield (music), Ben Jonson (words, arr. Oldfield)
Appears on: Episodes, The Complete Mike Oldfield, Elements: The Best Of Mike Oldfield, XXV: The Essential Mike Oldfield, Collection, The Platinum Collection, Mike Oldfield – The Collection, Icon
This is the full "Ode To Cynthia" movement that ends "Incantations (Part Four)" and the album itself. This excerpt appears on a variety of Oldfield collections, starting with *Episodes*.

"Hergest Ridge (Part Two – Boxed Remix) (Episodes Extract)" 4:10
Written by Mike Oldfield
Appears on: Episodes
This is an excerpt from the 3rd movement of "Part Two," from about 8:32 to 12:42 (the heavy, distorted guitar part). As collections go, *Hergest Ridge* doesn't usually get a lot of love, and when it does, it's usually an excerpt from "Part One," so it's nice to hear this part getting some attention. The track fades out early.

"Platinum (Part One): Airborn (Episodes Edit)" 4:59
Written by Mike Oldfield
Appears on: Episodes
In an unusual turn, this edit of the album track simply fades out as it reaches the end, before "Part Two: Platinum" kicks in.

-June 24-
Mike Oldfield performs at Palaise des Sports, Paris, France.

-June 25-
Mike Oldfield performs in Lille, France.

-June 26-
Mike Oldfield performs at Palais des Sports, Paris, France.

-June 27-
Mike Oldfield performs in Concarneau, France.

-June 28-
Mike Oldfield performs at Amphi Descartes, Poitiers, France.

-June 29-
Mike Oldfield performs at Palais d'Hiver, Lyon, France.

-June 30-
Mike Oldfield performs at Hall Rhenus, Strasbourg, France.

-July 1-
Mike Oldfield performs in Luxembourg City, Luxembourg.

-July 2-
Mike Oldfield performs at Stadthalle, Freiburg, Germany.

-July 3-
Mike Oldfield performs at Messehalle, Sindelfingen, Germany.

-July 5-
Mike Oldfield performs two shows at Montreux Casino, Montreux, Switzerland, as part of the Montreux Jazz Festival. One of the two shows is recorded and later released as part of the *Live At Montreux* DVD series.

-July 6-
Mike Oldfield performs at Velodromo Vigorelli, Milan, Italy.

-July 7-
Mike Oldfield performs at Open Air Festival, Jesolo, Italy.

-July 8-
Mike Oldfield performs in Bologna, Italy.

-July 9-
Mike Oldfield performs at Palasport, Rome.

-July 10-
Mike Oldfield performs at Stadio Armando Picchi, Livorno.

-July 12-
Mike Oldfield performs in Rimini, Italy.

-July 13 & 14-
Mike Oldfield performs in Tel Aviv, Israel.

-July 16 & 17-
Mike Oldfield performs at the Roman Ruins, Athens, Greece.

-July 20-
Mike Oldfield performs at Stadthalle, Vienna, Austria.

-July 22-
Mike Oldfield performs at Hala Arena, Poznań, Poland.

-July 24-
Mike Oldfield performs at Strahov Stadium, Praga, Czechoslovakia.

-July 28-
Mike Oldfield performs at Guildhall Yard, London, England, at The Royal Wedding Concert.

> "Royal Wedding Anthem" 2:56
> Written by Mike Oldfield
> Appears on: Unreleased
> This live recording comes from a concert Oldfield and his group performed during the Royal Wedding festivities the evening before the marriage of Prince Charles and Lady Diana Spencer. The piece has a very Baroque feel to it, with a jaunty tempo similar to "Portsmouth," only with more march-like drum parts. Bootleg copies of this performance are floating around in varying qualities. It's not known if a proper studio recording was ever made. Interesting to hear.

-July 30-
Mike Oldfield performs at the Rainbow Theatre, London, England, ending The European Adventure.

-August-
Mike Oldfield is featured on the *Musical Express* TV show, Barcelona, Spain.

-August 9-
Mike Oldfield performs at Theatre Royal, Nottingham, England. This concert is said to have been recorded.

-Date Unknown-
Ariola Benelux B.V. releases a compilation of **Mike Oldfield** tracks in The Netherlands and Germany, titled *Music Wonderland*. This appears to replace the *Mike Oldfield's Wonderland* release of earlier in the year, though it has a different track listing, as follows:

The Netherlands cassette (7 86943 4)
Germany LP (204 000-610), LP Club Edition (91 265 9), cassette (404 000-352)
"Arrival" - a cover of the 1976 ABBA instrumental.
"Portsmouth"
"Sheba"
"Blue Peter" - a cover of the 1958 TV show theme.
"Tubular Bells (Part One - Boxed Remix) (Episodes Extract)"
"The Sailor's Hornpipe (Single Version)"
"Punkadiddle (Original Version)"
"Wonderful Land" - a cover of The Shadows' 1962 instrumental.
"In Dulci Jubilo"
"Ommadawn (Part One) (Episodes Extract)"
"On Horseback (Single Version)"
"Guilty (Exposed - Music Wonderland Edit)"
"Platinum (Part Four): North Star/Platinum Finale"

-Summer-
Mike Oldfield starts work on his next album at his home studio in Denham, Buckinghamshire, England (*Five Miles Out* sessions).
"Five Miles Out" – Apparently, this was the first track written and worked on during these sessions, directly inspired by his aviation experience on September 20th, 1980. **Oldfield** says in his biography that recording this song takes "about three months" with "about six different versions." One such version with Maggie Reilly singing it in a '30 style (according to **Mike** in a 1998 *Mojo* magazine article).

> "Five Miles Out (Demo Version)" 4:10
> Written by Mike Oldfield
> Appears on: Five Miles Out (2013 Deluxe Edition)
> One of the early recordings, this version is very different from the final album version. It features some different lyrics and is sung entirely by Maggie Reilly. The backing tracking is completely different in places, though the song roughly follows the same structure. There are choral vocals, multitracked by Reilly. The opening includes part of the "Introduction" melody of *Tubular Bells* briefly.

-September-
Mike Oldfield and his touring group (Maggie Reilly, Morris Pert, Tim Cross, Rick Fenn and Mike Frye) work on the following at his home studio in Denham, Buckinghamshire, England.
"Five Miles Out" – The group continues to work on this track. Graham Broad plays drums on the track and strings are arranged by Pert and conducted by Martyn Ford. The track is co-produced by **Oldfield** and Tom Newman.
"Taurus II" – this track is recorded between September 1981 and February 1982, according to the tracking sheet pictured on the sleeve (which credits the piece to **"Mike Oldfield Groop."** Paddy Moloney plays uilleann pipes on this track. It contain a lullaby titled "The Deep Deep Sound," sung by Reilly.
"Family Man" – co-written by **Oldfield**, Cross, Fenn, Frye, Reilly and Pert. Accounts differ as to who wrote what parts and in what order. **Mike** says he wrote the chorus and Maggie wrote the verses after. Tim Cross says *he* (Cross) wrote the song based on Rick Fenn's attitude toward to groupies and that **Oldfield** and Reilly only added a verse each after his lyrics were written.
"Oorabidoo" – co-written by **Oldfield**, Cross, Fenn, Frye, Reilly and Pert.

-Date Unknown-
Dougal Oldfield is born to **Mike Oldfield** and Sally Cooper.

Five Miles Out

1982

-Winter 1982-
Mike Oldfield works with Carl Palmer (of Emerson, Lake & Palmer) at Denham, Buckinghamshire, England:
"Mount Teidi"
"Ready Mix"

> "Ready Mix" 3:55
> Written by Carl Palmer and/or Mike Oldfield
> Appears on: Anthology - One More Time
> This is an interesting instrumental track, with a repeating, heavy guitar melody over a strong drum backing track. It may be a little incomplete, which would explain why it didn't surface until 2001 on the Carl Palmer *Anthology* set. Still, as a session outtake, it's worth owning and Mike's work is clearly spotted, particularly on the bass.

-Date Unknown-
Mike Oldfield rechristens his touring band of Maggie Reilly, Tim Renwick, Morris Pert and Pierre Moerlen, Rick Fenn, Virginia Clee and Devra Robitaille as **The Mike Oldfield Group**. They rehearse for the upcoming Five Miles Out World Tour.

-February-
Mike Oldfield completes work on his album *Five Miles Out* at Denham, Buckinghamshire, England. It is mastered at The Town House Studios, London, England.

-February 18-
Mike Oldfield releases his "Five Miles Out" 7" singles on Virgin Records in Europe and Canada.

Spain 7" single (0283) promo:
"Five Miles Out"
"Live Punkadiddle" The Mike Oldfield Group

Spain 7" single (B-103 920):
"Five Miles Out"
"Live Punkadiddle" The Mike Oldfield Group

Scandinavia 7" single (VS-464):
"Five Miles Out"
"Live Punkadiddle" The Mike Oldfield Group

France 7" single (103920):
"Five Miles Out"
"Live Punkadiddle" The Mike Oldfield Group

Portugal 7" single (506005):
"Five Miles Out"
"Live Punkadiddle" The Mike Oldfield Group

Germany 7" single (1039 20):
"Five Miles Out (Early Mix)"
"Live Punkadiddle" The Mike Oldfield Group

Canada 7" single (VS 1150):
"Five Miles Out"
"Mount Teide"

> "Five Miles Out (Early Mix)" 4:18
> Written by Mike Oldfield
> Appears on: Germany 7" single; Australia 7" single; New Zealand 7" single; The Complete Mike Oldfield
> Probably an early mix of the song, this version's differences are apparent right from the start. There are some stereo effects not present in the standard version, Maggie Reilly sings along with Mike during the opening, various instruments have greater prominence at different parts and

overall the mix is a little busier throughout, meaning you'll hear little details more clearly. This is definitely worth tracking down as a great alternative to the album mix.

-March 5-
Mike Oldfield releases his "Five Miles Out" 7" singles on Virgin Records in the UK, Europe and Canada.

UK 7" single (VS 464):
"Five Miles Out"
"Live Punkadiddle" The Mike Oldfield Group

UK 7" single (VSY 464) Picture disc:
"Five Miles Out"
"Live Punkadiddle" The Mike Oldfield Group

Ireland 7" single (VS 464):
"Five Miles Out"
"Live Punkadiddle" The Mike Oldfield Group

-March 19-
Mike Oldfield releases his album *Five Miles Out* on LP on Virgin Records in the UK (V2222), Europe and the Canada (VL 2237), and in the US (ARE 37983). Track listing as follows:

"Taurus II"
"Family Man"
"Orabidoo"
"Mount Teidi"
"Five Miles Out"

Around this time, American Forces Radio And Television Service (AFRTS), part of the US Dept. of Defense, releases a Radio Promo LP including excerpts from *Five Miles Out*, track listing as follows:

Side One: *Five Miles Out* Mike Oldfield
"Taurus II (AFRTS Radio Promo Excerpt)" – listed as "Taurus (Excerpt)"
"Family Man"
"Mount Teidi"
"Five Miles Out"

Side Two: *Stars On Long Play III* Stars On
"Stars On Long Play III Part 2 (In Tribute To Stevie Wonder)" Stars On
"Stars On Long Play III Part 3 (In Tribute To Stevie Wonder)" Stars On
"The Stars Will Never Stop"

Note: the material on Side Two does not feature **Mike Oldfield**, instead being performed by the Dutch soundalike group Stars On 45 (who do cover tributes to famous artists). In the US, the record company changed both the name of the band (from Stars On 45 to just Stars On) and the name of their album (from *The Superstars* to *Stars On Long Play III*). Side Two of this Radio Promo LP is composed of excerpts from that album. *The Superstars* (aka *Stars On Long Play III*) was released in March 1982, further supporting that this Radio Promo LP dates from the same time as it and *Five Miles Out*.

> "Taurus II (AFRTS Radio Promo Excerpt)" 6:53
> Written by Mike Oldfield
> Appears on: AFRTS Radio Promo LP
> I have not heard this excerpt, but the promo LP notes a 14 second lead-in time next to the track length, which could indicate this is the 1st movement of "Taurus II," ending early on the bagpipes.

-Date Unknown-
Powderworks re-releases **The Sallyangie** album *Children Of The Sun*, credited to **Mike & Sally Oldfield** and titled *The Sally Angie* (POW 3014) in Australia and New Zealand on LP.

-April-
Mike Oldfield releases his "Five Miles Out" 7" singles on Virgin Records in Australia.

Australia 7" single (VS 464):
"Five Miles Out (Early Mix)"
"Live Punkadiddle" The Mike Oldfield Group

New Zealand 7" single (VS 464):
"Five Miles Out (Early Mix)"
"Live Punkadiddle" The Mike Oldfield Group

-April 8-
The Mike Oldfield Group performs at My Father's Place, Roslyn, New York, US, starting the Five Miles Out World Tour.

-April 10-
The Mike Oldfield Group performs at the National Arts Centre, Ottawa, Ontario, Canada.

-April 11-
The Mike Oldfield Group performs two shows at the Ryerson Polytechnical Institute Main Stage, Toronto, Ontario, Canada.

-April 13-
The Mike Oldfield Group performs at Place des Arts, Montreal, Quebec, Canada.

-April 14-
The Mike Oldfield Group performs at Palais Montcalm, Quebec, Canada.

-April 16-
The Mike Oldfield Group performs at Tower Theatre, Philadelphia, Pennsylvania, US.

-April 17-
The Mike Oldfield Group performs at the Berkley Performance Arts Centre, Boston, Massachusetts, US.

-April 18-
The Mike Oldfield Group performs at The Ritz, New York City, New York, US.

-April 21-
The Mike Oldfield Group performs at Park West, Chicago, Illinois, US.

-April 25-
The Mike Oldfield Group performs at the Orpheum, Vancouver, British Columbia, US.

-April 28-
The Mike Oldfield Group performs at the Civic Auditorium, Los Angeles, California, US.

-April 30-
The Mike Oldfield Group performs at the Warfield Theatre, San Francisco, US.

-May 6-
The Mike Oldfield Group performs at Dunden Town Hall, Dunden, New Zealand.

-May 7-
The Mike Oldfield Group performs at Christchurch Town Hall, Christchurch, New Zealand.

-May 9-
The Mike Oldfield Group performs at St. James Theatre, Wellington, New Zealand.

-May 10-
The Mike Oldfield Group performs two shows at Oakland Town Hall, Oakland, New Zealand.

-May 13-
The Mike Oldfield Group performs at the Festival Centre, Brisbane, Australia.

-May 15 & 16-
The Mike Oldfield Group performs at the Palais Theatre, Melbourne, Australia.

-May 18-
The Mike Oldfield Group performs at the Thebarton Theatre Hall, Adelaide, Australia.

-May 20, 21 & 22-
The Mike Oldfield Group performs at the Capitol Theatre, Sydney, Australia.

-May 26-
The Mike Oldfield Group performs at Shibuya Koukaidou, Tokyo, Japan, ending the Five Miles Out World Tour.

-May 28-
Mike Oldfield releases his 7" single "Family Man" in the UK, Europe and North America.

UK 7" single (VS 489):
"Family Man"
"Mount Teidi"

UK 7" single (VSY 489) Picture disc:
"Family Man"
"Mount Teidi"

Ireland 7" single (VS 489):
"Family Man"
"Mount Teidi"

Scandinavia 7" single (VS-489):
"Family Man"
"Mount Teidi"

Spain 7" single (B-103.793):
"Family Man"
"Mount Teidi"

Spain 7" single (VS-489):
"Family Man"
"Mount Teidi"

US 7" single (14-02877):
"Family Man"
"Mount Teidi"

US 7" single (14-02877) promo:
"Family Man" - listed as "Long Version"
"Family Man (Short Version)"

Canada 7" single (VS 1141):
"Family Man"
"Live Punkadiddle"

New Zealand 7" single (VS 489):
"Family Man"
"Mount Teidi"

"Family Man (Short Version)" 3:26
Written by Mike Oldfield / Tim Cross / Rick Fenn / Mike Frye / Maggie Reilly / Morris Pert
Appears on: US Promo 7" single
This edit removes some of the guitar instrumental before the second verse, from 0:45 to about to 0:59, as well as some the repeating chorus near the end.

-Summer-
The Mike Oldfield Group records the following at Denham, Buckinghamshire, England:
"Waldberg (The Peak)" – Co-produced by **Oldfield** and David Hentschel.
"In High Places" – This song is started during this period, as an early version is performed on several dates of the upcoming leg of the tour. It's not known if **The Mike Oldfield Group** recorded a version of it. The song would be re-visited during the *Crises* sessions.
"Recuerdos de la Alhambra" – This piece, written by Francisco Tárrega, would later become known to **Oldfield** fans later as "Étude," from *The Killing Fields* soundtrack album. Apparently, this recording was begun as a studio improv with **Oldfield** and Morris Pert.

-July-
The Mike Oldfield Group records the following at Denham, Buckinghamshire, England:
"Mistake" – Apparently, this was recorded the day before the *6:55* BBC Special taping. It is co-produced by **Oldfield** and David Hentschel, who also plays keyboards on the track. **Mike** writes both the words and music.

-July 3-
The Mike Oldfield Group performs at Roskilde Open Air Festival, Copenhagen, Denmark.

-July 28-
The Mike Oldfield Group performs on the broadcast of the *6:55* Special on BBC TV, London, England. They perform "Five Miles Out" (mimed) and "Mistake."

> "Mistake (6:55 Version)" 3:12
> Written by Mike Oldfield
> Appears on: Five Miles Out (2013 Deluxe Edition DVD)
> This performance is a very rough, since the song is brand new and the group had not played it often live. They had just recently (the day before) recorded it for the single.

-August 20-
The Mike Oldfield Group releases its 7" and 12" singles "Mistake" in the UK and Europe.

UK 7" single (VS 541):
"Mistake"
"Waldberg (The Peak)"

UK 7" single (VSY 541) Picture disc:
"Mistake"
"Waldberg (The Peak)"

Ireland 7" single (VS 541):
"Mistake"
"Waldberg (The Peak)"

Scandinavia 7" single (VS 541):
"Mistake"
"Waldberg (The Peak)"

Portugal 7" single (509705):
"Mistake"
"Waldberg (The Peak)"

Spain 7" single (B-104.640):
"Mistake"
"Waldberg (The Peak)"

Spain 7" single (B-104.640) promo:
"Mistake"
"Waldberg (The Peak)"

The Mike Oldfield EP
Germany 7" single (104 678):
"Mistake" The Mike Oldfield Group
"Waldberg (The Peak)" The Mike Oldfield Group
"Family Man" Mike Oldfield
"Mount Teidi" Mike Oldfield

The Mike Oldfield EP
Germany 12" single (600 690):
"Mistake" The Mike Oldfield Group
"Waldberg (The Peak)" The Mike Oldfield Group
"Family Man" Mike Oldfield
"Mount Teidi" Mike Oldfield

"Mistake" 2:57
Written by Mike Oldfield
Appears on: 7" single, The Mike Oldfield EP, Crises (North American LP Edition), The Complete Mike Oldfield, The Platinum Collection, Crises (2013 Deluxe Edition)
The only single release by The Mike Oldfield Group, though later releases simply include it and "Waldberg" as Mike Oldfield tracks. A great piece, with Maggie Reilly offering stellar lead vocals and Mike wailing on the guitar, it's well worth finding! Less elaborately arranged than other Oldfield '80s singles, it sounds like the group decided to go for it and rock out.

"Waldberg (The Peak)" 3:27
Written by Mike Oldfield
Appears on: Mistake 7" single, The Mike Oldfield EP, The Complete Mike Oldfield, Elements boxed set, Five Miles Out (2013 Deluxe Edition)
This is an instrumental in the classic Oldfield style, with repeating melodies and layering synths and guitar. Even the drums follow the tune, rather than simply keeping the beat. It's not too hard to find, as it's been on a few collections and appears as a bonus track on the 2013 re-issue of *Five Miles Out*. Also of note, the title is originally rendered as "(Waldberg) The Peak," though this is changed on later releases.

-September 8-
The Mike Oldfield Group performs at the Apollo, Manchester, England, kicking off the Who's Next Tour.

-September 9-
The Mike Oldfield Group performs at the Playhouse Theatre, Edinburgh, Scotland. The group plays an early version of "In High Places" and "Recuerdos de la Alhambra."

-September 10-
The Mike Oldfield Group performs at Sheffield City Hall, Sheffield, England.

-September 11-
The Mike Oldfield Group performs at Newcastle City Hall, Newcastle, England.

-September 12 & 13-
The Mike Oldfield Group performs at the Odeon, Birmingham, England.

-September 14-
The Mike Oldfield Group performs at Guildhall, Portsmouth, England.

-September 15-
The Mike Oldfield Group performs at New Theatre, Oxford, England.

-September 16-
The Mike Oldfield Group performs at the Hammersmith Odeon, London, England. The group plays "In High Places" and "Recuerdos de la Alhambra."

"Medley: In High Places / Recuerdos de la Alhambra (AKA Étude)"
Written by Mike Oldfield (In High Places) / Tárrega (Recuerdos de la Alhambra)
Appears on: Unreleased
A decent bootleg of this show exists and one of the highlights is this medley. It starts with an early version of "In High Places," featuring some different lyrics predating Jon Anderson's involvement with the song (he later co-wrote the C*rises* version). The arrangement and performance is similar to the album version. Some of the lyrics are hard to make out, but Mike introduces it as "a song that hasn't been recorded on an album before," suggesting either the group has only rehearsed it and not recorded their own version, or he's simply telling the fans in a roundabout way that it has

yet to appear on an album, basically it's a new song. He also says it's about "leprechauns and magic people, very small," which suggests the original, pre-Anderson lyrics were fairy tale-themed. The group then plays a discordant interlude, similar to the live jams of The Whole World, before going into "Recuerdos de la Alhambra." Whether Mike called the piece "Étude" at this early stage is not known. In classical music, an étude is a piece written in order to practice a skill. "Recuerdos de la Alhambra" is not a technically an étude in that sense, though Oldfield may use it as such ("étude" is French for "study"), hence his re-titling.

-September 20-
The Mike Oldfield Group performs in Oslo, Norway.

-September 22-
The Mike Oldfield Group performs at Jähalli, Helsinki, Finland.

-September 23-
The Mike Oldfield Group performs at Drammenshallen, Stockholm, Sweden.

-September 25-
The Mike Oldfield Group performs at the Scandinavium, Göteborg, Sweden.

-September 26-
The Mike Oldfield Group performs in Copenhagen, Denmark.

-September 27-
The Mike Oldfield Group performs in Alborg, Denmark.

-September 28-
The Mike Oldfield Group performs at the Olympen, Lund, Sweden.

-September 29-
The Mike Oldfield Group performs in Arhus, Sweden.

-September 30-
The Mike Oldfield Group performs at Osteehalle, Kiel, Germany.

-October 1-
The Mike Oldfield Group performs at Deutschlandhalle, Berlin, Germany.

-October 2 & 3-
The Mike Oldfield Group performs at Congress Center Hamburg, Hamburg, Germany.

-October 4-
The Mike Oldfield Group performs at Stadhalle, Bremen, Germany.

-October 6-
The Mike Oldfield Group performs at Eilenriedhalle, Hannover, Germany.

-October 7-
The Mike Oldfield Group performs at Halle Münsterland, Münster.

-October 8 & 9-
The Mike Oldfield Group performs at Grugahalle, Essen, Germany.

-October 10-
The Mike Oldfield Group performs at Eissporthalle, Kassel, Germany.

-October 11-
The Mike Oldfield Group performs at Saarlandhalle, Saarbrücken, Germany.

-October 12-
The Mike Oldfield Group performs at Schwarzwaldhalle, Karlsruhe, Germany.

-October 13-
The Mike Oldfield Group performs at Rhein-Neckar-Halle, Heidelberg, Germany.

-October 14-
The Mike Oldfield Group performs at Sporthalle, Köln, Germany.

-October 15 & 16-
The Mike Oldfield Group performs at Walter-Körbel- Halle, Rüsselsheim, Germany.

-October 17-
The Mike Oldfield Group performs at Carl-Dien-Halle, Würzburg, Germany.

-October 18 & 19-
The Mike Oldfield Group performs at Hemmerleinhalle, Nürnberg, Germany.

-October 20-
The Mike Oldfield Group performs at Sporthalle, Böblingen, Stuttgart, Germany.

-October 21-
The Mike Oldfield Group performs at Freiburg, Stadthalle, Germany.

-October 23-
The Mike Oldfield Group performs at Nibelungenhalle, Passau, Germany.

-October 24-
The Mike Oldfield Group performs at Olympiahalle, München, Germany.

-October 25-
The Mike Oldfield Group performs at Donauhalle, Ulm, Germany.

-October 26-
The Mike Oldfield Group performs at Messehalle, Friedrichshafen, Germany.

-October 27-
The Mike Oldfield Group performs at Sporthalle, Augsburg, Germany.

-October 28-
The Mike Oldfield Group performs at Freiheitshalle, Hof, Germany.

-October 29-
The Mike Oldfield Group performs at Orthenauhalle, Offenburg, Germany.

-October 31-
The Mike Oldfield Group performs at Eilenriedhalle, Hannover, Germany.

-November-
Mike Oldfield begins work on his next album, at Denham, Buckinghamshire, England (*Crises* sessions). This date and location is noted on the album sleeve, but it should be pointed out that **Mike** is in the middle of a tour throughout mainland Europe this month. Regardless, the album sessions last until April 1983.
"Crises" – Phil Spalding later notes that a live rehearsal recording, from this period, is used as a reference in February of 1983 when working on part of this track.

-November 1-
The Mike Oldfield Group performs at Stadhalle, Bremerhaven, Germany.

> "Mount Teidi (Live in Germany, 1982)" 4:34
> Written by Mike Oldfield
> Appears on: The Complete Mike Oldfield; The Complete Mike Oldfield Promo 12" single
> A good live version of the track from the Who's Next Tour (itself an extension of the Five Miles Out World Tour). There seems to be no consensus as to what date on this leg of the tour this recording hails from, and quite frankly I myself can offer little insight. Seemingly reliable sources cite different shows and I'm content to let them hash it out in online forums.
> Other possible dates seem to be:
> - October 14th at Sporthalle, Köln, Germany.
> - November 2nd at Sporthalle, Köln, Germany.
> - December 6th at Sporthalle, Köln, Germany, which was released on the 2013 *Five Miles Out* Deluxe Edition, possibly mixed differently than the recording heard on *The Complete Mike Oldfield*.

-November 2-
The Mike Oldfield Group performs at Sporthalle, Köln, Germany.

-November 5-
The Mike Oldfield Group performs at Orthenauhalle, Offenburg, Germany.

-November 6-
The Mike Oldfield Group performs in Innsbruck, Austria.

-November 7-
The Mike Oldfield Group performs in Linz, Austria.

-November 8-
The Mike Oldfield Group performs at Stadthalle, Wien, Germany.

-November 9-
The Mike Oldfield Group performs at Hallenstadion, Zürich, Germany.

-November 10-
The Mike Oldfield Group performs in Mulhouse, France.

-November 11-
The Mike Oldfield Group performs at Hall Rhenus, Strasbourg, France.

-November 13-
The Mike Oldfield Group performs in Paris, France.

-November 14-
The Mike Oldfield Group performs in Dijon, France.

-November 15-
The Mike Oldfield Group performs in Nancy, France.

-November 16-
The Mike Oldfield Group performs in Utrecht, The Netherlands.

-November 18-
The Mike Oldfield Group performs in Caen, France.

-November 19-
The Mike Oldfield Group performs in Rennes, France.

-November 20-
The Mike Oldfield Group performs in Quimper, France.

-November 21-
The Mike Oldfield Group performs in Nantes, France.

-November 22-
The Mike Oldfield Group performs in Poitiers, France.

-November 23-
The Mike Oldfield Group performs at Palais des Sports, Clermont-Ferrand, France.

-November 24-
The Mike Oldfield Group performs at Complexe Compans Casarelli, Toulouse, France.

-November 26-
The Mike Oldfield Group performs at Velódromo de Anoeta, San Sebastián, Spain.

-November 27-
The Mike Oldfield Group performs in Madrid, Spain.

-November 28-
The Mike Oldfield Group performs at Plaza España, Barcelona, Spain.

-November 29-
The Mike Oldfield Group performs in Montpellier, France.

-November 30-
The Mike Oldfield Group performs at Palais d'Hiver, Lyon, France.

-December 2-
The Mike Oldfield Group performs in Rouen, France.

-December 3-
The Mike Oldfield Group performs in Lille, France.

-December 4-
The Mike Oldfield Group performs at Forest National, Brussels, Belgium.

-December 5-
The Mike Oldfield Group performs in Luxembourg City, Luxembourg.

-December 6-
The Mike Oldfield Group performs at Sporthalle, Köln, Germany. This concert is recorded and partly released in 2013 on the *Five Miles Out* Deluxe Edition.

-December 9-
The Mike Oldfield Group performs at Rudi-Sedelmayer Halle, München, Germany. This date ends the Who's Next Tour.

-Mid-December-
Mike Oldfield works on his next album, at Denham, Buckinghamshire, England (*Crises* sessions). He co-produces the album with Simon Phillips, (who also plays Tama drums and assorted percussion).
"Moonlight Shadow" – reportedly, one of the first pieces **Mike** wrote, though the final lyrics would come much later in the album sessions.

Crises

1983

-Late January-
Producer Simon Phillips calls bassist Phil Spalding and asks him to join **Mike Oldfield**'s *Crises* album sessions.

-February 1-
Phil Spalding begins his sessions for **Mike Oldfield**'s *Crises* album, at Denham, Buckinghamshire, England. Spalding later notes on his website that Rick Fenn, Tim Renwick and Simon Phillips are present.
"Crises" – the group works on what would become part of this track, the "Crises, crises…I can't get away" section. Spalding says it developed from a soundcheck recording made on the previous tour.

-February 2-
Mike Oldfield and his session group (Phil Spalding, Tim Renwick and Simon Phillips) continue work on the *Crises* album, at Denham, Buckinghamshire, England.
"Moonlight Shadow" – The backing track is recorded on this date, according to Phil Spalding. **Mike** later tries out different singers and lyrics over the following months. One version, notably recorded with Hazel O'Connor, is titled "Moment of Passion."

-Early 1983-
Sessions continue for **Mike Oldfield**'s next album, *Crises*.

-Date Unknown-
Mike Oldfield produces David Bedford's album *Star Clusters, Nebulae And Places In Devon*, featuring the recordings made in 1978 of the following:
"Star Clusters, Nebulae And Places In Devon"
"The Song Of The White Horse"

Oldfield decides to put the album out on his own newly-created label Oldfield Music Ltd.

-April-
Mike Oldfield completes work on his album *Crises*, at Denham, Buckinghamshire, England. Tracks worked on since (apparently) November 1982 include:
"Man In The Rain" – It's been suggested that this song was written (or started) around this time. The song is worked on later during the *Islands* sessions.
"In High Places" – Having performed the track live on the previous tour, **Mike** invites Jon Anderson (of Yes) to co-write and sing the new version of the song. Pierre Moerlen plays vibraphone.
"Moonlight Shadow" – After failed attempts to match the existing backing track with a singer and suitable lyrics, **Oldfield** recruits Maggie Reilly to sing lyrics he pens the night before the session.
"Foreign Affair" – Co-written by **Oldfield** and Maggie Reilly.
"Shadow On The Wall" – Roger Chapman sings on this track.
"Rite Of Man" – The lyrics are co-written by **Oldfield** and Jeremy Parker. Parker and Pierre Moerlen provide backing vocals and percussion.
"Taurus 3" – This track is sometimes titled "Taurus III."
"Unused Crises Segments" – **Mike** apparently is on record saying there are pieces intended for the track "Crises" which he either didn't use or removed.

-Spring-
Mike Oldfield assembles a touring group for his Crises Tour, consisting of Maggie Reilly, Roger Chapman, Simon Phillips, Pierre Moerlen, Phil Spalding, Graeme Pleeth and Simon House. Sally Cooper manages the

tour. Barry Palmer notes later that he was asked to join the tour as a singer, but that he was unable because he busy recording his own album.

-Date Unknown-
Virgin Records releases **Mike Oldfield**'s album *Tubular Bells* on CD in Europe (CDV 2001), Canada (CDV 2001) and the US (V2 90589).

-May 6-
Mike Oldfield releases his "Moonlight Shadow" 7" and 12" in the UK, Europe, Australia and Canada.

UK 7" single (VS 586):
"Moonlight Shadow"
"Rite Of Man"

UK 12" single (VS 58 612):
"Moonlight Shadow (Extended Version)"
"Rite Of Man"

Europe 7" single (105 390):
"Moonlight Shadow"
"Rite Of Man"

Europe 12" single (600 928):
"Moonlight Shadow (Extended Version)"
"Rite Of Man"

Spain 7" single (B-105 390):
"Moonlight Shadow"
"Rite Of Man"

Scandinavia 7" single (VS 586):
"Moonlight Shadow"
"Rite Of Man"

Portugal 7" single (513305):
"Moonlight Shadow"
"Rite Of Man"

Australia 7" single (VS 586):
"Moonlight Shadow"
"Rite Of Man"

Australia 1-side 7" single (V FLEX 1) Flexidisc:
"Moonlight Shadow"

New Zealand 7" single (VS 586):
"Moonlight Shadow"
"Rite Of Man"

Canada 7" single (VS 1172):
"Moonlight Shadow"
"Taurus 3"

"Moonlight Shadow (Extended Version)" 5:16
Written by Mike Oldfield
Appears on: 12" single; 1993 Moonlight Shadow (Elements) CD single; Crises (2013 1CD, Deluxe & 30th Anniversary boxed set Editions)
This version breaks down the song by its musical elements, rebuilding it again by layers as the track progresses. It features an additional verse at the end not heard on the standard version. The extended version retains all the power and beauty of the original and arguably improves on what was already a nearly perfect song.

"Rite Of Man" 2:23
Written by Mike Oldfield & Jeremy Parker
Appears on: Moonlight Shadow 7" & 12" singles; Canada 7" single; 1988 Moonlight Shadow CD single
A fun little folk number that sounds like it was recorded live in the studio. The track is presented without polish, pretty much as it was recorded, complete with the group ending the song by simply stopping. It's a shame this track wasn't included on either the *Elements* boxed set or the 2013 Editions of *Crises*.

-Mid-May-
Mike Oldfield does an interview on the BBC TV show *Breakfast Show*, demonstrating various guitars he owns.

-May 26-
Mike Oldfield performs at Hall Rhenus, Strasbourg, France, beginning the Crises Tour.

-May 27-
Mike Oldfield releases his album *Crises* in the UK, Europe and Canada. This is his first album to be originally released on compact disc. Track listing as follows:

UK *Crises* LP (205 500)
UK *Crises* LP (V 2262)
UK *Crises* LP (70115)
UK & Europe *Crises* CD (CDV 2262)
"Crises"
"Moonlight Shadow"
"In High Places" Mike Oldfield Featuring Jon Anderson
"Foreign Affair"
"Taurus 3"
"Shadow On The Wall" Mike Oldfield And Roger Chapman

Canada *Crises* LP (VL 2262)
"Mistake" The Mike Oldfield Group
"In High Places" Mike Oldfield Featuring Jon Anderson
"Foreign Affair"
"Taurus 3"
"Shadow On The Wall" Mike Oldfield And Roger Chapman
"Moonlight Shadow"
"Crises"

Mike Oldfield performs in Dijon, France.

-May 28-
Mike Oldfield performs in Evry, France.

-May 30-
Mike Oldfield performs in Metz, France.

-May 31-
Mike Oldfield performs at Chapiteau de Pantin, Paris, France.

-June-
Virgin Records releases **Mike Oldfield**'s single "Moonlight Shadow" in Italy.

Italy 7" single (VIN 45076):
"Moonlight Shadow"
"Rite Of Man"

Italy 12" single (VINX 20):
"Moonlight Shadow"
"Rite Of Man"

-June 1-
Mike Oldfield performs at Palais d'Hiver, Lyon, France.

-June 2-
Mike Oldfield performs at Palais des Sports, Clermont-Ferrand, France.

-June 3-
Mike Oldfield performs at Patinoire de Meriadeck, Bordeaux, France.

-June 4-
Mike Oldfield performs at Estadi Narcís Sala, Barcelona, Spain.

-June 5-
Mike Oldfield performs at Pabellón de La Casilla, Bilbao, Spain.

-June 7-
Mike Oldfield performs at Palais des Sports, Toulouse, France.

-June 8-
Mike Oldfield performs in Nantes, France.

-June 9-
Mike Oldfield performs in Quimper, France.

-June 10-
Mike Oldfield performs in Le Mans, France.

-June 11-
Mike Oldfield performs at Foire de Lille, Lille, France.

-June 12-
Mike Oldfield performs at Forest National, Brussels, Belgium.

-June 13-
Mike Oldfield performs in Nijmegen, The Netherlands.

-June 14-
Mike Oldfield performs at the Midsummernight Festival, Wilhelm-Koch-Stadion, Hamburg, France.

-June 15-
Mike Oldfield performs at the Midsummernight Festival, Walbühne, Berlin, Germany.

-June 17-
Mike Oldfield performs at the Midsummernight Festival, Georg-Melches-Stadion, Essen, Germany.

-June 18-
Mike Oldfield performs at the Midsummernight Festival, Stadion am Böllenfalltor, Darmstadt, Germany.

-June 19-
Mike Oldfield performs at the Midsummernight Festival, Rosenaustadion, Augsburg, Germany.

-June 20-
Mike Oldfield performs in Luxembourg City, Luxembourg, ending the Crises Tour.

-July 3-
An article published this date in The Observer, by Ena Kendall, notes that after the forthcoming July 22 concert, **Mike Oldfield** will begin working on *The Killing Fields* score.

-July 22-
Mike Oldfield performs at Wembley Arena, London, England. This concert celebrates the 10th Anniversary of *Tubular Bells*. This show is audio and video recorded. The complete audio of the concert is released on

the *Crises* 30th Anniversary Edition boxed set, as is a 40 minute excerpt video of the concert, titled *Crises At Wembley*.

-Late July-
Mike Oldfield begins recording the score for the film *The Killing Fields* at his home studio, Denham, Buckinghamshire, England. These sessions last until December. **Mike** also starts working on ideas for his next studio album.

Possibly around this time, **Mike** works on the following, at Denham, Buckinghamshire, England.
"Shadow On The Wall" - Phil Spalding's later description of his contribution to the extended version indicates the new material is recorded later in the year after the album version was finished. Spalding provides backing vocals and probably bass on the extended version for the planned single.

-August-
This month, the Wembley Arena, July 22, 1983, concert recording is mixed at The Manor, Shipton-on-Cherwell, Oxfordshire, England.

-Date Unknown-
Oldfield Music Ltd releases David Bedford's album *Star Clusters, Nebulae And Places In Devon* in the UK. There are apparently distribution issues and it appears not many copies of the album actually get released.

-September-
Mike Oldfield And Roger Chapman release the "Shadow On The Wall" 7" and 12" singles in the UK and Europe.

UK 7" single (VS 625):
"Shadow On The Wall" Mike Oldfield And Roger Chapman
"Taurus 3" Mike Oldfield

UK 12" single (VS 625-12):
"Shadow On The Wall (12" Version)" Mike Oldfield And Roger Chapman
"Taurus 3" Mike Oldfield

Ireland 7" single (VS 625):
"Shadow On The Wall" Mike Oldfield And Roger Chapman
"Taurus 3" Mike Oldfield

Italy 7" single (VIN 45085):
"Shadow On The Wall" Mike Oldfield And Roger Chapman
"Taurus 3" Mike Oldfield

Spain 7" single (B-600 977):
"Shadow On The Wall" Mike Oldfield And Roger Chapman
"Taurus 3" Mike Oldfield

Spain 7" single (B-600 977) promo:
"Shadow On The Wall" Mike Oldfield And Roger Chapman
"Taurus 3" Mike Oldfield

Portugal 7" single (517505):
"Shadow On The Wall" Mike Oldfield And Roger Chapman
"Taurus 3" Mike Oldfield

Scandinavia 7" single (VS 625):
"Shadow On The Wall" Mike Oldfield And Roger Chapman
"Taurus 3" Mike Oldfield

Europe 12" single (600 977):
"Shadow On The Wall (12" Version)" Mike Oldfield And Roger Chapman
"Taurus 3" Mike Oldfield

Australia 7" single (VS 625):
"Shadow On The Wall" Mike Oldfield And Roger Chapman
"Taurus 3" Mike Oldfield

Australia 7" single (VS 625) promo:
"Shadow On The Wall" Mike Oldfield And Roger Chapman
"Taurus 3" Mike Oldfield

New Zealand 7" single (VS 625):
"Shadow On The Wall" Mike Oldfield And Roger Chapman
"Taurus 3" Mike Oldfield

> "Shadow On The Wall (12" Version)" 5:09
> Written by Mike Oldfield
> Appears on: 12" single, The Complete Mike Oldfield; A Virgin Compilation; Elements: The Best Of Mike Oldfield; Elements boxed set; Collection; The Platinum Collection; Crises (2013 1CD, Deluxe & 30th Anniversary boxed set Editions)
> The first part of this version is identical to the album version, but instead of fading out, new backing vocals come in, repeating "Like a shadow..." and there's a second, shorter guitar solo. This seems to have become Mike's preferred version as it appears on a number of his collections and is the version he later mixed in 5.1 Surround for the Crises Deluxe Edition.

This month, **Mike Oldfield** appears on the Italian TV shows *Superflash* and *Bis*.

-Date Unknown-
Virgin Records releases **The Mike Oldfield Group** 7" single (credited to only **Mike Oldfield**) "Mistake" in Canada.

Canada 7" single (VS 1168):
"Mistake" The Mike Oldfield Group
"Rite Of Man" Mike Oldfield

-Autumn-
Mike Oldfield works on the following at his home studio, Denham, Buckinghamshire, England (produced **Oldfield**):
"Crime Of Passion" - **Mike** recruits singer Barry Palmer for this track.
"Jungle Gardenia"

At some point not long after the tour and the start of *The Killing Fields* sessions, **Mike Oldfield** decides to live for a year in Villars-sur-Ollon, Switzerland, as a tax exile, having renegotiated his contract with Virgin Records.

Note: With eight of his contracted ten studio albums now released, the new contract included reimbursement for the previously low royalty rates and managerial fees from the original Virgin contract, as well as higher rates for an additional three albums. This reimbursement (a sudden influx of a large sum of money from Virgin) was a big part of the motivation to live abroad for a year.

-October-
Mike Oldfield appears on the German TV show *Bananas*, performing "Shadow On The Wall."

-Date Unknown-
Mike Oldfield appears on the Italian TV show *Premiatissima*, performing "Moonlight Shadow" and "Shadow On The Wall"

-December-
Mike Oldfield completes work on *The Killing Fields* score at Villars-sur-Ollon, Switzerland.

Discovery

1984

-January-
Mike Oldfield begins working on his *Discovery* album this month, at Villars-sur-Ollon, Switzerland.

-January 3-
Mike Oldfield releases his "Crime Of Passion" 7" and 12" singles in the UK and Europe.

UK 7" single (VS 648):
"Crime Of Passion"
"Jungle Gardenia"

UK 12" single (VS 648-12):
"Crime Of Passion (Extended Version)"
"Jungle Gardenia"

Ireland 7" single (VS 648):
"Crime Of Passion"
"Jungle Gardenia"

Italy 7" single (VIN 45092):
"Crime Of Passion"
"Jungle Gardenia"

Italy 12" single (VINX 32):
"Crime Of Passion (Extended Version)"
"Jungle Gardenia"

Portugal 7" single (517705):
"Crime Of Passion"
"Jungle Gardenia"

Australia 7" single (VS 648) promo:
"Crime Of Passion"
"Jungle Gardenia"

Spain 7" single (A-106102):
"Crime Of Passion"
"Jungle Gardenia"

Spain 12" single (F-601133):
"Crime Of Passion (Extended Version)"
"Jungle Gardenia"

Greece 12" single (062-VG 2008Z):
"Crime Of Passion (Extended Version)"
"Jungle Gardenia"

France 7" single (90096):
"Crime Of Passion"
"Jungle Gardenia"

France 12" single (80033):
"Crime Of Passion (Extended Version)"
"Jungle Gardenia"

"Crime Of Passion" 3:37
Written by Mike Oldfield
Appears on: 7" single, The Complete Mike Oldfield, Elements boxed set, The Platinum Collection
A very acoustic-driven rock track, "Crime Of Passion" doesn't try to do too much and the result is pretty good. In many ways, it's the spiritual successor of "Moonlight Shadow," with a similar sound, feel and theme (an ambiguous murder mystery). Some critics at the time accused it of trying to copy "Shadow" and whether that was Mike's intention or not, the single did okay in European charts, but wasn't a UK hit. Still, it's a good song.

"Crime Of Passion (Extended Version)" 4:11
Written by Mike Oldfield
Appears on: 12" single, Crises (2013 1CD, Deluxe & 30th Anniversary boxed set Editions)
This is mostly identical to the standard version, but featuring a few short extended instrumental parts between verses. The ending has been noticeably remixed and extended nicely. It's interesting that Oldfield selected this version and not the regular cut for the 2013 *Crises* re-issue, as until that point, it was harder to come by, as opposed to the standard version, which was relatively easy to find on different collections.

"Jungle Gardenia" 2:47
Written by Mike Oldfield
Appears on: Crime Of Passion 7" & 12" singles, The Complete Mike Oldfield, In High Places 12" single, A Virgin Compilation, 1988 Moonlight Shadow CD single, Elements boxed set
Another classic short Oldfield instrumental, full of mood and atmosphere, this piece is written in 3/4 time, making it move along at a brisk pace without losing its charm. The melodies repeat a few times before fading out quickly.

-Early 1984-
A few weeks after composing music for the new studio album at Villars-sur-Ollon, Switzerland, **Mike Oldfield** is join there by Simon Phillips.

Producer David Puttnam contacts **Mike Oldfield**, needing **Oldfield** to do more work on *The Killing Fields* score (**Mike** later says he was half way through the *Discovery* album when Puttnam contacted him). **Mike** has to set his work on the new studio album aside to work on *The Killing Fields*. This work lasts "a couple of months" by **Oldfield**'s estimate and he has David Bedford assist in recording orchestral score for the film in Munich, Germany.

-March-
Mike Oldfield resumes work on his studio album around this point, at Villars-sur-Ollon, Switzerland. Barry Palmer says in a September 1997 interview that his sessions were either March or April.
"Discovery" - According to Palmer, he was working on this song his second day in the studio when he experienced vocal problems, struggling through this track.
"Saved By A Bell" - Palmer also says he was still experience issues with his voice and the cold weather during part of the sessions for this track.
"Poison Arrows"
"Tricks Of The Light" - Palmer says he recorded his parts before Maggie Reilly recorded hers, with the two never actually meeting during the sessions.

-Spring-
Mike Oldfield continues to record his *Discovery* album at Villars-sur-Ollon, Switzerland. He recruits Maggie Reilly to record on the following:
"Tricks Of The Light" - Reilly records her parts after Barry Palmer finished his work on the track.
"To France"
"Talk About Your Life"
"The Lake"

Mixing of the album takes place over about ten days in Frankfurt, Germany.

-Date Unknown-
Virgin Records re-issues the following **Mike Oldfield** albums on CD in the UK, Europe and Canada

Europe & UK *Hergest Ridge* (1976 Boxed Edition) (CDV 2013).
Canada *Hergest Ridge* (1976 Boxed Edition) (CDVM 2013)

Europe *Platinum* CD (CDV 2141)
"Platinum (Parts 1 – 4) (with Extract from North Star)"
"Woodhenge"
"Into Wonderland (with "Sally Intro")" - incorrectly listed as "Sally."
"Punkadiddle (Original Version)"
"I Got Rhythm" - a version of the 1930 Gershwin song.

Note: the back sleeve track listing is noted above, whereas the CD label notes the individual parts of "Platinum" as follows:

Part 1: Airborne
Part 2: Platinum
Part 3: Charleston
Part 4: North Star/Platinum Finale

Europe *QE2* (CDV 2181)

Also re-issued in Europe on LP:

Europe *Platinum* LP (201 206)
Spain *Platinum* LP (I-201-206)
France *Platinum* LP (70016)

"Platinum (Part One): Airborne"
"Platinum (Part Two): Platinum"
"Platinum (Part Three): Charleston"
"Platinum (Part Four): North Star/Platinum Finale"
"Woodhenge"
"Into Wonderland (with "Sally" Outro)" – incorrectly listed as "Sally."
"Punkadiddle (Original Version)"
"I Got Rhythm" – a version of the 1930 Gershwin song.

-Date Unknown-
Virgin Records releases the **Mike Oldfield** 7" promo single "Foreign Affair" in Argentina.

Argentina 7" single (S-0425) promo:
"Foreign Affair"
"Crises (Argentina Promo Edit)"

> "Crises (Argentina Promo Edit)" 3:50
> Written by Mike Oldfield
> Appears on: Argentina 7" single
> I have not heard this excerpt, but would guess it's perhaps the first 3:50 of "Crises," ending at the tempo change that comes in at this point on the album.

-June-
Mike Oldfield finishes working on his *Discovery* album this month, at Villars-sur-Ollon, Switzerland (noted in a September 1984 article for *Guitarist* magazine).
"The Royal Mile" – Later identified as a "re-discovered" track in 2016, this recording is a longer version of the "Afghan" recording, with additional material at the beginning and end.

Other tracks hinted at via the album sleeve, from a photo of producer Simon Phillips' notes, include:
"Into The Snow"
"In The Pool" – This would be released as an instrumental, non-album b-side, though it's been suggested that there may be two other vocal versions, one with Maggie Reilly and one with Barry Palmer.
"Afghan" – This had the working title "Celtic Thing," and would be released as an instrumental, non-album b-side.
"China"

-June 16-
Mike Oldfield releases his "To France" 7" and 12" singles in the UK and Europe.

UK 7" single (VS 686):
"To France (Single Version)"
"In The Pool"

UK 12" single (VS 686-12):
"To France (Extended Version)"
"In The Pool"
"Bones"

Italy 7" single (VIN 45116):
"To France (Single Version)"
"In The Pool"

Italy 12" single (VINX 65):
"To France (Extended Version)"
"In The Pool"
"Bones"

Spain 7" single (A-106.590):
"To France (Single Version)"
"In The Pool"

France 7" single (106 590):
"To France (Single Version)"
"In The Pool"

France 7" single (90134):
"To France (Single Version)"
"In The Pool"

France 12" single (80117):
"To France (Extended Version)"
"In The Pool"
"Bones"

Australia 7" single (VS 686) promo:
"To France (Single Version)"
"In The Pool"

New Zealand 7" single (VS 686) promo:
"To France (Single Version)"
"In The Pool"

Canada 7" single (VS 1225):
"To France (Single Version)"
"In The Pool"

Canada 12" single (VSX 1225):
"To France (Extended Version)"
"In The Pool"
"Bones"

"To France (Single Version)" 4:44
Written by Mike Oldfield
Appears on: 7" single; 1988 Moonlight Shadow CD single; Elements: The Best Of Mike Oldfield; Elements boxed set; Collection, Two Sides: The Very Best Of Mike Oldfield
This well-known version is identical to the album cut until the very end, where it fades out during the bridge to "Poison Arrows."

"To France (Extended Version)" 5:35
Written by Mike Oldfield
Appears on: 12" single; The Platinum Collection; Discovery (2016 Deluxe Edition)
This version plays out like the album version for the first 3:37, then it changes to a new extended breakdown of the backing track that reworks the last portion of the song. It ends on a fade out, with no audible bridge to "Poison Arrows."

"In The Pool" 3:42
Written by Mike Oldfield
Appears on: To France 7" & 12" singles, 1993 Moonlight Shadow (Elements) CD single; Discovery (2016 Remaster) Deluxe Edition
An instrumental track, possibly a backing track intended to feature vocals (and there are rumors that both Maggie Reilly and Barry Palmer recorded a version each). It certainly seems to be constructed with the intention of there being lyrics as part of the song. The album sleeve's photo of Simon Phillips' notes suggests some version of the piece was in serious contention for the album, but didn't make it on, for whatever reason. Thankfully, Mike decided to release it as a b-side.

"Bones" 3:17
Written by Mike Oldfield
Appears on: To France 12" single, 1993 Moonlight Shadow (Elements) CD single; Discovery (2016 Remaster) Deluxe Edition

A more unusual Oldfield instrumental here, "Bones" starts relatively "normally," with percussion, synth and some vocals, before the rapid chanting and discordant synths take over and, despite remaining percussive, it becomes less-rhythmic. Far less melodic than other Oldfield instrumentals, it may not be to everyone's taste. It's still worth tracking down.

-June 25-
Mike Oldfield releases his album *Discovery* in the UK, Australia, Europe and Canada on Virgin Records. Curiously, the back cover has the track listing under the heading *Discovery And The Lake*.

UK & Australia *Discovery* LP (V 2308)
UK & Europe *Discovery* CD (CDV 2308)
Canada LP (VL 2294)
"To France"
"Poison Arrows"
"Crystal Gazing"
"Tricks Of The Light"
"Discovery"
"Talk About Your Life"
"Saved By A Bell"
"The Lake"

Around this time, a promo 12" single of "Discovery" in Canada.

Canada 12" single (VDJ006) promo:
"Discovery"
"Tricks Of The Light"

-Summer-
Mike Oldfield assembles his touring group for the Discovery Tour 1984. It consists of Maggie Reilly, Barry Palmer, Simon Phillips, Phil Spalding, Mickey Simmonds and Harold Zuschrader.

-August 19-
Mike Oldfield performs at Hemmerleinhalle, Nürnberg, Germany, beginning the Discovery Tour.

-August 21-
Mike Oldfield appears on the German TV shows *Bananas* and *Flashlight*, promoting "To France."

-August 23-
Mike Oldfield performs at Velódromo de Anoeta, San Sebastián, Spain.

-August 25-
Mike Oldfield performs at Estadio de San Andrés, Barcelona, Spain.

-August 27-
Mike Oldfield performs at CF Moscardó, Madid, Spain.

-August 29-
Mike Oldfield performs at Les Arênes, Dax, France.

-August 31-
Mike Oldfield performs at Théatre Antique, Orange, France.

-September 1-
Mike Oldfield releases his "Tricks Of The Light" singles in the UK and Europe.

UK 7" single (VS 707):
"Tricks Of The Light"
"Afghan"

UK 12" single: (VS 707-12):
"Tricks Of The Light"
"Afghan"
"Tricks Of The Light (Instrumental)"

Ireland 7" single (VS 707):
"Tricks Of The Light"
"Afghan"

Spain 7" single (A-106813):
"Tricks Of The Light"
"Afghan"

Spain 12" single (F-601.520):
"Tricks Of The Light"
"Afghan"
"Tricks Of The Light (Instrumental)"

Italy 7" single (VIN 45130):
"Tricks Of The Light"
"Afghan"

Italy 12" single (VINX 77):
"Tricks Of The Light"
"Afghan"
"Tricks Of The Light (Instrumental)"

France 7" single (90210):
"Tricks Of The Light"
"Afghan"

France 12" single (80 131):
"Tricks Of The Light"
"Afghan"
"Tricks Of The Light (Instrumental)"

Europe 7" single (106 810):
"Tricks Of The Light"
"Afghan"

Europe 12" single (601 520):
"Tricks Of The Light"
"Afghan"
"Tricks Of The Light (Instrumental)"

"Tricks Of The Light (Instrumental)"
Written by Mike Oldfield
Appears on: 12" single; Elements boxed set; Discovery (2016 Deluxe Edition)
This isn't just the backing track without Reilly and Palmer's vocals. Instead, the vocals are replaced with a glockenspiel, giving the track a lighter, playful feel and making for an interesting alternative.

"Afghan" 2:45
Written by Mike Oldfield
Appears on: Tricks Of The Light 7" & 12" single; Elements boxed set; Discovery (2016 Deluxe Edition)
This instrumental has a very Oldfield-folk sound, with uilleann bagpipe and a jaunty 3/4 time signature. The Discovery picture of Simon Phillips' notes which lists a piece titled "Celtic Thing" may be referring this track, as it would fit the description and Mike is known to have working titles like that for his instrumentals.

Mike Oldfield performs at Parc de l'Ouest, Nice, France.

-September 4-
Mike Oldfield performs at Palasport, Rome, Italy.

-September 6-
Mike Oldfield performs at Palasport, Genova, Italy.

-Date Unknown-
Mike Oldfield performs "To France" on the Italian TV show *Saint Vincent Estate*, likely during the Italian leg of the tour.

-September 8-
Mike Oldfield performs at Bussoladomani, Viareggio, Italy.

-September 10-
Mike Oldfield performs at Palasport, Milan, Italy.

-September 12 & 13-
Mike Oldfield performs at Verona Arena, Verona, Italy.

-September 16-
Mike Oldfield performs at Scandinavium, Göteberg, Sweden.

-September 17-
Mike Oldfield performs at Fyns Forum, Odense, Denmark.

-September 18-
Mike Oldfield performs at Bröndbyhallen, Copenhagen, Denmark.

-September 20-
Mike Oldfield performs at Olympen, Lund, Sweden.

-September 21-
Mike Oldfield performs at Ekeberg Idrettshall, Oslo, Norway. According to Anita Hegerland, it's during his Norway concert date during the Discovery Tour that she is introduced to him backstage before his show (Hegerland says the concert was at Drammenshallen, Drammen, Norway, but **Oldfield** didn't perform there this tour, so Anita may be mistaken about the venue). Hegerland joins **Mike** and his band for dinner afterwards, providing him with her new album, as he was curious about her singing ability.

-September 22-
Mike Oldfield performs at Isstadion, Stockholm, Sweden.

-September 24-
Mike Oldfield performs at Siegerlandhalle, Siegen, Germany.

-September 26-
Mike Oldfield performs at Eistadion, Mannheim, Germany.

-September 27-
Mike Oldfield performs at Festhalle, Frankfurt, Germany.

-September 29-
Mike Oldfield performs at Sporthalle St. Jakobs, Basel, Switzerland.

-October-
During the German dates, **Mike Oldfield** decides he likes the acoustics of the tiles in some of the venue dressing rooms and plans to use the same kind of tiles in his Denham studio. Also around this time, as the tour nears its end, **Mike** begins suffering from lingering stress and emotional issues.

-October 1-
Mike Oldfield performs at Stadhalle, Wein, Austria.

-October 3-
Mike Oldfield performs at Schleyer - Halle, Stuttgart, Germany.

-October 4-
Mike Oldfield performs at Schwarzwaldhalle, Karlsruhe, Germany.

-October 5-
Mike Oldfield performs at Westfalenhalle, Dortmund, Germany.

-October 7-
Mike Oldfield performs at Eissporthalle, Kassel, Germany.

-October 8-
Mike Oldfield performs at Köln, Sporthalle, Germany.

-October 9-
Mike Oldfield performs at Phillipshalle, Düsseldorf, Germany.

-October 11-
Mike Oldfield performs at Forest National, Brussels, Belgium.

-October 12-
Mike Oldfield performs at Europahalle, Hannover, Germany.

-October 13-
Mike Oldfield performs at Carl-Diem-Halle, Würzburg, Germany.

-October 15-
Mike Oldfield performs at Halle Münsterland, Münster, Germany.

-October 16-
Mike Oldfield performs at Alsterdorfer Sporthalle, Hamburg, Germany.

-October 17-
Mike Oldfield performs at Stadthalle, Bremen, Germany.

-October 19-
Mike Oldfield performs at Palais de Beaulieu, Lausanne, Switzerland.

-October 21-
Mike Oldfield performs at Hallenstadion, Zürich, Switzerland.

-October 23-
Mike Oldfield performs at Ortenauhalle, Offenburg, Germany.

-October 24-
Mike Oldfield performs at Messehalle, Friedrichshafen, Germany.

-October 26-
Mike Oldfield performs at Olympiahalle, München, Germany.

-October 27-
Mike Oldfield performs at Nibelungenhalle, Passau, Germany.

-October 29-
Mike Oldfield performs at Deutschlandhalle, Berlin, Germany.

-October 30-
Mike Oldfield performs at Ostseehalle, Kiel, Germany.

-November 1-
Mike Oldfield performs at Ahoy, Rotterdam, The Netherlands.

-November 2-
Mike Oldfield performs at Saarlandhalle, Saarbrücken, The Netherlands.

-November 4-
Mike Oldfield performs at Parc de Penfeld, France.

-November 5-
Mike Oldfield performs at Palais Omnisports de Paris Bercy, Paris, France.

-November 6-
Mike Oldfield performs at Palais des Sports, Lyon, France.

-November 7-
Mike Oldfield performs at Complexe Compans, Casarelli, Toulouse, France.

-November 8-
Mike Oldfield performs at Patinoire de Meriadeck, Bordeaux.

-November 9-
Mike Oldfield performs at Maison des Sports, Clermont Ferrand, France.

-November 10-
Mike Oldfield performs at Hall Rhenus, Strasbourg, France. This ends the Discovery Tour.

-November 26-
Mike Oldfield releases his Original Film Soundtrack album *The Killing Fields* on Virgin Records in the UK, Europe, Australia and North America. David Bedford wrote and recorded the tracks "The Year Zero" and "The Year Zero 2." Track listing as follows:

UK, Europe & Australia *The Killing Fields* Original Film Soundtrack LP (V2328)
UK & Europe *The Killing Fields* Original Film Soundtrack CD (CDV2328)
Europe *The Killing Fields* Original Film Soundtrack LP (206 707)
US *The Killing Fields* Original Film Soundtrack LP (90591-1)
US *The Killing Fields* Original Film Soundtrack CD (2-90591)
Canada *The Killing Fields* Original Film Soundtrack LP (VL 2317)
France *The Killing Fields* Original Film Soundtrack LP (70 301)

"Pran's Theme"
"Requiem For A City"
"Evacuation"
"Pran's Theme 2"
"Capture"
"Execution"
"Bad News"
"Pran's Departure"
"Worksite"
"The Year Zero" David Bedford
"Blood Sucking"
"The Year Zero 2" David Bedford

"Pran's Escape / The Killing Fields"
"The Trek"
"The Boy's Burial / Pran Sees The Red Cross"
"Good News"
"Étude"

Mike Oldfield also releases his "Étude" *Theme From The Killing Fields* 7" and 12" singles in the UK and Europe.

UK 7" single (VS 731):
"Étude (Single Edit)"
"Evacuation (Single Edit)"

UK 12" single (VS 731-12):
"Étude"
"Evacuation"

Europe 7" single (106 980):
"Étude (Single Edit)"
"Evacuation (Single Edit)"

Europe 12" single (601 610):
"Étude"
"Evacuation"

rope 7" single (VS 731) promo:
"Étude (Single Edit)"
"Evacuation (Single Edit)"

Spain 7" single (A-106980):
"Étude (Single Edit)"
"Evacuation (Single Edit)"

France 7" single (SA 1032):
"Étude (Single Edit)"
"Evacuation (Single Edit)"

Argentina 7" single (S-0471) promo:
"Étude (Argentina Single Edit)"
"Étude (Argentina Single Edit)"

"Étude (Single Edit)" 3:07
Written by Francisco Tárrega (arr. Oldfield)
Appears on: 7" single, The Complete Mike Oldfield, The Complete Mike Oldfield 7" Promo single, A Virgin Compilation, Elements: The Best Of Mike Oldfield, Elements boxed set, Collection; *The Killing Fields* (2016 Remaster)
The single edit removes some sections, mostly from the beginning, and you likely won't notice that a minute and a half of the piece has been removed, as it's very well done. This version is pretty easy to find, appearing on a good number of collections over the years.

"Evacuation (Single Edit)" 4:11
Written by Mike Oldfield
Appears on: 7" single, The Complete Mike Oldfield
This edit removes several sections of music throughout, most noticeably at the beginning, where the track loses the opening discordant percussion part.

"Étude (Argentina Single Edit)" 3:50
Written by Francisco Tárrega (arr. Oldfield)
Appears on: Argentina 7" Promo single
Apparently a different edit of the track, if the runtime on the label is to believed. I have not heard this version, so can not say what makes it unique.

-Late 1984-
Mike Oldfield and his family return to England. **Oldfield** seeks out professional psychotherapy to deal with his stress and emotional baggage.

Mike also sets about tiling his home studio at Denham, Buckinghamshire, England.

Pictures In The Dark

1985

Note: It appears **Mike Oldfield** took a break from recording, releasing and live/TV appearances during the early part of this year, likely to rest after the tour, focus on his psychotherapy and to work on his studio.

-Date Unknown-
Virgin Records re-issues **Mike Oldfield** albums in the UK and Europe on CD.

UK *Incantations* CD (CVDT 101)
"Incantations (Part One)" - includes "Hymn To Diana"
"Incantations (Part Two)" - includes "Hymn To Diana (Reprise)" and "The Song Of Hiawatha"
"Incantations (Part Three) (Original CD Edit)"
"Incantations (Part Four)" - includes "Canon For Two Vibraphones" and "Ode To Cynthia"

> "Incantations (Part Three) (Original CD Edit)" 13:49
> Written by Mike Oldfield
> Appears on: Incantations 1985 CD Edition; Incantations 1986 Virgin Megastore Edition
> Despite only clocking in at a little over 72 minutes in total length, it was decided to edit *Incantations* down to fit on CD when it was first released (early CDs could hold up to 74 minutes, so one wonders why they needed to cut anything out). The first 3 minutes or so of "Part Three" are removed, so the track starts during the percussion part. Later CDs re-releases restore the full track.

UK *Exposed* 2xCD (CDVD 2511)
Germany *Music Wonderland* CD (610 387-222)
The Netherlands *Music Wonderland* CD (0777 7 86943 2 8)

-April-
Mike Oldfield pursues his interest in music video-making, having video editing equipment installed in his home studio in Denham, Buckinghamshire, England. He also begins writing and recording the following:
"Pictures In The Dark" - Barry Palmer and Aled Jones record their vocals before Anita Hegerland. According to Palmer, he recorded more vocal parts which were later re-recorded by Hegerland. Also, Palmer notes that **Mike** wanted to get Enya (at the time a member of Clannad) to record harmony parts, but was unable to enlist her. In interviews, **Oldfield** says he worked on this track with the intention of combining the song with the video he was creating for it (rather than the video being made after). Video director Peter Claridge works with **Oldfield** on this project.

-Mid-1985-
Mike Oldfield works on the following at his home studio in Denham, Buckinghamshire, England:
"Legend" - this track would be used as a non-album B-side.
"The Trap" - this track would be used as a non-album B-side.
"Sutton Hoo" - the exact recording details are pretty scarce, but it seems at some point this year, **Mike** was asked by the BBC to provide some music for a re-cut of the 1965 documentary titled *Sutton Hoo: The Million Pound Grave*.

-Late Summer-
The 1985 re-cut BBC documentary *Sutton Hoo: The Million Pound Grave* airs in the UK, featuring new music by **Mike Oldfield**. The date listed comes from Peter Evans' **Oldfield** biography *Music From The Darkness*. The documentary is released on VHS the following year.

-Autumn-
Mike Oldfield invites Anita Hegerland to record on the following, at Denham, Buckinghamshire, England: "Pictures In The Dark" – Hegerland re-records some of Barry Palmer's vocal parts. She later says she never met Aled Jones during her session and when she shot her video footage. The sessions take place over a weekend.

-October 1-
Virgin Records releases a compilation titled *The Complete Mike Oldfield*, on 2xLP, 2xCD and 2xcassette. This release was assembled by Dirk Hohmeyer, who also mixed the live tracks. Since he received no help from **Oldfield** himself, Hohmeyer used whatever copies of the tracks he could get a hold of, with some master tapes having been mislabelled.

UK 2xLP Edition (MOC 1)
Ireland 2xLP Edition (MOC 1)
Italy 2xLP Edition (MOC 1)
Australia 2xLP Edition (MOC 1)

LP 1:
The Instrumental Side
"Arrival" – a cover of the 1976 ABBA instrumental.
"In Dulci Jubilo"
"Portsmouth"
"Jungle Gardenia"
"Guilty"
"Blue Peter" – a cover of the 1958 TV show theme.
"Waldberg (The Peak)" The Mike Oldfield Group
"Wonderful Land" – a cover of The Shadows' 1962 instrumental.
"Étude (Single Edit)"

The Vocal Side
"Moonlight Shadow"
"Family Man"
"Mistake" The Mike Oldfield Group
"Five Miles Out (Early Mix)"
"Crime Of Passion"
"To France (The Complete... Edit)"
"Shadow On The Wall (12" Version)" Mike Oldfield And Roger Chapman

LP 2:
The Complex Side
"Ommadawn (Part One) (Episodes Extract)"
"Excerpt from Tubular Bells
        (Part One – Boxed Remix) (The Complete...Edit)"
"Excerpt from Hergest Ridge
        (Part One - Boxed Remix) (The Complete... Edit)"
"Incantations (Part Four) ('Ode To Cynthia')"
"Evacuation (Single Edit)"

The Live Side
"Sheba (Live At Essen, 1981)"
"Mirage (Live At Essen, 1981)"
"Platinum (Live At Essen, 1981)"
"Mount Teidi (Live in Cologne 1982)" The Mike Oldfield Group

UK [Version 1] & Europe Edition 2xCD (CDMOC1)
1988 Japan 2xCD (VJD-25019)

CD 1:
The Instrumental Section
"Arrival" – a cover of the 1976 ABBA instrumental.
"William Tell Overture"
"Cuckoo Song" Mike Oldfield with Les Penning
"In Dulci Jubilo"
"Portsmouth"
"Jungle Gardenia"
"Guilty"
"Blue Peter" – a cover of the 1958 TV show theme.
"Waldberg (The Peak)" The Mike Oldfield Group
"Wonderful Land" – a cover of The Shadows' 1962 instrumental.
"Étude (Single Edit)"

The Vocal Section
"Moonlight Shadow"
"Family Man"
"Mistake" The Mike Oldfield Group
"Five Miles Out (Early Mix)"
"Crime Of Passion"
"To France (The Complete... Edit)"
"Shadow On The Wall (12" Version)" Mike Oldfield And Roger Chapman

CD 2:
The Complex Section
"Ommadawn (Part One) (Episodes Extract)"
"Excerpt from Tubular Bells (Part One) (The Complete...Edit)"
"Excerpt from Hergest Ridge
        (Part One - Boxed Remix) (The Complete... Edit)"
"Incantations (Part Four) ('Ode To Cynthia')"
"Evacuation (Single Edit)"

The Live Side / The Live Section
"Sheba (Live At Essen, 1981)"
"Mirage (Live At Essen, 1981)"
"Platinum (Live At Essen, 1981)"
"Mount Teidi (Live in Cologne 1982)" The Mike Oldfield Group

UK 2xCD Edition (CDMOC1) Version 2
Matrix CD 1: CD MOC 1A 2895 860 01
Matrix CD 1: CD MOC 1A 2895 861 01

CD 1:
The Instrumental Section
"Arrival" – a cover of the 1976 ABBA instrumental.
"William Tell Overture"
"Cuckoo Song" Mike Oldfield with Les Penning
"In Dulci Jubilo"
"Portsmouth"
"Jungle Gardenia"
"Guilty"
"Blue Peter" – a cover of the 1958 TV show theme.
"Waldberg (The Peak)" The Mike Oldfield Group
"Wonderful Land" – a cover of The Shadows' 1962 instrumental.
"Étude (Single Edit)"

The Vocal Section
"Moonlight Shadow"
"Family Man"
"Mistake" The Mike Oldfield Group
"Five Miles Out (Early Mix)"
"Crime Of Passion"
"To France (The Complete... Edit)"
"Shadow On The Wall (12" Version)" Mike Oldfield And Roger Chapman

CD 2:
The Complex Section
"Ommadawn (Part One) (Episodes Extract)"
"Excerpt from Tubular Bells
         (Part One – Boxed Remix) (The Complete... Edit)"
"Excerpt from Hergest Ridge
         (Part One - Boxed Remix) (The Complete... Edit)"
"Incantations (Part Four) ('Ode To Cynthia')"
"Evacuation (Single Edit)"

The Live Side / The Live Section
"Sheba (Live At Essen, 1981)"
"Mirage (Live At Essen, 1981)"
"Platinum (Live At Essen, 1981)"
"Mount Teidi (Live in Cologne 1982)" The Mike Oldfield Group

Spain 2xLP Edition (XL302678)
Germany 2xLP Edition (302689-503)
Germany 2xLP Edition (302678-503)
Portugal 2xLP Edition (635405)
Canada 2xLP Edition (VD 2345)

LP1:
The Instrumental Side
"Arrival" – a cover of the 1976 ABBA instrumental.
"William Tell Overture"
"Cuckoo Song" Mike Oldfield with Les Penning
"Jungle Gardenia"
"Guilty"
"Blue Peter" – a cover of the 1958 TV show theme.
"Waldberg (The Peak)" The Mike Oldfield Group
 Wonderful Land" – a cover of The Shadows' 1962 instrumental.
"Étude (Single Edit)"

The Vocal Side
"Moonlight Shadow"
"Family Man"
"Mistake" The Mike Oldfield Group
"Five Miles Out (Early Mix)"
"Crime Of Passion"
"To France (The Complete... Edit)"
"Shadow On The Wall (12" Version)" Mike Oldfield And Roger Chapman

LP2:
The Complex Side
"Excerpt from The Orchestral Tubular Bells (The Complete... Version)"
"Excerpt from Tubular Bells
         (Part One – Boxed Remix) (The Complete...Edit)"
"Excerpt from Hergest Ridge (Part One - Boxed Remix Edit)"
 "Incantations (Part Four) ('Ode To Cynthia')"
 "Evacuation (Single Edit)"

The Live Side
"Sheba (Live At Essen, 1981)"
"Mirage" (Live At Essen, 1981)"
"Platinum (Live At Essen, 1981)"
"Mount Teidi (Live in Cologne 1982)" The Mike Oldfield Group

France 2xLP Edition (60041)
France 2xLP Edition (PM917)
Greece 2xLP Edition (162-501 38/39)

LP1:
The Instrumental Side
"Arrival" – a cover of the 1976 ABBA instrumental.
"William Tell Overture"
"Cuckoo Song" Mike Oldfield with Les Penning
"Jungle Gardenia"
"Guilty"
"Blue Peter" – a cover of the 1958 TV show theme.
"Waldberg (The Peak)" The Mike Oldfield Group
 Wonderful Land" – a cover of The Shadows' 1962 instrumental.
"Étude (Single Edit)"

The Vocal Side
"Moonlight Shadow"
"Family Man"
"Mistake" The Mike Oldfield Group
"Five Miles Out (Early Mix)"
"Crime Of Passion"
"To France (The Complete... Edit)"
"Tricks Of The Lights"

LP2:
The Complex Side
"Excerpt from The Orchestral Tubular Bells (The Complete... Version)"
"Excerpt from Hergest Ridge
         (Part One - Boxed Remix) (The Complete... Edit)"
"Excerpt from Taurus II (The Complete... Version)"
 "Incantations (Part Four) ('Ode To Cynthia')"
 "Evacuation (Single Edit)"

The Live Side
"Sheba (Live At Essen, 1981)"
"Mirage (Live At Essen, 1981)"
"Platinum (Live At Essen, 1981)"
"Mount Teidi (Live in Cologne 1982)" The Mike Oldfield Group

Argentina 2xLP Edition (MOC1)
1986 Argentina 2xLP Edition (TLP 60197/98)
Yugoslavia 2xLP Edition (LSVIRG75103/4)

LP1:
The Instrumental Side
"Arrival" – a cover of the 1976 ABBA instrumental.
"In Dulci Jubilo" – Yugoslavia sleeve lists "William Tell Overture"
"Portsmouth" - Yugoslavia sleeve lists "Cuckoo Song"
"Jungle Gardenia"
"Guilty"
"Blue Peter" – a cover of the 1958 TV show theme.
"Waldberg (The Peak)" The Mike Oldfield Group
 Wonderful Land" – a cover of The Shadows' 1962 instrumental.
"Étude (Single Edit)"

The Vocal Side
"Moonlight Shadow"
"Family Man"
"Mistake" The Mike Oldfield Group
"Five Miles Out (Early Mix)"
"Crime Of Passion"
"To France (The Complete... Edit)"
"Tricks Of The Lights"

LP2:
The Complex Side
"Excerpt from The Orchestral Tubular Bells (The Complete... Version)"
"Excerpt from Tubular Bells (Part One) (The Complete... Edit)"
"Excerpt from Hergest Ridge (Part One - Boxed Remix Edit)"
 "Incantations (Part Four) ('Ode To Cynthia')"
 "Evacuation (Single Edit)"

The Live Side
"Sheba (Live At Essen, 1981)"
"Mirage" (Live At Essen, 1981)"
"Platinum (Live At Essen, 1981)"
"Mount Teidi (Live in Cologne 1982)" The Mike Oldfield Group

Virgin Records also releases promo singles for *The Complete Mike Oldfield* in the UK and Spain:

UK 7" single (SWALLOW 1) promo:
"Étude (Single Version)"
"Moonlight Shadow"
"Portsmouth"
"In Dulci Jubilo"

Spain 12" single (VP 020) promo:
"William Tell Overture"
"Moonlight Shadow"
"Ommadawn (Part One) (Episodes Extract)"
"Mount Teidi (Live in Cologne 1982)" The Mike Oldfield Group

>"To France (The Complete... Edit)" 4:33
>Written by Mike Oldfield
>Appears on: The Complete Mike Oldfield
>This version fades out a bit earlier than the single version, but is otherwise the same as the album and single.
>
>"Excerpt from Tubular Bells (Part One) (The Complete... Edit)" 7:59
>Written by Mike Oldfield
>Appears on: The Complete Mike Oldfield, The Platinum Collection

This excerpt starts with the "Russian" movement and continues into the "Finale," fading out before the end of "Part One."

"Excerpt from Tubular Bells (Part One – Boxed Remix) (The Complete... Edit)" 8:34
Written by Mike Oldfield
Appears on: UK, Ireland, Italy, Australia, Spain, Germany, Portugal & Canada The Complete Mike Oldfield 2xLP; UK The Complete Mike Oldfield 2xCD [Version 2]
This is a longer edit of the "Russian" and "Finale" movements from the Boxed remix version.

"Excerpt from Hergest Ridge (Part One - Boxed Remix) (The Complete... Edit)" 4:20
Written by Mike Oldfield
Appears on: The Complete Mike Oldfield
The *Boxed* Remix is used here, with this excerpt starting in the middle of the 3rd movement and ending halfway through the 4th movement of "Part One." It fades in at the beginning and fades out at the end.

"Excerpt from The Orchestral Tubular Bells (The Complete... Edit)" 8:44
Written by Mike Oldfield, arr. David Bedford
Appears on: The Complete Mike Oldfield (European Edition)
Honestly, I haven't heard this excerpt, so I can't even guess what section is used.

"Excerpt from Taurus II (The Complete... Edit)" 6:30
Written by Mike Oldfield
Appears on: The Complete Mike Oldfield (European Edition)
I haven't heard this excerpt either.

-November 15-
Mike Oldfield releases his single "Pictures In The Dark" in the UK, Europe and Canada on Virgin Records and Edisom. Some labels incorrectly title "Legend" as "Legends."

UK 7" single (VS 836):
"Pictures In The Dark"
"Legend"

UK 12" single (VS 836-12):
"Pictures In The Dark (Extended Version)"
"Legend"
"The Trap"

UK Limited Edition 2x7" single (VSD 836):
7" single 1:
"Pictures In The Dark"
"Legend"

7" single 2:
"Moonlight Shadow"
"Rite Of Man"

Ireland 7" single (VS 836):
"Pictures In The Dark"
"Legend"

Europe 7" single (107 850):
"Pictures In The Dark"
"Legend"

Italy 12" single (VINX 96):
"Pictures In The Dark (Extended Version)"
"Legend"
"The Trap"

Spain 7" single (A-107 850):
"Pictures In The Dark"
"Legend"

Spain 12" single (F 602070):
"Pictures In The Dark (Extended Version)"
"Legend"
"The Trap"

Portugal 7" single (533605):
"Pictures In The Dark"
"Legend"

Portugal 12" single (433705):
"Pictures In The Dark (Extended Version)"
"Legend"
"The Trap"

France 7" single (008367):
"Pictures In The Dark"
"Legend"

Canada 12" single (VSD 1299):
"Pictures In The Dark (Extended Version)"
"Legend"
"The Trap"

"Pictures In The Dark" 4:10
Written by Mike Oldfield
Appears on: 7" single, The Complete Mike Oldfield (Various Re-issues), Collection
This is Mike's first collaboration with Anita Hegerland, who shares the lead vocal duties with Barry Palmer and Aled Jones. This is Mike at his most '80s, which can turn some fans off. It has all his trademark changes and layering, though, and you may find you appreciate it more after a few listens.

"Pictures In The Dark (Extended Version)" 5:56
Written by Mike Oldfield
Appears on: 12" single, The Platinum Collection
This extended version has some additional verses, expanded sections and a longer guitar solo. Instead of fading out, the track finishes at full volume, with a definitive ending.

"Legend" 2:24
Written by Mike Oldfield
Appears on: Pictures In The Dark 7" & 12" singles, Elements boxed set, The Platinum Collection
There are two distinct movements to this piece, the first an upbeat medieval-sounding folk section, followed by a darker part with synth strings and guitars. This track is most easily found on the *Elements* boxed set and *The Platinum Collection* (where it is a hidden track at the end of disc 2).

"The Trap" 2:32
Written by Mike Oldfield
Appear on: Pictures In The Dark 12" single

A spooky, minor key waltz this, that builds in intensity (and madness) as it progresses. Nightmarish and awesome!

-November 30-
Mike Oldfield, Anita Hegerland, Aled Jones and Barry Palmer appear on the German TV show *Peter's Pop Show*, performing "Poison Arrows" and "Pictures In The Dark."

-Date Unknown-
Mike Oldfield appears on the UK TV series *Wide Awake Club*, promoting "Pictures In The Dark."

-December 7-
Mike Oldfield appears on the BBC TV show *The Old Grey Whistle Test*, discussing the making of the "Pictures In The Dark" video.

-Date Unknown-
Mike Oldfield appears on the Swedish TV show *Razzle* with Anita Hegerland, performing "Moonlight Shadow" and "Jungle Gardenia."

-Date Unknown-
Mike Oldfield and Anita Hegerland appear on the Austrian TV show *Winterwelt Mit Hits*, performing "Arrival" and "Pictures In The Dark."

-Date Unknown-
Virgin Records re-issues *The Complete Mike Oldfield* 2xLP (MOC 1) set in Germany, replacing "Mistake" with "Pictures In The Dark."

LP1:
The Instrumental Side
"Arrival" – a cover of the 1976 ABBA instrumental.
"William Tell Overture"
"Cuckoo Song" Mike Oldfield with Les Penning
"Jungle Gardenia"
"Guilty"
"Blue Peter" – a cover of the 1958 TV show theme.
"Waldberg (The Peak)" The Mike Oldfield Group
"Wonderful Land" – a cover of The Shadows' 1962 instrumental.
"Étude (Single Edit)"

The Vocal Side
"Moonlight Shadow"
"Family Man"
"Pictures In The Dark"
"Five Miles Out (Early Mix)"
"Crime Of Passion"
"To France (The Complete... Edit)"
"Shadow On The Wall (12" Version)" Mike Oldfield And Roger Chapman

LP2:
The Complex Side
"Excerpt from Ommadawn (Part One - Boxed Remix)"
"Excerpt from Tubular Bells (Part One) (The Complete... Edit)"
"Excerpt from Hergest Ridge (Part One - Boxed Remix) (The Complete... Edit)"
"Incantations (Part Four) ('Ode To Cynthia')"
"Evacuation (Single Edit)"

The Live Side
"Sheba (Live At Essen, 1981)"
"Mirage (Live At Essen, 1981)"
"Platinum (Live At Essen, 1981)"
"Mount Teidi (Live in Cologne 1982)" The Mike Oldfield Group

Shine

1986

-February 2 & 6-
Mike Oldfield performs with Marillion at the Hammersmith Odeon, London, England.

-February 9-
Mike Oldfield performs at the Colombian Volcano Appeal Concert, at the Royal Albert Hall, London, England.

-Date Unknown-
Virgin Records re-issues **Mike Oldfield**'s album *Incantations* via its Oxford Street, London, England, Megastore on CD (CDVDT 101) in the UK.

1986 *Incantations* Virgin Megastore Edition
"Incantations (Part One)" - includes "Hymn To Diana"
"Incantations (Part Two)" - includes "Hymn To Diana (Reprise)" and "The Song Of Haiwatha"
"Incantations (Part Three) (Original CD Edit)"
"Incantations (Part Four)" - includes "Canon For Two Vibraphones" and "Ode To Cynthia"

Note: This edition is identifiable by the text 'Virgin Megastore' on the matrix runout. The same catalogue number (CDVDT 101) is used in 1988 for the European CD re-issue of the album.

-Date Unknown-
Mike Oldfield and Anita Hegerland appear on a German TV show performing "Pictures In The Dark."

-Date Unknown-
Mike Oldfield separates from Sally Cooper.

-April 11-
Luke Oldfield is born to **Mike Oldfield** and Sally Cooper.

-Early 1986-
Mike Oldfield and Jon Anderson work on the following at **Oldfield**'s home studio, Denham, Buckinghamshire, England:
"Shine" - Like "Pictures In The Dark," **Mike** approaches this project with both music and the video images at the same time. Peter Claridge also assists with the video work. The track is co-written by the two and according to Anita Hegerland, the song is written for her. **Mike** says he worked on the song first over the phone with Anderson, who lives in Barbados, and later at **Oldfield**'s Denham studio. Working titles for the song are "She Was She Was," "If Rainbows Can Dance" and "Made In Heaven."

-Date Unknown-
Mike Oldfield and Jon Anderson shoot their performance segments for the "Shine" music video in Barbados. Anita Hegerland joins **Oldfield** on the trip.
"The Wind Chimes" - **Oldfield** says he was directly inspired to later write this piece when he heard the wind chimes' outside the bedroom during this trip.

-May 2-
Mike Oldfield with Jon Anderson release their 7" and 12" singles for "Shine" in the UK and Europe.

UK 7" single (VS863):
"Shine" Mike Oldfield with Jon Anderson
"The Path" Mike Oldfield

UK 7" single (VSS 863) Shaped Picture disc:
"Shine" Mike Oldfield with Jon Anderson
"The Path" Mike Oldfield

UK 12" single (VS 863-12):
"Shine (Extended Version)"
    Mike Oldfield with Jon Anderson
"The Path" Mike Oldfield

UK 7" single (VIN 45194):
"Shine" Mike Oldfield with Jon Anderson
"The Path" Mike Oldfield

Italy 12" single (VINX 127):
"Shine (Extended Version)"
    Mike Oldfield with Jon Anderson
"The Path" Mike Oldfield

Europe 7" singles (108 134):
"Shine" Mike Oldfield with Jon Anderson
"The Path" Mike Oldfield

Europe 12" singles (608 134):
"Shine (Extended Version)"
    Mike Oldfield with Jon Anderson
"The Path" Mike Oldfield

Spain 7" singles (A 108134):
"Shine" Mike Oldfield with Jon Anderson
"The Path" Mike Oldfield

Spain 7" singles (A 108134) promo:
"Shine" Mike Oldfield with Jon Anderson
"The Path" Mike Oldfield

Spain 12" singles (F 608134):
"Shine (Extended Version)"
    Mike Oldfield with Jon Anderson
"The Path" Mike Oldfield

"Shine" 3:21
Written by Mike Oldfield (words & music) & Jon Anderson (words)
Appears on: 7" single
This second collaboration with Jon Anderson (the other being "In High Places") sees Mike thoroughly focused on combining music with visuals, an idea that would later culminate with the Islands/Wind Chimes project the following year (and then later when Mike got heavily into computers). If you like Mike's '80s singles period, you may like this track, but don't be surprised if it doesn't grab you at first.

"Shine (Extended Version)" 4:58
Written by Mike Oldfield (words & music) & Jon Anderson (words)
Appears on: 12" single; The Platinum Collection
The Extended Version is similar to other '80s Extended Versions, with additional passages not heard in the standard version.

-Date Unknown-
Mike Oldfield appears on the UK TV show *Saturday Morning*, explaining his video studio gear and animation techniques for "Pictures In The Dark" and "Shine."

-Date Unknown-
Virgin Records re-issues the following **Mike Oldfield** and related albums on CD, picture disc CD and LP in the UK, Europe and Canada.

US *The Orchestral Tubular Bells* CD (2-90894) Royal Philharmonic Orchestra (with Mike Oldfield)
North America *The Orchestral Tubular Bells* CD (0777 7 86049 2 1)
    Royal Philharmonic Orchestra (with Mike Oldfield)
Canada *The Orchestral Tubular Bells* CD (CDVM 2026) Royal Philharmonic Orchestra (with Mike Oldfield)
UK *The Orchestral Tubular Bells* Picture Disc CD (CDV 2026)
    Royal Philharmonic Orchestra (with Mike Oldfield)
UK *The Orchestral Tubular Bells* CD Picture Disc (CDVP 2026)
    Royal Philharmonic Orchestra (with Mike Oldfield)

Ommadawn CD (CDV 2043)
"Ommadawn (Part One)"
"Ommadawn (Part Two)"

Ommadawn Picture Disc CD (CDVP 2043)
"Ommadawn (Part One)"
"Ommadawn (Part Two - Edit)"
"On Horseback (Single Version)" - unlisted on the sleeve.

Ommadawn Picture Disc CD (CDVM 2043)
"Ommadawn (Part One)"
"Ommadawn (Part Two - Edit)"
"On Horseback (Single Version)" - unlisted on the sleeve.

QE2 CD (CDV 2181)

-Autumn-
Mike Oldfield moves to Megeve, France, with Anita Hegerland. There, he begins working on his next album (*Islands* sessions) and the accompanying video project, *The Wind Chimes*. Hegerland says in a 1989 interview that she and **Mike** didn't live together until Autumn of this year.

-October-
Sunrise Records releases the LP collection *Where Would You Rather Be Tonight?* (A40111M) in the UK as a benefit for Broadreach House, a drug and alcohol rehab centre. It features the **Phil Beer And Mike Oldfield** track "Passed You By."

> "Passed You By" 3:13
> Written by Phil Beer
> Appears on: Where Would You Rather Be Tonight?
> This is a great track, highly recommended. It's a Celtic-flavoured folk rock number and Mike's work on the backing track is perfectly suited to it. You can hear all his trademarks and instrumentation, with things like such as his bodrhán (Celtic drum), and the result so much fun.

-Date Unknown-
Mike Oldfield works on tracks for his next album in France (*Islands* sessions):
"When The Night's On Fire" - Barry Palmer records vocals for an early version. The song evolves and later becomes both this and "Islands."
"Man In The Rain" - This is the earliest version definitely confirmed to exist (though it's possible the song dates from earlier). Barry Palmer says he worked on the track in Switzerland with **Mike** on keyboards and guitars accompanied by a German band, but the results were "horrible" and the track is not used on the album.
"Magic Touch" - Barry Palmer suggests to **Oldfield** that he employ singer John Pain (a friend of Palmer's) to record on this track. It's possible Fish (of Marillion) had recorded his version by this point. Pain's version was a contender for the album until very late in production.
"Flying Start" - **Oldfield** works with Kevin Ayers (on vocals) for this track and Palmer later suggests that **Mike** attempted to recreate Kevin's loose production style during the album sessions. This approach would be counter to **Mike**'s usual method of tight production on tracks, hence the many later re-recordings of parts before the album's completion. Interestingly, Ayers would later re-record his own version of the song (with no **Oldfield** involvement) between May and June of 1987 for his own album *Falling Up*.
"Islands" - Anita Hegerland notes that Bonnie Tyler did her vocals for the track in France. The track is co-produced by **Oldfield**, Tom Newman and Alan Shacklock. In 2000 (on VH-1 *Greatest Hits*), **Mike** says he spent months on this track, recording it with different artists, reworking it, taking it apart and putting it back together (this process likely originates with "When The Night's On Fire")
"The Wind Chimes" - **Mike** writes (at least part of) this piece inspired the wind chimes he heard on his trip to Barbados earlier in the year.

"When The Night's On Fire (Barry Palmer Demo)" 4:58
Written by Mike Oldfield
Appears on: Unreleased
Barry Palmer sings on this is an early stage recording, with a simple synth backing track and work-in-progress lyrics. Nonetheless, it's recognizable as containing what would also become "Islands." As demos go, this offers an interesting glimpse into the development of the two songs.

"When The Night's On Fire (Bonnie Tyler Demo)" 4:52
Written by Mike Oldfield
Appears on: Unreleased
Bonnie Tyler sings on this version, which is getting closer to "Islands," while retaining the original ideas for "When The Night's On Fire." It could almost be the finished "Islands," save for the lack of the familiar chorus and various other differences. At a later point in the recording sessions for the album, Mike developed the ideas heard here into the two aforementioned separate songs.

Note: The exact time period for these sessions is unclear and likely extended into 1987.

Note: Barry Palmer says in a later interview that his sessions were in Switzerland. Megève and Montbéliard (where **Oldfield** lived and worked at the time) are both French towns on the Swiss border in The French Alps, so it's possible his sessions were actually in France. Or he might have recorded in Switzerland.

Islands

1987

-Date Unknown-
Mike Oldfield begins work on his new home studio, Roughwood Croft, Chalfont St. Giles, Buckinghamshire, England.

-Date Unknown-
Mike Oldfield travels to Bali, Indonesia with a film crew to capture audio and film of local musicians for both the *Islands* album and *The Wind Chimes* video project.

-Dates Unknown-
Mike Oldfield works with Peter Claridge of CAL Video Graphics, with whom he previously worked on the "Pictures In The Dark" and "Shine" videos. **Oldfield** writes and records the following (venue unknown):
"Music For The Video Wall" - it's speculated that **Mike** wrote this piece as part of the company's campaign (a Video Wall) to sell its video graphics and editing equipment.

-May-
Mike Oldfield continues work on both *Islands* and *The Wind Chimes*, at Montbéliard, France.
 "The Wind Chimes (Part Two)" - Pierre and Benoit Moerlen record their vibraphone parts this month.

-Summer-
Mike Oldfield completes his album *Islands* in Megeve, France. A working title for the album was *North Point*.
"When The Night's On Fire" - re-worked now, the track is recorded with Anita Hegerland on vocals.
"North Point" - Anita on vocals, produced by **Oldfield**.
"The Time Has Come" - Anita on vocals, produced by **Oldfield** and Michael Cretu.
"Magic Touch" - Max Bacon records a version of the song, as does Jim Price. Co-produced by **Oldfield** and Geoffrey Downes.
"The Wind Chimes (Part One)" - produced Mike Oldfield.
"The Wind Chimes (Part Two)" - Simon Phillips plays drums and co-produces the track with **Oldfield**, living with him and Anita (who provides the chants) in Megeve for a month. **Oldfield** uses audio recorded in Bali, Indonesia, in the track, as well as footage for *The Wind Chimes* video project.

Virgin Records releases the **Mike Oldfield featuring Jon Anderson** singles "In High Places" in the UK and Spain, commemorating Richard Branson's trans-Atlantic hot air balloon flight.

UK 7" single (VS 955):
"In High Places" Mike Oldfield Featuring Jon Anderson
"Poison Arrows (Single Version)" Mike Oldfield

UK 12" single (VS 955-12):
"In High Places" Mike Oldfield Featuring Jon Anderson
"Poison Arrows (Single Version)" Mike Oldfield
"Jungle Gardenia" Mike Oldfield

Spain 7" single (F 609 205):
"In High Places" Mike Oldfield Featuring Jon Anderson
"Poison Arrows (Single Version)" Mike Oldfield

Spain 12" single (A-109 205):
"In High Places" Mike Oldfield Featuring Jon Anderson
"Poison Arrows (Single Version)" Mike Oldfield
"Jungle Gardenia" Mike Oldfield

> "Poison Arrows (Single Version)"
> Written by Mike Oldfield
> Appears on: In High Places 7" & 12" singles
> This version fades in during the bridge from "To France" and continues normally to the end of the track. If you're looking for a good stand-alone version, this is it.

-September 7-
Mike Oldfield releases his album *Islands* in the UK, Europe and North America on Virgin Records. Most of the related singles make a point of co-crediting the singers of the different tracks next to **Oldfield**, as has been done occasionally on past releases. Also, the UK and European CDs combine both Parts of "The Wind Chimes" into a single track, despite being two separate pieces. Track listing as follows:

UK *Islands* LP (V 2466) & Europe LP
"The Wind Chimes (Part One)"
"The Wind Chimes (Part Two)"
"Islands" Mike Oldfield Featuring Bonnie Tyler
"Flying Start" Mike Oldfield (with Kevin Ayers)
"North Point" Mike Oldfield Featuring Anita Hegerland
"Magic Touch"
"The Time Has Comes" Mike Oldfield Featuring Anita Hegerland

UK *Islands* CD (CDV 2466)
Europe *Islands* CD (CDV 2466)
"The Wind Chimes (Part One and Part Two)"
"Islands" Mike Oldfield Featuring Bonnie Tyler
"Flying Start" Mike Oldfield (with Kevin Ayers)
"North Point" Mike Oldfield Featuring Anita Hegerland
"Magic Touch"
"The Time Has Comes" Mike Oldfield Featuring Anita Hegerland
"When The Night's On Fire" Mike Oldfield Featuring Anita Hegerland

US *Islands* LP (7 90645-1)
US *Islands* CD (7-90645-2)
Canada *Islands* LP (VL 2466)
"The Wind Chimes (Part One)"
"The Wind Chimes (Part Two)"
"Magic Touch (Original Mix)"
"The Time Has Come" Mike Oldfield Featuring Anita Hegerland
"North Point" Mike Oldfield Featuring Anita Hegerland
"Flying Start" Mike Oldfield (with Kevin Ayers)
"Islands" Mike Oldfield Featuring Bonnie Tyler

Note: the North American editions of the album feature completely different, black and white artwork.

> "Magic Touch (Original Mix)" 4:13
> Written by Mike Oldfield
> Appears on: Islands (1987 US Edition), 7" & 12" singles, A Virgin Compilation; Lo Mejor De... Mike Oldfield
> The "Original Mix," as it's called on various releases, is identical to the standard version featuring Jim Price on vocals, but is instead Max Bacon singing. The story goes that Virgin could not release

Price's version in North America for contractual reasons, so it used Bacon's. Take your pick which you like better!

-September 14-
Mike Oldfield Featuring Bonnie Tyler releases the "Islands" singles in the UK and Europe.

UK 7" singles (VS 990):
"Islands" Mike Oldfield Featuring Bonnie Tyler
"The Wind Chimes (Part One)" Mike Oldfield

UK 12" single (VS 990 12):
"Islands (12" Mix)" Mike Oldfield Featuring Bonnie Tyler
"When The Night's On Fire" Mike Oldfield Featuring Anita Hegerland
"The Wind Chimes (Part One)" Mike Oldfield

UK CD single (CDEP 6) promo:
"Islands" Mike Oldfield Featuring Bonnie Tyler
"When The Night's On Fire" Mike Oldfield Featuring Anita Hegerland
"The Wind Chimes (Part One)" Mike Oldfield
"Islands (12" Mix)" Mike Oldfield Featuring Bonnie Tyler

France 7" singles (009907):
"Islands" Mike Oldfield Featuring Bonnie Tyler
"The Wind Chimes (Part One)" Mike Oldfield

France 12" single (009906):
"Islands (12" Mix)" Mike Oldfield Featuring Bonnie Tyler
"When The Night's On Fire" Mike Oldfield Featuring Anita Hegerland
"The Wind Chimes (Part One)" Mike Oldfield

Spain 12" single (F 609 351):
"Islands (12" Mix)" Mike Oldfield Featuring Bonnie Tyler
"When The Night's On Fire" Mike Oldfield Featuring Anita Hegerland
"The Wind Chimes (Part One)" Mike Oldfield

Europe 12" single (609 351):
"Islands (12" Mix)" Mike Oldfield Featuring Bonnie Tyler
"When The Night's On Fire" Mike Oldfield Featuring Anita Hegerland
"The Wind Chimes (Part One)" Mike Oldfield

Portugal 7" singles (505506):
"Islands" Mike Oldfield Featuring Bonnie Tyler
"The Wind Chimes (Part One)" Mike Oldfield

Portugal 12" single:
"Islands (12" Mix)" Mike Oldfield Featuring Bonnie Tyler
"When The Night's On Fire" Mike Oldfield Featuring Anita Hegerland
"The Wind Chimes (Part One)" Mike Oldfield

Italy 7" singles (VIN 45241):
"Islands" Mike Oldfield Featuring Bonnie Tyler
"The Wind Chimes (Part One)" Mike Oldfield

Italy 12" single (VINX 45241):
"Islands (12" Mix)" Mike Oldfield Featuring Bonnie Tyler
"When The Night's On Fire" Mike Oldfield Featuring Anita Hegerland
"The Wind Chimes (Part One)" Mike Oldfield

Canada 7" singles (VS 1409):
"Islands" Mike Oldfield Featuring Bonnie Tyler
"The Wind Chimes (Part One)" Mike Oldfield

South Africa 7" singles (VS 718):
"Islands" Mike Oldfield Featuring Bonnie Tyler
"The Wind Chimes (Part One)" Mike Oldfield

> "Islands (12" Mix)" 5:36
> Written by Mike Oldfield
> Appears on: 12" & Promo CD singles
> This mix is a little beefier throughout, but the biggest different comes at the end. The track does not fade out but finishes at full volume followed by a pause and a new reprise with additional vocals and music not heard in the standard version.

-Date Unknown-
Mike Oldfield and Bonnie Tyler appear on the BBC TV show *It's Wicked* promoting the single "Islands".

-Date Unknown-
Mike Oldfield and Bonnie Tyler appear on the BBC TV show *Live from Her Majesty's*, Palladium, London, England.

-Date Unknown-
Mike Oldfield and Bonnie Tyler appear on the BBC TV show

-November-
Virgin Records America releases a promo CD **Mike Oldfield** collection titled *A Virgin Compilation* (PRCD2113) in North America. Track listing as follows:

"Magic Touch (Original Mix)"
"Magic Touch (Original Mix Promo Edit)"
"Tubular Bells (A Virgin Compilation Edit)"
"Family Man"
"Flying Start" Mike Oldfield (with Kevin Ayers)
"Moonlight Shadow"
"Shadow On The Wall (12" Version)" Michael Oldfield And Roger Chapman
"Five Miles Out"
"Étude (Single Edit)"
"Jungle Gardenia"
"North Point" Mike Oldfield Featuring Anita Hegerland

> "Magic Touch (Original Mix Promo Edit)" 3:37
> Written by Mike Oldfield
> Appears on: 7" & 12" Promo single, A Virgin Compilation
> This promo edit of the Max Bacon version removes bits of the song throughout and fades out early. Despite that, it's still pretty listenable.

> "Tubular Bells (A Virgin Compilation Edit)" 3:18
> Written by Mike Oldfield
> Appears on: A Virgin Compilation

This edit attempts to recreate the original 1974 "Now..." version and comes pretty close, employing fewer cuts. All in all, it doesn't really help.

Virgin Records America also releases the "Magic Touch" singles in North America.

US 7" single (7-99402):
"Magic Touch (Original Mix Promo Edit)"
"Wind Chimes (Part One)"

US 7" single (7-99402) promo:
"Magic Touch (Original Mix Promo Edit)"
"Magic Touch (Original Mix Promo Edit)"

Note: "The Wind Chimes (Part One)" is incorrectly listed on the sleeve as the B-side.

US 12" single (PR2113):
"Magic Touch (Original Mix)"
"Magic Touch (Original Mix Promo Edit)"

Also released by Virgin Records around this time is a "Magic Touch" single in Australasia.

-November 9-
Mike Oldfield Featuring Anita Hegerland release the single "The Time Has Come" in the UK and Europe.

UK 7" single (VS 1013):
"The Time Has Come" Mike Oldfield Featuring Anita Hegerland
"Final Extract From The Wind Chimes (Part Two)" Mike Oldfield

UK 12" single (VST 1013):
"The Time Has Come" Mike Oldfield Featuring Anita Hegerland
"The Time Has Come (12" Version)" Mike Oldfield Featuring Anita Hegerland
"Final Extract From The Wind Chimes (Part Two)" Mike Oldfield

Portugal 7" single (505539):
"The Time Has Come" Mike Oldfield Featuring Anita Hegerland
"North Point" Mike Oldfield Featuring Anita Hegerland

France 12" single (80351):
"The Time Has Come (12" Version)" Mike Oldfield Featuring Anita Hegerland
"The Time Has Come" Mike Oldfield Featuring Anita Hegerland
"North Point" Mike Oldfield Featuring Anita Hegerland

Spain 12" single (F-609 542):
"The Time Has Come" Mike Oldfield Featuring Anita Hegerland
"The Time Has Come (12" Version)" Mike Oldfield Featuring Anita Hegerland
"Final Extract From The Wind Chimes (Part Two)" Mike Oldfield

Europe 7" single (109 542):
"The Time Has Come" Mike Oldfield Featuring Anita Hegerland
"North Point" Mike Oldfield Featuring Anita Hegerland

Europe 12" single (609 542):
"The Time Has Come (12" Version)" Mike Oldfield Featuring Anita Hegerland
"The Time Has Come" Mike Oldfield Featuring Anita Hegerland
"North Point" Mike Oldfield Featuring Anita Hegerland

Note: Curiously, the 7" single doesn't credit Anita Hegerland on the track "North Point," whereas the 12" does.

>"The Time Has Come (12" Version)" 4:25
>Written by Mike Oldfield
>Appears on: 12" single, The Platinum Collection
>The 12" Version is only extended by about 30 seconds, with a longer percussion opening.

>"Final Extract From The Chime Wind (Part Two)" 3:14
>Written by Mike Oldfield
>Appears on: The Time Has Come 7" & 12" single
>Despite the name, this wouldn't be the last extract from "The Wind Chimes" to appear on an *Islands* single. It's possible, though, that it is actually referring (with ambiguous syntax) to the fact that the extract is of the finale of "The Wind Chimes (Part Two)". It is the last 3:14 of the piece.

-Date Unknown-
Mike Oldfield, Bonnie Tyler and Anita Hegerland appear on Goldene Europa 1987, Saarbrücken, Germany, showcasing tracks from *Islands*.

-Date Unknown-
Mike Oldfield, Bonnie Tyler and Anita Hegerland appear on the German TV show *Wetten Dass*.

-Date Unknown-
Mike Oldfield appears on the Spanish TV show *Semáforo Pop*.

-Date Unknown-
Mike Oldfield appears on the Spanish TV show *Tocata*.

-December 31-
Mike Oldfield, Bonnie Tyler and Anita Hegerland perform on Peter's Pop Show, Germany.

The Wind Chimes

1988

-Date Unknown-
Mike Oldfield, Bonnie Tyler and Anita Hegerland appear on the Spanish TV show *Sabado Noche*.

-Date Unknown-
Virgin Records re-issues **Mike Oldfield**'s album *Incantations* on CD in Europe (CDVDT 101). This edition restores the full version of "Incantations (Part Three)." Track listing as follows:

"Incantations (Part One)" - includes "Hymn To Diana"
"Incantations (Part Two)" - includes "Hymn To Diana (Reprise)" and "The Song Of Hiawatha"
"Incantations (Part Three)"
"Incantations (Part Four)" - includes "Canon For Two Vibraphones" and "Ode To Cynthia"

Note: The same catalogue number (CDVDT 101) was used previously for the 1986 Virgin Megastore CD re-issue of the album.

-Date Unknown-
Virgin Records releases a Club Edition of **Mike Oldfield**'s *Islands* album on CD (V2-90645) in the US. Track listing as follows:

US *Islands* CD Club Edition
"The Wind Chimes (Part One)"
"The Wind Chimes (Part Two)"
"Magic Touch (Original Mix)"
"The Time Has Come" Mike Oldfield Featuring Anita Hegerland
"North Point" Mike Oldfield Featuring Anita Hegerland
"Flying Start" Mike Oldfield (with Kevin Ayers)
"Islands" Mike Oldfield Featuring Bonnie Tyler

Note: This edition features the same black and white artwork as the previous North American releases.

-Date Unknown-
Virgin Records releases CD singles of "Moonlight Shadow" in the UK.

UK CD single (CDF 7):
"Moonlight Shadow (Extended Version)"
"Rite Of Man"
"To France (Single Version)"
"Jungle Gardenia"

UK 3"CD single (CDT 7):
"Moonlight Shadow (Extended Version)"
"Rite Of Man"
"To France (Single Version)"
"Jungle Gardenia"

-February 1-
Mike Oldfield (with Kevin Ayers) releases his "Flying Start" singles in the UK and Europe.

UK 7" single (VS 1047):
"Flying Start" Mike Oldfield (with Kevin Ayers)
"The Wind Chimes (Part Two) (Edit)" Mike Oldfield

UK 12" single (VST 1047):
"Flying Start (12" Version)" Mike Oldfield (with Kevin Ayers)
"The Wind Chimes (Part Two) (Edit)" Mike Oldfield

France 7" single (90388):
"Flying Start" Mike Oldfield (with Kevin Ayers)
"The Wind Chimes (Part Two) (Edit)" Mike Oldfield

Europe 12" single (609 718):
"Flying Start (12" Version)" Mike Oldfield (with Kevin Ayers)
"The Wind Chimes (Part Two) (Edit)" Mike Oldfield

Germany 7" single (109 718):
"Flying Start" Mike Oldfield (with Kevin Ayers)
"The Wind Chimes (Part Two) (Edit)" Mike Oldfield

> "Flying Start (12" Version)" 4:39
> Written by Mike Oldfield
> Appears on: 12" single
> With an extended instrumental intro that adds a good deal of atmosphere, this version improves on an already good song. After the into, the rest of the song is identical to standard version. It's nice to hear to Kevin and Mike working together again and Ayers seemed to like the song so much he recorded his own version for his own album the same year.
>
> "The Wind Chimes (Part Two) (Edit)" 4:01
> Written by Mike Oldfield
> Appears on: Flying Start 7" & 12" singles
> This edit is the first 4 minutes of "Part Two," fading out at the end over the percussion.

-February 22-
Mike Oldfield releases his "Magic Touch" singles in Europe and Australasia.

Germany 7" single (109 872):
"Magic Touch (Original Mix Single Edit)"
"Music For The Video Wall"

Australasia 12" single (VST1069):
"Magic Touch (Original Mix Single Edit)"
"Music For The Video Wall"
"Magic Touch (Original Mix)"

> "Magic Touch (Original Mix Single Edit)" 4:04
> Written by Mike Oldfield
> Appears on: 12" singles
> This is the Max Bacon version, with the edit being that it fades out ten seconds early.
>
> "Music For The Video Wall"
> Written by Mike Oldfield
> Appears on: European 7" & 12" single
> This music was seemingly meant to accompany images, on the Video Wall, with the two promoting video graphics software and equipment, so taken by itself, it can seem a bit disjointed, but it's

certainly worth getting a hold of! It reuses some sequences that appear in other Oldfield tracks, such as a bit of "Evacuation" at one point.

-Date Unknown-
Transatlantic Records re-releases **The Sallyangie** album *Children Of The Sun* in Germany (TACD 9.00586 O) on CD.

-April 28-
Greta Marie Hegerland Oldfield is born to **Mike Oldfield** and Anita Hegerland.

-May 31-
Mike Oldfield appears on the BBC TV show *Good Morning Britain*.
"Mandolin (Reprise 2)" – On the show, **Mike** plays a bit of "Taurus 3" and then goes into this piece, which would later appear in "Amarok". He also plays a bit of the "Introduction" from *Tubular Bells*.

-June-
In an interview released this month in *Music, Computers & Software* magazine with **Mike Oldfield** indicates that he is still working on *The Wind Chimes* video project to accompany the *Islands* album.

-July 15-
Mike Oldfield and Anita Hegerland appear on the German TV show *Showfenster*

-Date Unknown-
BGO re-issues the Kevin Ayers album *Whatevershebringswesing* on LP (BGO LP11) and CD (BGO CD11), featuring **Mike Oldfield**.

-Date Unknown-
Mike Oldfield completes work on his video project *The Wind Chimes*, which contains music videos for all of the songs on the *Islands* album (except for "When The Night's On Fire"). **Oldfield** enlists Peter Claridge to work with him on editing *The Wind Chimes* video project.

-October-
Mike Oldfield releases his video album *The Wind Chimes* on VHS and laserdisc. It also contains the videos for "Pictures In The Dark," "Shine," "Five Miles Out," "Moonlight Shadow" and "Shadow On The Wall."

-Late 1988-
Mike Oldfield begins work on his next album. **Mike** decides to make the album entirely vocal, with no instrumental tracks. The earliest tracks are written in Greece, inspired by the scenery of the Greek mountain view from his veranda. **Oldfield** later cites the following tracks as directly inspired by the view:
"Bridge To Paradise"
"Holy"
"See The Light"
"Earth Moving"

Note: **Mike** says he worked on the album for nine months

Earth Moving

1989

-June-

Mike Oldfield finishes work on his album *Earth Moving* at Roughwood Croft, Chalfont St. Giles, Buckinghamshire, England. Since December, **Mike** works on the following:

"Far Country" - Three versions are recorded, one with Fish, one with Max Bacon and one with Mark Williamson, whose version is used on the album. Adrian Belew plays the guitar solo.
"Blue Night" – features Maggie Reilly on vocals.
"Innocent" – features Anita Hegerland on vocals. This track was inspired by their daughter Greta (who also appears in the music video). Mike says in a *Melody Maker* interview this year that the backing "took an afternoon" to do.
"Hostage" – features Max Bacon on vocals.
"Bridge To Paradise" – features Max Bacon and Phil Spalding on vocals.
"Hostage" – features Max Bacon on vocals.
"Holy" – several remixes are made for this track, which features Adrian Belew and Phil Spalding on vocals.
"Earth Moving" – features Nikki 'B' Bentley and Carl Wayne on vocals. Different Bentley vocal takes are used on the two different released mixes of the song.
"Nothing But" – features Carol Kenyon on vocals.
"Runaway Son" – features Chris Thompson on vocals.
"See The Light" – features Chris Thompson and Phil Spalding on vocals.

-June 23-
Virgin Records releases **Mike Oldfield**'s "Innocent" singles in the UK and Europe.

UK CD single (VSCD 1214):
"Innocent" – listed as the "7" Version."
"Innocent (12" Mix)"
"Earth Moving (Disco Version)"

Europe 7" single (112 383):
"Innocent"
"Earth Moving (Disco Version)"

Europe 12" single (612 383):
"Innocent (12" Mix)"
"Innocent (7" Version)"
"Earth Moving (Disco Version)"

Europe 12" single (612 383-213):
"Innocent (12" Mix)"
"Innocent"
"Earth Moving (Disco Version)"

Europe CD single (662 383):
"Innocent (7" Version)"
"Innocent (12 Mix)"
"Earth Moving (Disco Version)"

France 7" single (90529):
 "Innocent (7" Version)"
"Earth Moving (Disco Version)"

France 12" single (80466):
"Innocent (12" Mix)"
"Innocent (7" Version)"
"Earth Moving (Disco Version)"

Italy 7" single (VIN 45307):
"Innocent (7" Version)"
"Earth Moving (Disco Version)"

Italy 12" single (VINX 244):
"Innocent (12" Mix)"
"Innocent (7" Version)"
"Earth Moving (Disco Version)"

Spain 7" single (SP-112 383):
"Innocent (7" Version)"
"Earth Moving (Disco Version)"

Spain 12" single (F-612 383):
"Innocent (7" Version)"
"Innocent (12" Mix)"
"Earth Moving (Disco Version)"

Note: It's been observed that different European single contain the album version and some contain the 7" Version, so one or more of the listed singles here may not be accurate.

"Innocent (7" Version)" 3:27
Written by Mike Oldfield
Appears on: 7",12" & CD singles
This stripped down mix of the song lightens it up considerably, so if you thought the album version was too densely layered, this version is for you. It's not noted on the sleeve or label whether Bob Kraushaar is responsible for this version, but it does have some mixing similarities to the 12" Mix he did.

"Innocent (12" Mix)" 5:33
Written by Mike Oldfield, Remix by Bob Kraushaar
Appears on: 12" & CD singles, The Platinum Collection
A very dance-oriented mix from Bob Kraushaar (whose name is sometimes misspelled on the sleeve as "Krausmaar"). The intro and instrumental parts throughout are extended, adding more than 2 minutes to the run time. Overall, like the 7" Version, this mix is lighter than the album version.

-Summer-
Mike Oldfield releases his "Earth Moving" singles in the UK and France.

UK 7" single (VS 1189):
"Earth Moving (7" Version)"
"Bridge To Paradise"

UK 12" single (VST 1189):
"Earth Moving (Disco Mix)"
"Earth Moving (7" Version)"
"Bridge To Paradise"

UK CD single (VSCD 1189):
"Earth Moving (7" Version)"
"Earth Moving (Disco Mix)"
"Bridge To Paradise"

France One-side 7" single (SA 1270) promo:
"Earth Moving (7" Version)"

"Earth Moving (7" Version)" 4:04
Written by Mike Oldfield
Appears on: 7", 12" & CD singles
Very similar to the standard album version, this version features a few mixing differences, particularly at the beginning with an added instrumental layer and the end with an extra guitar layer.

"Earth Moving (Disco Mix)" AKA "Club Version" 4:04
Written by Mike Oldfield
Appears on: 12" & CD singles; Innocent 7", 12" & CD singles
Don't be fooled into thinking this is simply a dance remix of the track. This is, in fact, a much different recording and mix, with heavier guitars and more aggressive, alternate vocals by Nikki Bentley. It might have been more accurate to label this the "Rock Mix," because that's basically what it is. Seek this out!

"Bridge To Paradise" 4:39
Written by Mike Oldfield
Appears on: UK Earth Moving 7", 12" & CD singles
Since "Nothing But" and "Bridge To Nowhere" are two individual songs, with no material linking them, either literally or thematically, one wonders why they were put on the same track on the album. Here is a standalone cut of "Bridge To Paradise" that is otherwise identical to the album version. "Nothing But" would also be released by itself on a promo single in Spain.

-July-
Mike Oldfield and Anita Hegerland appear on the BBC TV show *Good Morning Britain*, being interviewed and performing an acoustic version of "Innocent." It's noted their daughter Greta is 14 months old and they are expecting their second child. **Oldfield** says he's "chucking out" all the computers for when he works on his next album. He also states, when asked about a follow up to *Tubular Bells*, that he considers the first album to be Parts 1 & 2 and is planning to start writing Part 3 & 4 "in a few weeks," with no synths or computers.

-July 5-
Mike Oldfield and Anita Hegerland appear on the German TV show *Na Siehste* performing "Innocent."

-July 10-
Mike Oldfield releases his album *Earth Moving* in the UK, Europe and North America on CD and LP on Virgin Records. The songs "Nothing But" and "Bridge To Paradise" are unrelated, but appear as a single track. Daniel Lazerus and **Mike Oldfield** co-produce the album. Track listing as follows:

UK *Earth Moving* CD (CDV2610)
UK *Earth Moving* LP (V 2610)
Europe *Earth Moving* CD (CDV2610)
Europe *Earth Moving* LP (209 982)
US *Earth Moving* CD (2-91270)
US *Earth Moving* LP (1-91270)
Canada *Earth Moving* LP (VL 2610)

"Holy" Mike Oldfield (with Adrian Belew)
"Hostage"
"Far Country"
"Innocent"
"Runaway Son"
"See The Light"
"Earth Moving"
"Blue Night"
"Nothing But / Bridge To Paradise"

-Date Unknown-
Virgin Records releases 7" promo singles of **Mike Oldfield**'s "Blue Night" and "Nothing But" in Spain.

Spain 7" single (SP-MIKE 1) promo:
"Blue Night"
"Blue Night"

Spain 7" single (SP-MIKE 2) promo:
"Nothing But"
"Nothing But"

> "Nothing But"
> Written by Mike Oldfield
> Appears on: Spain 7" promo single
> Lending further credence to the fact that this song and "Bridge To Paradise" are otherwise unrelated, here it is by itself, suffering no ill effects from being separated from the latter. Aside from that, it's identical to the album version.

-July 21-
Virgin Records re-issues **Mike Oldfield**'s album *Platinum* on CD (VJD-23006) in Japan. Track listing as follows.

"Platinum (Part One): Airborne"
"Platinum (Part Two): Platinum"
"Platinum (Part Three): Charleston"
"Platinum (Part Four): North Star/Platinum Finale"
"Woodhenge"
"Into Wonderland (with "Sally" Outro)" – listed as "Sally."
"Punkadiddle" – now includes the "Sally" ending at the start.
"I Got Rhythm" – a version of the 1930 Gershwin song.

-Date Unknown-
Mike Oldfield, Anita Hegerland and Maggie Reilly appear on the Spanish TV show *La Luna*, performing "Blue Night" and "Innocent."

-Date Unknown-
Virgin Records re-issues *The Orchestral Tubular Bells* album by The Royal Philharmonic Orchestra (with **Mike Oldfield**) on CD via their Virgin VIP label (VVIPD 101).

-Date Unknown-
BGO Records re-issues the **Kevin Ayers And The Whole World** album *Shooting At The Moon* on LP (BGO LP13) in the UK.

-August 23-
The Nicky Campbell Show on BBC Radio 1 airs the following, recorded at an earlier date:

"Tubular Bells (The Nicky Campbell Show)"
"Far Country (The Nicky Campbell Show)"
"Innocent (The Nicky Campbell Show)"
"Earth Moving (The Nicky Campbell Show)"

> "Tubular Bells (The Nicky Campbell Show)" 6:34
> Written by Mike Oldfield
> Appears on: N/A
> Mike recorded this and the three other tracks for The Nicky Campbell Show, This version starts with the "Introduction" and then moves right into the "Finale." It's an excellent, condensed version of "Part One" and is the highlight of the four. John Peel introduces the instruments, doing so live on the air (the master tape has no vocals).
>
> "Far Country (The Nicky Campbell Show)" 4:04
> Written by Mike Oldfield
> Appears on: N/A
> This version is pretty close to the album version, possibly using elements of the original backing track. There are new parts, too, such as the vocals and guitar work.
>
> "Innocent (The Nicky Campbell Show)" 3:26
> Written by Mike Oldfield
> Appears on: N/A
> Like "Far Country", this is very similar to the album version. Anita's vocals and some of the instrumentation is new, while some instrumentation could be a re-use of the original backing track.
>
> "Earth Moving (The Nicky Campbell Show)" 3:44
> Written by Mike Oldfield
> Appears on: N/A

Unlike "Far Country" and "Innocent," this version sounds like an entirely new recording, instrumentation, vocals and all. Most interesting is that Anita sings the song (this isn't confirmed, but it sounds a lot like her and she really goes for it at the very end).

Note: in later interviews, **Oldfield** says work on the "Tubular Bells" track from this session, with (almost) all hand-played instruments at least partly inspired his interest in moving away from computers in his music for his next album.

-September-
Mike Oldfield begins working on his new album at Roughwood Croft, Chalfont St. Giles, Buckinghamshire, England (*Amarok* sessions). After the entirely vocal *Earth Moving*, **Oldfield** decides to make this album a return to mostly instrumental, as well as abandoning synths and computers for it. He also recruits many of the artists who appeared on *Ommadawn*. In later interviews, **Mike** says the sessions lasted six months.

Note: It would seem that two factors changed the direction of the album from being the *Tubular Bells* sequel **Mike** had previously mentioned: he decided to wait until his Virgin Records contract was up, and he changed his musical direction. The result is that **Oldfield** crafts the new album more as a sequel to *Ommadawn* than of *Tubular Bells*. His autobiography says he had a lot of fun working on it, throwing in everything he could think of.

-September 18-
Mike Oldfield releases his "Innocent" singles in the UK.

UK 7" single (VS1214):
"Innocent (7" Version)"
"Earth Moving (Disco Version)" - listed as "Club Version"

UK 12" single (VST 1214):
"Innocent (12" Mix)"
"Innocent (7" Version)"
"Earth Moving (Disco Version)" - listed as "Club Version"

UK 12" single (VST 1214) White label:
"Innocent (12" Mix)"
"Innocent (7" Version)"
"Earth Moving (Disco Version)" - listed as "Club Version"

UK CD single (VSCD 1214):
"Innocent (7" Version)"
"Innocent (12 Mix)"
"Earth Moving (Disco Version)" - listed as "Club Version"

-Date Unknown-
Mike Oldfield, Anita Hegerland and Adrian Belew appear on the German TV show *Peter's Pop Show*, performing "Holy" and "Innocent."

-October-
William Murray photographs **Mike Oldfield** for the cover of the forthcoming album. It is planned as an "updated" recreation of the *Ommadawn* cover artwork, according to Murray in a 1990 interview with David Porter.

In an interview this month for *Keyboards* magazine, **Mike Oldfield** again states that the "new *Tubular Bells*" album will be more traditional instruments (no computers) and will comprise "Parts 3 & 4."

Virgin Records re-issues **Mike Oldfield**'s *Boxed* in a 3xCD set (CDBOX1), track listing as follows:

CD 1: *Tubular Bells*
"Tubular Bells (Part One – Boxed Remix)"
"Tubular Bells (Part Two – Boxed Remix)"
"The Rio Grande (Boxed Version)" David Bedford
"Portsmouth"
"In Dulci Jubilo"

CD 2: *Hergest Ridge*
"Hergest Ridge (Part One – Boxed Remix)"
"Hergest Ridge (Part Two – Boxed Remix)"
"An Extract from 'Star's End'" David Bedford
"Argiers"
"Speak (Tho' You Only Say Farewell)" – a version 1926 Ray Morello & Horatio Nicholls song.

CD 3: *Ommadawn*
Ommadawn (Part One – Boxed Remix)"
Ommadawn (Part Two – Boxed Remix)"
 "The Phaeacian Games" David Bedford
"First Excursion"

Note: the CDs contain all the material from the original LP edition, but eliminates the separate *Collaborations* disc by dividing those tracks up and placing them on the albums' discs to save space.

-October 21-
In the issue of *Melody Maker* published on this date, **Mike Oldfield** says in the interview that he is currently working on a "completely uncommercial" instrumental album, distancing himself from a lot of electronics on it. He also explicitly states that he is not happy with Virgin Records and once his contract is up, he plans to work on the sequel to *Tubular Bells* with another record company.

-October 30-
Virgin Records releases the **Mike Oldfield with Adrian Belew** singles "One Glance Is Holy" in Germany.

Germany 7" single (112 761):
"One Glance Is Holy (Edit)"
"One Glance Is Holy (Remix)"

Germany 12" single (612 761):
"One Glance Is Holy (Hard And Holy Mix)"
"One Glance Is Holy (Remix)"
"One Glance Is Holy (Edit)"
"One Glance Is Holy (Holy Groove Instrumental)"

Germany CD singles (:
"One Glance Is Holy (Hard And Holy Mix)"
"One Glance Is Holy (Remix)"
"One Glance Is Holy (Edit)"
"One Glance Is Holy (Holy Groove Instrumental)"

Note: the singles list the title of the song as "One Glance Is Holy," rather than how it appears everywhere else as just "Holy."

> "One Glance Is Holy (Hard And Holy Mix)" 4:53
> Written by Mike Oldfield; Remixed by Martyn Ware (assisted by Phil Spalding)
> Appears on: 12" & CD single

This version re-works the backing track to give it a more rock-oriented sound, with more prominent rhythm guitar, percussion and punchier drums. Instead of fading out, the track ends with the rhythm guitar playing out to the last note.

"One Glance Is Holy (Remix)" 3:50
Written by Mike Oldfield; Remixed by Martyn Ware (assisted by Phil Spalding)
Appears on: 7", 12" & CD singles; Elements boxed set
Like the "Hard And Holy Mix," this features the same rock-oriented backing track, but it doesn't stop there. It re-arranges the lyric structure, the first chorus between the first two verses and having the guitar solo come in later. It also tightens up the running time by shortening the end with an early fade out.

"One Glance Is Holy (Edit)" 3:40
Written by Mike Oldfield
Appears on: 7", 12" & CD singles
This edit removes a few seconds from the beginning, takes out the middle eight and guitar solo, and fades out early. Not bad, but if you want a shorter version, I suggest going with the "Remix," its more fun.

"One Glance Is Holy (Holy Groove Instrumental)" 4:51
Written by Mike Oldfield
Appears on: 12" & CD singles
It takes a bit to get going, but once it does, it's a good instrumental remix of the backing track. All of the synth parts appear to have been removed, as have the lead guitar and solo, leaving just the rhythm section.

-November 17-
Mike Oldfield and Anita Hegerland perform "Moonlight Shadow" at the Diamond Awards Festival, Antwerp, Belgium. Also of note, Roy Orbison gives his only live performance of "You Got It" at the Awards, three weeks before his death.

Amarok

1990

-Early 1990-
Mike Oldfield returns to psychotherapy. He starts by reading books suggested by his therapist and then begins session, which last nines months.

-Date Unknown-
Noah Daniel Hegerland Oldfield is born to **Mike Oldfield** and Anita Hegerland.

-March-
Mike Oldfield completes work on his album *Amarok*. Bridget St. John, Paddy Moloney, Clodagh Simonds, Janet Brown and Jabula appear on the album. Jabula record their parts in London, England. Tom Newman engineers the album and does the cover's lettering. Sessions likely take place at Roughwood Croft, Chalfont St. Giles, Buckinghamshire, England.
"Irish Air" – the actual title of the track is not confirmed, but this is reportedly a piece recorded with Bridget St. John which ultimately went unused on the album. It's very likely not the only unused piece **Oldfield** recorded during these sessions.
"Mandolin (Reprise 2)" – the little tune that makes up this piece was previously played by **Mike** on *Good Morning Britain* (31-05-88).
"Branches" – this **Sallyangie** guitar improvisation, recorded but yet-unreleased at the time, features a segment **Mike** would work into the "Mad Bit" of *Amarok*.
"Hoover" – **Oldfield** supposedly had a demo piece he'd planned for *Tubular Bells*, which was left unused. It featured a vacuum cleaner (a "Hoover"). That demo might be the inspiration for this segment.
"Africa III" – some of the tribal music heard in this segment sounds identical to part of "Bones," which may indicate that **Mike** sampled or used bits of the original recording for this part of *Amarok*.

Note: Virgin Records wanted to call the album *Tubular Bells II*, but **Oldfield** was against it, wanting it to be *Amarok*. As much as he liked the album, he didn't feel it was the *Tubular Bells* sequel.

-Date Unknown-
Thinking about his next album, the last under his Virgin Record contract, **Mike Oldfield** decides to sing all the lead vocals himself (because he'd never done that before on his past albums). He spends months getting vocal training to learn to sing properly.

-Date Unknown-
Mike Oldfield records guitar on the track "Break Through The Rock" for Sally Oldfield's new album (*Natasha* sessions).

-Mid-1990-
Mike Oldfield begins work on his last Virgin Records album of his original contracts (*Heaven's Open* sessions). The session last until late 1990, at Roughwood Croft, Chalfont St. Giles, Buckinghamshire, England.

-May-
Virgin Records releases **Mike Oldfield**'s *Amarok* promo CD singles in the UK and Germany.

German CD single (663 271-000) promo:
"Amarok (Excerpt I: Boat)"
"Amarok (Excerpt II: Slow Waltz + Lion [Reprise] + Mandolin [Reprise])"
"Amarok (Excerpt III: Africa I & II)"
"Amarok (Excerpt IV: Fast Riff [Edit])"
"Amarok (Excerpt V: Boat (Reprise) to Green (Reprise)"

Amarok X-Trax
UK 5"CD single (AMACD1J) promo:
"Amarok (Excerpt I: Fast Riff Intro + Intro)"
"Amarok (Excerpt II: Fast Waltz to Intermission)"
"Amarok (Excerpt III: Intro [Reprise] + Big Roses + Green Green [Excerpt])"
"Amarok (Excerpt IV: Lion (Reprise) to Hoover / Scot)"
"Amarok (Excerpt V: Africa III)"

Amarok X-Trax
UK 3" CD single (AMACD 1) promo:
"Amarok (Excerpt I: Fast Riff Intro + Intro)"
"Amarok (Excerpt II: Fast Waltz to Intermission)"
"Amarok (Excerpt V: Africa III)"

Note: The 3" CD single comes from the HW Smith store magazine, *Insight*, and was redeemable for £1 off the price of the *Amarok* album, but customers had to hand over the promo CD in order to get the discount (like a coupon, you weren't allowed to keep it). Since only some fans kept them, while more simply traded theirs in, not many of the 3" CD singles are in circulation.

"Amarok (Excerpt I: Boat)" 3:09
Written by Mike Oldfield
Appears on: German Promo CD single; Heaven's Open 7", 12" & CD singles
This edits fades in over the last few seconds of "Intermission" before "Boat" starts and fades out before "Intro (Reprise)."

"Amarok (Excerpt II: Slow Waltz + Lion [Reprise] + Mandolin [Reprise])" 3:26
Written by Mike Oldfield
Appears on: German Promo CD single; Gimme Back 7", `12" & CD single
No fade in or fade outs here, the track starts cleanly on "Slow Waltz" and ends cleanly after "Mandolin (Reprise)."

"Amarok (Excerpt III: Africa I & II)" 9:36
Written by Mike Oldfield
Appears on: German Promo CD single; Gimme Back 7", `12" & CD single
Here are the first two "Africa" movements. It fades in on "Africa I" and ends cleanly after "Africa II."

"Amarok (Excerpt IV: Fast Riff [Edit])" 1:53
Written by Mike Oldfield
Appears on: German Promo CD single
This edit starts after the glass shattering which starts the segment on the album and fades out a few seconds early.

"Amarok (Excerpt V: Boat [Reprise] to Green Green [Reprise]" 2:29
Written by Mike Oldfield
Appears on: German Promo CD single; Heaven's Open 7", 12" & CD singles
Fading in on the start of "Boat (Reprise)," this excerpt continues through to "Green (Reprise)," ending cleanly before "Africa I".

"Amarok (Excerpt I: Fast Riff Intro + Intro)" 3:05
Written by Mike Oldfield
Appears on: Amarok X-Trax 5" CD & 3" CD singles
Starting the same as the album, with "Fast Riff Intro," the track fades out 30 seconds into the next segment, "Intro."

"Amarok (Excerpt II: Fast Waltz to Intermission)" 4:16
Written by Mike Oldfield
Appears on: Amarok X-Trax Promo 5" CD & 3" CD singles
Fading in on "Fast Waltz" and fading out as "Intermission" draws to a close, this excerpt crams in a few of the shorter segments of the album.

"Amarok (Excerpt III: Intro [Reprise] + Big Roses)" 3:47
Written by Mike Oldfield
Appears on: Amarok X-Trax Promo 5" CD single
Fading in on the "Intro (Reprise)" segment and continuing into "Big Roses" before ending cleanly.

"Amarok (Excerpt IV: Lion [Reprise] to Hoover / Scot)" 5:18
Written by Mike Oldfield
Appears on: Amarok X-Trax Promo 5" CD single
Starting cleanly at "Lion (Reprise)" and continuing through to "Hoover / Scot," this track ends cleanly after that segment.

"Amarok (Excerpt V: Africa III)" 5:38
Written by Mike Oldfield
Appears on: Amarok X-Trax Promo 5" CD & 3" CD singles
This is the complete "Africa III" segment, starting cleanly with "Hello Everyone" and going right through to the "Finale," ending as the album does.

-June 7-
An article published on this date in *The Age* (Australia) states that **Mike Oldfield**'s next album is near completion (*Heaven's Open* sessions). It describes the album as a mix of songs and instrumentals. It also notes that **Oldfield** plans to start *Tubular Bells II* in January. The article explicitly quotes **Mike** as saying *Amarok* is a sequel to *Ommadawn*.

-June 14-
Mike Oldfield releases his album *Amarok* in the UK. Some sources give the European release as May 21st. Tom Newman co-produced the album.

William Murray writes the amusing short story featured in the original release of the album (it is removed for the 2000 re-issue).

Mike institutes a contest wherein he offers a £1,000 of his own money to whoever finds the hidden message. The contest is eventually won by Roy Rashbrook, who was unaware of the prize and never claimed the money.

Track listing as follows:

UK *Amarok* CD (CDV 2640):
UK *Amarok* Promo CD (CDV 2640 WL)
Europe *Amarok* CD (CDV 2640)
"Amarok"

Europe LP (V 2640)
"Amarok (Side One)"
"Amarok (Side Two)"

Note: **Mike**'s plan for the album was for it to be the uninterrupted 60:02 minute track. Since records and tapes can't accommodate that, "Amarok" is split in two on those releases. The LP and cassette don't give the two sides any sort of differentiation, simply calling both sides "Amarok," with 30 minute run times.

The inner sleeve photo notes the track names and lengths for most of the individual pieces of music that appear. Not all the notation is accurate, due to later changes made by **Oldfield**, but here is the correct, adjusted listing:

00:00 "Fast Riff Intro"
02:32 "Intro"
05:46 "Climax I – 12 Strings"
06:18 "Soft Bodrhan"
07:20 "Rachmaninov's I"
07:38 "Soft Bodrhan 2"
07:59 "Rachmaninov's II"
08:35 "Roses"
10:42 "Intro (Reprise 1)"
12:45 "Scot"
13:16 "Didlybom"
15:00 "Mad Bit" – melody from **The Sallyangie** piece "Branches."
15:56 "Russian"
16:11 "Hoover"
18:00 "Fast Riff"
19:57 "Lion"
21:57 "Fast Waltz"
23:43 "Stop"
24:33 "Mad Bit 2"
24:46 "Fast Waltz 2"
25:06 "Mandolin"
26:07 "Intermission"
26:19 "Boat"
29:27 "Intro (Reprise)" – LP/tape break point at 30:00.
32:07 "Big Roses"
33:13 "Green Green"
34:24 "Slow Waltz"
36:04 "Lion (Reprise)"
37:05 "Mandolin (Reprise 1)"
37:47 "TV-AM"
39:16 "Mandolin (Reprise 2)" – tune heard on *Good Morning Britain* (May 1988).
39:50 "Fast Riff (Reprise)"
41:03 "Hoover / Scot"
42:22 "Boat (Reprise)"
43:32 "12 Strings (Reprise)"
43:50 "Intro Waltz"
44:12 "Green (Reprise)"
44:46 "Africa I: Far Build"
48:00 "Africa I: Far Dip" – the secret message appears in this segment.
48:46 "Africa I: Pre-Climax"
49:33 "Africa I: 12 Climax"
50:24 "Africa I: Climax I"
51:00 "Africa II: Bridge"

51:17 "Africa II: Riff"
51:34 "Africa II: Boat III"
51:52 "Africa II: Bridge II"
52:10 "Africa II: Climax II"
54:23 "Africa III: Hello Everyone"
55:50 "Africa III: Choir" – has part of what sounds like "Bones" at the end.
57:30 "Africa III: Recorder"
58:14 "Africa III: Happy"
58:43 "Africa III: Finale"

Note: credit goes to the contributors of the Mike Oldfield FAQ at Amadian.net and to Tubular.net for their respective breakdowns, both of which I drew from, in addition to my own analysis of the music, to devise what I feel is an accurate track listing.

Note: the secret message originally uncovered by Roy Rashbrook is Morse Code spelling out: F-U-C-K-O-F-F-R-B, generally accepted by fans as directed towards Richard Branson and, by extension, Virgin Records.

-Date Unknown-
Mike Oldfield is interviewed by Anne Nightingale for *One To One* on ITV, UK.

-Summer-
Simon Draper records his drum parts for **Mike Oldfield**'s next album (*Heaven's Open* sessions), at Roughwood Croft, Chalfont St. Giles, Buckinghamshire, England. The session take a week, according to the October *Sym-Info* magazine interview.

Mike Oldfield lives in a tent outside his house (Roughwood Croft, Chalfont St. Giles, Buckinghamshire, England) in protest of overly-synthetic/computerized music. It is mentioned in several period interviews. The duration of this protest is said to be about three months.

-October-
In an interview published this month in *Sym-Info* magazine, it states that **Mike Oldfield** is working on finishing his new album (*Heaven's Open* sessions). This interview quotes **Oldfield** as saying *Amarok* began with the idea of being *Ommadawn II*.

-Late 1990-
Mike Oldfield finishes work on his new album, *Heaven's Open*. Other artists who appear on the album include Anita Hegerland, Nikki 'B' Bentley and Tom Newman (deliberately credited as "Thom Newman") and Simon Phillips. Newman also co-produces and engineers the album. The sessions take place at Roughwood Croft, Chalfont St. Giles, Buckinghamshire, England.
Tracks worked on include:
"Fed Up, Fed Up" – The original version of what became "Gimme Back."
"Man In The Rain" – This *Islands*-era (possibly earlier) song is re-worked/re-written into "Heaven's Open."
"Music From The Balcony" – This instrumental uses a sample from the Zero G sampler, specifically the "No!" vocals.

> "Fed Up, Fed Up" 4:30
> Written by Mike Oldfield
> Appears on: Unreleased
> This track is pretty much complete, featuring a different, earlier vocal by Mike and no "gimme back" backing vocal part. Instead, the backing vocals chant "fed up, fed up." The mix is rougher than "Gimme Back" and is missing some of the flourishes that appear in the album version. Mike's vocal performance is more angry here than the frustrated desperation heard on the "Gimme Back" version. I highly recommend this outtake.

-Date Unknown-
Virgin Records re-issues **Mike Oldfield**'s album *Five Miles Out* on CD (VVIPD 106) in the UK.

-Date Unknown-
Sally Natasha Oldfield releases her album *Natasha* in Europe (CD 467407 1, LP 467407 2) on CBS Records, featuring **Mike Oldfield** on guitar on "Break Through The Rock."

Note: "Natasha" is not Sally's actual middle name (it's Patricia), but the Natasha pseudonym is used throughout the album's credits, such her songwriting credit listed as "N. Oldfield." Her next album in 1992, *The Flame*, is released under the name "Natasha Oldfield," before she returned to using Sally Oldfield for subsequent albums. This coincides with **Mike**'s brief period of releasing his work under the name "Michael Oldfield" for *Heaven's Open* and its singles (for which co-producer Tom Newman calls himself "Thom Newman"). Mike refers to this period as his "half-hearted" attempt to re-invent himself.

> "Break Through The Rock" 4:18
> Written by N. Oldfield (AKA Sally Oldfield)
> Appears on: Natasha
> Unlike Sally's previous folk stylings, this song and this album sees her with a more prog rock sound. The backing track is very mid-tempo percussion-driven and Mike's guitar work stands out.

-December 31-
Mike Oldfield's contract with Virgin Records ends on this date, having delivered his *Heaven's Open* album. The terms of the contract do state that **Oldfield** can't release a new album with a new record company before May 1992 (**Mike** quotes this stipulation in his October *Sym-Info* interview).

Heaven's Open

1991

-January-
Michael Oldfield releases his "Heaven's Open" single in the UK and Europe on Virgin Records.

UK 7" single (VS 1341):
"Heaven's Open" Michael Oldfield
"Amarok (Excerpt I: Boat + Intro [Reprise])" Mike Oldfield

Europe 7" single (VS 1341):
"Heaven's Open" Michael Oldfield
"Amarok (Excerpt I: Boat + Intro [Reprise])" Mike Oldfield

UK 12" single (VST 1341):
"Heaven's Open" Michael Oldfield
"Amarok (Excerpt I: Boat + Intro [Reprise])" Mike Oldfield
"Heaven's Open (12" Version)" Michael Oldfield
"Amarok (Excerpt V: Boat [Reprise] to Green [Reprise]" Mike Oldfield

Europe 12" single (VST 1341):
"Heaven's Open" Michael Oldfield
"Amarok (Excerpt I: Boat + Intro [Reprise])" Mike Oldfield
"Heaven's Open (12" Version)" Michael Oldfield
"Amarok (Excerpt V: Boat [Reprise] to Green [Reprise]" Mike Oldfield

UK CD single (VSCDT 1341):
"Heaven's Open" Michael Oldfield
"Amarok (Excerpt I: Boat + Intro [Reprise])" Mike Oldfield
"Heaven's Open (12" Version)" Michael Oldfield
"Amarok (Excerpt V: Boat [Reprise] to Green [Reprise]" Mike Oldfield

Europe CD single (VSCDT 1341):
"Heaven's Open" Michael Oldfield
"Amarok (Excerpt I: Boat + Intro [Reprise])" Mike Oldfield
"Heaven's Open (12" Version)" Michael Oldfield
"Amarok (Excerpt V: Boat [Reprise] to Green [Reprise]" Mike Oldfield

> "Heaven's Open (12" Version)" 4:33
> Written by Michael Oldfield
> Appears on: 12" & CD single
> Rather than going the traditional 12" Mix route, this version rebuilds much of the song. It replaces some the guitar parts with new ones, adds some additional ones and removes some of the vocals. The end result is a pretty different version of the track. Of note, this version is used on the video, rather then the standard version.

-Early 1991-
Mike Oldfield begins writing and recording what he plans to be *Tubular Bells II*, at Roughwood Croft, Chalfont St. Giles, Buckinghamshire, England. At some point during these early album sessions, **Oldfield** is filmed working on the tracks, likely for later promotional material, given he knows *Tubular Bells II* is highly anticipated. Tom Newman co-produces these sessions.

Note: Some sources put the start of the sessions in September, but Mike says in his autobiography that he decided to do another tax exile year in Los Angeles, California, US, while working on the album (so he could work with Trevor Horn there, too). As he had about half the album recorded before moving and was back in England the next summer rehearsing for the Edinburgh concert, he must have started much earlier in 1991.

> "Early Stages" 4:07
> Written by Mike Oldfield
> Appears on: Sentinel 7", 12" & CD singles
> The opening movement of *Tubular Bells II*, heard hear at the "early stage," is what would become "Sentinel" on that album. You can hear part of the theme in there, but you can also hear that Oldfield and Tom Newman were producing a sound texture much closer to the first *Tubular Bells* than how *TBII* would end up. And though this is the only early portion officially released, excerpts from some of the other movements (leaked onto YouTube) show that they, too, were of a similar sound, recognizable as what would end up on *TBII*, but much more densely layered and more reminiscent of the first *Tubular Bells*.

-February 18-
Michael Oldfield releases his album *Heaven's Open* in the UK, Europe and Canada, his last album with Virgin Records. On the sleeve **Oldfield** and co-producer Tom Newman go by alternate versions of their first names ("Michael" and "Thom" respectively). The artwork adapts the Trevor Key image previously planned for *Tubular Bells* when Virgin Records toyed with the title *Breakfast In Bed* for that album in 1973. Track listing as follows:

UK *Heaven's Open* CD (CDVIP 153)
Europe *Heaven's Open* CD (CDV 2653)
Europe *Heaven's Open* LP (V 2653)
Canada *Heaven's Open* CD (CDV 2653)

"Make Make"
"No Dream"
"Mr. Dream"
"Gimme Back"
"Heaven's Open"
"Music From The Balcony"

-Date Unknown-
Mike Oldfield and Anita Hegerland split up.

-Date Unknown-
Virgin Records re-issues the **Mike Oldfield** compilation *The Complete Mike Oldfield* in France on CD (CDMOC 1).

Note: this features the same track listing as the 1985 French 2xCD (CDMOC 1) set.

Also released in France is a "Moonlight Shadow" single:

France 7" single (SA 9020) promo:
"Moonlight Shadow"
"To France (Single Version)"

France cassette single (55060):
"Moonlight Shadow"
"To France (Single Version)"

France CD single (35060):
"Moonlight Shadow"
"To France (Single Version)"
"Jungle Gardenia"

-Date Unknown-
Virgin Records re-issues the following **Mike Oldfield** albums on LP in the UK:

UK 1991 *Platinum* LP (OVED 233)
"Platinum (Part One): Airborne"
"Platinum (Part Two): Platinum"
"Platinum (Part Three): Charleston"
"Platinum (Part Four): North Star/Platinum Finale"
"Woodhenge"
"Into Wonderland" – incorrectly listed as "Sally."
"Punkadiddle"
"I Got Rhythm" – a version of the 1930 Gershwin song.

-Date Unknown-
Caroline Blue Plate re-issues the following **Mike Oldfield** albums on CD in the US.

Ommadawn CD (CAROL 1855-2)
"Ommadawn (Part One)"
"Ommadawn (Part Two – Edit)"
"On Horseback (Single Version)" – unlisted on the sleeve.

Exposed 2xCD (CAROL 1852-2)
Five Miles Out (CAROL 1853-2)
Discovery (CAROL 1851-2)

-June 10/11-
Virgin Records releases **Michael Oldfield**'s "Gimme Back" singles in Germany.

Germany 7" single (114 943):
"Gimme Back (Edit)" Michael Oldfield
"Amarok (Excerpt II: Slow Waltz + Lion [Reprise] + Mandolin [Reprise])" Mike Oldfield

Germany 12" single (614 430):
"Gimme Back" Michael Oldfield
"Amarok (Excerpt II: Slow Waltz + Lion [Reprise + Mandolin [Reprise])" Mike Oldfield
"Amarok (Excerpt III: Africa I & II)" Mike Oldfield

Germany CD single (664 430):
"Gimme Back" Michael Oldfield
"Amarok (Excerpt II: Slow Waltz + Lion [Reprise + Mandolin [Reprise])" Mike Oldfield
"Amarok (Excerpt III: Africa I & II)" Mike Oldfield

> "Gimme Back (Edit)" 3:44
> Written by Michael Oldfield
> Appears on: 7" single
> A simple edit, though rare, since it only appears on this 7" German single, it simply fades out early, so the very end of the song is absent. At least one collector found a Virgin Records "Fact Sheet" (in German) in their copy's sleeve (which I'm guessing to be a promotional insert). The Fact Sheet discusses the song and its reggae/Barbados influence. And refers to Mike as

"Michael," keeping with that trend for all things related to the *Heaven's Open* album. It's not known how common this insert was.

-Summer-
Mike Oldfield moves to Los Angeles, California, US, to continue work on *Tubular Bell II* (and to do a tax exile year so as not to lose the advance he anticipates for this album). He enlists Trevor Horn to produce the album. They work on the material separately, each their own home studios. It's been reported that **Mike** had about the first half of the album done before going to LA, where it was then re-worked with Horn's production techniques. These sessions last until June 1992.

-Date Unknown-
Mike Oldfield signs with WEA (Warner/Elektra/Atlantic, now Warner Music Group) for two albums (*Tubular Bells II* and what would be *The Songs Of Distant Earth*).

-Date Unknown-
Virgin Records re-issues **Mike Oldfield**'s album *Crises* in the UK on CD (VVIPD 116)

Tubular Bells II

1992

-January-
Kevin Ayers releases his album *Still Life With Guitar* in the UK on CD (PERM CD5) & LP (PERM LP5) on Permanent Records, featuring **Mike Oldfield** on the track "I Don't Depend On You."

>"I Don't Depend On You" 3:36
>Written by Kevin Ayers
>Appears on: Still Life With Guitar
>A typically laid back Kevin Ayers track, written in 3/4 time, with minimalist guitar by Mike.

-June-
Mike Oldfield completes work on his *Tubular Bells II* album in Los Angeles, California, US. Tracks worked on since September 1991 include:
"The Bell" – several vocalists record the part of introducing the instruments. They are: Vivian Stanshall, Alan Rickman, Billy Connelly, Otto Waalkes, (in both German and English) and Carlos Finely (in Spanish).
"Altered State" – features John Robinson on drums.
"Red Dawn" – a working title for this track is "Russian," in keeping with its sister movement on the original *Tubular Bells*.

Oldfield notes in an interview this year that the second half of the album was recorded in about a week.

-Date Unknown-
Windsong International releases the **Kevin Ayers And The Whole World** January 6th, 1972, BBC session as *BBC Radio 1 Live In Concert* in the UK on CD (WIN CD 018).

-Date Unknown-
Virgin Records releases **Mike Oldfield**'s album *Tubular Bells* on Digital Compact Cassette (DCC) in Europe and the UK. Remastered by Simon Heyworth.

Note: DCC was short-lived magnetic tape format that attempted to compete with Digital Audio Tape (DAT), MiniDisc and CD technology. DCC was discontinued by 1996.

-Date Unknown-
Virgin Records re-issues the **Mike Oldfield** album *Earth Moving* on CD (0777 7 86332 2 8) in the US.

-Date Unknown-
Virgin Records re-issues the following **Mike Oldfield** albums on CD in the UK and Europe.

Discovery (CDV 2308)
The Killing Fields Original Film Soundtrack (CDV 2328)

-Summer-
Mike Oldfield and his ensemble rehearse at Roughwood Croft, Chalfont St. Giles, Buckinghamshire, England, for the live premier of *Tubular Bells II* at Edinburgh Castle, Edinburgh, Scotland. The ensemble is:

Robyn Smith	Jay Stapley	Hugh Burns	Alan Limbrick
Craig Pruess	Dave Hartley	Adrian Thomas	Yitkin Seow
Lawrence Coddle	Ian Thomas	Ben Huffnung	Alasdair Malloy
Jerry McKenna	Pete Clarke	John Parricelli	Jackie Queen
Linda Taylor	Edie Lehmann	Susannah Melvoin	John Gordon Sinclair

Mike Oldfield appears on the BBC Radio show *The Break*, discussing his career, *Tubular Bells II* and the upcoming Edinburgh Castle concert.

Mike Oldfield records the following (venue unknown). **Oldfield** produces the session.
"Silent Night" – it's not known exactly when **Mike** recorded this version of the carol. It could either have been during the *Tubular Bells II* sessions or shortly after.

-July-
Reprise Records releases an advance CD copy of **Mike Oldfield**'s album *Tubular Bells II* Promo CD (PRO-CD-5705) in the US.

-August 27-
An article published on this date discusses the release of *Tubular Bells II* and the rehearsals of **Mike Oldfield** and his ensemble for the upcoming Edinburgh concert.

-August 31-
Mike Oldfield releases his album *Tubular Bells II* in the UK, Europe and North America on WEA and Reprise Records. It contains Alan Rickman's vocals on "The Bell," credited as 'A Strolling Player.' Track listing as follows:

UK & Europe *Tubular Bells II* LP (4509 90618-1)
UK & Europe *Tubular Bells II* CD (4509 90618-2)
US *Tubular Bells II* CD (9 45041-2)
Canada *Tubular Bells II* CD (CD 90618)

"Sentinel"
"Dark Star"
"Clear Light"
"Blue Saloon"
"Sunjammer"
"Red Dawn"
"The Bell"
"Weightless"
"The Great Plain"
"Sunset Door"
"Tattoo"
"Altered State"
"Maya Gold"
"Moonshine"

Note: **Oldfield** says in an interview this year that both the idea of splitting up the two halves into shorter tracks on the album, and giving each of these movements a title, came when a friend told him it was hard to listen to a small part alone of a long instrumental track on his past albums.

-September 4-
Mike Oldfield and his ensemble premier *Tubular Bells II* live at Edinburgh Castle, Edinburgh, Scotland. It is a charity concert attended by Prince Charles. There is a party following the show. Several tracks from this concert are released individually over the years and the concert is later released on home video.

> "Sentinel (Live At Edinburgh Castle)" 8:07
> Written by Mike Oldfield
> Appears on: Tattoo CD single (Part 1 of 2)

A really good live version (from the album's premier, where Mike and his ensemble played the entire *Tubular Bells II* album from start to finish), it doesn't really deviate from the album version, but it's still impressive to hear it played by a live group.

"The Bell (Live At Edinburgh Castle)" 4:20
Written by Mike Oldfield
Appears on: UK CD single
John Gordon Sinclair acts as MC for this performance, introducing the instruments. The track fades out before the end of the movement, which is a shame. Hopefully, one day the uncut concert will be released on CD.

"Tattoo (Live At Edinburgh Castle)" 3:46
Written by Mike Oldfield
Appears on: Tattoo: Live At Edinburgh Castle EP CD, Two Sides: The Very Best Of Mike Oldfield
This live version fades out before the end of the piece, just after the build-up reaching its climax, so the dénouement is gone.

"Maya Gold (Live At Edinburgh Castle)" 4:10
Written by Mike Oldfield
Appears on: Tattoo: Live At Edinburgh Castle EP CD
A faithful recreation of the album version and rather than fading out, it flows into the next movement (and track), "Moonshine," so as a standalone track, it cuts suddenly at the end.

"Moonshine (Live At Edinburgh Castle)" 1:42
Written by Mike Oldfield
Appears on: Tattoo: Live At Edinburgh Castle EP CD
Picking up where the previous track ends, this is the group having a lot of fun playing the piece. The track cuts off at the end for the next piece, the "Reprise" of "The Bell" to come in.

"Reprise (Live At Edinburgh Castle)" 1:21
Written by Mike Oldfield
Appears on: Tattoo: Live At Edinburgh Castle EP CD
Rather than finishing with "Moonshine," the ensemble performs a "Reprise" of "The Bell," so the concert ends with tubular bells and a grand finale.

-September 5-
Mike Oldfield holds a press conference in Edinburgh, Scotland, for the media previously invited to the premier.

-September 10-
John Gordon Sinclair (MC at the Edinburgh Castle concert) does an interview on *TVAM Breakfast Show*, UK, discussing the *Tubular Bells II* premier.

-September 12-
Mike Oldfield appears on the Italian TV show *Viendomos TVE1*, promoting "Sentinel."

-September 22-
Mike Oldfield releases his "Sentinel" singles in the UK, Europe and North America.

UK 7" singles (YZ 698):
"Sentinel (Single Restructure)"
"Early Stages"

UK CD single (YZ 698CD):
"Sentinel (Single Restructure)"
"Sentinel (The ORB 7" Mix)" Mike Oldfield vs The ORB
"Early Stages"

Europe 7" singles (YZ 698):
"Sentinel (Single Restructure)"
"Early Stages"

Europe CD single (YZ 698CD):
"Sentinel (Single Restructure)"
"Sentinel (The ORB 7" Mix)" Mike Oldfield vs The ORB
"Early Stages"

France CD single (YZ 698CD):
"Sentinel (Single Restructure)"
"Sentinel (The ORB 7" Mix)" Mike Oldfield vs The ORB
"Early Stages"

UK CD single (SAM 1085):
"Sentinel (Single Restructure)"

US CD single (PRO-CD-5800) promo:
"Sentinel (Single Restructure)"

> "Sentinel (Single Restructure)" 3:56
> Written by Mike Oldfield
> Appears on: 7", 12", CD & Promo CD singles; Elements: The Best Of Mike Oldfield; XXV: The Essential Mike Oldfield; Collection; The Platinum Collection; The Best Of: 1992 - 2003
> For the single, "Sentinel" is edited down by half, but loses nothing in the process. As the title suggests, the track in restructured, removing the opening piano, cutting out some bits in the middle and the change to the Major key at the end. A new, remixed ending then closes the track, making for a good, radio friendly cut.
>
> "Sentinel (The ORB 7" Mix)" 4:03
> Written by Mike Oldfield; Remixed by The ORB
> Appears on: 12" & CD singles, Sentinel (Total Overhaul) 12" Promo & CD single
> This is the first of the Mike Oldfield remixes released, wherein a DJ/producer (or team) completely re-works one of his tracks and does additional production (this practice would be fairly common at the time for many other artists). In this case, it appears only a small fraction of the remix is remotely recognizable as anything performed by Mike. The rest is ambient; almost trance music, with no backbeat. As remixes go, it's not bad, just not much Oldfield in there.

-September 26-
Mike Oldfield appears on the German TV show *Wretten Dass*, promoting "Sentinel."

-September 27-
Mike Oldfield appears at "Pavarotti International" Charity Gala Concert, Medona, Italy, promoting "Sentinel." Also on the bill is Brian May, Sting and others

> "Sentinel (Live at Pavarotti International)" 3:53
> Written by Mike Oldfield
> Appears on: Pavarotti & Friends

Because the track is so complex, Mike simply mimed the performance to the "Single Restructure." There's no new material here, no overdubs or additional instrumentation. The track starts and ends with the crowd applauding.

-September 28-
Mike Oldfield vs The ORB release the *Sentinel (Total Overhaul)* singles in the UK, Europe and North America.

UK & Europe CD single (YZ698CDX):
"Sentinel (Nobel Prize Mix)"
"Sentinel (Orbular Bells)"
"Sentinel (The ORB 7" Mix)"

UK 12 single (SAM 1094) promo:
"Sentinel (Nobel Prize Mix)"
"Sentinel (Orbular Bells)"
"Sentinel (The ORB 7" Mix)"

Europe CD single (YZ698CDX):
"Sentinel (Nobel Prize Mix)"
"Sentinel (Orbular Bells Mix)"
"Sentinel (The ORB 7" Mix)"

> "Sentinel (Nobel Prize Mix)" 14:28
> Written by Mike Oldfield; Remixed by The ORB
> Appears on: 12" Promo & CD singles
> Similar to the 7" Mix in production, but vastly extended and incorporating bits not just of "Sentinel," but of "Altered State" and "Blue Saloon" among others. However, those familiar bits are buried within the ORB's remixing and you'll only catch brief flashes of Mike throughout. It all still sounds trance-y and though 14 and a half minutes long, it's still not bad. It's not for everyone, though.
>
> "Sentinel (Orbular Bells Mix)" 12:28
> Written by Mike Oldfield; Remixed by The ORB
> Appears on: 12" Promo & CD singles; The Best Of: 1992 - 2003
> This mix is very organic and swishy throughout, with watery effects, then wind-like sounds, all interspersed with jungle-like samples. The "Blue Saloon" processor sound weaves in and out and there's no percussion or backbeat. The 7" Mix appears to be a shortened version of this mix, but all three ORB mixes use the same aesthetic, so it's hard to say. If you like the others, you might like this.

Note: some listings have this released on September 21st.

-October-
Mike Oldfield appears on the MTV show *Most Wanted (with Ray Cookes)*, promoting "Sentinel," in the US.

Warner Music releases **Mike Oldfield**'s live VHS *Tubular Bells II: The Performance Live At Edinburgh Castle*, from the September 4, 1992 concert.

-October 2-
Mike Oldfield appears on the Tele5 German TV show *Süsser Die Glocken Nie Klingen*, promoting *Tubular Bells II*.

-October 13-
Mike Oldfield appears on the French TV show *Top*, promoting "Sentinel."

-Date Unknown-
Reprise Records releases **Mike Oldfield**'s *The Bell / Sentinel (Restructure)* in the US.

US 12" single (0-40749):
"Sentinel (Trance Mix)"
"Sentinel (Tubular Beats)"
"The Bell (Edit)"
"Sentinel (Satoshi Tomii Interpretation)"
"Sentinel (Global Lust Mix)"

US CD single (9 40749-2):
"The Bell (Edit)"
"Sentinel (Trance Mix)"
"Sentinel (Satoshi Tomii Interpretation)"
"Sentinel (Global Lust Mix)"
"Sentinel (Nobel Prize Mix)" Mike Oldfield vs The ORB
"Sentinel (Tubular Beats)"

US 12" single (SAM1150) promo:
"Sentinel (Satoshi Tomii Interpretation)"
"Sentinel (Global Lust Mix)"
"Sentinel (Trance Mix)"
"Sentinel (Tubular Beats)"

"Sentinel (Trance Mix)" 5:43
Written by Mike Oldfield; Remixed by Tommy Musto
Appears on: The Bell / Sentinel (Restructure) 12" & CD single; The Bell 7", 12" & CD single
This mix features sample from Tubular Bells II underpinned by a percussion backing track. There's more recognizable Mike pieces here, but as with the other period remixes, it may not be everyone's taste.

"Sentinel (Tubular Beats)" 4:12
Written by Mike Oldfield; Remixed by Tommy Musto
Appears on: The Bell / Sentinel (Restructure) 12" & CD single
Similar to the trance mix, but eliminating the ambient vocal parts, this version is instead more reliant on its percussion backing track. There's still a fair amount of Mike's material in the mix, including the main "Sentinel" piano line.

"The Bell (Edit)" 4:08
Written by Mike Oldfield
Appears on: The Bell / Sentinel (Restructure) 12" & CD single
This edit of the album version (with MC 'Strolling Player' AKA Alan Rickman) removes a portion of the intro and the introductions to the Venetian Effect and the Digital Sound Processor. It fades out early.

"Sentinel (Satoshi Tomii Interpretation)" 7:42
Written by Mike Oldfield; Remixed by Satoshi Tomii
Appears on: The Bell / Sentinel (Restructure) 12" & CD single; The Bell 7", 12" & CD single
Why this isn't simply called "Altered State" instead of "Sentinel" is the most obvious question, because that's what it is. The "Altered State" samples are used liberally over an otherwise nondescript dance track.

"Sentinel (Global Lust Mix)" 5:56
Written by Mike Oldfield; Remixed by Mark Lewis
Appears on: The Bell / Sentinel (Restructure) 12" & CD single; The Bell 7", 12" & CD single
This is probably the most dated of the "Sentinel" remixes, sounding very much of its time, with Oldfield samples sprinkled throughout a '90s synth-rhythm production.

-November-
Mike Oldfield appears on the Australian TV series *The Steve Wizzard Show*, promoting *Tubular Bells II*.

Mike Oldfield appears on the Australian TV series *The Today Show*, promoting *Tubular Bells II*.

-December 7-
Mike Oldfield releases his "Tattoo" singles in the UK and Europe on WEA.

UK 7" single (YZ 708):
"Tattoo (Edit)"
"Silent Night"

UK cassette (YZ 708C):
"Tattoo (Edit)"
"Silent Night"

Europe CD single (YZ 708CD) (Part 1 of 2):
"Tattoo (Edit)"
"Silent Night"
"Sentinel (Live At Edinburgh Castle)"

UK 1-track CD single (PROMO CD YZ 708):
"Tattoo (Edit)"

"Tattoo (Edit)" 3:44
Written by Mike Oldfield
Appears on: 7", cassette & CD single; The Best Of: 1992 - 2003
This is an excellent version of the track. Not just an edit (and the track is very minorly edited for time, mostly near the beginning), but a different mix, with some extra guitar parts appearing subtly throughout. Not so subtly, the melody is changed in parts, going up the scale in places instead of dropping down.

"Silent Night" 4:21
Written by Franz Xaver Gruber (music) & Joseph Mohr (words) (arr. Mike Oldfield)
Appears on: Tattoo 7", cassette & CD single; The Best Of: 1992 - 2003
Mike's rendition of this classic carol is nothing short of stunning. The arrangement is layered, but not overpowering (less is more). And Oldfield of course uses his distinctive guitar wail to great effect. If you haven't heard this recording, seek it out. With all the bland, repetitious Christmas music played every year, putting this in your holiday rotation will leave many others in the dust (throw "In Dulci Jubilo" in there, too, just for good measure!)

-Mid-December-
Mike Oldfield releases his CD single *Tattoo: Live At The Edinburgh Castle EP* CD.

UK CD single (YZ 708 CDX) (Part 2 of 2):
"Tattoo (Live At Edinburgh Castle)"
"Maya Gold(Live At Edinburgh Castle)"
"Moonshine (Live At Edinburgh Castle)"
"Reprise (Live At Edinburgh Castle)"

-December 14-
Mike Oldfield appears on the UK TV series *This Morning* promoting *Tubular Bells II*.

Elements

1993

-February 17-
Mike Oldfield appears at the Carnival of Santa Cruz de Tenerife, Spain, promoting "Sentinel" and "Tattoo."

-March 1-
Mike Oldfield performs the US premier of *Tubular Bells II* at Carnegie Hall, New York City, New York, US.

-March 20-
Mike Oldfield appears on the *Private Eye Bofty Awards*, BBC TV show, promoting "The Bell."

-March 22-
Mike Oldfield performs at Olympiahalle, München, Germany, starting the 1st leg of the Tubular Bells II Tour.

-March 23-
Mike Oldfield performs at Schleyer - Halle, Stuttgart, Germany.

-March 25-
Mike Oldfield performs at the Alsterdorfer Sporthalle, Hamburg, Germany.

-March 26-
Mike Oldfield performs at Westfalenhalle, Dortmund, Germany.

-March 27-
Mike Oldfield performs at Forest National, Brussels, Belgium.

-March 31-
Mike Oldfield performs at Zenith, Paris, France.

-April 1-
Mike Oldfield performs at Statenhal, Den Haag, The Netherlands.

-April 2-
Mike Oldfield performs at Festhalle, Frankfurt, Germany.

-April 3-
Mike Oldfield performs at Hallenstadion, Zürich, Switzerland.

-April 5-
Mike Oldfield releases his singles for "The Bell" in the UK and Europe.

UK 7" single (YZ 737):
"The Bell (MC Vivian Stanshall)"
"Sentinel (Trance Mix)"

UK cassette (YZ 737C):
"The Bell (MC Vivian Stanshall)"
"Sentinel (Trance Mix)"

UK CD single (YZ 737CD) (Part 1 of 2):
"The Bell (MC Viv Stanshall)"
"Sentinel (Trance Mix)"
"Sentinel (Global Lust Mix)"
"Sentinel (Satoshi Tomii Interpretation)"

UK CD single (YZ 737CDX) (Part 2 of 2):
"The Bell (Live At Edinburgh Castle)"
"The Bell (MC Billy Connolly)"
"The Bell (MC Otto – German Version)"
"The Bell (MC Strolling Player)"
"The Bell (Instrumental Version)"

Europe CD single (4509-92262-2):
"The Bell (MC Viv Stanshall)"
"The Bell (MC Billy Connolly)"
"Sentinel (Trance Mix)"

Germany CD single (4509-92247-2):
"The Bell (MC Viv Stanshall)"
"The Bell (MC Otto – English Version)"
"The Bell (MC Otto – German Version)"

Spain CD single (1639) Limited Edition:
"The Bell (MC Carlos Finaly)"
Note: exclusive to the Spanish radio station Cadena 100.

"The Bell (MC Viv Stanshall)" 3:31
Written by Mike Oldfield
Appears on: UK 7" & CD single, European CD single, German CD single, Spanish CD single; The Best Of: 1992 - 2003
Having been the iconic MC on the original *Tubular Bells*, it was only natural for Mike to invite Viv back to record the introductions for the instruments in *Tubular Bells II*. Ultimately, Oldfield decided to use Alan Rickman on the album, but honoured Stanshall by using his vocal take on the music video for "The Bell." It's great to hear the man do the introductions "yet again..." There are no intros for the Venetian Effect and the Digital Sound Processor, and the track fades out early.

"The Bell (MC Billy Connolly)" 3:31
Written by Mike Oldfield
Appears on: CD single (Part 2 of 2); The Best Of: 1992 - 2003
Mike's new manager after leaving Virgin Records was Clive Banks, who was also Connolly's manager at the time, which probably contributed to Billy having a go at the MC duties. This backing track is identical to the edit which appears on the Viv Stanshall version.

"The Bell (MC Otto – English Version)" 3:30
Written by Mike Oldfield
Appears on: German CD single
Otto introduces the instruments in English, to the same backing track at the Stanshall and Connolly versions.

"The Bell (MC Otto – German Version)" 3:31
Written by Mike Oldfield
Appears on: CD single (Part 2 of 2), German CD single
Otto introduces the instruments in German, with the same backing track as above.

"The Bell (MC Carlos Finaly)" 3:30
Written by Mike Oldfield
Appears on: Spain CD single
Finaly introduces the instruments in Spanish, with the same backing track as above.

"The Bell (MC Strolling Player)" 5:01
Written by Mike Oldfield
Appears on: CD single (Part 2 of 2)
Alan Rickman's complete vocal appears here, unlike the earlier edit versions, including the Venetian Effect and the Digital Sound Processor. It has a longer intro, but fades out at the same time as the other MC versions.

"The Bell (Instrumental Version)" 3:30
Written by Mike Oldfield
Appears on: CD single (Part 2 of 2)

This is the backing track that appears on the Stanshall, Connolly, Otto and Finaly versions, only MC-free. All the different MCs give something different to the track, but it's also nice to hear the music by itself, so I highly recommend this version.

Mike Oldfield performs at the Royal Albert Hall, London, England.

-April 6, 7 & 8-
Mike Oldfield performs at the Royal Albert Hall, London, England. This ends the 1st leg of the Tubular Bells II Tour.

-June-
Mike Oldfield begins working on his new album, based on the novel *The Songs Of Distant Earth* by Arthur C. Clarke. The idea for doing this came from Rob Dickins at WEA. **Oldfield** writes and records from his new home in Los Angeles, California, US.

-Date Unknown-
Virgin Records re-issues the following **Mike Oldfield** albums in the UK and Europe.

UK & Europe 1993 *Platinum* CD (CDV 2141)
"Platinum (Part One): Airborne"
"Platinum (Part Two): Platinum"
"Platinum (Part Three): Charleston"
"Platinum (Part Four): North Star/Platinum Finale"
"Woodhenge"
"Into Wonderland (with "Sally" Outro)" - listed as "Sally."
"Punkadiddle (Original Version)"
"I Got Rhythm" - a version of the 1930 Gershwin song.

UK 1993 *Crises* CD (CDVIP 118)

-Summer-
Mike Oldfield visits Arthur C. Clarke at Clarke's home in Sri Lanka to discuss **Oldfield**'s recording of music based on *The Songs Of Distant Earth*.

-September 13-
Virgin Records releases the collection *The Best Of Mike Oldfield: Elements* in the UK, Europe and US. It is issued on CD, LP and cassette. The tracks have been remastered by Chris Blair, at Abbey Road Studios, London, England. Track listing as follows:

UK *The Best Of Mike Oldfield: Elements* CD (VTCD18)
Europe *The Best Of Mike Oldfield: Elements* CD (VTCD18)
US *The Best Of Mike Oldfield: Elements* CD (7243 8 39069 2 5)

"Tubular Bells (Opening Theme)"
"Family Man"
"Moonlight Shadow"
"Heaven's Open" Michael Oldfield
"Five Miles Out"
"To France (Single Version)"
"Foreign Affair"
"In Dulci Jubilo"
"Shadow On The Wall (12" Version)" Mike Oldfield And Roger Chapman
"Islands" Mike Oldfield Featuring Bonnie Tyler
"Étude (Single Edit)"
"Sentinel (Single Restructure)"

"Ommadawn (Part One) (Elements Excerpt)"
"Incantations (Part Four) ('Ode To Cynthia')"
"Amarok ('Africa I [Edit]')"
"Portsmouth"

"Tubular Bells (Opening Theme)" 4:16
Written by Mike Oldfield
Appears on: The Best Of Mike Oldfield: Elements; Spain 1-track CD Promo single; XXV: The Essential Mike Oldfield; The Platinum Collection; Mike Oldfield's Single (2013 Record Store Day Edition)
A good edit if you want just the first half of the "Introduction." It fades out right before the build up. This is could well be the best edit of the "Introduction" and is vastly superior to an of the "Now the Original..." versions.

"Ommadawn (Part One) (Elements Excerpt)" 3:40
Written by Mike Oldfield
Appears on: The Best Of Mike Oldfield: Elements; UK 1-track CD single; Collection; The Platinum Collection; Icon; Lo Mejor De... Mike Oldfield
This is the 1st movement of "Part One," fading out before the build up. Like the "Tubular Bells (Opening Theme)" on the same collection, it's a well-timed edit.

"Amarok ('Africa I [Edit]')" 4:45
Written by Mike Oldfield
Appears on: The Best Of Mike Oldfield: Elements
It would have been nice to just include the complete "Africa I" segments that later appeared on the boxed set (it's not like there wasn't room), but all in all, this isn't bad and is a good introduction to the album for new Mike Oldfield fans.

-September 14-
Mike Oldfield performs at Palais des Sports, Toulous, France. This starts the 2nd leg of the Tubular Bells II Tour.

-September 15-
Mike Oldfield performs at Plaza de Toros Monumental, Barcelona, Spain.

-September 17-
Mike Oldfield performs at Plaza de Toros de las Ventas, Madrid, Spain.

-September 18-
Mike Oldfield performs at Plaza de Toros de Oviedo, Oviedo, Spain.

-September 19-
Mike Oldfield performs at the Auditorio de Castrelos, Vigo, Spain.

-September 22-
Mike Oldfield performs at Dramático de Cascais, Lisbon, Portugal.

-September 23-
Mike Oldfield performs at Coliscu, Oporto, Portugal

-September 24-
Mike Oldfield performs at Plaza de Toros El Plantó, Burgos, Spain.

-September 25-
Mike Oldfield performs at Plaza de Toros Vista Alegre, Bilbao, Spain.

-October-
Virgin Records releases the VHS collection *Elements: The Best Of Mike Oldfield* in the UK, Europe and North America. It features some of **Mike Oldfield**'s videos and other material:
"Tubular Bells (excerpt from The 2nd House performance)"
"In Dulci Jubilo"
"Incantations (Part Four – 'Ode To Cynthia')" - excerpt from *The Space Movie*.
"Étude"
"Five Miles Out"
"Moonlight Shadow"
"Islands"
"Shadow On The Wall"
"Sentinel"
"Tattoo (Live At Edinburgh Castle)"
Exclusive interview footage

-October 10-
Mike Oldfield performs at John Ansem Ford Theatre, Los Angeles, California, US, ending the 2nd leg of the Tubular Bells II Tour.

-Late 1993-
Mike Oldfield continues work on his new album, *The Songs Of Distant Earth*, at his home studio in Los Angeles, California, US.

-November 10-
Mike Oldfield releases his 4xCD boxed set *Elements* in the UK, Europe and North America. The tracks have been remastered by Chris Blair, at Abbey Road Studios, London, England. It features a mix of released, unreleased and rare material. Track listing as follows:

UK *Elements* 4xCD boxed set (CDBOX 2)
Europe *Elements* 4xCD boxed set (CDBOXY 2)

CD 1:
"Tubular Bells (Part One)"
"Tubular Bells (Part Two)"
"Hergest Ridge (Part One – Boxed Remix) (Elements Excerpt)"
"In Dulci Jubilo"
"Portsmouth"
"Vivaldi Concerto In C"

CD 2:
"Ommadawn (Part One)"
"On Horseback (Single Version)"
"William Tell Overture"
"Argiers"
"First Excursion"
"The Sailor's Hornpipe (Single Version)"
"Incantations (Part Two) ('Hymn To Diana [Reprise]' + 'The Song Of Hiawatha')"
"Guilty"
"The Path"
"Blue Peter" - a cover of the 1958 TV show theme.
"Woodhenge (Single Version)"
"Live Punkadiddle" The Mike Oldfield Group
"Polka (Live in Vienna, 1980)"

CD 3:
"Platform
 (Part Three): Charleston
 (Part Four): North Star/Platinum Finale"
"Arrival" – a cover of the 1976 ABBA instrumental.
"Taurus 1"
"QE2"
"Wonderful Land (Single Version)" – a cover of The Shadows' 1962 instrumental.
"Sheba"
"Five Miles Out"
"Taurus II (Elements Excerpt)"
"Family Man"
"Mount Teide"
"Waldberg (The Peak)" The Mike Oldfield Group
"Crises (Elements Excerpt)"
"Moonlight Shadow"
"Foreign Affair"

CD 4:
"Shadow On The Wall (12" Version)" Mike Oldfield And Roger Chapman
"Taurus 3"
"Crime Of Passion"
"Jungle Gardenia"
"To France (Single Version)"
"Afghan"
"Tricks Of The Light (Instrumental)"
"Étude (Single Edit)"
"Evacuation"
"Legend"
"Islands" Mike Oldfield Featuring Bonnie Tyler
"The Wind Chimes (Part One)"
"Flying Start" Mike Oldfield (with Kevin Ayers)
"Magic Touch"
"Earth Moving"
"Far Country"
"One Glance Is Holy (Remix)" – Incorrectly listed as the "Hard And Holy Mix"
"Amarok ('Africa I')"
"Heaven's Open" Michael Oldfield

Note: It's been reported that the collection went through various stages before the final version was released, with the original plan being to include more rare material (such as "Froggy Went A'Courting"). It is also worth noting that there are no tracks featuring Anita Hegerland and "The Sailor's Hornpipe" appears twice, once as part of "Tubular Bells (Part Two)" and again with the "Single Version."

 "Hergest Ridge (Part One – Boxed Remix) (Elements Excerpt)" 9:32
 Written by Mike Oldfield
 Appears on: Elements boxed set
 This is the entire 1st movement and the first minute of the 2nd movement of the Boxed Remix of Part One.

 "Incantations (Part Two) ('Hymn To Diana [Reprise]' + 'The Song Of Hiawatha')" 12:19
 Written by Mike Oldfield ("The Song Of Hiawatha" words by Longfellow (arr. Oldfield)
 Appears on: Elements boxed set
 This is the 2" and 3rd movements of Part Two, the "Hymn To Diana (Reprise)"" and "The Song Of Hiawatha."

"Platinum (Part Three): Charleston"
"Platinum (Part Four): North Star/Platinum Finale" 8:02
Written by Mike Oldfield ("North Star" by Glass, arr. Oldfield)
Appears on: Elements boxed set
This is Parts Three and Four of *Platinum* combined as one track. It starts with "Charleston," though you can hear that last part of "Part Two: Platinum" from the segue under the beginning of the track.

"Taurus II (Elements Excerpt)" 7:59
Written by Mike Oldfield
Appears on: Elements boxed set
This is the 1st movement of the piece, fading out just before the crescendo that leads into the 2nd movement.

"Crises (Elements Excerpt)" 5:25
Written by Mike Oldfield
Appears on: Elements boxed set
This is an edit of the 1st movement, fading out before the vocals come in.

"Amarok ('Africa I')" 6:17
Written by Mike Oldfield
Appears on: Elements boxed set, The Platinum Collection
It's been said on numerous occasions that Virgin Records found it difficult to use excerpts of *Amarok* to promote the album, and it's true that Mike designed the album partly for that reason (to give Virgin a headache). Various excerpts were issued previously, but the "Africa I" segments, played as a single piece, come the closest to a standalone representation of the album. Perhaps Virgin would have been wise to use this part for a single, with something close to the edit that appears on the *Elements* Best Of... collection for a shorter version (for a 7" single) and this for the longer singles (like a 12" or CD single).

Around this time, Virgin Records issues CD singles to support the boxed set in the UK and Europe.

UK CD single (VSCDT1477):
"Moonlight Shadow"
"Moonlight Shadow (Extended Version)"
"In The Pool"
"Bones"

Europe CD single (VSCDT1477):
"Moonlight Shadow"
"Moonlight Shadow (Extended Version)"
"In The Pool"
"Bones"

France CD single (FROLD 1) promo:
"Tubular Bells (Opening Theme)"
"Moonlight Shadow"

Europe 1-track CD single (SPOLD1) promo:
"Tubular Bells (Opening Theme)"

Europe 1-track CD single (SPOLD2) promo:
"Moonlight Shadow"

UK & Europe 1-track CD single (SPOLD3) promo:
"Ommadawn (Part One) (Elements Excerpt)"

Europe 1-track CD single (SPOLD4) promo:
"Family Man"

Europe 1-track CD single (SPOLD5) promo:
"To France (Single Version)"

Europe 1-track CD single (SPOLD6) promo:
"Islands"

-November 19-
Virgin Records releases *The Mike Oldfield Christmas EP* in the UK in support of the *Elements* releases.

UK & Europe CD single (VSCDT1486):
"In Dulci Jubilo"
"Wonderful Land (Single Version)" - a cover of The Shadows' 1962 instrumental.
"Portsmouth"
"Vivaldi Concert In C"

UK cassette single (VSC 1486):
"In Dulci Jubilo"
"Wonderful Land (Single Version)" - a cover of The Shadows' 1962 instrumental.
"Portsmouth"
"Vivaldi Concert In C"

The Songs Of Distant Earth

1994

-February 8-
Virgin Music Canada releases the **Mike Oldfield** compilation *The Best Of Mike Oldfield: Elements* on CD (V2 39069).

-Early 1994-
Mike Oldfield continues to work on his new album, *The Songs Of Distant Earth*, at Roughwood Croft, Chalfont St. Giles, Buckinghamshire, England. **Mike** begins working on the CD-ROM interactive portion simultaneously to recording the album. **Mike** says in a 1995 interview that the CD-ROM content took five months to produce.

-Date Unknown-
Virgin Records releases promo CD singles of **Mike Oldfield** tracks to promote the *Elements* boxed set and compilation.

Europe 1-track CD single (SPOLD7) promo:
"Five Miles Out"

Europe 1-track CD single (SPOLD 8) promo:
"Foreign Affair"

Europe 1-track CD single (SPOLD 9) promo:
"Heaven's Open"

-Date Unknown-
Love Records re-issues the Pekka Pohjola album *Keesojen Lehto* (AKA *Mathematician's Air Display*) on CD in Finland (MAR 95110 / LRCD 219). CD mastered by Otto Donner.

-June-
Mike Oldfield completes work on his album *The Songs Of Distant Earth* at Roughwood Croft, Chalfont St. Giles, Buckinghamshire, England. **Mike** says in 1995 that the album was a bit rushed while finishing it. Tom Newman is one of the engineers on the album. Tracks worked on since June of 1993 include:
"In The Beginning" – this track excerpts astronaut Bill Anders reading the Bible (Genesis 1:1-4), from the December 24, 1968, which was broadcast from the moon's orbit by Apollo 8.
"Let There Be Light" – this samples the phrase from the Apollo 8 broadcast.
"Supernova" – the explosion heard in this track is one of the stock explosions heard on *Star Trek: The Original Series*, lifted straight from an episode (heard when **Mike** spent a weekend watching the show while working on the album).
"Magellan" – the drum track heard here is sampled from Led Zeppelin's "When The Levee Breaks."
"Only Time Will Tell" – the sampled voice comes from the narration of an episode of *Lost In Space*. It might also have appeared on a Zero-G sample collection **Mike** used, rather than him taking it straight from an episode.
"Prayer For The Earth" – this piece is almost entirely comprised of the opening titles music and vocals (by Nils-Aslak Valkeapaa) from the Norwegian film *Ofelas* (English title: *Pathfinder*). The only change **Oldfield** made was to add guitar and some percussion over the existing recording.
"The Chamber" – **Oldfield** notes in a 1995 interview that Molly Oldfield has the distinction of triggering on keyboard the Russian cosmonaut sample heard in this piece. She was also **Mike**'s "sounding board" for the album.
"Tubular World" – the phrase "Enter..." comes from an edit (of "Enterprise") made of a vocal sample from the Zero-G sample collection.

"Crystal Clear" – **Oldfield** samples Michael Joseph's self-hypnosis cassette for the countdown. This track is sometimes referred to as "Hypnotist," which may have been a working title.
"A New Beginning" – this track is an excerpt from the French Polynesian Tubuai Choir's 2005 recording of "Vahine Taihara."
"The Spectral Army" – this track would become a non-album B-side.
"The Song Of The Boat Men" - this track would become a non-album B-side.
"Indian Lake" - this track would become a non-album B-side.
"Tomorrow's World" – it's been reported that this BBC TV science series asked **Mike** for theme music and he re-worked a melody used on the album. His piece was not used.

Arthur C. Clarke also writes the liner notes for the album.

-November 21-
Mike Oldfield releases his album *The Songs Of Distant Earth* in the UK, Europe, Canada and Australia on WEA. Two editions are issued, one a standard CD (in the UK, Europe, Canada and Australia), the other containing an interactive CD-ROM track (Europe). Track listing as follows:

UK *The Songs Of Distant Earth* CD (SAM 1477)
Europe *The Songs Of Distant Earth* CD (4509 98581-2)
Europe *The Songs Of Distant Earth* CD (4509 98582-2) Enhanced
Canada *The Songs Of Distant Earth* CD (CD 98581)
Australia *The Songs Of Distant Earth* CD (4509 98581-2)

Enhanced Edition-only: CD-ROM
"In The Beginning"
"Let There Be Light"
"Supernova"
"Magellan"
"First Landing"
"Oceania"
"Only Time Will Tell"
"Prayer For The Earth"
"Lament For Atlantis"
"The Chamber"
"Hibernaculum"
"Tubular World"
"The Shining Ones"
"Crystal Clear"
"The Sunken Forest"
"Ascension"
"A New Beginning"

Note: the CD-ROM is only playable on Macintosh computers. It features interactive environments based on the music and the original Clarke novel.

WEA releases the following in Europe to promote the album.

The Netherlands *Highlights From The Album The Songs Of Distant Earth* promo cassette (WARNER 2)
"Highlights From The Album The Songs Of Distant Earth"

> "Highlights From The Album The Songs Of Distant Earth" 13:00
> Written by Mike Oldfield
> Appears on: Highlights From The Album The Songs Of Distant Earth
> A 13-minute medley of the tracks from the album. The track appears on both sides on the cassette.

Sweden *The Songs Of Distant Earth* CD (WMSPROM68) Promo sampler
"The Chamber"
"Hibernaculum"
"The Sunken Forest"
"Ascension"
"A New Beginning"

-December 5-
Mike Oldfield releases his "Hibernaculum" singles in the UK and Europe on WEA.

UK CD single (YZ 871CDX) (Part 1 of 2):
"Hibernaculum (Single Version)"
"Moonshine (Festive Mix)"
"Moonshine (Solution Hoedown Mix)"
"Moonshine (Jungle Mix)"

UK CD single (YZ8771CD) (Part 2 of 2):
"Hibernaculum (Single Version)"
"The Spectral Army"
"The Song Of The Boat"

UK CD single (YZ871CDDJ) promo:
"Hibernaculum (Single Version)"

A Shot Of Moonshine DJ Promo
UK 12" single (SAM 1470) promo:
"Moonshine (Solution Hoedown Mix)"
"Moonshine (Jungle Mix)"
"A Shot Of Moonshine (Jungle Instrumental)"

Europe CD single (YZ 871CDX) (Part 1 of 2):
"Hibernaculum (Single Version)"
"Moonshine (Festive Mix)"
"Moonshine (Solution Hoedown Mix)"
"Moonshine (Jungle Mix)"

Europe single (YZ871CD) (Part 2 of 2):
"Hibernaculum (Single Version)"
"The Spectral Army"
"The Song Of The Boat"

Note: the DJ Promo 12" single lists all the song titles as "A Shot Of Moonshine" and no mention is made on the sleeve or label of Mike Oldfield. It does appear to be an official WEA release.

> "Hibernaculum (Single Version)" 3:38
> Written by Mike Oldfield
> Appears on: CD single (Part 1), CD Single (Part 2); The Platinum Collection; The Best Of: 1992 - 2003
> A good standalone version, the Single Version fades in slightly earlier than the album version and fades out on the last vocal before the "Enter" that starts "Tubular World."

"The Spectral Army" 2:43
Written by Mike Oldfield
Appears on: Hibernaculum CD single (Part 1); The Best Of: 1992 - 2003
Another grand Oldfield folk instrumental, this bagpipe march starts slow before breaking into a gallop halfway through, building to a powerful, satisfying ending. Highly recommended.

"The Song Of The Boat Men" 2:53
Written by Mike Oldfield
Appears on: Hibernaculum CD single (Part 1); The Best Of: 1992 - 2003
A gentle, serene instrumental, evoking a quiet evening by the water. If it sounds familiar, that's because Mike would rewrite this piece 20 years later, adding lyrics and rechristening it "Moonshine" for his *Man On The Rocks* album (not to be confused with the track "Moonshine" on *Tubular Bells II*).

"Moonshine (Festive Mix)" 3:42
Written by Mike Oldfield; Remixed by The Solution For Small World Productions
Appears on: Hibernaculum CD single (Part 2)
Oh, hell yeah! This is one of the best remixes of an Oldfield track ever done! If it doesn't move you to get up and dance a hoedown, you may well have no soul. It loops the main riffs and lets the original banjo and fiddle parts shine, while offering a few new breakdowns throughout, never losing its energy or fun. Seek this out! Also, there appears to be an indexing glitch at the end, so the first second of the "Solution Hoedown Mix" appears at the end of the track, after this mix ends.

"Moonshine (Solution Hoedown Mix)" 5:29
Written by Mike Oldfield; Remixed by The Solution For Small World Productions
Appears on: Hibernaculum CD single (Part 2), A Shot Of Moonshine UK 12" Promo single
Because of the aforementioned indexing glitch, the first second of the mix is cut off. This mix is basically an extended version of the Festive Mix, repeating sections throughout, though there is a new breakdown added in the middle. If the Festive Mix wasn't long enough for you, hunt this down. It has a similar indexing glitch, with the track ending with the start of the "Jungle Mix).

"Moonshine (Jungle Mix)" 4:17
Written by Mike Oldfield; Remixed by The Solution For Small World Productions
Appears on: Hibernaculum CD single (Part 2), A Shot Of Moonshine UK 12" Promo single
If you're familiar with the Oldschool Jungle genre, this track probably won't surprise you. If you're not familiar with it, well, you're in for something different. The main riff of "Moonshine" is sampled and incorporated into a bass and drum heavy backing track. Fans of the genre will recognize the famous "Amen Break" samples (or a very close approximation) as the foundation of the backing track. Featuring Peter Lee and Rankin' Sean on vocals.

"A Shot Of Moonshine (Jungle Instrumental)" 4:17
Written by Mike Oldfield
Appears on: A Shot Of Moonshine UK 12" Promo single
The lesser-known A Shot Of Moonshine 12" Promo features this unique mix, the instrumental version of the Jungle Mix.

Variations On A Rhythm

1995

-Date Unknown-
Mike Oldfield begins work on a computer project combining music with virtual reality environments, at Roughwood Croft, Chalfont St. Giles, Buckinghamshire, England. He works with designers from the London-based company Balanda on texture mapping, which itself takes "four to five months," as **Oldfield** notes in an interview later this year with the German magazine *Multimedia Screen*.

-Date Unknown-
Warner Music UK Ltd. releases the Enhanced Edition of **Mike Oldfield**'s album *The Songs Of Distant Earth* on CD (4509-9 8524-2) in the UK. This edition features alternate cover artwork.

-Date Unknown-
Reprise Records releases the Enhanced Edition of **Mike Oldfield**'s album *The Songs Of Distant Earth* on CD (9 45933-2) in the US, also as a promo CD (9 45933-2). This edition features alternate cover artwork.

-March 5-
Vivian Stanshall dies in his sleep, the result of an electrical fire at his flat, Muswell Hill, London. Stanshall was the MC on *Tubular Bells* (and recorded the unused original monologue for "The Sailor's Hornpipe") and on one of the single versions of "The Bell" from *Tubular Bells II*.

-June 1-
Mike Oldfield does an interview with Gareth Randall, discussing among other things his current Music Virtual Reality computer project.

-Date Unknown-
Griffin Music re-issues **Mike Oldfield**'s album *Islands* on CD (GCD-352-2) in the US. Track listing as follows:

"The Wind Chimes (Part One and Part Two)"
"Islands" Mike Oldfield Featuring Bonnie Tyler
"Flying Start" Mike Oldfield (with Kevin Ayers)
"North Point" Mike Oldfield Featuring Anita Hegerland
"Magic Touch"
"The Time Has Comes" Mike Oldfield Featuring Anita Hegerland
"When The Night's On Fire" Mike Oldfield Featuring Anita Hegerland

-Date Unknown-
Virgin Records re-issues the **Mike Oldfield** compilation *The Complete Mike Oldfield* in Europe on CD (CDMOC 1). This features a different photo of the swallow on the cover.

CD 1:
The Instrumental Section
"Arrival" – a cover of the 1976 ABBA instrumental.
"William Tell Overture"
"Cuckoo Song" Mike Oldfield with Les Penning
"In Dulci Jubilo"
"Portsmouth"
"Jungle Gardenia"
"Guilty"
"Blue Peter" – a cover of the 1958 TV show theme.
"Waldberg (The Peak)" The Mike Oldfield Group

"Wonderful Land" – a cover of The Shadows' 1962 instrumental.
"Étude (Single Edit)"

The Vocal Section
"Moonlight Shadow"
"Family Man"
"Mistake" The Mike Oldfield Group
"Five Miles Out (Early Mix)"
"Crime Of Passion"
"To France (The Complete... Edit)"
"Shadow On The Wall (12" Version)" Mike Oldfield And Roger Chapman

CD 2:
The Complex Section
"Excerpt from Ommadawn (Part One)"
"Excerpt from Tubular Bells (Part One) (The Complete...Edit)"
"Excerpt from Hergest Ridge
            (Part One - Boxed Remix) (The Complete... Edit)"
"Incantations (Part Four) ('Ode To Cynthia')"
"Evacuation (Single Edit)"

The Live Side / The Live Section
"Sheba (Live At Essen, 1981)"
"Mirage" (Live At Essen, 1981)"
"Platinum (Live At Essen, 1981)"
"Mount Teidi (Live in Cologne 1982)" The Mike Oldfield Group

-August 21-
Mike Oldfield releases his "Let There Be Light" singles in the UK, Europe and North America on WEA and Reprise Records.

UK 12" single (0630-11701-0):
"Let There Be Light (BT's Pure Luminescence Remix)"
"Let There Be Light (Hardfloor Remix)"
"Let There Be Light (Hardfloor Dub)"

UK CD single (YZ880CD) (Part 1 of 2):
"Let There Be Light (Single Version)"
"Let There Be Light (BT's Pure Luminescence Remix)"
"Let There Be Light (The Ultraviolet Mix)"
"Let There Be Light (Hardfloor Remix)"

UK CD single (YZ880CDX) (Part 2 of 2):
"Let There Be Light (Single Version)"
"Indian Lake"
"Let There Be Light (BT's Entropic Dub)"

UK CD single (SAM 1639) promo:
"Let There Be Light (Single Version)"

UK 2x12" single (SAM 1650) promo:
12" single 1:
"Let There Be Light (BT's Pure Luminescence Remix)"
"Let There Be Light (The Ultraviolet Mix)"

12" single 2:
"Let There Be Light (Hardfloor Remix)"
"Let There Be Light (Hardfloor Dub)"
"Let There Be Light (BT's Entropic Dub)"

US 12" single (0-43561):
"Let There Be Light (BT's Pure Luminescence Remix)"
"Let There Be Light (BT's Entropic Dub)"

US 2x12" single (PRO-A-7992) promo:
12" single 1:
"Let There Be Light (BT's Pure Luminescence Remix)"
"Let There Be Light (The Ultraviolet Mix Edit)"

12" single 2:
"Let There Be Light (Hardfloor Remix)"
"Let There Be Light (Hardfloor Dub)"
"Let There Be Light (BT's Entropic Dub)"

US CD single (9435612):
"Let There Be Light (Single Version)"
"Let There Be Light (BT's Pure Luminescence Remix)"
"Let There Be Light (The Ultraviolet Mix Edit)"
"Let There Be Light (Hardfloor Remix)"
"Let There Be Light (Hardfloor Dub)"
"Let There Be Light (BT's Entropic Dub)"

Europe CD single (0630-11732-2):
"Let There Be Light (Single Version)"
"Let There Be Light (Hardfloor Remix)"
"Let There Be Light (Hardfloor Dub)"
"Let There Be Light (BT's Pure Luminescence Remix)"

Spain CD single (2004):
"Let There Be Light (Single Version)"

"Let There Be Light (Single Version)" 4:21
Written by Mike Oldfield
Appears on: UK CD single (Parts 1 & 2), US CD single, European CD Single, Promo CD single, XXV: The Essential Mike Oldfield; The Best Of: 1992 - 2003
This version shaves off about 30 seconds throughout, but loses none of its beauty, making for an excellent standalone version.

"Indian Lake" 3:41
Written by Mike Oldfield
Appears on: UK CD single (Part 2 of 2); The Best Of: 1992 - 2003
This non-album instrumental features a 3/4 time percussion backing track over which the melody is played with synth and guitar, finishing with some classic Mike guitar wailing.

"Let There Be Light (BT's Pure Luminescence Remix)" 13:24
Written by Mike Oldfield
Appears on: UK 12" single, UK 12" Promo 2 disc single, UK CD single (1 of 2), US 12" single, US 12" Promo 2 disc single, US CD single, European CD single; The Best Of: 1992 - 2003
Heavy on the additional production and light on Mike samples, featuring only the "Burning...Melting...Dissolving" and "Let there be light" vocals and some bits of guitar, this mix

only really gets interesting when the track goes into a breakdown and the backbeat eases off, but it's a dance remix, so what do you expect?

"Let There Be Light (Hardfloor Remix)" 11:21
Written by Mike Oldfield
Appears on: UK 12" single, UK 12" Promo 2 disc single, UK CD single (1 of 2), US 12" Promo 2 disc single, US CD single, European CD single
This mix starts off promisingly, with some synth and "Let there be light" samples, then goes into full-on dance remix mode. It then shifts gears and slows down, now featuring more Mike music, around the 5:10 mark. At the 8:10 mark, it changes again, picking up the pace once more and we're back into dance club territory, abandoning all the Mike parts, except the "Let there be light" sample.

"Let There Be Light (Hardcore Dub)" 9:35
Written by Mike Oldfield
Appears on: UK 12" single, UK 12" Promo 2 disc single, US 12" Promo 2 disc single, US CD single, European CD single
Dub mixes are achieved by removing the vocals, leaving the mix entirely or mostly instrumental. In some cases, such as here, it's removing the samples of the original artist, leaving only the additional production. It allows other DJ and producers to take what is essentially the backing track and do their own thing with it. All well and good, but what we're left with here is a Mike Oldfield remix with no Mike Oldfield in it. There aren't even any Bill Anders "Let there be light" samples. So, yeah, this is a "Let There Be Light" remix in name only, a dub of the "Hardfloor Remix."

"Let There Be Light (Ultraviolet Mix)" 15:07
Written by Mike Oldfield
Appears on: UK 12" Promo 2 disc single, UK CD single (1 of 2), US 12" Promo 2 disc single, US CD single, European CD single
This mix tries to do something a bit different. Still long on dance electronica, it offsets this somewhat by lacing the woodwind samples (which don't appear to be from the original) throughout, giving it a sort of Eastern feel. The only recognizable Oldfield samples are the riff and the vocal "Burning…Dissolving…"

"Let There Be Light (Ultraviolet Mix Edit)" 10:44
Written by Mike Oldfield
Appears on: UK CD single (1 of 2), US 12" Promo 2 disc single, US CD single
This is a shortened version of the "Ultraviolet Mix," fading out early.

"Let There Be Light (BT's Pure Entropic Dub)" 14:39
Written by Mike Oldfield
Appears on: UK 12" Promo 2 disc single, US 12" single, US 12" Promo 2 disc single, US CD single
A different BT remix, this time going for a computer-y sound.

-Date Unknown-
Voiceprint releases the David Bedford composition *Variations On A Rhythm Of Mike Oldfield* in the UK on CD (VP191CD). Track listing as follows:

"Variations On A Rhythm Of Mike Oldfield" David Bedford
"Superman (Demo)" Tom Newman
"Day Of The Percherons (Demo)" Tom Newman
"Have Mercy On My Eyes" Tom Newman

Note: The piece was recorded in 1973 by Bedford and itself does not feature **Oldfield** playing or his involvement at all. Listed here because the additional tracks do feature **Mike** (though are unrelated to the

"Variations..." piece, as they are Tom Newman demos and an outtake from the *Fine Old Tom* sessions) and because it sometimes gets lumped in with **Mike**'s work, even though he really has nothing to do with it. It's a good place to find the "Day Of The Percherons" demo, which doesn't appear on the *Fine Old Tom* re-issue of this year.

-Date Unknown-
Voiceprint Records re-issues Tom Newman's album *Fine Old Tom* on CD in the UK and Europe. In addition to **Mike Oldfield** appearing on the standard tracks "Sad Sing," Suzie," and "Ma Song," this re-issue features outtakes and demos from the album sessions, three of which also feature **Mike**.
"Superman (Demo)"
"Sweet 16"
"Have Mercy On My Eyes"

-Date Unknown-
Voiceprint Records issues Tom Newman's previously unreleased 1976 album *Live At The Argonaut* in the UK and Europe on CD (VP 168 CD). It features **Mike Oldfield** on the track "Just For Old Times."

-Date Unknown-
Mike Oldfield begins work on his new album, at Roughwood Croft, Chalfont St. Giles, Buckinghamshire, England (*Voyager* sessions).

-Date Unknown-
Disky re-issues **Mike Oldfield**'s album *Crises* in Europe on CD (VI 863002).

Voyager

1996

-January 30-
WEA & Reprise Records re-issues *The Songs Of Distant Earth* with a new cover and updated CD-ROM content.

-Winter-
While working on the Music Virtual Reality project and his new album, **Mike Oldfield** purchases a plot of land at Es Cubells, on the island of Ibiza, Spain. He begins having a new house built.

-March-
Mike Oldfield completes work on his new studio album, *Voyager*, at Roughwood Croft, Chalfont St. Giles, Buckinghamshire, England. Tom Newman is one of the assistant engineers. A working title for the album was *Celtic Cross*. Tracks worked on during the album sessions include:
"The Song Of The Sun" – a cover of the 1988 song "O son do ar" by Luar Na Lubre, written by Bieito Romero.
"The Hero" – a version of the 1903 song "Hector The Hero" by James Scott Skinner.
"She Moves Through The Fair" – a traditional Irish piece.
"Women Of Ireland" – the original song was based on an 18th Century Irish poem by Peadar Ó Doirnín, set to music by Seán Ó Riada in 1969. **Oldfield** adapts an arrangement used in the film *Barry Lyndon*, using a segment of Handel's "Keyboard suite in D minor."
"Dark Island" – a 1958 Scottish piece written by Iain Maclachlan, with lyrics later added by David Silver.
"Flowers Of The Forest" – a traditional Scottish folk tune.
"Mont St. Michel" – the London Symphony Orchestra records at Air Studios, London, England.
"Mike's Reel" – this track would appear as a non-album B-side.

-Date Unknown-
MSI (Music Scene Incorporated) re-releases **The Sallyangie** album *Children Of The Sun* in Japan (MSI 16089). Track listing as follows:

"Strangers"
"Lady Mary"
"Children Of The Sun"
"A Lover For All Seasons"
"River Song"
"Banquet On The Water"
"Balloons"
"Midsummer Night's Happening"
"Love In Ice Crystals"
"Changing Colours"
"Chameleon"
"Milk Bottle"
"Murder Of The Children Of San Francisco"
"Strangers (Reprise)"
Bonus Tracks
"Children Of The Sun (Minus Intro)"
"Two Ships" – a cover of the 1968 Maria Dallas song.
"Colour Of The World"

"Children Of The Sun (Minus Intro)" 4:11
Written by Sally Oldfield
Appears on: Children Of The Sun (2002, 2003, 2011 & 2017 Reissues)
This edit omits the spoken word intro by Sally and some of Mike's guitar. It works.

-Summer-
Mike Oldfield moves to Es Cubells, Ibiza, Spain. While his new house there is under construction, he lives in a hotel.

According to articles, it is this year, in Ibiza, that **Mike** first meets Fanny Vandekerckhove. However, by the time of *Tubular Bells III*, he is dating Miriam Felber.

-August 21-
WEA Records releases **Mike Oldfield**'s "The Voyager" Promo CD single in Germany.

Promo CD single (PRO 6201) promo:
"The Voyager (Radio Edit)"
"The Voyager (Single Edit)"
"The Voyager"

"The Voyager (Radio Edit)" 2:59
Written by Mike Oldfield
Appears on: German Promo CD single
Not much to say about this edit, some material was removed and it fades out early, losing the last 1:25.

"The Voyager (Single Edit)" 3:59
Written by Mike Oldfield
Appears on: German Promo CD single
Like the "Radio Edit," this version removes some material in addition to fading out early, though it only loses the last 25 seconds.

-August 26-
Mike Oldfield releases his album *Voyager* in the UK, Europe and North America on WEA and Reprise Records. Track listing as follows:

UK & Europe *Voyager* CD (0630-15896-2)
Europe *Voyager* Promo CD (PROP180)
US *Voyager* CD (9 46487-2)
US *Voyager* Promo CD (9 46487-AB)
Canada *Voyager* CD (CD 15896)

"The Song Of The Sun" - a cover of the 1988 song "O son do ar" by Luar Na Lubre.
"Celtic Rain"
"The Hero" - a version of the 1903 song "Hector The Hero" by James Scott Skinner.
"Women Of Ireland" - a cover of the 1969 music by Seán Ó Riada.
"The Voyager"
"She Moves Through The Fair"
"Dark Island" - a cover of the 1958 piece written by Iain Maclachlan.
"Wild Goose Flaps Its Wings"
"Flowers Of The Forest"
"Mont St. Michel"

-Date Unknown-
Warmer Music Spain releases a promo CD of **Mike Oldfield**'s "Mont St. Michel" in Spain.

Spain 1-track CD single (PRCD 363):
"Mont St. Michel (Promo Edit)"

> "Mont St. Michel (Promo Edit)" 3:35
> Written by Mike Oldfield
> Appears on: Spain Promo CD single
> This edit (cut from 12:18 down to 3:35) just goes to show that it's extremely hard to pare down Mike's longer pieces (made up of different, distinct movements) and not have the edit sound disjointed. More often than not, it's better to simply take a section of music and let it play out as recorded, rather than trying to cram everything into a short runtime. This version starts off alright, with some subtle edits, then around the 1:16 mark it jumps to a faster section and it's all down hill from there as the edits don't give the music a chance to breathe at all.

-Date Unknown-
WEA releases a promo CD of **Mike Oldfield**'s cover of "The Song Of The Sun" in Spain.

Spain 1-track CD single (PRCD 486):
"The Song Of The Sun" - a cover of the 1988 song "O son do ar" by Luar Na Lubre.

-Dates Unknown-
Virgin Records re-issues **Mike Oldfield**'s album *Ommadawn* in the UK on CD (CDVIP 185).

Disky re-issues the following **Mike Oldfield** albums on CD in the UK and Europe:

Ommadawn CD (VI 873762)
"Ommadawn (Part One)"
"Ommadawn (Part Two - Edit)"
"On Horseback (Single Version)" - unlisted on the sleeve.

Heaven's Open CD (VI 874894)

-Date Unknown-
Mike Oldfield moves into his new home in Es Cubells, Ibiza, Spain, building a studio as well, but must wait until after Sally Oldfield finishes recording her new album (*Secret Songs*) at Roughwood Croft, Chalfont St. Giles, Buckinghamshire, England, before the gear can be transported.

-October 12-
WEA Records releases **Mike Oldfield**'s "Women Of Ireland" singles in Germany.

Germany 12" single (0630-16819-0):
"Women Of Ireland (12" Lurker Mix)" - a cover of the 1969 music by Seán Ó Riada.
"Women Of Ireland (Transient Mix)" - a cover of the 1969 music by Seán Ó Riada.

Germany CD single (0630-16820-2):
"Women Of Ireland (Lurker Edit)" - a cover of the 1969 music by Seán Ó Riada.
"Women Of Ireland (12" Lurker Mix)" - a cover of the 1969 music by Seán Ó Riada.
"Women Of Ireland (Transient Mix)" - a cover of the 1969 music by Seán Ó Riada.

Germany CD single (PRCD 415):
"Women Of Ireland (Lurker Edit)" - a cover of the 1969 music by Seán Ó Riada.

> "Women Of Ireland (Lurker Edit)" 3:37
> Written by Seán Ó Riada / Handel (arr. Oldfield); Remixed by George Shilling/Henry Jackman
> Appears on: CD single; Promo CD single; XXV CD singles; The Best Of: 1992 - 2003

Not a bad remix of the track, mainly adding a dance backbeat to Mike's piece. It does a good job of maintaining the atmosphere of the original. One of the more tastefully done remixes.

"Women Of Ireland (12" Lurker Mix)" 9:09
Written by Seán Ó Riada / Handel (arr. Oldfield); Remixed by George Shilling/Henry Jackman
Appears on: 12" & CD single; XXV CD singles
Where the "Lurker Edit" restrains itself from overdoing the dance remix parts of the track, this mix lets loose, adding more production, outside samples and extending the track to 9 minutes.

"Women Of Ireland (Transient Mix)" 9:39
Written by Seán Ó Riada / Handel (arr. Oldfield); Remixed by George Shilling/Henry Jackman
Appears on: 12" & CD single; XXV CD singles
Is it just me or do the swooshy effects sound like TIE fighters flying past? This mix is a variant of the Lurker mixes, with a slightly different arrangement.

-October 30-
Mike Oldfield is interviewed from his home in Es Cubells, Ibiza, Spain, for the German TV show RTL.

-December-
Mike Oldfield begins work on his new album, *Tubular Bells III*, at his home studio in Es Cubells, Ibiza, Spain. His sessions there last until March 1998. Around this time, too, he puts a hold on his Music Virtual Reality project.

-December 6-
Trevor Key, photographer (*Tubular Bells, Hergest Ridge, Boxed, Incantations, Platinum, Heaven's Open, Tubular Bells II*, "Sentinel" single, as well as for many other artists), passes away.

XXV

1997

Note: **Mike** spends about a year and a half working on *Tubular Bells III*, resulting in very little to report during this year.

-Date Unknown-
BGO Records re-issues the following **Kevin Ayers And The Whole World** and Kevin Ayers solo albums in the UK on CD:

Whatevershebringswesing (BGOCD 11)
Shooting At The Moon (BGOCD 13)

-May-
System 7 remixes **Mike Oldfield**'s recording of "Women of Ireland" for a forthcoming single release.

-Date Unknown-
Virgin Records re-issues **Mike Oldfield**'s album *Tubular Bells* on 180 gram vinyl LP (724384280017) in the UK, as part of the EMI 100 Series (LPCENT18), using Direct Metal Mastering.

-Dates Unknown-
Immersing himself in the dance club culture of Ibiza, Spain, while working on *Tubular Bells III*, **Mike Oldfield** has his works-in-progress anonymously played by club DJs in their sets.
"Tubular Bells III (Original Side One)" - According to the programme notes for the *Tubular Bells III* premiere, **Mike** records an entire side of the album in the club style before realizing it was too much and he trimmed it down. This was also, it seems, the point where the other movements began to develop.
"The Serpent Dream" – In the later Jools Holland 1998 interview, **Mike** says this track developed as he played impromptu sets at Ibiza clubs, bringing his Spanish guitar and joining the local performers.
"The Top Of The Morning" - Originally written on guitar, before Mike tried it out on piano.
"A Bag Of Secrets" - this is reportedly a working title for what became "The Source Of Secrets."

-November 10-
WEA Records releases **Mike Oldfield**'s *XXV: Women Of Ireland* singles in the UK and Europe. One features CD-ROM material which includes the "Women Of Ireland" video, a biography and discography.

UK 12" single (WEA 093 T):
"Women Of Ireland (System 7 12" Mix)" - a cover of the 1969 music by Seán Ó Riada.
"Women Of Ireland (12" Lurker Mix)" - a cover of the 1969 music by Seán Ó Riada.
"Women Of Ireland (Lurker Edit)" - a cover of the 1969 music by Seán Ó Riada.

UK 12" single (SAM 3096) promo:
"Women Of Ireland (System 7 12" Mix)"
	- a cover of the 1969 music by Seán Ó Riada. Listed as "System 7 Mix."
"Women Of Ireland (12" Lurker Mix)" - a cover of the 1969 music by Seán Ó Riada. Listed as "Lurker Mix"
"Women Of Ireland (Transient Mix)"
	- a cover of the 1969 music by Seán Ó Riada. Listed as "12" Extended Mix."

UK CD single (WEA 093):
"Women Of Ireland (Lurker Edit)" - a cover of the 1969 music by Seán Ó Riada.
"Women Of Ireland" - a cover of the 1969 music by Seán Ó Riada.
"Mike's Reel"
CD-ROM

UK CD single (WEA 093 CDX):
"Women Of Ireland (Lurker Edit)" – a cover of the 1969 music by Seán Ó Riada.
"Women Of Ireland (System 7 12" Mix)" – a cover of the 1969 music by Seán Ó Riada.
"Women Of Ireland (12" Lurker Mix)" – a cover of the 1969 music by Seán Ó Riada.
"Women Of Ireland (Transient Mix)" – a cover of the 1969 music by Seán Ó Riada.

UK CD single (WEA 093 CDDJ) Promo:
"Women Of Ireland (Lurker Edit)" – a cover of the 1969 music by Seán Ó Riada. Listed as "Radio Edit."

Germany CD single (PRCD 415) Promo:
"Women Of Ireland (Lurker Edit)" – a cover of the 1969 music by Seán Ó Riada. Listed as "Radio Edit."

> "Mike's Reel" 3:50
> Written by Mike Oldfield
> Appears on: XXV: Women Of Ireland CD single (WEA 093); The Best Of: 1992 - 2003
> A reel in music is a specific type of folk tune in England, Wales, Ireland and Scotland, accompanied by a reel dance. It is designed with even beats and is very uptempo, quickly alternating tight musical phrases. Given Mike's background in folk, it's unsurprising he'd write and record one himself. This is one of only two new pieces of his music released this year, the other being an excerpt from his in-progress *Tubular Bells III* sessions (see below).
>
> "Women Of Ireland (System 7 12" Mix) 9:02
> Written by Seán Ó Riada / Handel (arr. Oldfield); Remixed by System 7
> Appears on: XXV: Women Of Ireland 12" & CD single (2 of 2); The Best Of: 1992 - 2003
> This is a pretty bland dance mix, with a basic backbeat and only a few samples of the melody strung together here and there. It's not that it's terrible, it's just dull. Sorry, System 7.

-November 11 & 17-
WEA Records releases the **Mike Oldfield** collection *XXV: The Essential Mike Oldfield* in the Europe and Australia. Track listing as follows:

UK & Europe *XXV: The Essential Mike Oldfield* CD (3984 21218 2)
Europe *XXV: The Essential Mike Oldfield* Promo CD (PROP 371)
Australia *XXV: The Essential Mike Oldfield* CD (3984 21218 2)

"Tubular Bells (Opening Theme)"
"Hergest Ridge (Part One - Boxed Remix) (XXV Excerpt)"
"Ommadawn (Part One) (Episodes Extract)"
"Incantations (Part Four) ('Ode To Cynthia')"
"Moonlight Shadow"
"Portsmouth"
"Good News"
"Sentinel (Single Restructure)"
"The Bell (MC Viv Stanshall Edit)"
"Let There Be Light (Single Version)"
"Only Time Will Tell (XXV Version)"
"The Voyager"
"Women Of Ireland" – a cover of the 1969 music by Seán Ó Riada.
"Tubular Bells III (Excerpt)"

> "Hergest Ridge (Part One - Boxed Remix) (XXV Excerpt)" 4:58
> Written by Mike Oldfield
> Appears on: XXV: The Essential Mike Oldfield
> This is the 2nd movement of the "Part One - Boxed Remix," from about 8:33 to 13:31.

"The Bell (MC Viv Stanshall Edit)" 3:22
Written by Mike Oldfield
Appears on: XXV: The Essential Mike Oldfield
In a curious move, this version edits out about 22 seconds of the track, from right after Stanshall says "yet again...tubular bells." The rest of the track continues as the single version does. Honestly, why did they bother?

"Only Time Will Tell (XXV Version)" 4:39
Written by Mike Oldfield
Appears on: XXV: The Essential Mike Oldfield
Another good standalone version, this edit fades in at the start and fades out at the end, losing none of the original track.

"Tubular Bells III (Excerpt)" 3:39
Written by Mike Oldfield
Appears on: XXV: The Essential Mike Oldfield
At the time of this collection, Mike was working on *Tubular Bells III*, with sections heavily influenced by the club scene in Ibiza. It shows here, in his most dance-oriented original piece to date (setting aside the many recent DJ remixes). It gave a taste of what he had in mind for TBIII and many fans didn't know what to make of it. At the time, it sounded like Oldfield had remixed *Tubular Bells* and fans wondered if the entire album would sound like this, all club music. This excerpt is an early mix of what would become "The Source Of Secrets" on the finished album, with Mike himself providing the vocal parts and featuring some subtly different mixing and edits in places.

Tubular Bells III

1998

-March-
Mike Oldfield decides to leave his home in Es Cubells, Ibiza, Spain and returns to Roughwood Croft, Chalfont St. Giles, Buckinghamshire, England.

-Spring-
Ten Thirteen Productions asks **Mike Oldfield** to record the following for the forthcoming film *The X-Files*:
"Tubular X" – **Mike** combines "The X-Files" theme with elements of the "Introduction" of *Tubular Bells*, creating a new arrangement.

-Date Unknown-
William Murray dies, in Dublin, Ireland. Murray played drums on the Kevin Ayers' album, *Whatevershebringswesing*, on which **Mike Oldfield** also played. He was a housemate of **Mike**'s at Througham Slad during the recording of *Ommadawn* (on which he played percussion and co-wrote "On Horseback") and was photographer and writer of the funny short story for the sleeve of *Amarok*.

-April-
Mike Oldfield continues work on *Tubular Bells III* in London, England. These sessions last until June.

-May 22-
Virgin Records re-issues **Mike Oldfield**'s album *Tubular Bells* on CD in Europe (CDVx2001) as a 25th Anniversary limited edition gold disc. Remaster by Simon Heyworth at Chop'Em Out Mastering, London, England.

-June-
Mike Oldfield completes work on *Tubular Bells III*. The album's liner notes say these sessions are in London, but his autobiography says they are at his home studio, Roughwood Croft, Chalfont St. Giles, Buckinghamshire, England. Since December 1996, tracks worked on include:
"Man In The Rain" – this song from the mid-'80s is revisited again. It previously evolved into "Heaven's Open." This is **Mike**'s next attempt to get the song closer to its original idea. Reportedly, Maggie Reilly was approached to record on it, but there were issues with her management. Cara Dillon (of Polar Star) records lead vocals, while Heather Burnett provides additional vocals.
"The Inner Child" – Rosa Cedrón sings on this track. She also recorded a cello part simultaneously, but **Mike** says in an interview this year that the vocals stood on their own and the cello was mixed out. Cedrón is a member of the band Luar Na Lubre, whom **Mike** covered with "The Song Of The Sun."
"The Source Of Secrets" – This track is completed and Amar records her vocals, replacing **Mike**'s as heard on the *XXV* excerpt. The working title for this track is "A Bag Of Secrets."
"Jewel In The Crown" – features Amar on vocals.
"Secrets" – features Amar on vocals. The working title for this track is "More Secrets."
"Far Above The Clouds" – features Clodagh Simonds and Francesca Robertson (goddaughter of a WEA executive Rob Dickins) on vocals. Robertson does the narration.
"Outcast" – the working title for this track is "The Mighty Fall."

In an interview for *Music Media Verlag* in 1999, **Oldfield** says he recorded about 70 minutes for the album, but pared it down to 46 minutes for release and that there are "quite a lot of out-takes." He also says none of that unused material appears on *Guitars* or *The Millennium Bell*.

-June 2-
20th Century Fox releases *The X-Files: The Album*, one of two soundtrack albums on CD for the film (the other being the score soundtrack album) in the UK (7559-62266-2) and Europe (7559-62266-2), and a promo CD. It features **Mike Oldfield**'s "Tubular X."

20th Century Fox also releases *The X-Files: The Album Sampler* in North America on CD (3331000027), with also features **Mike Oldfield**'s "Tubular X."

Note: despite being on the sampler, "Tubular X" does not appear on the North American soundtrack album.

> "Tubular X"
> Written by Mark Snow (arr. Oldfield)
> Appears on: UK & Europe Promo & Standard The X-Files: The Album CD, US The X-Files: The Album Sampler
> Mike weaves Mark Snow's theme with his own *Tubular Bells* stylings, creating a wonderful hybrid of the two, where in *The X-Files* theme and Oldfield's music compliment each other perfectly. The name "Tubular X" apparently came from Fox or the studio, though Mike doesn't seem to object in interviews and says he had fun making this track. Fans should definitely seek this out and play it at Hallowe'en.

-June 8-
20th Century Fox releases *The X-Files Theme* EP CD single (AMCY-2917) in Japan, featuring both "Tubular X" and "The Source Of Secrets" by **Mike Oldfield**.

> "The Source Of Secrets (Single Version)" 5:33
> Written by Mike Oldfield
> Appears on: The X-Files Theme EP
> This version is identical to the version that later appeared on the album, but ends right after the explosion, removing the low rumble that segues into "The Watchful Eye." This release came out the same month Oldfield was finishing the album and several months before the album's release, indicating it was one of the first tracks finished for the album, which makes sense since the *XXV* excerpt appeared mostly finished in November of 1997.

Note: Some sources list the release date as Dec. 16th.

-July-
Mike Oldfield assembles his group for the live premiere of *Tubular Bells III*, scheduled for September 4, 1998. The rehearsals last 2 months. The ensemble is:

Robyn Smith	Adrian Thomas	Hugh Burns	Carrie Melbourne
Katherine Rockhill	Jody Linscott	Alasdar Malloy	Pepsi Demacque
Amar	Rosa Cedrón		

-Date Unknown-
WEA Records issues a promo CD of **Mike Oldfield**'s album *Tubular Bell III* in the UK. Track listing as follows:

"The Source Of Secrets" – listed as "A Bag Of Secrets."
"The Watchful Eye"
"Jewel In The Crown"
"Outcast" – listed as "The Mighty Fall."
"Serpent Dream"
"The Inner Child"
"Man In The Rain" Mike Oldfield Featuring Cara
"The Top Of The Morning"
"Moonwatch" – listed as "Moon Watch."

"Secrets" – listed as "More Secrets."
"Far Above The Clouds"

-August 31-
Mike Oldfield releases his album *Tubular Bells III* on WEA/Warner on CD in the UK, Europe and Australia. Engineered and produced by **Oldfield**. Track listing as follows:

UK & Europe *Tubular Bells III* CD (3984243492)
UK *Tubular Bells III* Promo CD (3984-24349-2)
Australia *Tubular Bells III* CD (3984243492)

"The Source Of Secrets"
"The Watchful Eye"
"Jewel In The Crown"
"Outcast"
"Serpent Dream"
"The Inner Child"
"Man In The Rain" Mike Oldfield Featuring Cara
"The Top Of The Morning"
"Moonwatch"
"Secrets"
"Far Above The Clouds"

-Date Unknown-
WEA releases a promo CD single of **Mike Oldfield**'s "The Top Of The Morning" in Spain.

Spain CD single (PRO1116):
"The Top Of The Morning"

-Date Unknown-
WEA releases a promo CD single of **Mike Oldfield**'s "Secrets" in the UK.

UK CD single (333000672):
"Secrets"

-September 4-
Mike Oldfield premiers *Tubular Bells III* live at the Horse Guards Parade ground, London, England. There is a party after the show. The concert is filmed and later released on home video. Several individual tracks from the concert are released:

> "Serpent Dream (Live at Horse Guard Parade)" 3:00
> Written by Mike Oldfield
> Appears on: Man In The Rain CD single
> As he'll tell you, Mike is first and foremost a guitarist and this flamenco piece showcases his impressive skills as an acoustic player. The track ends on crowd noise as it segues into "The Inner Child."

> "The Inner Child (Live at Horse Guard Parade)" 4:39
> Written by Mike Oldfield
> Appears on: Man In The Rain CD single
> Rosa Cedrón gives a stunning vocal performance here, as on the album. It's pretty faithful to the studio recording, retaining all the power of the original. With the help of modern technology and excellent ensembles, Mike was getting pretty good at recreating his albums onstage by this point.

-September 5-
Mike Oldfield holds a press conference for the media who attended the *Tubular Bells III* premiere the evening before. **Oldfield** states he wants to do an album of only guitars at some point in the future.

-September 22-
Mike Oldfield releases his album *Tubular Bells III* in Canada.

Canada *Tubular Bells III* CD (2 24349)
Canada *Tubular Bells III* Promo CD (W2 24349)

-September 27-
Mike Oldfield appears on *Across The Threshold* on Classic FM radio, UK.

-October-
Mike Oldfield begins working on his new album, with the aim being able to perform the entire thing with only guitars (and guitar samples). Recording takes places at Roughwood Croft, Chalfont St. Giles, Buckinghamshire, England. The sessions last until February 1999. In an interview the following year, **Mike** says he is already planning his millennium album project at this time, but decided to record *Guitars* to clear his contract with Warner in the meantime.

Warner Music releases the VHS and Laserdisc of *Tubular Bells III (The Premiere Performance Recorded Live At Horse Guards Parade London)* in the UK. It is an edit of the concert, removing the non-TBIII tracks which appeared in the encore.

-October 25-
Mike Oldfield Featuring Cara releases his "Man In The Rain" singles in the UK and Europe.

UK 1-track CD single (PRO00028) promo:
"Man In The Rain" Mike Oldfield Featuring Cara

Europe CD single (WEA194CD):
"Man In The Rain" Mike Oldfield Featuring Cara
"Serpent Dream (Live at Horse Guard Parade)" Mike Oldfield
"The Inner Child (Live at Horse Guard Parade)" Mike Oldfield

Europe CD single (3984-25185-9):
"Man In The Rain" Mike Oldfield Featuring Cara
"The Inner Child (Live at Horse Guard Parade)" Mike Oldfield

Europe 1-track CD single (WEA194CDDJ) promo:
"Man In The Rain" Mike Oldfield Featuring Cara

-October 31-
Mike Oldfield and his ensemble appear live on *Later With...Jools Holland* in BBC TV, performing "The Serpent Dream," "Secrets" and "Far Above The Clouds."

> "The Serpent Dream" 4:01
> "Interview" 4:32
> "Secrets + Far Above The Clouds" 8:15
> Written by Mike Oldfield
> Appears on: N/A
> Unlike most television appearances Mike made over the years, which required him to simply mime to whichever single he was promoting, on this evening he and his band actually played the tracks live. Like the TBIII premiere, the result is pretty stellar (if not better than the September show).

-November 12-
Mike Oldfield appears on *Premios Ondas* (Spanish Music Awards), Spain.

-November 22-
Mike Oldfield appears on the award show *Goldene Europa*, Saarlandhalle, Saarbrucken, Germany.

Guitars & The Millennium Bell

1999

-January-
Mike Oldfield visits Peru, investigating the Inca culture, according to *The Millennium Bell* liner notes. "Pacha Mama" – directly inspired by his visit, using Ancient Inca lyrics given to him by his local guide.

-January 23-
An article published in *The Times* (UK) on this date notes that **Mike Oldfield** is currently finishing off his *Guitars* album at Roughwood Croft, Chalfont St. Giles, Buckinghamshire.

-February-
Mike Oldfield completes work on *Guitars* at Roughwood Croft, Chalfont St. Giles, Buckinghamshire. The album features only guitars and guitar-performed elements (such as guitar samples and drum beats triggered by guitar-MIDI).
"Out Of Sight" – the drum sample heard here is again from "When The Levee Breaks" by Led Zeppelin, previously used on the track "Magellan."

-March – April-
Oldfield begins recording his next album, *The Millennium Bell*, at Roughwood Croft, Chalfont St. Giles, Buckinghamshire. This session lasts until November. He says specifically in a November interview that he spent these months writing the new material.

-Spring-
Mike Oldfield assembles his touring group and begins rehearsals for the upcoming Then & Now '99 Tour. The ensemble is:

Adrian Thomas	Pepsi Demacque	Claire Nicholson	Carrie Melbourne
Fergus Garrand			

-April-
WEA issues a press release for the forthcoming **Mike Oldfield** *Guitars* album. It also notes the upcoming tour. They also issue a press release for the forthcoming "Far Above The Clouds" singles.

-April 12-
Mike Oldfield releases his "Far Above The Clouds" singles in the UK and Spain.

UK 12" single (WEA206T):
"Far Above The Clouds (Jam & Spoon Mix)"
"Far Above The Clouds (Timewriter's Big Bag Of Secrets)"

UK 12" single (WEA206T):
"Far Above The Clouds (Jam & Spoon Mix)"
"Far Above The Clouds (Timewriter's Big Bag Of Secrets)"

UK 2x12" single (SAM 00054) promo:
12" single 1:
"Far Above The Clouds (Jam & Spoon Mix)"
"Far Above The Clouds (Timewriter's Big Bag Of Secrets)"

12" single 2:
"Far Above The Clouds (Jam & Spoon Deep Inside The Club Mix)"
"Far Above The Clouds (Jam & Spoon Far Below The Bass Mix)"

UK CD single (PRO1276):
"Far Above The Clouds (Timewriter's Radio Edit)" – listed as "Timewriter's Radio Mix."
"Far Above The Clouds (Jam & Spoon Mix)" – listed as "Jam & Spoon Radio Edit."

UK CD Maxi-single (WEA206CDDJ) promo:
"Far Above The Clouds (Timewriter's Radio Edit)"
"Secrets + Far Above The Clouds (Promo Edit)" – listed as "Album Version – Single Edit."
"Far Above The Clouds (Jam & Spoon Radio Edit)"
"Far Above The Clouds (Timewriter's Big Bag Of Secrets)"
"Far Above The Clouds (Jam & Spoon Mix)"
"Far Above The Clouds (Jam & Spoon Deep Inside The Club Mix)"
"Far Above The Clouds (Jam & Spoon Far Below The Bass Mix)"
"Secrets + Far Above The Clouds" – listed as "Album Version."

Spain 1-track CD single (3984-24349-2:
"Far Above The Clouds (Spanish Promo Edit)"

"Secrets + Far Above The Clouds" 8:48
Written by Mike Oldfield
Appears on: UK Promo CD Maxi-single
This is the two tracks "Secrets" and "Far Above The Clouds" combined as a single track, with no change to the music itself, the same as they appear on the album.

"Secrets + Far Above The Clouds (UK Promo Edit)" 3:40
Written by Mike Oldfield
Appears on: UK Promo CD Maxi-single
In an interesting move, rather than using one of the other edits of "Far Above The Clouds," this mix was created, condensing the two tracks into a very short single track. Not a bad idea, but it's perhaps condensed a bit too much, where the "Secrets" portion doesn't have a lot of breathing room and ends just as it gets going.

"Far Above The Clouds (UK Single Edit)" 4:48
Written by Mike Oldfield
Appears on: UK CD single (1 of 2), The Platinum Collection
The sleeve calls this the "Original Version," but in fact it's an edit. About ten seconds from the beginning are removed and about 30 seconds of the nature effects at the end gone after an early fade out.

"Far Above The Clouds (Spanish Promo Edit)" 3:52
Written by Mike Oldfield
Appears on: Spanish Promo CD single
This edit removes the first minute of the track and begins with the narration. It fades out forty seconds early on the nature sounds at the end.

"Far Above The Clouds (Jam & Spoon Mix)" 9:57
Written by Mike Oldfield; Remixed by Jam & Spoon
Appears on: UK 12" single, UK 12" Promo 2 disc single, UK Promo CD Maxi-single, UK CD (1 of 2), US 12" single; The Best Of: 1992 - 2003
From an album that began life heavily influence by dance club music, it now comes full circle with the DJ remixes on the singles. This mix, by Jam & Spoon, shifts moods a few times throughout to keep things interesting, using different samples in different areas, though favouring the tubular

bells. As with all the dance remixes of the period, if you like them, you'll probably like this. If not, it's probably because there isn't a lot of Mike in the track, just the short samples.

"Far Above The Clouds (Jam & Spoon Radio Edit)" 5:08
Written by Mike Oldfield; Remixed by Jam & Spoon
Appears on: UK Promo CD Maxi-single
This version reduces the Jam & Spoon Mix down by half, shortening each section and making it much for listenable for non-fans of these remixes. The track has enough variety and different parts to keep casual fans interested.

"Far Above The Clouds (Jam & Spoon Deep Inside The Club Mix)" 10:25
Written by Mike Oldfield; Remixed by Jam & Spoon
Appears on: UK 12" Promo 2 disc single, UK Promo CD Maxi-single, UK CD single (2 of 2), US 12" single
The exact opposite of the Jam & Spoon Edit, this is the extended version of the Jam & Spoon Mix, drawing the track out another minute and a half.

"Far Above The Clouds (Jam & Spoon Far Below The Bass Mix)" 7:38
Written by Mike Oldfield; Remixed by Jam & Spoon
Appears on: UK 12" Promo 2 disc single, UK Promo CD Maxi-single, UK CD single (2 of 2), US 12" single
This mix emphasizes the bass lines in the backing track and adds a few new elements. If you've come this far, you now get something a bit new!

"Far Above The Clouds (Timewriter's Big Bag Of Secrets)" 6:20
Written by Mike Oldfield; Remixed by The Timewriter
Appears on: UK 12" single, UK 12" Promo 2 disc single, UK Promo CD Maxi-single, UK CD single (2 of 2), US 12" single
A much more laid back mix, which uses the narration, the piano melody and tubular bells samples. The narration is pitched down in places, making it sound like an old man, giving a contrast to Francesca Robertson's natural vocals when they're played back to back in the mix. Otherwise, it's a bit repetitive.

"Far Above The Clouds (Timewriter's Radio Edit)" 3:41
Written by Mike Oldfield; Remixed by The Timewriter
Appears on: UK Promo CD single, UK Promo CD Maxi-single, UK CD single (1 of 2); The Best Of: 1992 - 2003
This is a shorter variation of the "Big Bag Of Secrets Mix."

-Date Unknown-
Mike Oldfield records the London Session Orchestra, conducted by Robyn Smith for his album *The Millennium Bell* at Abbey Road Studios, London, England. The session takes one day.
"The Doge's Palace"
"Lake Constance"
"Broad Sunlit Uplands"

-Date Unknown-
Tempus Fugit in Germany re-releases the Tom Newman album *Faerie Symphony* as *Faerie Symphony And Other Stories*, including bonus tracks. **Mike Oldfield** (probably) appears on the album track "Dance Of The Daoine Sidhe" and (definitely) appears on the bonus tracks "Sad Sing" (originally from *Fine Old Tom*), "Day Of The Percherons" (from the *Fine Old Tom* sessions).

-Date Unknown-
Harvest re-issues the Kevin Ayers album *Whatevershebringswesing* on CD (7243 5 21197 21), featuring **Mike Oldfield.**

-May-
WEA releases the 2-part **Mike Oldfield** "Far Above The Clouds" CD singles in the UK.

UK CD single (WEA206CD1) (1 of 2):
"Far Above The Clouds (Timewriter's Radio Edit)"
"Far Above The Clouds (Jam & Spoon Mix)"
"Far Above The Clouds (UK Single Edit)"

UK CD single (WEA206CD2) (2 of 2):
"Far Above The Clouds (Jam & Spoon Deep Inside The Club Mix)"
"Far Above The Clouds (Timewriter's Big Bag Of Secrets)"
"Far Above The Clouds (Jam & Spoon Far Below The Bass Mix)"

UK CDr single promo:
"Far Above The Clouds (Timewriter's Radio Edit)" - listed as "Radio Mix."
"Far Above The Clouds (Jam & Spoon Deep Inside The Club Mix)"
"Far Above The Clouds (Jam & Spoon Far Below The Bass Mix)"

-May 20-
An interview with **Mike Oldfield** in *Estrella Digital* is published on this date. It notes the name of the new album as *Millennium* and discusses the following:
"Nativity" - not mentioned by name, but noted that the album starts with Christ.
"Pacha Mama" - not mentioned by name, but the next part is about the Incas.
"Excalibur" - indirectly named, as **Mike** includes "Excalibur and King Arthur" next.
"Santa Maria" - not mentioned by name, but as a piece about the discovery of America.
"Sunlight Shining Through Clouds" - not mentioned by name, but as a piece about slavery.
"Lake Constance" - not mentioned by name, but as a "classic romantic" piece.
"Broad Sunlit Uplands" - not mentioned by name, but as a World War II piece.
"Unnamed Space Piece" - **Mike** notes a piece about space travel.
"The Millennium Bell" - indirectly named, as he says the whole thing will finish with new millennium bells.

-May 24-
Mike Oldfield releases his album *Guitars* in the UK, Europe, Canada and Australia. Track listing as follows:

UK *Guitars* CD (3984274012)
Europe *Guitar* CD (3984274012)
Germany *Guitar* Promo CD (PROP05055)
Spain *Guitar* Promo CDr
Canada *Guitars* CD (2 27401)
Australia *Guitars* CD (3984274012)

"Muse"
"Cochise"
"Embers"
"Summit Day"
"Out Of Sight"
"B. Blues"
"Four Winds"
"Enigmatism"
"Out Of Mind
"From The Ashes"

-June 6-
Mike Oldfield does an interview for Power ON magazine on this date, at Roughwood Croft, Chalfont St. Giles, Buckinghamshire. He identifies indirectly the aforementioned known pieces planned for the album. He also says *The Millennium Bell* is nearly finished and that he's writing the concert version simultaneously for a New Year's Eve concert.

-June 15-
Oldfield Music presses a CD of early versions of tracks from *The Millennium Bell*, which **Mike Oldfield** is currently working on. The date appears on the sleeve of some copies, but the tracks themselves (some or all) appear to be mixes dating from a bit earlier, as evidenced by things like **Mike** saying specifically in a July 29 press conference that the opening hymn of "Amber Light" had been recorded. Track listing as follows:

"Nativity"
"Pacha Mama (Early Version)"
"Excalibur"
"Santa Maria (Early Mix)"
"Sunlit Shining Through Cloud (Early Mix)"
"The Doge's Palace (Early Mix)"
"Lake Constance (Early Mix)"
"Mastermind (Early Mix)"
"Board Sunlit Uplands (Early Mix)"
"Emancipation"
"The Millennium Bell (Early Mix)"
"Amber Light (Early Mix)"

> "Nativity" 5:05
> Written by Mike Oldfield
> Appears on: Unreleased
> This track would later become "Peace On Earth," compared to whom, this sounds very much unfinished. There are no lyrics, just the chorus of "Na...na na na-na-na-na" over and over. There is also no guitar, so it sounds more like a partly-finished backing track (which is exactly what is).
>
> "Pacha Mama (Early Version)" 5:10
> Written by Mike Oldfield
> Appears on: Unreleased
> Some noticeable differences include the chanting starting earlier in place of the sampled "ee-ah-ee-ah-ee-ah..." vocal. The chanting also goes on longer in places, which was reduced on the final mix, accounting for it being over a minute longer.
>
> "Excalibur" 3:42
> Written by Mike Oldfield
> Appears on: Unreleased
> This a wholly unused piece, based on the King Arthur mythology, It features a brief lyric near the beginning. Very slow and dramatic, evoking the majesty of the legendary king, it builds to a climax and then cuts during the dénouement as the next track "Santa Maria" comes in. The flow of the two tracks actually works well, but the cut-off doesn't make for an ideal standalone version.
>
> "Santa Maria (Early Mix)" 4:02
> Written by Mike Oldfield
> Appears on: Unreleased
> Right from the start, this mix sounds clearer than the album version. It also features a much more layered backing track which only adds to the piece. There are no lyrics when the Handel Choir comes in, so they only sing low notes. The next section, the build-up, has no lyrics either and the

track continues afterwards with a reprise of the opening portion before cutting off as "Sunlight Shining Through Cloud" comes in.

"Sunlight Shining Through Cloud (Early Mix)" 5:50
Written by Mike Oldfield
Appears on: Unreleased
Before Mike incorporated the words from "Amazing Grace," this track featured a rap about facing adversity. Some of the rap lyrics survived to the album, reworked with the "Amazing Grace" lyrics and overall the track is longer, with some good guitar work by Mike.

"The Doge's Palace (Early Mix)" 4:15
Written by Mike Oldfield
Appears on: Unreleased
There's no choir or organ here, so the music just jugs along on its own. It also features some parts not heard in the final album version, with a recorder part coming in around the 1:47 mark. The ending is also different, more drawn out. For some reason, the track cuts off suddenly at the end, though not because of a segue way to the next track.

"Lake Constance (Early Mix)" 5:26
Written by Mike Oldfield
Appears on: Unreleased
Nearly identical to the later album version, the "Early Mix" features a few extra bars of moodier strings at the beginning.

"Mastermind (Early Mix)" 3:15
Written by Mike Oldfield
Appears on: Unreleased
This mix feature some audio samples not heard in the final version (in addition to "Mastermind" and "What is love") but is otherwise identical to the album mix. An indexing difference appears at the end. The album version cuts right after the last "What is love," going abruptly into "Broad Sunlit Uplands." Here, that abrupt change, drum roll and the first 12-13 seconds of "Broad Sunlit Uplands" is at the end of this track. This bit is the same as on the album version of "Broad Sunlit Uplands," but features an additional sample of Winston Churchill saying "United as never before," not heard on the album.

"Broad Sunlit Uplands (Early Mix)" 3:50
Written by Mike Oldfield
Appears on: Unreleased
Beginning with the echo of the line "United as never before," which an indexing error placed at the end of "Mastermind," this version is the same as the album version (minus those first 12-13 seconds), but features an additional quote by Churchill, him saying "broad sunlit uplands" throughout. Like on the finished album, this track segues into the next, "Emancipation."

"Emancipation" 3:27
Written by Mike Oldfield
Appears on: Unreleased
The precursor to "Liberation," this early mix has no spoken word poem and no quiet vocal section near the beginning Instead, it's African drumming and Mike's guitar for the first 2 minutes, followed by vocals over some keyboard flanging until the end.

"The Millennium Bell (Early Mix)" 5:36
On the album, "The Millennium Bell" is basically a club remix-sounding reprise of all the previous tracks on the album. This track is something completely different. A original dance mix first (not the same as on the album) with a new, uptempo vocal parts from "Nativity" and "Sunlit Shining Through Cloud." It cuts off before the last crash, which starts the next track, "Amber Light."

"Amber Light (Early Mix)" 3:52
Written by Mike Oldfield
Appears on: Unreleased
Beginning with the cymbal crash the segues from "The Millennium Bell," this version doesn't feature the "Amber light..." lyrics at the beginning. Instead, it starts with some quiet synths before the tribal chanting starts. The rest of the track is similar to the album version, but is still rough, with a different arrangement and guitar parts

-June 18-
Mike Oldfield performs at Kisstadion, Budapest, Hungary. This starts the Then & Now '99 Tour.

-June 19-
Mike Oldfield performs at Stadhalle, Wien, Austria.

-June 20-
Mike Oldfield performs at August-Schattner-Halle, Hanau, Germany.

-June 21-
Mike Oldfield performs at Sporthalle, Böblingen, Germany.

-June 23-
Mike Oldfield releases his "Far Above The Clouds" singles in North America on Kinetic Records.

US 12" single (0-44669):
"Far Above The Clouds (Jam & Spoon Mix)"
"Far Above The Clouds (Timewriter's Big Bag Of Secrets)"
"Far Above The Clouds (Jam & Spoon Deep Inside The Club Mix)"
"Far Above The Clouds (Jam & Spoon Far Below The Bass Mix)"

US 12" single (PRO-A-9752-A) promo:
"Far Above The Clouds (Jam & Spoon Mix)"
"Far Above The Clouds (Timewriter's Big Bag Of Secrets)"
"Far Above The Clouds (Jam & Spoon Deep Inside The Club Mix)"
"Far Above The Clouds (Jam & Spoon Far Below The Bass Mix)"

Mike Oldfield performs at ICC, Berlin, Germany.

-June 24-
Mike Oldfield performs at Freilichtbühne, Dresden, Germany.

-June 25-
Mike Oldfield performs at Stadpark, Hamburg, Germany.

-June 26-
Mike Oldfield performs at Stadhalle, Rostock, Germany.

-June 27-
Mike Oldfield performs at Stadhalle, Bielefeld, Germany.

-June 28-
Mike Oldfield performs at Museuemeilem, Bonn, Germany. In an interview before the show for *Music Media Verlag*, **Mike** says he has a "skeleton" of *The Millennium Bell* finished, with some pieces done and some not. He notes the forthcoming New Year's Eve concert is set for the Jubilee Gardens, London, England.

"The Millennium Bell" – **Mike** says he wants to work on this track with DJs in the style of a remix of his own work (Note: the syntax of the translation is a little vague, but that seems to be what he's getting at).

-June 29-
Mike Oldfield performs at Ahoy, Rotterdam, The Netherlands.

-July 1-
Mike Oldfield performs at Plaza de Toros de Illumbre, San Sebastián, Spain. The support band is Luar Na Lubre.

-July 2-
Mike Oldfield performs at Jardín de Viveros, Valencia, Spain. The support band is Luar Na Lubre.

-July 3-
Mike Oldfield performs at Polideportivo San Javier, San Javier, Spain. The support band is Luar Na Lubre.

-July 4-
Mike Oldfield performs at Campo de Fútbol San Miguel, Ubeda, Spain. The support band is Luar Na Lubre.

-July 6-
Mike Oldfield performs at Palau Sant Jordi, Barcelona, Spain. The support band is Luar Na Lubre.

-July 7-
Mike Oldfield performs at Plaza de Toros, Palma de Mallorca, Spain. The support band is Luar Na Lubre.

-July 8-
Mike Oldfield performs at Plaza de Toros de Leganés, Leganés, Spain. The support band is Luar Na Lubre.

-July 9-
Mike Oldfield performs at Salamanca FC Stadium, Salamanca, Spain. The support band is Luar Na Lubre.

-July 10-
Mike Oldfield performs at Estadio Riomar, Castro Urdiales, Spain. The support band is Luar Na Lubre.

-July 12-
Mike Oldfield performs at Grand Rex, Paris, France. The support act is Mark Nevin.

-July 13-
Mike Oldfield performs at Wembley Arena, London, England. The support act is Mark Nevin.

-July 14-
Mike Oldfield performs at New NEC, Birmingham, England. The support act is Mark Nevin.

-July 15-
Mike Oldfield performs at The Point, Dublin, Ireland. The support act is Mark Nevin.

-July 17-
Mike Oldfield performs at the Folk Festival, Undine Castle, Undine, Italy.

-July 19-
Mike Oldfield performs at the Hohentwiel Festival, Singen, Germany.

-July 20-
Mike Oldfield performs at Stadhalle, Furth, Germany.

-July 21-
Mike Oldfield performs at the Colosseum, Munich, Germany.

-July 22-
Mike Oldfield performs at the Sunset, Zürich, Switzerland.

-July 23-
Mike Oldfield performs at Parkbuhne, Leipzig, Germany.

-July 24-
Mike Oldfield performs at the Sports Hall, Prague, Czech Republic.

-July 25-
Mike Oldfield performs at Spodek Hall, Katowice, Poland.

-July 27-
Mike Oldfield performs at Cirkus, Stockholm, Sweden.

-July 29-
Mike Oldfield performs at Langelands Festival, Fünen, Denmark. At a pre-show press conference, **Mike** discusses ideas for the New Year's Eve concert as well as *Millennium* album project.
"Amber Light" - **Mike** describes the hymn he wrote and recorded with a boy soprano (Andrew Johnson).

-July 31-
Mike Oldfield performs at Playa Santa Cristina, La Coruña, Spain.

-August-
Mike Oldfield resumes work on *The Millennium Bell* album sessions at Roughwood Croft, Chalfont St. Giles, Buckinghamshire, England. He notes this date in a November interview.

-September 17-
The London Handel Choir records its parts for *The Millennium Bell* at Roughwood Croft, Chalfont St. Giles, Buckinghamshire, England. The singers are selected by Roy Rashbrook (**Oldfield**'s engineer is Ben Darlow, whose father knows Rashbrook is a singer and asks him to assemble a choir with a week's notice). The session lasts 3 hours.

Note: Rashbrook writes a detailed account of the day's session, which appears on the Mike Oldfield Mailing List. Curiously, no mention is made of Rashbrook having solved the *Amarok* Morse Code contest, despite Rashbrook being a professed big fan of **Mike**'s work and mentioning that album by name.

-November 5-
Mike Oldfield completes work on his album *The Millennium Bell* at Roughwood Croft, Chalfont St. Giles, Buckinghamshire, England. He specifies the exact date in an interview this month. Among the artists appearing on the album are Cimilla Darlow, Nicola Emmanuel, David Serame, Miriam Stockley, Martay, Pepsi Demacque, Gota Yashiki, Andrew Johnson and the London Handel Choir. **Mike** also employs some more Zero-G samples.
"Peace On Earth" - this track evolved from "Nativity" and now features the London Handel Choir.
"Liberation" - this track evolved from "Emancipation" and features Greta Hegerland-Oldfield doing the narration, reading from Anne Frank's diary.
"Untitled Van Gogh Piece" - In an interview this year with a Spanish newspaper, **Mike** notes this piece is "simple, pretty and violent" (reported by The Mike Oldfield Mailing List).
"Untitled Aristotle Piece" - also reported by The Mike Oldfield Mailing List. **Oldfield** and Fanny Vandekerckhove (his girlfriend) apparently researched Aristotle for possible lyrics.

-Early November-
Mike Oldfield signs to do his New Year's Eve concert in Berlin, Germany. **Mike**'s agent has been in touch with the lighting effects company Art In Heaven, to arrange a collaboration between them and **Oldfield**

Around this time, **Oldfield** has a meeting with Art In Heaven director Gert Hof, at **Oldfield**'s home (Roughwood Croft, Chalfont St. Giles, Buckinghamshire). This meeting is filmed and appears in the Special Features section of *The Art In Heaven Concert* DVD. **Mike**'s handwritten notes show the evening's set list in progress as:

> 10:30 – "Hypnotist"
> "Ommadawn"
> "Shadow On The Wall"
> "Moonlight Shadow"
> 11:10 - *The Millennium Bell*
> 11:58
> 12:00 - Bell
> 12:10 – *The Songs Of ...*
> "Nova"
> *T.B.1 / 3* [illegible] version
> [Here "Berlin 2000" is crossed out in blue pen, with "Art In Heaven" written in blue pen below it as a correction]
> [The notes from 12:00 onwards are also bracketed as "LIGHTSHOW," indicating that is the "Art In Heaven" lightshow segment of the evening.]

"Untitled Synth Arpeggio Piece" – Heard during the Art In Heaven meeting (the unofficial title comes from The Mike Oldfield Mailing List), when **Mike** plays the selection for Gert Hof.

Oldfield's live ensemble is:

Robyn Smith	Adrian Thomas	Claire Nicolson	Carrie Melbourne
Fergus Gerrard	Jody Linscott	Pepsi Demacque	Miriam Stockley
Nicola Emmanuelle	David Serame	St. Petersburg State Symphony Orchestra	
The Glinka State Choir			

-Late-November-
Warner Music Spain releases **Mike Oldfield**'s "Pacha Mama" promo single(s) in Spain.

Spain CD single (SP008W):
"Pacha Mama"
"The Millennium Bell"

(Possible) Spanish Promo CD single 2 (SP008W):
"Pacha Mama"
"The Millennium Bell (Radio Edit)"

Note: these two singles may be one and the same. Some discographies list the edition with the "Radio Edit," but scans of the single itself list the running time as the same as the album version and don't mention an edit at all. Both singles are listed with the same catalogue number (SP008W). The "Radio Edit" does exist (I have the track on *The Platinum Collection*, but not the single itself), so it could be that the single's label is wrong.

> "The Millennium Bell (Radio Edit)" 3:45
> Written by Mike Oldfield
> Appears on: Spanish Promo CD single; The Platinum Collection

Not just an edit here, but a re-edit, focusing on the opening dance groove and extending it in places (such before the piano kicks in). It re-cuts the next few passages, including the "beep beep beep Zero!" and reworks the ending.

-November 29-
Mike Oldfield releases his album *The Millennium Bell* in the UK, Europe and Canada on WEA on CD.

UK *The Millennium Bell* CD (8573808852)
Europe *The Millennium Bell* CD (8573808852)
Europe *The Millennium Bell* Promo CDr
Germany *The Millennium Bell* Promo CD (PROP05149)
Canada *The Millennium Bell* CD (2 80885)

"Peace On Earth"
"Pacha Mama"
"Santa Maria"
"Sunlight Shining Through The Cloud"
"The Doge's Palace"
"Lake Constance"
"Mastermind"
"Broad Sunlit Uplands"
"Liberation"
"Amber Light"
"The Millennium Bell"

-December 22-
Mike Oldfield does a live interview with Steve Wright on BBC Radio 2, London, England. He talks about the upcoming New Year's Eve concert in Berlin, Germany.
"Art In Heaven" – Wright plays a segment of a studio recording of the piece **Oldfield** composed for the Berlin concert, introducing it as "Berlin 2000". Since the CD it was on was given to him by **Mike** for this interview (he says so during the broadcast), I suspect that's what **Mike** wrote on the disc to identify it ("Berlin 2000"), like a basic working title. The later concert DVD refers to the project (light show and music) as "Art In Heaven."

> "Art In Heaven (Studio Version)" 13:37
> Written by Mike Oldfield (Symphony No. 9 by Beethoven, arr. Oldfield)
> Appears on: Unreleased
> This version was put together by Mike presumably for his musicians and the lighting techs to rehearse with. It starts with a minute and a half-long low rumbling note, then "In The Beginning" comes in, a slightly different mix than is on the album. After that part ends, the song goes into the new material, which sounds familiar because it later evolved into "Thou Art In Heaven." Some of the backing track elements that appear in the album version are present, but there are different parts, too, such as the heavy, driving percussion and grinding guitars. There are few synth breaks, but for the most part, once the track shifts into high gear, it doesn't let up until the end. The end sees the performance of an excerpt of Beethoven's *Symphony No. 9 in D Minor*. It's pretty much the way it is played at the concert, but it's great that a full studio recording exists.

-December 26-
On this date, the technical crew begins setting up for *The Millennium Bell* New Years Eve concert at Siegessäule, Berlin, Germany.

-December 31-
Mike Oldfield premières *The Millennium Bell* at Siegessäule, Berlin, Germany, with his ensemble. The concert runs past midnight, as the end of *The Millennium Bell* is timed to be at 12 AM sharp, before the show continues into the Art In Heaven lightshow portion. This concert is filmed and later released as *The Art In Heaven Concert*.

Music Virtual Reality

2000

-January-
In an interview with *Classic Rock* magazine published this month, **Mike Oldfield** says his next project is his Music Virtual Reality computer game and that he'll do an album with music from it when the game is done. He estimates it will be a year or two before anything new is released.

-Date Unknown-
Mike Oldfield resumes work on his Music Virtual Reality project, starting from scratch with a newly programmed platform. Work on the project lasts until 2002. **Mike** also writes new music for the program, at Roughwood Croft, Chalfont St. Giles, Buckinghamshire, England.

-February 10-
Warner Music releases **Mike Oldfield**'s *The Art In Heaven Concert: Live In Berlin*, a concert DVD of the December 31, 1999 show.

-March-
For a planned re-issue of *Tubular Bells* by Virgin Records, engineer David Glasser works on the master tapes at Air Show Mastering, Boulder, Colorado, US.

-March 6-
An interview published on this date in *The Guardian* newspaper sees **Mike Oldfield** discuss his car and driving habits (noted here because as **Mike** spent the next two years on his MusicVR project, there isn't much else to report).

-March – April-
For the forthcoming remaster series of re-issue of **Mike Oldfield**'s back catalogue by Virgin Records, Simon Heyworth remasters the albums *Tubular Bells* to *Heaven's Open* at Chop'Em Out Mastering, London, England.

-Date Unknown-
Warner Music Spain releases a promo CD single of **Mike Oldfield**'s "Amber Light" in Germany.

Germany CD single (PRO1783) promo:
"Amber Light (Edit)"
"Sunlight Shining Through Cloud (Radio Edit)"
"Mastermind"

> "Amber Light (Edit)"
> Written by Mike Oldfield
> Appears on: Promo CD single
> I have not heard this and the sleeve does not list the time.
>
> "Sunlight Shining Through Cloud (Radio Edit)"
> Written by Captain John Newtown (words) & Mike Oldfield (music & words)
> Appears on: Promo CD single
> I have not heard this and the sleeve does not list the time.

-May 9-
VH-1 in the US airs an episode of *Greatest Hits* featuring **Mike Oldfield** introducing some of his videos. For the record, they are:

"Let There Be Light"
"Man In The Rain (Live at Horse Guards Parade)"
"Pictures In The Dark"
"Moonlight Shadow"
"Islands"
"To France"

Mike also talks about the future music videos as possibly being virtual reality-based.

-May 29 & 31-
Virgin Records (UK & Europe) and Caroline Records (North America) re-issues the first batch of **Mike Oldfield**'s albums on HDCD. This series features new liner notes by David Lang (which are inaccurate at times) and does not recreate the original sleeve artwork inside. The spines of the CDs are designed to create the Tubular Bell image when all the albums from *Tubular Bells* to *Heaven's Open* are placed in chronological order (see *Islands* HDCD). The HDCD format is playable on a regular CD player, in addition to an HDCD player (which gives a bit better sound).

Tubular Bells (CDVR2001)
Hergest Ridge (1976 Boxed Remix) (UK MIKECD2) (US CAR 49398)
The Orchestral Tubular Bells (UK MIKECD3) Royal Philharmonic Orchestra (with Mike Oldfield)
Ommadawn (UK MIKECD4) (US CAR 1855) - features an error on "Part Two."
Incantations (UK MIKECD5) (US CAR 1854)
Exposed (UK MIKECD6) (US CAR 1852)

Platinum (UK MIKECD7) (US CAR 1856)
"Platinum (Part One): Airborne"
"Platinum (Part Two): Platinum"
"Platinum (Part Three): Charleston"
"Platinum (Part Four): North Star/Platinum Finale"
"Woodhenge"
"Into Wonderland" - incorrectly listed as "Sally."
"Punkadiddle"
"I Got Rhythm" - a version of the 1930 Gershwin song.

QE2 (UK MIKECD8) (US CAR 1857)

> "Ommadawn (Part Two) (HDCD Error)" 17:14
> Written by Mike Oldfield, "On Horseback" written by Mike Oldfield (words & music) & William Murray (words)
> This remaster features a noticeable error at 11:12, during the 3rd movement of "Part Two."

-July 3-
Virgin Records re-issues the second batch of **Mike Oldfield**'s albums on HDCD in the UK, Europe and North America.

Five Miles Out (UK MIKECD9) (US CAR 1853)
Crises (UK MIKECD10) (US CAR 1850) - "Foreign Affair" not listed, but it is on the CD.
Discovery (UK MIKECD11) (US CAR 1851)
The Killing Fields Original Film Soundtrack (UK MIKECD12)

-July 31-
Virgin Records re-issues the third batch of **Mike Oldfield**'s albums on HDCD in the UK, Europe and North America.

Islands (UK MIKECD13) (US CAR49383)

"The Wind Chimes (Part One and Part Two)"
"Islands" Mike Oldfield Featuring Bonnie Tyler
"Flying Start" Mike Oldfield (with Kevin Ayers)
"North Point" Mike Oldfield Featuring Anita Hegerland
"Magic Touch"
"The Time Has Comes" Mike Oldfield Featuring Anita Hegerland
"When The Night's On Fire" Mike Oldfield Featuring Anita Hegerland

Note: The spine on this re-issue of *Islands* does not coordinate with the Tubular Bell image of the rest of the series. The album's artwork is based on the original 1987 UK and European editions.

Earth Moving (UK MIKECD14) (US CAR49384)

-August 22-
Virgin Records re-issues the fourth batch of **Mike Oldfield**'s albums on HDCD in the UK, Europe and North America.

Amarok (UK MIKECD 15) (US CAR49385)
- Omits William Murray's short story from the liner notes.

Heaven's Open (UK MIKECD 16) (US CAR49386) Michael Oldfield

Note: **Mike** continues to work on the MusicVR project for much of the next year and a half.

The Best Of Tubular Bells

2001

Note: **Mike** is busy working on his Music Virtual Reality computer program all year. The few **Oldfield**-related releases issued in 2001 are noted below. He also does interviews which coincide with the release of *The Best Of Tubular Bells*.

-January-
WEA releases the Enhanced Edition of **Mike Oldfield**'s album *The Songs Of Distant Earth* on CD (4509-9 8524-2) in Europe. This edition features alternate cover artwork.

-April 8-
MusicVR.com releases a demo of **Mike Oldfield**'s Music Virtual Reality program.

-April 26-
BBC Radio 2 broadcasts the programme *Seven More Days That Rocked The World*, which examines *Tubular Bells* and features interview clips of **Mike Oldfield** and others, including Simon Heyworth.

-May 28-
Carl Palmer releases his double album *Anthology: One More Time*, which features the **Mike Oldfield** track "Mount Teidi" (on which Palmer collaborated) and the previously unreleased "Ready Mix,' recorded during the *Five Miles Out* sessions.

-Mid-2001-
Mike Oldfield buys a house near Marlow, Buckinghamshire, England, as inspiration for his MusicVR project (*Tr3s Lunas* sessions). Ultimately, he spends little time there as his regular residence is nearby. He sells the new house 18 months later, in January of 2003.

-Date Unknown-
Virgin Records re-issues **Mike Oldfield**'s album *Tubular Bells* as an SACD in Europe (SACDV 2001). This release is a remaster by Simon Heyworth of the 1975 quadraphonic mix.

-Date Unknown-
Simply Vinyl re-issues **Mike Oldfield**'s album *Ommadawn* on 180 gram vinyl in the UK on LP (SVLP 322).

-June-
Mike Oldfield and his designers complete rendering of the MusicVR environments.

-June 5-
Virgin Records releases the **Mike Oldfield** collection *The Best Of Tubular Bells* in the UK, Europe and North America. The collection is compiled by Simon Heyworth. Track listing as follows:

"Tubular Bells (Part One - 'Introduction') (Original - Edit)"
"Tubular Bells (Part One - 'Fast Guitars + Basses') (Orchestral - Edit)"
    Royal Philharmonic Orchestra (with Mike Oldfield)
"Tubular Bells (Part One - 'Latin + A Minor Tune') (Original – Edit)"
"Tubular Bells (Part One – 'Blues + Thrash') (Exposed – Edit)"
"Tubular Bells (Part One – 'Finale') (Original – Edit)"
"Tubular Bells (Part Two – 'Caveman') (Original – Edit)"
"Tubular Bells (Part Two – 'Ambient Guitars') (Exposed – Edit)"
"Sentinel"
"The Bell"

"Far Above The Clouds (Tubular Bells III – Edit)"
"The Millennium Bell"
"The Sailor's Hornpipe (Single Version)"

> "Tubular Bells (Part One – 'Introduction') (Original - Edit)" 4:42
> Written by Mike Oldfield
> Appears on: The Best Of Tubular Bells
> An interesting experiment, to present segments of the three *Tubular Bells* albums and *The Millennium Bell* and to try to link most of them together (at least for the "Part One" pieces). This edit of the "Introduction" is a bit longer than the version found on Elements and fades out after the build-up and the change to a major key.
>
> "Tubular Bells (Part One - 'Fast Guitars + Basses') (Orchestral – Edit)" 4:42
> Written by Mike Oldfield
> Appears on: The Best Of Tubular Bells
> This collection is the only one that dares place and excerpt from the Orchestral version of the album along side Oldfield's original work. Mike is on record not liking The Orchestral Tubular Bells and his involvement was minimal. Nonetheless, Virgin boldly placed the album along side his while they controlled that part of his back catalogue. If you've not heard this rendition, this edit gives you a good idea of what to expect. There's no fade in or out, because the tracks on the album were meant to flow from one to the other, and they do reasonably well. In the context of the collection, it's interesting to hear this version.
>
> "Tubular Bells (Part One – 'Latin + A Minor Tune') (Original – Edit)" 3:47
> Written by Mike Oldfield
> Appears on: The Best Of Tubular Bells
> As noted, this is the "Latin" and "A Minor Tune" movements. They don't fade in or out.
>
> "Tubular Bells (Part One – 'Finale') (Original – Edit)" 8:29
> Written by Mike Oldfield
> Appears on: The Best Of Tubular Bells
> This is the complete 'Finale,' starting where the previous track, the Exposed Edit, ends off.
>
> "Tubular Bells (Part Two – 'Caveman') (Original – Edit)" 4:46
> Written by Mike Oldfield
> Appears on: The Best Of Tubular Bells
> If you want a good standalone edit of the "Caveman" song, this would be it. No fade in or out.
>
> "Far Above The Clouds (Tubular Bells III – Edit)" 5:30
> Written by Mike Oldfield
> Appears on: The Best Of Tubular Bells
> This edit fades in and continues normally to the end.

-July-
In an interview published this month for *Record Collector* magazine, **Mike Oldfield** discusses the history of *Tubular Bells*. The interview takes place at Roughwood Croft, Chalfont St. Giles, Buckinghamshire, England. **Mike** also shows interviewer Joel McIver a preview of the Music Virtual Reality computer program and notes that the next album will be "pure ambient music" and released with a copy of the program.

-August-
In an interview published this month in *Q* magazine, **Mike Oldfield**, Tom Newman and Simon Heyworth discuss the history of *Tubular Bells*.

-October-
In an interview published this month in *Total Guitar* magazine (Issue 98), **Mike Oldfield** discusses the technical details of his guitar playing style. The interview takes place at Roughwood Croft, Chalfont St. Giles, Buckinghamshire, England.

Tr3s Lunas

2002

-January-
Plan 1 Studios, Germany, announces that **Mike Oldfield** will be recording music there for his MusicVR and album project.

-February 26-
Virgin Records releases a compilation of **Mike Oldfield**'s work simply titled *Collection* as a 2xCD set in the UK (7243 8 12212 2 8). Track listing as follows:

UK *Collection* (7243 8 12212 2 8)
Denmark *The Danish Collection* (7243 8 12145 2 7)
Scandinavia *The Danish Collection* (7243 8 12145 2 7)

CD 1:
"Moonlight Shadow"
"To France (Single Version)"
"Five Miles Out"
"Shadow On The Wall" Mike Oldfield And Roger Chapman
"Foreign Affair"
"Sentinel (Single Restructure)"
"Family Man"
"Heaven's Open" Michael Oldfield
"Pictures In The Dark"
"Innocent"
"Islands" Mike Oldfield (featuring Bonnie Tyler)
"Incantations (Part Four) ('Ode To Cynthia')"

CD 2:
"Tubular Bells (Opening Theme)"
"Étude (Single Edit)"
"Ommadawn (Part One) (Elements Excerpt)"
"In Dulci Jubilo"
"Good News"
"Pran's Theme 1 & 2"
"Pran's Departure"
"Hergest Ridge (Part One – Boxed Remix)"
"Portsmouth"

> "Pran's Theme 1 & 2" 2:24
> Written by Mike Oldfield
> Appears on: Collection
> This is both parts of "Pran's Theme" combined as one track.

-March 21-
Mike Oldfield posts on his website (MikeOldfield.com) that he his finishing off his new album.

-Spring-
Mike Oldfield completes work on his *MusicVR* computer game and his album *Tr3s Lunas*, at Plan 1 Studios, Germany. Featured in the game and album are the vocals of Sally Oldfield, Amar and Jude Sim. Between 2000 and 2002, **Oldfield** composes a good deal of music for the game and reworks some of that music into

the album proper. In the *Tr3s Lunas* electronic press kit, **Oldfield** says "the music for the album doesn't fit with the game," that there isn't enough room on the CD-ROM for densely layered material.

"Thou Art In Heaven" – this track evolved from the "Art In Heaven" music **Mike** wrote from the 1999 Berlin New Year's Eve concert. It features Sally Oldfield on vocals and the St. Petersburg State Symphony Orchestra's strings.

"To Be Free" – The album version features Jude Sim singing the song in English, but she also recorded versions in Spanish, French and German.

Tracks not appearing on the album include the following (with unofficial titles taken from their appearance in the game):

"The Earth Spirit" 2:31
Written by Mike Oldfield
Appears on: MusicVR 1st Episode – Tr3s Lunas (Computer Game)
A mellow, percussion-driven piece, which includes the whispering of "The Earth Spirit is watching you" and "Make a wish" (the latter also appears in "To Be Free"). Mike uses a lot of organic instruments (drums, woodwind, vocal harmonies, etc.) on this track, addition to the synths and guitar.

"Spirit Dance" 2:25
Written by Mike Oldfield
Appears on: MusicVR 1st Episode – Tr3s Lunas (Computer Game)
A rhythmic piece, using sampled beats, layered with synths and guitar. It grooves along nicely, staying evenly in chill-out mode before ending with a fade out a little abruptly.

"Snow Cavern Flight" 5:22
Written by Mike Oldfield
Appears on: MusicVR 1st Episode – Tr3s Lunas (Computer Game)
This piece will sound a bit familiar, it is basically a longer version or alternate mix of the piece that became "Ringscape" on the later album *Light + Shade*.

"Redwings" 2:30
Written by Mike Oldfield
Appears on: MusicVR 1st Episode – Tr3s Lunas (Computer Game)
The wind samples at the beginning sound like they come from "The Source Of Secrets." Over them, Mike plays some moody guitar.

"Sprites" 4:15
Written by Mike Oldfield
Appears on: MusicVR 1st Episode – Tr3s Lunas (Computer Game)
The guitar heard here is very similar to the melody played on the album track "Tr3s Lunas," though it is a different performance. The track starts off melancholy and somewhat downbeat before it picks up halfway through, when the sprites arrive. This track would also later be incorporated into "First Steps" on the *Light + Shade* album.

"Solar System" 5:31
Written by Mike Oldfield
Appears on: MusicVR 1st Episode – Tr3s Lunas (Computer Game)
This track uses a lot of backing track elements also heard in the album track "No Man's Land," but also has its own unique features and different guitar parts. At the 2 minute mark, it shift more into a segment that sounds identical to part of "No Man's Land," before the piano takes over, joined by the guitar, creating a magnificent last movement. The dénouement reprises another segment which also appears in "No Man's Land."

"Requiem Of The Sky" 2:23
Written by Mike Oldfield
Appears on: MusicVR 1st Episode - Tr3s Lunas (Computer Game)
A lot of dramatic layers of vocals in this track, some played backwards, creating a sort of choral whirlwind.

"Moonlight Stroll" 1:58
Written by Mike Oldfield
Appears on: MusicVR 1st Episode - Tr3s Lunas (Computer Game)
This is a short, gentle, piano-dominant piece, with a romantic flavour.

"Lunar Jam" 2:08
Written by Mike Oldfield
Appears on: MusicVR 1st Episode - Tr3s Lunas (Computer Game)
This mixes very computer-y sounds, fast, rhythmic percussion and some sweet guitar playing.

"Joy Ride" 2:50
Written by Mike Oldfield
Appears on: MusicVR 1st Episode - Tr3s Lunas (Computer Game)
A very fun piece, "Joy Ride" is really what it sounds like, a rollercoaster-like musical trip, with twists and turns between heavy synth dance segments and wailing guitar.

"Thou Art In Heaven II" 2:01
Written by Mike Oldfield
Appears on: MusicVR 1st Episode - Tr3s Lunas (Computer Game)
This is basically an edited version of what appears on the album. The edit point is very noticeable at the 29 second mark.

"The Journey" 7:57
Written by Mike Oldfield
Appears on: MusicVR 1st Episode - Tr3s Lunas (Computer Game)
This nearly 8 minute piece features subtly (and not so subtly) shifting moods and textures. Some parts are wholly ambient, some are piano-driven and some are dark and mysterious. There are guitar grooves and short synthetic melodies. The segments are often very short (think *Amarok*, but chilled out and more computer-based). A part around the 3:36 mark is similar to backing track of "Fire Fly" on the album. The ending does build to a longer dramatic conclusion, with wailing guitar and synths.

"Landing" 2:45
Written by Mike Oldfield
Appears on: MusicVR 1st Episode - Tr3s Lunas (Computer Game)
A very folk-styled piece this, despite the sampled heavy drum track.

"Underwater Castle" 1:35
Written by Mike Oldfield
Appears on: MusicVR 1st Episode - Tr3s Lunas (Computer Game)
Naturally, being underwater, Mike re-issues the whale effects heard on *The Songs Of Distant Earth* album. The synth strings are reminiscent of "The Wind Chimes (Part One);" a nice, short piece.

"Butterflies" 3:05
Written by Mike Oldfield
Appears on: MusicVR 1st Episode - Tr3s Lunas (Computer Game)
This piece uses the 3/4 timed backing element heard in "Snow Cavern Flight" and "Ringscape," though the rest of the music is different.

"Rebirth Tunnel" 1:43
 Written by Mike Oldfield
Appears on: MusicVR 1st Episode – Tr3s Lunas (Computer Game)
Another very folk piece, with a recorder, guitar, uilleann bagpipes and some synth strings. Pretty sweet.

-Date Unknown-
Mike Oldfield signs a contract with Warner Music Spain, including the release of *Tr3s Lunas*. The record company also commissions DJs/producers to remix "To Be Free" and "Thou Art In Heaven."

-May 10-
Mike Oldfield marries Fanny Vandekerckhove.

-May 20-
Mike Oldfield releases his "To Be Free" singles in Europe and the UK on WEA and EMI Music Publishing Ltd.

UK CDr single:
"To Be Free (Radio Edit)"
"To Be Free (Pumpin' Dolls Radio Friendly Edit)"

Germany *To Be Free: The Remixes* 12" single (0927 467750):
"To Be Free (Pumpin' Dolls To The Top Club Mix)"
"To Be Free (Pumpin' Dolls Argento Dub Mix)"
"To Be Free (Soultronik Hard Floor Cibervetido Mix)"
"To Be Free (Soultronik Mix-tical Mix)"

Spain *To Be Free: The Remixes* 12" single (0927 467750):
"To Be Free (Pumpin' Dolls To The Top Club Mix)"
"To Be Free (Pumpin' Dolls Argento Dub Mix)"
"To Be Free (Soultronik Hard Floor Cibervetido Mix)"
"To Be Free (Soultronik Mix-tical Mix)"

12" single (SAM 00659) promo:
"To Be Free (Soultronik Hard Floor Cibervetido Mix)"
"To Be Free (Soultronik Mix-tical Mix)"
Note: territory of release not noted on the label.

Europe CD single (0927483652):
"To Be Free (Pumpin' Dolls Radio Friendly Edit)"
"To Be Free (Radio Edit)"

Europe CD single (PRO 3208) promo:
"To Be Free (Pumpin' Dolls Radio Friendly Edit)"
"To Be Free (Soultronik Mix-tical Radio Edit)"
"To Be Free (Soultronik Hard Floor Cibervetido Radio Edit)"
"To Be Free (Pumpin' Dolls To The Top Club Mix)"
"To Be Free (Pumpin' Dolls Argento Dub Mix)"
"To Be Free (Soultronik Hard Floor Cibervetido Mix)"
"To Be Free (Soultronik Mix-tical Mix)"

Europe CD single (PRO 3152) promo:
"To Be Free (Radio Edit)"
"To Be Free"

Sweden *To Be Free: DJ Remixes* CDr single:
"To Be Free (Pumpin' Dolls Radio Friendly Edit)"
"To Be Free (Soultronik Mix-tical Radio Edit)"
"To Be Free (Soultronik Hard Floor Cibervetido Radio Edit)"
"To Be Free (Pumpin' Dolls To The Top Club Mix)"
"To Be Free (Pumpin' Dolls Argento Dub Mix)"
"To Be Free (Soultronik Hard Floor Cibervetido Mix)"
"To Be Free (Soultronik Mix-tical Mix)"

Spain *To Be Free: The Remixes* CD Maxi-single (0927467752):
"To Be Free (Radio Edit)"
"To Be Free (Pumpin' Dolls To The Top Club Mix)"
"To Be Free (Pumpin' Dolls Argento Dub Mix)"
"To Be Free (Soultronik Hard Floor Cibervetido Mix)"
"To Be Free (Soultronik Mix-tical Mix)"

"To Be Free (Radio Edit)" 3:56
Written by Mike Oldfield
Appears on: Tr3s Lunas, Promo CD single, CD single, CD Maxi-single; The Best Of: 1992 - 2003
This edit cuts a few seconds out in the middle and fades out early, but is otherwise identical to the album version.

"To Be Free (Pumpin' Dolls To The Top Club Mix)" 9:30
Written by Mike Oldfield; Remixed by Pumpin' Dolls
Appears on: *To Be Free: The Remixes* 12" single:
This is a great remix! It says faithful to the original in that it adds percussion and a more uptempo backbeat to the track and all of the additional production serves to enhance the song, rather than pulling a few samples and working them into a dance mix that has nothing to do with the song. Even if club mixes aren't your thing, I expect you'll find this a more than worthy effort.

"To Be Free (Pumpin' Dolls Radio Friendly Edit)" 3:25
Written by Mike Oldfield; Remixed by Pumpin' Dolls
Appears on: Promo CD single, To Be Free: The Remixes Promo CD single
A greatly shorted version of the "Pumpin' Dolls To The Top Club Mix" which doesn't lose any time getting to the point. If the full club mix is too long for you, this might be more up your alley.

"To Be Free (Pumpin' Dolls Argento Dub Mix) 8:11
Written by Mike Oldfield; Remixed by Pumpin' Dolls
Appears on: To Be Free - The Remixes 12", Promo and CD Maxi-single
Pumpin' Dolls takes their new backing track and amps up the additional production, creating a hard and heavy dub. There's only a few faint whispers of Jude Sim saying "Make a wish" and not much else that sounds like Mike Oldfield. After about halfway through, it really stops being interesting as it repeats individual sections.

"To Be Free (Soultronik Hard Floor Cibervetido Mix)" 7:02
Written by Mike Oldfield; Remixed by Soultronik
Appears on: To Be Free - The Remixes 12", 12" Promo, Promo CD & CD Maxi-single
A laid back mix that incorporates samples of Sim's vocals, a excerpt of the original backing vocal track (which is the only interesting few seconds on the piece) and nothing else of Oldfield's original piece, this version really demonstrates that the idea of making dance club mixes of Mike's music during this era was running its course.

"To Be Free (Soultronik Hard Floor Cibervetido Radio Edit)" 4:02
Written by Mike Oldfield; Remixed by Soultronik
Appears on: To Be Free: The Remixes Promo CD single:

This is a shortened version of the "Cibervetido Mix."

"To Be Free (Soultronik Mix-tical Mix)" 5:05
Written by Mike Oldfield; Remixed by Soultronik
Appears on: To Be Free – The Remixes 12", 12" Promo, Promo CD & Maxi-single; The Best Of: 1992 - 2003
Well, I'll say this much: this mix preserves Jude Sim's lead vocals, though it's slowed to match the tempo of the new backing track and is somewhat processed. The additional production is a bit bland, so having all the lyrics present really doesn't help.

"To Be Free (Soultronik Mix-tical Radio Edit)" 3:10
Written by Mike Oldfield; Remixed by Soultronik
Appears on: To Be Free: The Remixes Promo CD single:
This is a shorter variation of the "Mix-tical Mix".

-June 3-
Mike Oldfield releases his album *Tr3s Lunas* in Europe and Canada on WEA on both a CD (no CD-ROM material) and 2xCD set, with the second disc being a demo copy of *MusicVR*. Track listing as follows:

Europe *Tr3s Lunas* 2xCD (0927 458922)
Europe *Tr3s Lunas* CD (0927 476985)
Canada *Tr3s Lunas* 2xCD (W 2 45892)

CD 1: *Tr3s Lunas*
"Misty"
"No Man's Land"
"Return To The Origin"
"Landfall"
"Viper"
"Turtle Island"
"To Be Free"
"Fire Fly"
"Tr3s Lunas"
"Daydream"
"Thou Art In Heaven"
"Sirius"
"No Man's Land (Reprise)"
Bonus Track:
"To Be Free (Radio Edit)"

CD 2:
CD-ROM: *Music VR 1st Episode - Tr3s Lunas* (Demo)

Note: the CD-ROM is only PC compatible. To activate the full version, you had to follow the onscreen instructions and register with Tubular.net.

-June 18-
Mike Oldfield sets up his studio to work on the re-recording of *Tubular Bells*, at Roughwood Croft, Chalfont St. Giles, Buckinghamshire, England.

-Mid-June-
Mike Oldfield begins work on re-recording *Tubular Bells* for the 30th Anniversary in 2003. Sessions take place at Roughwood Croft, Chalfont St. Giles, Buckinghamshire, England, and last until February 2003

-August-
In an interview with BBC Radio London, **Mike Oldfield** says he's in the middle of the re-recording *Tubular Bells*.

-August 5-
Sanctuary re-issues **The Sallyangie**'s album *Children Of The Sun* as a 2xCD set in the US (06076 81209-2). Track listing as follows:

CD 1:
"Strangers"
"Lady Mary"
"Children Of The Sun"
"A Lover For All Seasons"
"River Song"
"Banquet On The Water"
"Balloons"
"Midsummer Night's Happening"
"Love In Ice Crystals"
"Changing Colours"
"Chameleon"
"Milk Bottle"
"Murder Of The Children Of San Francisco"
Bonus Track "Twilight"
Bonus Track "Song Of The Healer"
"Strangers (Reprise)"

CD 2:
"Children Of The Sun (Minus Intro)"
"Mrs. Moon And The Thatched Shop"
"Branches"
"A Sad Song For Rosie"
"Colour Of The World"
"Two Ships" - a cover of the 1968 Maria Dallas song.

-August 26-
Mike Oldfield releases his *Thou Art In Heaven: The Remixes* singles in Spain.

Spain Maxi-CD single (0927483732):
"Thou Art In Heaven (Radio Edit)"
"Thou Art In Heaven (Pumpin' Dolls vs Mighty Mike Club Mix) (Radio Edit)"
"Thou Art In Heaven (Soultronik-Stethoscope Radio Edit)"
"Thou Art In Heaven (Pumpin' Dolls vs Mighty Mike Club Mix)"
"Thou Art In Heaven (Soultronik-Stethoscope Mix)"
"To Be Free (Spanish Version - Radio Edit)"
"To Be Free (French Version - Radio Edit)"
"To Be Free (German Version - Radio Edit)"

> "Thou Art In Heaven (Radio Edit)" 3:43
> Written by Mike Oldfield
> Appears on: Spanish CD single; The Best Of: 1992 - 2003
> This song reunites Sally and Mike yet again. In the years since the end of The Sallyangie, they've appeared on each other's albums and both have come a long way in all that time. The song itself grew out of Mike's collaboration with the Art In Heaven lightshow at the Millennium concert and he tries recreate elements of that performance, but in keeping with the chill-out concept of the album. This edit, though, removes a large portion of the song from the beginning and the end,

including the saxophone guitar, which is unfortunate, because what's left kind of has nowhere new to go until it just fades out early.

"Thou Art In Heaven (Pumpin' Dolls vs Mighty Mike Club Mix)" 9:50
Written by Mike Oldfield; Remixed by Pumpin' Dolls / Mighty Mike
Appears on: Spanish CD single; The Best Of: 1992 - 2003
I'm not sure if it was intentional (you know, to reflect the "vs" credit of the two factions who remixed it. I know "vs" is a common credit in remix/DJ culture), but it really does seem that there are two forces at work in this mix, both wrestling for control. I don't know who's responsible for what parts, or if everyone just worked together happily, but the dance club mix elements and the more faithful remixing of the original really swing back and forth for nearly ten minutes, neither ever really gaining the upper hand.

"Thou Art In Heaven (Pumpin' Dolls vs Mighty Mike Radio Edit)" 4:39
Written by Mike Oldfield; Remixed by Pumpin' Dolls / Mighty Mike
Appears on: Spanish CD single
This version condenses the "Cub Mix" into an easier to manage four and a half minutes. The result is much better than the full "Club Mix," as it never has to chance deviate far from the idea that the mix should support the original. There's a lot of the original woven through the additional production material and for the most part it's a respectful harmony. Of all the "Thou Art In Heaven" mixes and edits, this possibly the best.

 "Thou Art In Heaven (Soultronik - Stethoscope Mix)" 8:25
Written by Mike Oldfield; Remixed by Soultronik
Appears on: Spanish CD single
This mix is pretty much the familiar piano and "Now...thou art in heaven" samples woven through a pretty standard-sounding backing track. At one point near the middle, it gets your hopes up when the original backbeat comes in, but it is overtaken again be the club mix and we're back in dance remix territory.

"Thou Art In Heaven (Soultronik - Stethoscope Radio Edit)" 3:44
Written by Mike Oldfield; Remixed by Soultronik
Appears on: Spanish CD single
This edit shortens the full "Stethoscope Mix".

"To Be Free (Spanish Version - Radio Edit)" 3:58
Written by Mike Oldfield
Appears on: Spanish CD single
Jude Sim sings the verses in Spanish. The chorus is identical to the standard version, as is the "Make a wish" whispering. The edit replicates the English version of the Radio Mix, fading out at the same point.

"To Be Free (French Version - Radio Edit)" 3:58
Written by Mike Oldfield
Appears on: Spanish CD single
Jude Sim sings the verses in French. The chorus and whispering remain in English. It fades out at the same point as the English Radio Edit.

"To Be Free (German Version - Radio Edit)" 3:57
Written by Mike Oldfield
Appears on: Spanish CD single
Same as above, only sung in German instead of Spanish or French.

-September 7-
John Cleese records his MC vocal for the *Tubular Bells* re-recording project, from Santa Barbara, California, US. Reportedly, **Mike Oldfield** is in touch with him via telephone for these sessions. The recordings are then sent to **Oldfield** via internet file transfer. **Mike** has a rough version of "Part One" completed and has started "Part Two" by this date.

-October 8-
Castle Music re-issues **The Sallyangie**'s album *Children Of The Sun* as a 2xCD set in the UK (CMDDD 545). Track listing as follows:

CD 1:
"Strangers"
"Lady Mary"
"Children Of The Sun"
"A Lover For All Seasons"
"River Song"
"Banquet On The Water"
"Balloons"
"Midsummer Night's Happening"
"Love In Ice Crystals"
"Changing Colours"
"Chameleon"
"Milk Bottle"
"Murder Of The Children Of San Francisco"
Bonus Track "Twilight"
Bonus Track "Song Of The Healer"
"Strangers (Reprise)"

CD 2:
"Children Of The Sun (Minus Intro)"
"Mrs. Moon And The Thatched Shop"
"Branches"
"A Sad Song For Rosie"
"Colour Of The World"
"Two Ships" - a cover of the 1968 Maria Dallas song.

-November-
In an article published this month in *Sound On Sound* magazine it is noted that **Mike Oldfield** is currently working on the re-recording of *Tubular Bells*.

-November 28-
Mike Oldfield is nearly finished re-recording *Tubular Bells* by this point, at Roughwood Croft, Chalfont St. Giles, Buckinghamshire, England. **Mike** also notes in the May 2003 issue of *Dark Star* (the Official Mike Oldfield magazine) that he has started the next MusicVR project by this date.

Tubular Bells 2003

2003

-January-
The following **Kevin Ayers And The Whole World** track is worked on at The Audio Archiving Company, London, England.
"Hat" – recorded in 1970 during the *Shooting At The Moon* sessions, Take 4 of this track is mixed for the forthcoming re-issue of the album.

-February-
Mike Oldfield completes work in his re-recording of *Tubular Bells* at Roughwood Croft, Chalfont St. Giles, Buckinghamshire, England. Sally Oldfield provides vocals on the album.

-Spring-
Mike Oldfield works on the following at for his MusicVR game *The Tube World*, at Roughwood Croft, Chalfont St. Giles, Buckinghamshire, England:
"Resolution" – **Mike** works on this song as the 2003 Invasion of Iraq occurs (according to his notes posted on his website for the release of *Light + Shade*).

-April 24-
Mike Oldfield releases his promo CD single "Tubular Bells 2003: Introduction" in Spain on WEA.

Spain 1-track CD single (PR03962):
"Tubular Bells 2003: Introduction (Radio Edit)"

> "Tubular Bells 2003: Introduction (Radio Edit)" 3:43
> Written by Mike Oldfield
> Appears on: Spain 1-track CD single; The Best Of: 1992 - 2003
> This remix rebuilds the "Introduction" of *TB2003* as a dance club track, but the result is actually pretty good. If you want an energetic rendition of the opening theme, this is the mix for you!

-May 22-
In a live radio interview in Spain on *Los40*, **Mike Oldfield** mentions he's working on a videogame titled *The Tube World*, planning for a release by the end of the year.

-May 26 & 27-
Mike Oldfield releases his album *Tubular Bells 2003* in Europe, the UK and North America. Various formats are issued. Track listing as follows:

Europe *Tubular Bells 2003* CD (2564-60204-2)
US *Tubular Bells 2003* CD (R2 60204)
US *Tubular Bells 2003* Promo CDr

Tubular Bells 2003 CD (Copy-protected CD)
"Introduction"
"Fast Guitars"
"Basses"
"Latin"
"A Minor Tune"
"Blues"
"Thrash"
"Jazz"

"Ghost Bells"
"Russian"
"Finale"
"Harmonics"
"Peace"
"Bagpipe Guitars"
"Caveman"
"Ambient Guitars"
"The Sailor's Hornpipe"

Canada *Tubular Bells 2003* CD (2 60204) (non-Copy-protected CD)

Europe & UK *Tubular Bells 2003* CD+DVD (2 49921)
CD: *Tubular Bells 2003* (Copy-protected CD)
DVD: 5.1 Digital tracks + Video
"Introduction" 5.1 Digital
"Fast Guitars" 5.1 Digital
"Basses" 5.1 Digital
"Tubular Bells 2003: Introduction (Radio Edit)" Video

Canada *Tubular Bells 2003* CD+DVD (0927499212)
CD: *Tubular Bells 2003* (non-Copy-protected CD)
DVD: 5.1 Digital tracks + Video
"Introduction" 5.1 Digital
"Fast Guitars" 5.1 Digital
"Basses" 5.1 Digital
"Tubular Bells 2003: Introduction (Radio Edit)" Video

Europe & UK *The Complete Tubular Bells* 4xCD+DVD Edition (2564602052)
CD 1: *Tubular Bells 2003* (Copy-protected CD)
CD 2: *Tubular Bells II*
CD 3: *Tubular Bells III*
DVD: 5.1 Digital tracks + Video

Note: the copy-protected CD, which is a new manufacturing technique in the industry (done so in an attempt to stop music piracy and file sharing), causes a lot of problems for buyers, who find the CDs won't play in computers and may even cause damage to CD and DVD players. *Tubular Bells 2003* was among many artists' albums released during this period with copy-protection and reports of playback issues were common. The Canadian pressing of TB2003 did not feature copy protection and played normally.

-Date Unknown-
EMI Gold re-issues *The Orchestral Tubular Bells* by The Royal Philharmonic Orchestra (with **Mike Oldfield**) in Europe, with new artwork and mastered at EMI Uden.

-Date Unknown-
Harvest re-issues the **Kevin Ayers And The Whole World** album *Shooting At The Moon* on copy-protected CD (07243-58353-2-0) in the UK. Track listing as follows:

"May I?"
"Rheinhardt & Geraldine/Colores Para Dolores"
"Lunatics Lament"
"Pisser Dans un Violon"
"The Oyster And The Flying Fish" – does not feature **Mike Oldfield**.
"Underwater" – does not feature **Mike Oldfield**.
"Clarence In Wonderland"

"Red Green And You Blue"
"Shooting At The Moon"
"Gemini Child"
"Puis Je?"
"Butterfly Dance"
"Jolie Madame" – does not feature **Mike Oldfield**.
"Hat"

-June-July-
An article in *High Fidelity Review* says that 5.1 Digital Surround Sound Mixes of *Tubular Bells 2003* are being worked on these months at Abbey Road Studios, London, England.

-June 10-
MikeOldfield.com releases a demo version of *The Tube World* MusicVR game for download.

-August 5-
Warner Music Spain and Rhino Records re-issue **Mike Oldfield**'s album *Tubular Bells 2003* on CD without copy protection, in Europe, the UK and North America.

Note: Much of the rest of the year is spent working on the next MusicVR project, currently titled *The Tube World*. Fanny Oldfield later discusses in her online diary her involvement in this project.

-Date Unknown-
Harvest re-issues the Kevin Ayers album *Whatevershebringswesing* (07243-582778-2-1) on CD, featuring **Mike Oldfield**. Track listing as follows:

"There Is Loving/Among Us/There Is Loving (Reprise)"
"Margaret"
"Oh My"
"Song From The Bottom Of A Well"
"Whatevershebringswesing"
"Stranger In Blue Suede Shoes"
"Champagne Cowboy Blues"
"Lullabye"
Bonus Tracks
"Stars"
"Don't Sing No More Sad Songs"
"Fake Mexican Tourist Blues"
"Stranger In Blue Suede Shoes (Early Mix)"

Note: "Stars" is the only bonus track to feature **Mike Oldfield**.

-November 28-
Transatlantic Records re-issues **The Sallyangie**'s album *Children Of The Sun* as a 2xCD set in Japan (ARC-7037/38). Track listing as follows:

CD 1:
"Strangers"
"Lady Mary"
"Children Of The Sun"
"A Lover For All Seasons"
"River Song"
"Banquet On The Water"
"Balloons"
"Midsummer Night's Happening"

"Love In Ice Crystals"
"Changing Colours"
"Chameleon"
"Milk Bottle"
"Murder Of The Children Of San Francisco"
 "Strangers (Reprise)"

CD 2:
"Children Of The Sun (Minus Intro)"
"Mrs. Moon And The Thatched Shop"
"Branches"
"A Sad Song For Rosie"
"Colour Of The World"
"Two Ships" – a cover of the 1968 Maria Dallas song.
"Twilight"
"Song Of The Healer"

-December 4-
MikeOldfield.com announces that *The Tube World* MusicVR project is nearing completion.

Maestro

2004

-January-
Mike Oldfield completes work on his new MusicVR project, previously titled *The Tube World*, but now called *Maestro*, at Roughwood Croft, Chalfont St. Giles, Buckinghamshire, England. Fanny Oldfield was also heavily involved in the project.

-January 26-
WEA & Warner Music Spain release editions of *Tubular Bells 2003* in Europe and the UK.

Europe & UK *Tubular Bells 2003* DVD-Audio (5.1 Digital) (2564 60204-5)
"Tubular Bells (Long)"
"Caveman Lead-In"
"Caveman"
"Peace Demo A"
"Peace Demo B"
"Sentinel (Live At Edinburgh Castle)"
"Far Above The Clouds (Live At Horse Guards Parade)"

Europe & UK *Tubular Bells 2003* CD+DVD (0927499212)
CD: *Tubular Bells 2003* (non-Copy-protected CD)
DVD: 5.1 Digital tracks + Video
"Introduction" 5.1 Digital
"Fast Guitars" 5.1 Digital
"Basses" 5.1 Digital
"Tubular Bells 2003: Introduction (Radio Edit)" Video

Also released on this date is the 3xDVD set *The Mike Oldfield DVD Collection* in Europe and the UK.

DVD 1: *Tubular Bells 2003* (5.1 Digital)

DVD 2: *Tubular Bells II (Live At Edinburgh Castle)*
Tubular Bells III (Live at Horse Guards Parade)

DVD 3: *The Art In Heaven Concert: Live In Berlin*

-January 31-
MikeOldfield.com is updated and the name of the new MusicVR game is announced as *Maestro*.

-February 24-
Warner Strategic Marketing releases the DVD-Audio (R9 60204) of *Tubular Bells 2003* in the US. It has the same content at the European and UK release.

-March 10-
Jake Oldfield is born to **Mike** and Fanny Oldfield

-March 14-
Mike Oldfield releases his MusicVR computer game *Maestro*, for download via his website. The official launch is April 12, though the game is made available for download in advance. The game features music written specifically for it.

"Maestro"
Written by Mike Oldfield
Appears on: MusicVR – Maestro
The music heard throughout the game, similar to the *Tr3s Lunas* compositions, vary between synthy computer-heavy pieces to upbeat chill out to moody atmospheric pieces. It pretty much sounds like what Mike was doing at the time in general, including elements recorded for *Tubular Bells 2003*. Some of the music would be worked into his double album *Light + Shade*.

-May 25-
Mike Oldfield posts a message on his online forum at MikeOldfield.com that he is in the middle of working on his new album.

-July-
Mike Oldfield contacts Fruity Loops, the software company whose program **Oldfield** is using on his new album, and asks if he can work with part of an existing piece of demo music available in the program.
"Slipstream – **Mike** created this piece from the existing Fruity Loops demo titled "Highpass," written by Jason Cluts. **Oldfield** contacted Cluts directly via email to discuss the track.

-August 12-
Mike Oldfield sends Jason Cluts a copy of the "first draft" of his "Highpass" remix, "Slipstream." The date is shared by Cluts during an online chat with fans in October 2005 and he says it was about a month after the initial contact by **Oldfield**.

"Slipstream (Early Mix)"
Written by Mike Oldfield ("Highpass" written by Jason Cluts)
Appears on: Unreleased
Cluts notes in the October 2005 chat that he has an early mix of "Slipstream" which is close to the finished version, but the piano part (near the 2 minute mark) is different.

-Mid-2004-
Mike Oldfield continues work on his new album. One of the working titles is *Quicksilver*. Another title he considers (according to a 2005 interview) is *Breakfast In Bed*. Recording takes place at Roughwood Croft, Chalfont St. Giles, Buckinghamshire, England. He reworks some tracks previously recorded for the MusicVR games *Tr3s Lunas* and *Maestro*.

-Date Unknown-
Mike Oldfield sells off most of the gear in his home studio at Roughwood Croft, Chalfont St. Giles, Buckinghamshire, England, converting it to a digital, computer software-based facility.

Light + Shade

2005

-February – March-
As Pope John Paul II falls ill, **Mike Oldfield** is working on the following for his next album, at Roughwood Croft, Chalfont St. Giles, Buckinghamshire, England:
"Our Father" – this started as a *Tr3s Lunas* MusicVR piece that **Oldfield** began rewriting at the time of the Pope's illness, wherein it became this track. The Pope dies on April 2 this year.

-Dates Unknown-
Mike Oldfield works on the following at Roughwood Croft, Chalfont St. Giles, Buckinghamshire, England:
"Nightshade" – Christopher von Deylen records additional bass and drum keyboard arrangements for the track. **Oldfield** and von Deylen agreed to each record on the other's album.

Mike Oldfield records guitar for von Deylen's album's *Tag und Nacht* (English: *Night And Day*), on the track "Morgentau." **Oldfield** works from Roughwood Croft, Chalfont St. Giles, Buckinghamshire, England, recording his parts at his home studio and sending them to von Deylen via internet file sharing. The *Tag und Nacht* sessions last four days, according to von Deylen.

-May 3-
Pierre Moerlen dies of natural causes. Moerlen was percussionist on the **Mike Oldfield** albums *Ommadawn*, *Incantations*, *Exposed*, *Platinum*, *Crises* and *Islands*, as well as appearing with him live.

-May 13-
Mike Oldfield announces that he is putting the finishing touches on his new double album, one disc of "Ambient" music and the other of "Chill Out" music, with 18 tracks in all. A tentative title is *Quicksilver*.

-Summer-
Mike Oldfield finishes recording his new album (*Light + Shade* sessions) at Roughwood Croft, Chalfont St. Giles, Buckinghamshire, England. Tracks worked on during the sessions since 2004 include:
"First Steps" – this is a mix of pieces written for the MusicVR game *Tr3s Lunas*, including "Sprites." The same melody also appears in the track "Tr3s Lunas."
"Sunset" – this is a variation on a *Maestro* piece.
"Romance" – this piece includes part of a classical guitar piece by the same name, the authorship of which is disputed by scholars and is currently classified as Anonymous.
"Ringscape" – This track is a re-edit/alternate mix of the *Tr3s Lunas* game piece "Snow Cavern Flight." Robyn Smith works on the track.
"Près De Toi" – this variation on "Closer" would be a bonus track on the album
"Lakme (Fruity Loops)" – this version of the "Flower Duet" from the 1883 opera *Lakmé* by Léo Delibes would be a bonus track on the album.
"Cook's Tune"

Mike reports that a 5.1 Mix of the album is also created, but it so far remains unreleased.

-Date Unknown-
Mike Oldfield signs a deal with Mercury Records.

-Date Unknown-
Mercury Records issues a 2xCDr promo edition of **Mike Oldfield**'s forthcoming album with the working title *Chillout + Cruise?*. Track listing as follows:

CD 1: *Chillout*
"Angelique"
"Blackbird"
"The Gate"
"Près De Toi" – listed as "Près De Toi (Traditional)."
"Surfing"
"First Steps"
"Sunset"
"Rocky"

CD 2: *Cruise?*
"Slipstream"
"Resolution"
"Quicksilver"
"Tears Of An Angels"
"Romance" – listed as "Romance (Traditional)."
"Ringscape"
"Nightshade"

> "Près De Toi" 3:56
> Written by Mike Oldfield
> Appears on: Chillout + Cruise? Promo CD; Light + Shade (UK Edition)
> This is an alternate version of the track "Closer," a different recording with different production. Mike says in the notes for each album track, posted on his website for the album's launch, that this was his first arrangement hymn he heard during a visit to Ypes.

-September 3-
Mike Oldfield releases the promo CD single "Surfing" in Spain.

Spain CD single (SURFCJ1) promo:
"Surfing (Promo Edit)"

> "Surfing (Promo Edit)" 3:00
> Written by Mike Oldfield
> Appears on: Spain Promo CD single
> This is an edit of the album version, removing nearly half the song. It still sounds okay. The sleeve does not list the edit. In fact, the sleeve incorrectly lists the album's track length of 5:37.

-September 26 & 27-
Mike Oldfield releases his 2xCD double album *Light + Shade* in the UK, Europe, Canada and Australia. Several editions are issued. Track listing as follows:

UK *Light + Shade* Enhanced 2xCD (9873642)

CD 1: *Light*
"Angelique"
"Blackbird"
"The Gate"
"First Steps"
"Closer"
"Our Father"
"Rocky"
"Sunset"
Bonus Track:
"Près De Toi"
CD-ROM: U-MYX
"Quicksilver (U-MYX)"
"Our Father (U-MYX)"
"Slipsteam (U-MYX)"
"Angelique (U-MYX)"

CD 2: *Shade*
"Quicksilver"
"Resolution"
"Slipstream"
"Surfing"
"Tears Of An Angels"
"Romance"
"Ringscape"
"Nightshade"
Bonus Track:
"Lakme (Fruity Loops)"

Note: U-MYX (now GoMix) is software that allows the user to mix the multitracks of the songs, creating their on remixes.

Europe *Light + Shade* 2xCD (9873810)
Australia *Light + Shade* 2xCD (9873810)
Canada *Light + Shade* 2xCD (0249873810)

CD 1: *Light*
"Angelique"
"Blackbird"
"The Gate"
"First Steps"
"Closer"
"Our Father"
"Rocky"
"Sunset"

CD 2: *Shade*
"Quicksilver"
"Resolution"
"Slipstream"
"Surfing"
"Tears Of An Angel"
"Romance"
"Ringscape"
"Nightshade"

German *Light + Shade* 2xCDr
CD 1: *Light*
"Angelique"
"Blackbird"
"The Gate"
"First Steps"
"Closer"
"Our Father"
"Rocky"
"Sunset"

CD 2: *Shade*
"Quicksilver"
"Resolution"
"Slipstream"
"Surfing"
"Tears Of An Angel"
"Romance"
"Ringscape"
"Nightshade (German Promo Version)"
German Digital Bonus Track: "Cook's Tune"

"Nightshade (German Promo Version)" 5:42
Written by Mike Oldfield
Appears on: Light + Shade (German Promo Edition)
This is a different mix than appears on the retail releases of the album. There's different production and additional elements unheard in the standard version. And the track is about 30 seconds longer.

"Lakme (Fruity Loops)"
Written by Léo Delibes (arr. Oldfield)
Appears on: Light + Shade (UK Edition)
From the opera *Lakmé*, this is a rendition of the "Flower Duet" from Act 1, sung by Lakmé and Millika. Mike used the software Fruity Loops to mix the track, hence the subtitle. It's a beautiful melody and Mike's version takes it into the electronic age.

"Cook's Tune" 3:15
Written by Mike Oldfield
Appears on: Light + Shade (German Digital Edition)
The release of this bonus track proved frustrating to fans as it was only released on a German website and limited the territories that could download it. There were also problem with the payment system, so even those fans in Germany seemed to have issues getting it. Fortunately, the few who did get it happily shared the track online and the rest of the work got to hear it eventually. The piece is upbeat folk number, like a jig, with a flavour along the lines of "Portsmouth" or "Rite Of Man."

-October 24-
Virgin Records releases **Mike Oldfield**'s live 2 disc DVD *Exposed*, from the April 25/26, 1979 Birmingham concert.

-October 28-
Christopher von Deylen releases his album *Tag und Nacht* as Schiller, in Germany on CD (06024 9874077 4) on Island Records, featuring **Mike Oldfield** on the track "Morgentau."

"Morgentau" 4:09
Written by Christopher von Deylen
Appears on: Tag und Nacht
Mike plays guitar on this spacey trance number and it fits perfectly. As Mike was doing a lot of computer-based music by this point, he clearly understood what von Deylen was going for and the collaboration between the two creates a piece that goes far beyond the "synthetic" music genre.

-Date Unknown-
Mike Oldfield begins working on a new music project at Roughwood Croft, Chalfont St. Giles, Buckinghamshire, England.

The Platinum Collection

2006

-January 14-
In a live online chat with Christopher von Deylen (AKA Schiller), he makes mention that **Mike Oldfield** recently moved from Roughwood Croft, Chalfont St. Giles, Buckinghamshire, to a new house in Bath, Somerset, England. **Oldfield** mentions the move with his family from Roughwood Croft in his autobiography.

-January 26-
Mike Oldfield posts on his website (MikeOldfield.com) that he is currently working on his autobiography with co-writer Jon Collins. He says he has three and a half more years to complete a new album, giving his current project time to "evolve and mature."

-February 23-
In an interview with Steve Wright, broadcast on this date on BBC Radio 2, **Mike Oldfield** says he's currently working on a long, three-part instrumental, with no drum loops.

-March 13-
Virgin Records releases the 3xCD set of **Mike Oldfield**'s work, *The Platinum Collection* in the UK and Europe. A number of the excerpts used previously appeared on past collections, such as *The Complete Mike Oldfield* and *Elements* (both the collection and the boxed set). Track listing as follows:

UK & Europe *The Platinum Collection* 3xCD (MIKECDX17)

CD 1:
"Tubular Bells (Opening Theme)"
"Excerpt from Tubular Bells (Part One) (The Complete...Edit)"
"The Sailor's Hornpipe (Single Version)"
"Hergest Ridge (Part One - Boxed Remix) (Elements Excerpt)"
"Ommadawn (Part One) (Elements Excerpt)"
"Ommadawn (Part One) (Episodes Extract)"
"In Dulci Jubilo"
"Don Alfonso"
"Portsmouth"
"William Tell Overture"
"Cuckoo Song" Mike Oldfield with Les Penning
"Incantations (Part Four) ('Ode To Cynthia')"
"Platinum (Part Four): North Star / Platinum Finale"
"Woodhenge (Single Version)"

CD 2:
"Moonlight Shadow (Extended Version)"
"Blue Peter" - a cover of the 1958 TV show theme.
"Guilty (Long Version)"
"Arrival" - a cover of the 1976 ABBA instrumental.
"Wonderful Land" - a cover of The Shadows' 1962 instrumental.
"Sheba"
"Five Miles Out"
"Family Man"
"Mistake" The Mike Oldfield Group
"Shadow On The Wall (12" Version)" Mike Oldfield And Roger Chapman

"Foreign Affair"
"In High Places" Mike Oldfield Featuring Jon Anderson
"Crime Of Passion"
"Tricks Of The Light"
"To France (Extended Version)"
"Étude"
"Evacuation + Legend" – "Legend" is a hidden track which appears after a bit of silence.

CD 3:
"Sentinel (Single Restructure)"
"Pictures In The Dark (Extended Version)"
"Shine (Extended Version)"
"Islands (12" Mix)" Mike Oldfield Featuring Bonnie Tyler
"Flying Start (12" Version)" Mike Oldfield (with Kevin Ayers)
"The Time Has Comes (12" Version)" Mike Oldfield Featuring Anita Hegerland
"Innocent (12" Mix)"
"Earth Moving (Club Version)"
"Amarok (Africa I)"
"Heaven's Open" Michael Oldfield – incorrectly listed as the 12" Mix
"Hibernaculum (Single Version)"
"Women Of Ireland" – a cover of the 1969 music by Seán Ó Riada.
"Far Above The Clouds (UK Single Edit)"
"The Millennium Bell (Radio Edit)"
"To Be Free (Radio Edit)"

-May 15-
Eagle Vision and Montreux Sounds release **Mike Oldfield**'s concert DVD *Live At Montreux 1981* as part of their *Live In Montreux* DVD series. The concert is the July 5, 1981, show at the Montreux Jazz Festival.

-Date Unknown-
Water re-issues the Kevin Ayers album *Whatevershebringswesing* on CD (water190), featuring **Mike Oldfield.**

-September-
Röyksopp begins work remixing tracks which would became their *Back To Mine* album. Two of the tracks worked on during the albums sessions (the duration of which is unknown) are **Mike Oldfield**'s "Platinum (Part Three): Charleston" and "Platinum (Part Four): North Star / Platinum Finale."

-October 27-
Mike Oldfield rehearses the Night Of The Proms concert festival at Sportpaleis, Antwerp, Belgium. Miriam Stockley is also among the ensemble and sings "Moonlight Shadow" for this and the upcoming shows. **Oldfield**'s segment is about 30 minutes long.

-December 1 & 2-
Mike Oldfield performs in the Night Of The Proms concert festival at Color Line Arena, Hamburg, Germany.

-December 3-
Mike Oldfield performs in the Night Of The Proms concert festival at TUI Arena, Hannover, Germany.

-December 5-
Mike Oldfield performs in the Night Of The Proms concert festival at Messehalle, Erfurt, Germany.

-December 7, 8, 9 & 10-
Mike Oldfield performs in the Night Of The Proms concert festival at Olymiahalle, München, Germany.

-December 12-
Mike Oldfield performs in the Night Of The Proms concert festival at AWD DOME, Bremen, Germany.

-December 13-
Mike Oldfield performs in the Night Of The Proms concert festival at Westfalenhalle, Dortmund, Germany.

-December 14-
Mike Oldfield performs in the Night Of The Proms concert festival at ISS DOME, Düsseldorf, Germany.

-December 15 & 16-
Mike Oldfield performs in the Night Of The Proms concert festival at Kölnarena, Köln, Germany.

-December 17-
Mike Oldfield performs in the Night Of The Proms concert festival at König-Pilsener-ARENA, Oberhausen, Germany.

-December 19-
Mike Oldfield performs in the Night Of The Proms concert festival at SAP Arena, Mannheim, Germany.

-December 20-
Mike Oldfield performs in the Night Of The Proms concert festival at Hanns-Martin-Schleyer-Halle, Stuttgart, Germany.

-December 21 & 22-
Mike Oldfield performs in the Night Of The Proms concert festival at Festhalle, Frankfurt, Germany.

Song For Survival

2007

-March-
In an interview published this month with *Infomacion.es*, **Mike Oldfield** notes he is currently writing his autobiography, *Changeling*. He also discusses his classical album project (*Music Of The Spheres* sessions),

In an interview published this month in *Resolution* magazine, **Mike** discusses his classical project, that he's writing and recording MIDI demos for what will be later recorded as orchestral pieces. He also notes he's currently talking to Karl Jenkins about a collaboration.

-March 30-
Mike Oldfield performs in the Night Of The Proms concert festival at Velódromo Luis Puig, Valencia, Spain.

-March 31-
Mike Oldfield performs in the Night Of The Proms concert festival at Palacio de Deportes de la Comunidad de Madrid, Madrid, Spain.

-April 22-
Upfront issues a promo CD edition of **Mike Oldfield**'s album *Tubular Bells* in Ireland (UPT 001) free with *The Irish Mail On Sunday* newspaper on this date. 2000 remaster by Simon Heyworth.

-May-
Mike Oldfield releases his autobiography *Changeling*.

-May 2-
Röyksopp releases its compilation album *Back To Mine* on CD (BACKCD25) in the UK on DMC, featuring two remixes of **Mike Oldfield**'s work.

> "Platinum (Part Three): Charleston (Röyksopp Remix)" 1:20
> "Meatball" 2:53
> Written by Mike Oldfield ("North Star" by Glass, arr. Oldfield)
> Appears on: Back To Mine
> The tracks on the album are designed to all flow and segue from one to the other, so the "Charleston" remix starts abruptly when listened to on its own. More "Charleston" music fades in at the end of the previous track, a remix of Mr. Flagio's "Take A Chance." As the "Charleston" remix starts a bit of the synth melody from "Take A Chance" can still be heard. Otherwise, not much is done to this track, really, apart from the tempo being sped up, so the last two minutes of Oldfield's piece run at under a minute and a half (it works, though). Then, as on the *Platinum* album, the next track comes in. This would be "Meatball," though why it's called that I couldn't even venture a guess. All the artists on *Back To Mine* who have their work remixed are properly credited, including Oldfield for "Charleston," yet this track, which is a remix of Oldfield's "North Star / Platinum Finale," is credited to Röyksopp's other alias Emmanuel Splice and titled "Meatball." The writing credit goes to Röyksopp members Svein Berge and Torbjøn Brundtland (rather than to Mike Oldfield and Phillip Glass). And it's not that Röyksopp used a few samples and that's it, they only added a bit of additional production to the Oldfield piece, made a few edits and mix changes and what we're left with is still very much "North Star / Platinum Finale." Very strange. Not bad remixes, though.

-May 15-
In an article published on this date in *The Standard*, **Mike Oldfield** confirms the name of his classical project as *Music Of The Spheres*, which he is collaborating on with Karl Jenkins.

-June 9-
Mike Oldfield appears on the ITV show *This Morning*, discussing his autobiography, *Changeling*, and his classical project, *Music Of The Spheres*. He notes this month he'll be recording with a full orchestra at Abbey Road Studios, London, England.

-August 10-
In an interview broadcast live on this date on *Classic FM*, **Mike Oldfield** says Lang Lang recorded his piano parts at Legacy Recording Studios, New York City, New York, US, via iChat.

-Date Unknown-
Virgin Records re-issues **Mike Oldfield**'s album *Tubular Bells* on 200 gram vinyl LP in the US as part of the Classic Records series (VS 2001). Mastered by BG.

-Summer-
Mike Oldfield completes work on his classical album *Music Of The Spheres*, at his home studio, Bath, Somerset, England. The orchestrations are transcribed by Karl Jenkins and performed by the Sinfonia Sfera Orchestra, Lang Lang plays piano throughout and Hayley Westenra provides vocals. **Oldfield** plays classical guitar. The planned release is Autumn, though it later gets pushed back to January, then to March.

-September 18-
Mike Oldfield makes a guest appearance at the Tape Club, Berlin, Germany, to promote *Music Of The Spheres*. Promotional material includes a brochure, heat-sensitive mug mat and EPK DVD with short promo clips about the writing of the album and the collaboration with Karl Jenkins.

-Date Unknown-
Mike Oldfield works on the following at his home studio, Bath, Somerset, England:
"Song For Survival" - **Mike** gets involved in the project via Molly Oldfield, who is assembling the album in support of Survival International, a tribal peoples-focused preservation charity. The aim with the album is to get contemporary recording artists to compose songs based on the tribes, each given samples of the tribes music. **Oldfield** selects the Anuta tribe's sample and records this piece, which incorporates the sample. **Mike**'s track is the second completed for the project.

-November-
Universal Music releases the 2xCD collection *The Number One Classical Album 2008* (480 035-7), featuring **Mike Oldfield**'s "On My Heart," in the UK.

> "On My Heart (Edit)" 2:28
> Written by Mike Oldfield
> Appears on: The Number One Classical Album 2008, Two Sides - The Very Best Of Mike Oldfield
> This version of the track fades in at the beginning, making for a good standalone version.

-Autumn-
Mike Oldfield and his family move from their home in Bath, Somerset, England to Palma de Mallorca, Spain. An October 21st, article notes he has only recently moved, disputing the recent changes in smoking legislation in England.

-October-
Universal Music releases a promo CD+DVD edition of **Mike Oldfield**'s album *Music Of The Spheres* in the UK in a tin case. Track listing as follows:

UK *Music Of The Spheres* Promo CD+DVD (4766206)

CD: *Music Of The Spheres*
"Harbinger"
"Animus"
"Silhouette"
"Shabda"
"The Tempest"
"Harbinger (Reprise)"
"On My Heart"
"Aurora"
"Prophecy"
"On My Heart (Reprise)"
"Harmonia Mundi"
"The Other Side"
"Empyrean"
"Musica Universalis"

DVD: *EPK Promo Clip*

Music Of The Spheres

2008

-January 22-
Eugene Oldfield is born to **Mike** and Fanny Oldfield.

-March 3-
Mike Oldfield releases his digital single "Spheres" on iTunes UK.

> "Spheres" 5:22
> Written by Mike Oldfield
> Appears on: iTunes UK single
> This piece is made up of Mike's working versions of the tracks on the album, the recordings he made prior to his collaboration with Karl Jenkins. The pieces heard here feature no orchestra. The mix gives a good taster for the album and shows how the album would've sounded if Mike had not gone the classical route

-March 7-
Mike Oldfield premieres *Music Of The Spheres* live at the Guggenheim Museum, Bilbao, Spain. It features **Oldfield** performing live with the Euskadiko Orkestra Sinfonikoa, the Biboa Choral Society and Hayley Westenra. The following track is released individually:

> "Aurora (Live At The Guggenheim 2008 Bilbao)" 3:39
> Written by Mike Oldfield
> Appears on: Lo Mejor De... Mike Oldfield
> I have not heard this excerpt, so can only guess that it's presented as a standalone version.

-March 14-
Mike Oldfield releases his album *Music Of The Spheres* in Europe on UCJ Music. Track listing as follows:

Europe *Music Of The Spheres* CD (4766206)

"Harbinger"
"Animus"
"Silhouette"
"Shabda"
"The Tempest"
"Harbinger (Reprise)"
"On My Heart"
"Aurora"
"Prophecy"
"On My Heart (Reprise)"
"Harmonia Mundi"
"The Other Side"
"Empyrean"
"Musica Universalis"

-March 17-
Mike Oldfield releases his album *Music Of The Spheres* in the UK.

-March 18-
Mike Oldfield releases his album *Music Of The Spheres* in North America.

US *Music Of The Spheres* Club Edition CD (Decca Records B0010925-02)
Canada *Music Of The Spheres* CD (Universal Music / UCJ Music 1749051)

Mike Oldfield and Hayley Westenra appear on The Alan Titchmarsh Show, ITV, promoting "On My Heart."

-Date Unknown-
Virgin Records re-issues **Mike Oldfield**'s album *Tubular Bells* on 200 gram clear vinyl LP in the US (VS 2001). Mastered by BG.

-September 15-
Kensaltown Records releases online (via iTunes, Amazon and Play.com) the charity album *Songs For Survival*, which includes the track "Song For Survival," by **Mike Oldfield featuring the Anuta tribe.**

> "Song For Survival" 4:04
> Written by Mike Oldfield ("Anuta Chant" trad.)
> Appears on: Songs For Survival
> Mike has a long history of working in what we now call World Music, going all the way back to *Ommadawn* and his work with Jabula. He's frequently revisited the genre, so was a natural choice for this project (apart from Molly being his daughter, which helps). Here, Mike simply builds a backing track around the existing tribal singing and the result is similar to "A New Beginning," with a dash of "Song Of The Boat Men" thrown in. Good stuff!

-October 13-
Kensaltown Records releases *Songs For Survival* on CD on Amazon.co.uk.

-November 21 & 24-
Universal Music re-issues *Music Of The Spheres* as a 2xCD set in the UK, including with it the live premiere performance from March 7th.

Europe *Music Of The Spheres* 2xCD (4766970)
CD 1: *Music Of The Spheres*
CD 2: *Music Of The Spheres - Live from Bilbao*

iTunes Edition
Music Of The Spheres
Music Of The Spheres - Live from Bilbao
"Mike Oldfield Interview"
"Karl Jenkins Interview"

Tubular Bells Revisited

2009

-Date Unknown-
Mike Oldfield moves with his family from Palma de Mallorca, Spain, to a houseboat in The Bahamas.

-March-
Mike Oldfield begins work on remixing the original *Tubular Bells* and its associated tracks, including creating a 5.1 Digital Surround Sound mix, for the planned re-issue under Mercury Records. This work takes place at his houseboat studio, The Bahamas. Remastering later takes place at Audio Archiving Company, London, England.

-June 5, 8 & 9-
Mike Oldfield releases *Tubular Bells* (2009 Stereo Mix) in the UK, Europe and North America on Mercury Records. The sleeve artwork, though similar to the original, is not identical to the 1973 release, noticeable on the bell itself, which appears to be computer generated (look closely at the reflection and the position) and the birds have been removed. Several editions are released. Track listings as follows:

Tubular Bells 180 gram vinyl LP Edition (0602527035314)
LP: *Tubular Bells* 180 gram vinyl (1973 Original Mix Remastered)
"Tubular Bells (Part One)" - 2009 Remaster
"Tubular Bells (Part Two)" - 2009 Remaster

CD: *Tubular Bells* (2009 Stereo Mix) (0602527035055)
"Tubular Bells (Part One - 2009 Stereo Mix)"
"Tubular Bells (Part Two - 2009 Stereo Mix)"
Bonus Tracks:
"Theme from Tubular Bells"
"The Sailor's Hornpipe (Original Version - 2009 Mix)"

Deluxe Edition (2xCD+DVD) (270 354-1)
CD 1: *Tubular Bells* (2009 Stereo Mix)
CD 2: *Tubular Bells* (1973 Original Mix Remastered)

DVD: *Tubular Bells* (2009 5.1 Digital Surround Sound Mix)
"Tubular Bells (Part One)" 5.1 Digital Surround Sound Mix
"Tubular Bells (Part Two)" 5.1 Digital Surround Sound Mix
"Theme From Tubular Bells" 5.1 Digital Surround Sound Mix
"The Sailor's Hornpipe (Original Version - 2009 Mix)" 5.1 Digital Surround Sound Mix
"Tubular Bells (The 2nd House Performance)" 5.1 Digital Surround Sound Mix

Ultimate Edition (3xCD+DVD+LP) (270 353-9)
CD 1: *Tubular Bells* (2009 Stereo Mix)
CD 2: *Tubular Bells* (1973 Original Mix Remastered)

CD 3: *The Demos*
"Tubular Bells (Long)"
"Caveman Lead-In"
"Caveman"
"Peace Demo A"
"Peace Demo B"
"Tubular Bells (Part One) (Scrapped Early Mix)"

DVD: *Tubular Bells* (2009 5.1 Digital Surround Sound Mix)
LP: *Tubular Bells* 180 gram vinyl (1973 Original Mix Remastered)

Also includes: 60-page book, poster and other paraphernalia.

"Tubular Bells (Part One – 2009 Stereo Mix)" 25:57
"Tubular Bells (Part Two – 2009 Stereo Mix)" 23:13
Written by Mike Oldfield ("The Sailor's Hornpipe" Unknown, arr. Oldfield)
Appears on: Tubular Bells (2009 Stereo Mix Edition, Deluxe Edition & Ultimate Edition), The Collection
With his old Virgin Records catalogue now back under his control, the first thing Mike did was to set to work re-mixing *Tubular Bells*, an album he'd long had technical concerns over. Mike rebuilds the two parts from the ground up, using the original elements and fixing timing issues and glitches. He also cleans up the sound and in the mix, gives instruments which were previously buried under layers of sound more definition and prominence. You *will* hear the difference between this and the original mix. In addition to all that, Mike makes an additional, noticeable change in "Part One": to the end of the "Blues" movement, at 14:05, the piano and vocal humming part repeats, adding 10 seconds to the track. It'll throw you off if you're not expecting it and are waiting for the "Thrash" guitars to burst in.

"The Sailor's Hornpipe (Original Version – 2009 Mix)" 2:48
Written by Mike Oldfield ("The Sailor's Hornpipe" Unknown, arr. Oldfield)
Appears on: Tubular Bells (2009 Stereo Mix Edition, Deluxe Edition & Ultimate Edition), The Collection, Icon
Despite its claim to be the original version, it's not. This new mix retains Viv Stanshall's full monologue in all its ridiculous glory, but removes the familiar "Sailor's Hornpipe" performance that followed the monologue (the part kept on the original album). For comparison, the *Boxed* set in 1976 has the full, complete version. Here, after the monologue, the track is edited and remixed, going from a bit of whistling guitar to the last few notes of the original piece. All that being said, it's always great to hear Viv Stanshall.

Also released on this date by Mercury Records is *Mike Oldfield – The Collection*, a 2xCD set in Europe and Australia, track listing as follows:

Europe *Mike Oldfield – The Collection* 2xCD (0602527035055)
Australia *Mike Oldfield – The Collection* 2xCD (0602527035055)

CD 1: *Tubular Bells* (2009 Stereo Mix)

CD 2: *The Collection*
"In Dulci Jubilo"
"Ommadawn (Part One) (Episodes Extract)"
"William Tell Overture"
"Incantations (Part Four) ('Ode To Cynthia')"
"Guilty (Long Version)"
"Blue Peter" – a cover of the 1958 TV show theme.
"Five Miles Out"
"Wonderful Land" – a cover of The Shadows' 1962 instrumental.
"Taurus II (The Collection Excerpt)"
"Family Man"
"Shadow On The Wall" Mike Oldfield And Roger Chapman

"Taurus II (The Collection Excerpt)" 11:16
Written by Mike Oldfield
Appears on: Mike Oldfield - The Collection
This excerpt is the first 11 minutes of the piece, ending in a fade out.

A promo CD single titled *Tubular Bells - Original And Best* is issued advertising the above releases.

UK 1-track CD single (BELLS 001) promo:
"Tubular Bells (Now The Original Theme from 'The Exorcist' - Version 1)"

-June 10-
In an article published on this date in *The Telegraph*, **Mike Oldfield** discusses the recording of *Tubular Bells*. The article notes that **Oldfield** and his family plan to travel south to spend time on an island near Mexico.

-Date Unknown-
Mike Oldfield begins work on remastering and creating the 5.1 surround sound mixes for his albums *Hergest Ridge* and *Ommadawn*, at his houseboat studio in The Bahamas.

-December-
Mike Oldfield and his family take up residence in St. Thomas on their houseboat.

Hergest Ridge & Ommadawn Revisited

2010

-Early 2010-
Mike Oldfield continues work on restoring his albums *Hergest Ridge* and *Ommadawn*, at his houseboat studio in The Bahamas. The "Lost Version" of *Ommadawn*, a copy of the first recording of the album which had been forgotten in the Virgin Record vaults, is rediscovered.

-January 11-
Parlophone releases the **Kevin Ayers And The Whole World** January 6th, 1972, BBC session as *Kevin Ayers: BBC In Concert* in the UK on CD (WIN CD 018).

-February 9-
In her online diary, Fanny Oldfield discusses her and **Mike**'s decision to stop living on a houseboat (currently in St. Thomas) and to buy a house in Nassau, The Bahamas.

-February 12-
In her online diary, Fanny Oldfield mentions **Mike Oldfield** is "excited" about a "'Telecaster' album" idea.

-March 14-
In her online diary, Fanny Oldfield notes on this date that they leave St. Thomas to move to Nassau, The Bahamas. The family lives in an apartment while they house.

-April 5-
In her online diary, Fanny Oldfield notes that **Mike Oldfield** has been working a lot on "the new album," describing it in terms of something new (not the remixing and remastering of his earlier material, but new compositions), likely the 'Telecaster' guitar album.

-Date Unknown-
Luke Oldfield, son of **Mike Oldfield**, restores the facilities at **Mike**'s former home, Denham, Buckinghamshire, England, christening the new studio as Tilehouse Studios.

-May 19-
In her online diary, Fanny Oldfield notes that **Mike Oldfield** is "working."

-Date Unknown-
Esotaric Records re-issues the Pekka Pohjola album *Keesojen Lehto* as *Mathematician's Air Display* on CD in the UK (ECLEC 2177), remastered by Pauli Saastamoinen. The album features **Mike Oldfield**.

-June 7-
Mike Oldfield releases his remastered albums *Hergest Ridge* and *Ommadawn* in the UK, Europe and North America. This re-issue features an updated cover (**Mike** was apparently never satisfied with the original sleeve artwork). Several editions are released. Track listing as follows:

Hergest Ridge

LP: *Hergest Ridge* (1974 Original Mix Remastered) (*Back To Black Vinyl Edition*) (0600753267585)
"Hergest Ridge (Part One)" 2010 Remaster
"Hergest Ridge (Part Two)" 2010 Remaster

CD: *Hergest Ridge* (2010 Stereo Mix) (532 675-5)
"Hergest Ridge (Part One – 2010 Stereo Mix)"
"Hergest Ridge (Part Two – 2010 Stereo Mix)"
Bonus Tracks
"In Dulci Jubilo (For Maureen)"
"Spanish Tune"

Deluxe Edition (2xCD+DVD) (532 675-4)
CD 1: *Hergest Ridge* (2010 Stereo Mix)

CD 2: *Hergest Ridge* (1974 Original Mix Remastered)
"Hergest Ridge (Part One)" 2010 Remaster
"Hergest Ridge (Part Two)" 2010 Remaster
Bonus Tracks
"Hergest Ridge (Part One) (1974 Demo)"
"Hergest Ridge (Part Two) (1974 Demo)"

DVD: *Hergest Ridge* 2010 5.1 Digital Surround Sound Mix
"Hergest Ridge (Part One)" 5.1 Digital Surround Sound Mix
"Hergest Ridge (Part Two)" 5.1 Digital Surround Sound Mix

Ommadawn

LP: *Ommadawn* 1975 Original Mix Remastered (*Back To Black Vinyl Edition*) (0600753267653)
"Ommadawn (Part One)" 2010 Remaster
"Ommadawn (Part Two)" 2010 Remaster

CD: *Ommadawn* (2010 Stereo Mix) (532 676-6)
"Ommadawn (Part One – 2010 Stereo Mix)"
"Ommadawn (Part Two – 2010 Stereo Mix)"
Bonus Tracks
"In Dulci Jubilo"
"First Excursion"
"Argiers"
"Portsmouth"

Deluxe Edition (2xCD+DVD) (532 676-1)
CD 1: *Ommadawn* (2010 Stereo Mix)

CD 2: *Ommadawn* (1975 Original Mix Remastered)
"Ommadawn (Part One)" 2010 Remaster
"Ommadawn (Part Two)" 2010 Remaster
Bonus Track
"Ommadawn (Lost Version)"

DVD: *Ommadawn* 2010 5.1 Digital Surround Sound Mix
"Ommadawn (Part One)" 5.1 Digital Surround Sound Mix
"Ommadawn (Part Two)" 5.1 Digital Surround Sound Mix

> "Hergest Ridge (Part One – 2010 Stereo Mix)" 19:18
> "Hergest Ridge (Part Two – 2010 Stereo Mix)" 18:47
> Written by Mike Oldfield
> Appears on: Hergest Ridge (2010 Stereo Mix & Deluxe Editions)
> The first thing you'll notice is that this is not the "Boxed Remix" but a new mix based on the original 1974 mix. The Remastered version also uses the original, so for the first time, the 1974

recording sees a digital release. The new stereo mix takes the same approach as the *Tubular Bells* 2009 remaster, of fixing small mistakes most of us probably couldn't hear in the first place and rebuilding the album with the original elements to make it what Mike viewed as an improved version.

"Spanish Tune (2010 Version)" 3:10
Written by Mike Oldfield
Appears on: Hergest Ridge (2010 Deluxe Edition); Icon
This version is almost the same as the original planned single A-side that appeared on a white label test pressing in 1974. The only difference is that this excerpt from "Hergest Ridge (Part Two)" fades in at the beginning, rather than starting at full volume, as it did on the 1974 test pressing.

"Ommadawn (Part One - 2010 Stereo Mix)" 19:03
"Ommadawn (Part Two - 2010 Stereo Mix)" 17:22
Written by Mike Oldfield
Appears on: Ommadawn (2010 Stereo Mix & Deluxe Editions)
Like *Tubular Bells* and *Hergest Ridge* before it, this new Stereo Mix rebuilds the album with the original elements to create an improved version. You'll hear a few things in the mix you didn't on the original, as different instruments have more presence, such as the recorder and acoustic guitar in places. "On Horseback" now sounds like it was recorded yesterday and you can clearly hear the lyrics (gone is the "mumble" that resulted from a low vocal mix that plagued the original version of the song). Overall, this mix sounds brighter and clearer without losing any of the album's power.

-June 14-
Mercury Records releases a Limited Edition set of *Hergest Ridge* (2010 Stereo Mix) in the UK (250 copies) on mikeoldfieldofficial.com. Track listing as follows:

Limited Edition set:
LP: *Hergest Ridge* (1974 Original Mix Remastered) (*Back To Black Vinyl Edition*)
CD 1: *Hergest Ridge* (2010 Stereo Mix)
CD 2: *Hergest Ridge* (1974 Original Mix Remastered)
DVD: *Hergest Ridge* 2010 5.1 Digital Surround Sound Mix
Also included is a numbered and signed (by **Mike Oldfield**) print of the updated sleeve artwork

-Date Unknown-
Mike Oldfield begins work on restoring his album *Incantations*, only to discover a large number of the original multitracks are damaged beyond repair and some have been lost, limiting his efforts. Work takes place at his home studio in The Bahamas.

-October-
Torsten Stenzel (AKA York) is introduced to **Mike Oldfield** by Thomas Scherer, VP of BMG Rights. They chat via Skype, followed by York visiting **Mike** in The Bahamas (York lives not far away, in Antigua). **Mike** is already working on remixes of his material and asks York to assist, beginning a collaboration of remixing **Oldfield**'s classic work, via file-sharing. These sessions last about two years.
"Islanders" - York brings a number of layout tracks for them to work on when he meets **Mike**, who selects this track and plays guitar right then in an used take. A couple weeks later, York receives **Oldfield**'s proper recording on the track.

-October 7-
Published on this date is a *Masterclass* feature on composer Don Black, in the online magazine *Music Week*, wherein Black says he's been writing with **Mike Oldfield**, who sent him a copy of *Tubular Bells*.

Incantations Revisited

2011

-Early 2011-
Mike Oldfield continues work on remastering the stereo album master tape on *Incantations* and remixing the salvageable multitracks, at his home studio, Nassau, The Bahamas.

-Date Unknown-
Esoteric Records re-issues **The Sallyangie**'s album *Children Of The Sun* on CD (ECLEC 22294) in the UK. Track listing as follows:

"Strangers"
"Lady Mary"
"Children Of The Sun"
"A Lover For All Seasons"
"River Song"
"Banquet On The Water"
"Balloons"
"Midsummer Night's Happening"
"Love In Ice Crystals"
"Changing Colours"
"Chameleon"
"Milk Bottle"
"Murder Of The Children Of San Francisco"
Bonus Track: "Twilight"
Bonus Track: "Song Of The Healer"
"Strangers (Reprise)"
Bonus Tracks:
"Children Of The Sun (Minus Intro)"
"Mrs. Moon And The Thatched Shop"
"Branches"
"A Sad Song For Rosie"
"Colour Of The World"
"Two Ships" – a cover of the 1968 Maria Dallas song.
"Child Of Allah"
"Lady Go Lightly"

-July 25-
Mike Oldfield releases *Incantations (2011 Remastered Edition)* in the UK, Europe and North America. Like *Hergest Ridge*, **Oldfield** has the sleeve artwork updated for this release. Track listing as follows:

2xLP: *Incantations (2011 Remastered Edition)* (533 463)
"Incantations (Part One)" 2011 Remaster
"Incantations (Part Two)" 2011 Remaster
"Incantations (Part Three)" 2011 Remaster
"Incantations (Part Four – 1st Pressing Error Version)" 2011 Remaster

CD: *Incantations (2011 Remastered Edition)* (533 463-6)
"Incantations (Part One)" 2011 Remaster
"Incantations (Part Two)" 2011 Remaster
"Incantations (Part Three)" 2011 Remaster
"Incantations (Part Four – 1st Pressing Error Version)" 2011 Remaster

Bonus Track
"Guilty (2011 'Slow' Version)"

Deluxe Edition (2xCD+DVD) (533 463-7)
CD 1: *Incantations (2011 Remastered Edition)*

CD 2: *2011 Stereo Mixes*
"Diana (2011 Stereo Mix)"
"Northumbrian (2011 Stereo Mix)"
"Piano Improvisation (2011 Stereo Mix)"
"Hiawatha (2011 Stereo Mix)"
"Canon For Two Vibraphones (2011 Stereo Mix)"
"William Tell Overture"
"Cuckoo Song"
"Pipe Tune"
"Wreckorder Wrondo"
"Guilty (Long Version 2011 Stereo Mix)"
"Diana – Desiderata (2011 Stereo Mix)"

DVD: 5.1 Digital Surround Sound Mix
"Diana" 5.1 Digital Surround Sound Mix
"Northumbrian" 5.1 Digital Surround Sound Mix
"Piano Improvisation" 5.1 Digital Surround Sound Mix
"Hiawatha" 5.1 Digital Surround Sound Mix
"Canon For Two Vibraphones" 5.1 Digital Surround Sound Mix
"Guilty" 5.1 Digital Surround Sound Mix
"William Tell Overture" – Promo Video
"Incantations (Parts One & Two)" Live at Wembley – from the *Exposed* DVD
"Incantations (Parts Three & Four)" Live at Wembley – from the *Exposed* DVD
"Guilty" – Promo Video

"Incantations (Part Four – 1st Pressing Error Version)" 17:00
Written by Mike Oldfield (music), Ben Jonson ("Ode To Cynthia," arr. Oldfield)
Appears on: Incantation (2011 Remastered Edition)
A pretty nasty glitch happens at about 12:36, where a percussion beat is missing, apparently due to a mastering problem. Universal Music was made aware of the glitch, responded to concerns and attempted a fix on the next pressing (though that correction is still not perfect). The missing beat throws the tempo and timing off, so the listener has to force themselves to pick the correct timing back up again. Naturally, when enjoying music, it's very distracting.

"Guilty (2011 'Slow' Version)" 4:14
Written by Mike Oldfield
Appears on: Incantation (2011 Remastered Edition), Two Sides – The Very Best Of Mike Oldfield, Moonlight Shadow – The Collection
For whatever reason, this version runs a bit too slow and appears to slow down even further as it goes along. It's a shame, because this version has now been appearing on new collections featuring Mike's latest remasters. After a while you do sort of get used to it, but it's not good. Stick with one of the previous remasters that run at the correct speed.

"Guilty (Long Version 2011 Stereo Mix)" 6:41
Written by Mike Oldfield
Appears on: Appears on: Incantation (2011 Deluxe Edition), Icon
This remix also runs a bit too slow. In addition to that, some production elements have been removed, such as the reverb. The resulting mix sounds crisper, but lacks the sonic depth of the original. There are a few new "I'm guilty" vocals in the middle, too.

"Diana (2011 Stereo Mix)" 6:35
Written by Mike Oldfield
Appears on: Appears on: Incantation (2011 Deluxe Edition), Moonlight Shadow – The Collection
This is a new remix by Mike combining both the "Hymn To Diana" movement in "Part One" and its "Reprise" in "Part Two." Mike adds a few new elements (such as new drum parts) and remixes others. This is a great piece.

"Hiawatha (2011 Stereo Mix)" 9:01
Written by Mike Oldfield
Appears on: Appears on: Incantation (2011 Deluxe Edition)
This is a remix of "The Song Of Hiawatha" movement of "Part Two." It's still pretty much the same, but Mike did remove the droning fuzzy sound that plays throughout the original and the last little bit of guitar is absent.

"Canon For Two Vibraphones (2011 Stereo Mix)" 2:50
Written by Mike Oldfield
Appears on: Appears on: Incantation (2011 Deluxe Edition)
This mix isolates part of the canon movement from "Part Four," fading in at the beginning after the guitar part and fading out before the end of the piece. Mike has said several times that this part was one of his favourite pieces on the album.

"Diana – Desiderata (2011 Stereo Mix)"
Written by Mike Oldfield ("Desiderata" by Erhmann, arr. Oldfield)
Appears on: Appears on: Incantation (2011 Deluxe Edition)
This would be a more or less straight excerpt of the "Hymn To Diana" movement of "Part One," if not for the inclusion of a new vocal part, a computerized reading of Max Erhmann's poem "Desiderata." The voice software used makes it sound like Prof. Stephen Hawking is reading the piece.

-Mid-2011-
Mike Oldfield begins work on remixing and remastering his album *Platinum*, at his home studio, Nassau, The Bahamas.

-July-
Mike Oldfield receives word that Danny Boyle, artistic director for the upcoming Summer Olympic Games in London, England, want him to participate in the Opening Ceremonies. Boyle emails **Oldfield** a few days later.

-August-
Hurricane Irene hits the Caribbean, including The Bahamas.
"Irene" – **Mike Oldfield** is inspired by the hurricane to write this song, also as a homage to The Rolling Stones style of rock.

-August 2-
In an interview published on this date on the *Downed In Sound* website, **Mike Oldfield** says he's working on the following, at his home studio, Nassau, The Bahamas:
"North Star (2012 Mike Oldfield Remix)" – this is the eventual name of the new mix, which is released the following year as part of the remastered *Platinum* album.

In the interview, he says a future project is the 5.1 Surround Sound mix of *Amaork*, which he hasn't gotten to yet. Nor has he started on *QE2* remastering. **Oldfield** also says he's now semi-retired.

-Date Unknown-
Danny Boyle flies to Nassau, The Bahamas, to meet with **Mike Oldfield** to discuss the Opening Ceremony. Around this time, **Mike** begins working on new arrangements of several existing pieces. Boyle later suggests a Swing arrangement of *Tubular Bells* and **Mike** writes one.

-October 1-
David Bedford dies of lung cancer. Bedford was a member of Kevin Ayers' band **The Whole World** with **Mike Oldfield**. Of Bedford's releases, **Oldfield** appears on *Star's End*, *The Rime Of The Ancient Mariner*, *The Odyssey*, *Instructions For Angels* and **Mike** engineered, produced and released *Star Clusters, Nebulae And Places In Devon*. Of **Oldfield**'s releases, Bedford appears on "Don Alfonso," "Speak (Tho' You Only Say Farewell)," "First Excursion" (which Bedford co-wrote), *Incantations* and *The Killing Fields*. Bedford toured with **Mike** for the Exposed Tour, was a member of the ensemble which premiered *Tubular Bells* at Queen Elizabeth and he also arranged and conducted both *The Orchestral Tubular Bells* and the unreleased *Orchestral Hergest Ridge*. Bedford also composed and recorded the piece *Variations Of A Rhythm Of Mike Oldfield*.

Islanders

2012

-Early 2012-
Mike Oldfield continues to work on remixing and remastering his *Platinum* album, as well as working on his *QE2* album, at his home studio in The Bahamas.

Mike also continues to collaborate with York on remixes of **Oldfield**'s track, via email and file sharing. York works at his own studio at English Harbour, Antigua.

Mike also works on the Olympics' Opening Ceremonies music, later sending it to be mixed by Underworld (the musical directors) at Abbey Road Studios, London, England.

Mike also works on compiling a new 2xCD collection of his work, what would become *Two Sides*.

-Date Unknown-
Mike Oldfield records guitar for Terry Oldfield's album *Journey Into Space*, on the tracks "Origin," "Flight Of The Eagle" and "Dancer In The Void."

-April – May-
Ben Wiseman and Mark Powell mix the Wembley Arena, May 28, 1980, and Essen, April 1, 1981, concerts at Blitz Productions, London, England.

-May 31-
Universal Music releases a collection of **Mike Oldfield** works as part of their *Icon* series on CD (5337949). Track listing as follows:

"Tubular Bells (Now The Original Theme from 'The Exorcist' – Version 1)"
"Moonlight Shadow"
"In Dulci Jubilo"
"Spanish Tune (2010 Version)"
"Harbinger"
"Ommadawn (Part One) (Elements Excerpt)"
"The Tempest (Icon Edit)"
"Angelique"
"Family Man"
"Guilty (Long Version 2011 Stereo Mix)"
"The Gate"
"The Sailor's Hornpipe (Original Version – 2009 Mix)"
"Portsmouth"
"Incantations (Part Four) ('Ode To Cynthia')"

> "The Tempest (Icon Edit)" 5:49
> Written by Mike Oldfield
> Appears on: Icon
> This edit fades out at the end.

-Summer-
Four weeks after sending his music off (according to an article in *The Telegraph*, July 29), **Mike Oldfield** and his family travel to London for rehearsals for the Opening Ceremonies.

-July 10-
Lol Coxhill dies. Coxhill was a member of Kevin Ayers' band **The Whole World**, with **Mike Oldfield** and **Oldfield** appears on Coxhill's album *Ear Of The Beholder*.

-July 27-
Mike Oldfield performs at the 2012 Olympic Summer Games' Opening Ceremonies *Isle Of Wonder*, London, England. Luke Oldfield plays guitars and keyboards in **Oldfield**'s ensemble.

-July 28-
At 12 AM Decca Music Group releases for download the Summer Olympics' Opening Ceremonies compilation album *Isle Of Wonder*, featuring **Mike Oldfield**'s track "Music For The Opening Ceremony Of The London 2012 Olympic Games."

> "Music For The Opening Ceremony Of The London 2012 Olympic Games" 11:29
> Written by Mike Oldfield ("In Dulci Jubilo" Trad. Arr. Oldfield, based on Pearsall)
> Appears on: Isles Of Wonder, Music For The Opening Ceremony Of The London 2012 Olympic Games
> 1-track download single & 12" single
> This medley, created for the Opening Ceremonies, features excerpts (with new and existing elements) of the following: "Tubular Bells (Part One): Introduction," "Swing Tubular Bells" (the new Swing arrangement), "Tubular Bells (Part Two): Peace," "Introduction (Reprise)," "Secrets / Far Above The Clouds" and "In Dulci Jubilo." If you really enjoyed the Opening Ceremonies with Mike (or if your broadcast had commentators who wouldn't shut the hell up so you could hear the music because they were talking over it the entire time), get a hold of this track. The Swing arrangement alone is worth it. During the "Peace" segment, J.K. Rowling read from *Peter Pan* onstage, setting the scene. Her vocals are not present in this mix.

-July 29-
In an article published on this date in *The Telegraph*, **Mike Oldfield** notes that one of his current projects is a "rock album."

-July 27 & 30-
Mike Oldfield releases the following in the UK, Europe and North America:

Platinum

Platinum 180 gram LP (2012 Remaster) (370 791-4) Blue vinyl
Platinum 180 gram LP (2012 Remaster) (370 883-6)
"Platinum (Part One): Airborne"
"Platinum (Part Two): Platinum"
"Platinum (Part Three): Charleston"
"Platinum (Part Four): North Star / Platinum Finale"
"Woodhenge"
"Into Wonderland"
"Punkadiddle"
"I Got Rhythm" – a version of the 1930 Gershwin song.

Platinum CD (2012 Remaster) (533 942-3)
"Platinum (Part One): Airborne"
"Platinum (Part Two): Platinum"
"Platinum (Part Three): Charleston"
"Platinum (Part Four): North Star / Platinum Finale"
"Woodhenge"
"Into Wonderland"
"Punkadiddle"
"I Got Rhythm" – a version of the 1930 Gershwin song.

Bonus Tracks
"Platinum (Live Studio Session)"
"North Star (2012 Mike Oldfield Mix)"
"Blue Peter" - a cover of the 1958 TV show theme.

Platinum 2xCD Deluxe Edition (533 942-2):
CD 1: *Platinum* (2012 Remaster)
CD 2: *Live At Wembley Arena (London - 28th May 1980)*

> "North Star (2012 Mike Oldfield Mix)" 8:08
> Written by Phillip Glass (arr. Oldfield)
> Appears on: Platinum (2012 Deluxe Edition)
> This remix extends the track two nearly twice as long as the original, drawing out the elements of the track and playing around with them a bit, with loops and repeats. Not too shabby.

QE2

LP: *QE2* (2012 Remaster) 180 gram vinyl (370 883-4)

LP: *QE2* (2012 Remaster) 180 gram White vinyl (370 791-3)

CD: *QE2* (2012 Remaster) (533 941-9)
"Taurus 1"
"Sheba"
"Conflict"
"Arrival" - a cover of the 1976 ABBA instrumental.
"Wonderful Land" - a cover of The Shadows' 1962 instrumental.
"Mirage"
"QE2/QE2 Finale"
"Celt"
"Molly"
Bonus Tracks
"Polka (Live in Vienna, 1980)"
"Wonderful Land (Single Version)" - a cover of The Shadows' 1962 instrumental.
"Shiva"

QE2 (2012 Remaster) Deluxe Edition (2xCD) (533 941-8)
CD 1: *QE2* (2012 Remaster)
CD 2: *Live From The European Adventure Tour* (Essen, April 1, 1981)

> "Shiva" 3:34
> Written by Mike Oldfield
> Appears on: *QE2* (2012 Remaster)
> This a new reworking of the track "Sheba," now featuring actual lyrics sung by Mike Oldfield. It's unclear if this new vocal part dates from the original *QE2* sessions or is more recent. Either way, it's an interesting new version and one of the great little treats on the remasters.

Europe *Two Sides - The Very Best Of Mike Oldfield* 2xCD (5339182)

CD 1:
"Tubular Bells (Part One) (Two Sides Excerpt)"
"Ommadawn (Part One) (Two Sides Excerpt)"
"Crises (Two Sides Excerpt)"
"The Lake (Two Sides Excerpt)"
"Amarok ('Fast Riff Intro' & 'Intro')"

"Amarok ('Africa I, II & III')"
"Sentinel (Two Sides Version)"
"Supernova (Two Sides Version)"
"Ascension (Two Sides Version)"
"The Tempest (Two Sides Version)"

CD 1:
"Guilty (2011 'Slow' Version)"
"Family Man"
"Five Miles Out"
"Moonlight Shadows"
"Shadow On The Wall" Mike Oldfield And Roger Chapman
"To France (Single Version)"
"Étude"
"Magic Touch"
"Islands" Mike Oldfield Featuring Bonnie Tyler
"Heaven's Open" Michael Oldfield
"Tattoo (Live at Edinburgh Castle)"
"The Song Of The Sun" – a cover of the 1988 song "O son do ar" by Luar Na Lubre.
"Summit Day"
"Lake Constance"
"Broad Sunlit Uplands"
"The Doges Palace"
"Amber Light (Two Sides Version)"
"Angelique"
"On My Heart (Edit)"

"Tubular Bells (Part One) (Two Sides Excerpt)" 13:28
Written by Mike Oldfield
Appears on: Two Sides - The Very Best Of Mike Oldfield, Moonlight Shadow - The Collection
This excerpt starts with the "Introduction" and continues through to "Blues" before fading out early.

"Ommadawn (Part One) (Two Sides Excerpt)" 6:47
Written by Mike Oldfield
Appears on: Two Sides - The Very Best Of Mike Oldfield
This excerpt is of the 4th and 5th movements of "Part One," almost the same as the earlier excerpt that appeared on *Wonderland*, *The Complete* and various others. Here, instead of a longer, gradual fade in, it's a faster fade at a later point in the 4th movement.

"Crises (Two Sides Excerpt)" 10:29
Written by Mike Oldfield
Appears on: Two Sides - The Very Best Of Mike Oldfield
This is the 4th and 5th movements of "Crises," basically the second half of the piece, fading in after the "Watcher and the tower" vocal movement.

"The Lake (Two Sides Excerpt)" 5:29
Written by Mike Oldfield
Appears on: Two Sides - The Very Best Of Mike Oldfield
This is the first five and a half minutes of the piece, fading out at the end.

"Amarok ('Fast Riff Intro' & 'Intro')" 5:04
Written by Mike Oldfield
Appears on: Two Sides - The Very Best Of Mike Oldfield
This is the first two segments of the album, fading out a bit early during "Intro."

"Amarok ('Africa I, II & II')" 15:15
Written by Mike Oldfield
Appears on: Two Sides – The Very Best Of Mike Oldfield
And this is the last section of the album, the complete three "Africa" movements.

"Sentinel (Two Sides Version)" 8:08
Written by Mike Oldfield
Appears on: Two Sides – The Very Best Of Mike Oldfield
This very minor edit fades out quickly at the end of the closing explosion.

"Supernova (Two Sides Version)" 3:23
Written by Mike Oldfield
Appears on: Two Sides – The Very Best Of Mike Oldfield
Instead of segueing from the previous track, as it does on the album, this version fades in nicely and fades out over the build up leading into "Magellan."

"Ascension (Two Sides Version)"
Written by Mike Oldfield
Appears on: Two Sides – The Very Best Of Mike Oldfield
This very minor edit fades out quickly at the end of the closing explosions.

"The Tempest (Two Sides Version)" 5:48
Written by Mike Oldfield
Appears on: Two Sides – The Very Best Of Mike Oldfield
Like "Supernova," this version fades in rather than starting with the segue from "Shabda"

"Amber Light (Two Sides Version)" 3:44
Written by Mike Oldfield
Appears on: Two Sides – The Very Best Of Mike Oldfield
On *The Millennium Bell* album, this track segues into the title track. Here, the piece fades out quickly at the end.

Also released by Mercury Records is **Mike Oldfield**'s *Classic Album Selection (Six Albums 1973 – 1980)* 6xCD boxed set.

CD 1: *Tubular Bells* (2009 Stereo Mix)
CD 2: *Hergest Ridge* (2010 Stereo Mix)
CD 3: *Ommadawn* (2010 Stereo Mix)
CD 4: *Incantations* (2011 Remastered Edition)
CD 5: *Platinum* (2012 Remaster)
CD 6: *QE2* (2012 Remaster)

-August-
Universal Music holds a contest for fans to remix the "Two Sides Excerpt" of *Tubular Bells*, using multitrack stems available on IndabaMusi.com. The winner (David Schornsheim) receives £1,000 and a merchandise package from **Mike Oldfield**.

-September 25-
York releases his album *Islanders* in Europe on CD (88765421032), featuring his **Mike Oldfield** collaboration "Islanders."

"Islanders (Chill Out Mix)" 9:12
Written by York & Mike Oldfield
Appears on: Islanders
Even with the recent re-issues of Mike Oldfield's albums and his Summer Olympics Opening Ceremony appearance, there hadn't been much new in the way of Mike Oldfield material since *Music Of The Spheres*. This collaboration was a welcome sight for fans, offering hope that something new might still be on the horizon. Don't let the title "Chill Out Mix" fool you, this isn't a dance club mix, it's a pleasant trance piece with plenty of Mike, a genuine co-production, with the two men creating the track between them. Mike's guitar really shines and the track grooves along beautifully for 9+ minutes, ebbing and flowing, creating a picturesque place of sun and clear water.

-October 8-
Mercury Records releases the 12" One-sided **Mike Oldfield** single "Music For The Opening Ceremony Of The London 2012 Olympic Games" in the UK.

UK 12" One-sided single (00602537159628):
"Music For The Opening Ceremony Of The London 2012 Olympic Games"

The sleeve and label breakdown the track by its movements as follows:

"Music For The Opening Ceremony Of The London 2012 Olympic Games
    Tubular Bells (Part One Excerpt)
    Tubular Bells (Part One - Swing)
    Tubular Bells (Part Two Excerpt)
    Tubular Bells III (Far Above The Clouds)
    Mary Poppins Arrival
    Fanfare For The Isle Of Wonder
    In Dulci Jubilo
    Olympic Tubular Bells Coda"

-October 12-
Terry Oldfield featuring Mike Oldfield releases the album *Journey Into Space* in the UK and North America. **Mike** features on the tracks "Origin," "Flight Of The Eagle" and "Dancer In The Void." The songwriting credits are a little vague, noting "All music by Terry Oldfield, Mike Oldfield and Soraya Saraswati," except for one traditional piece. I assume then that **Mike** didn't actually co-write the pieces he's not on.

"Origin" 4:49
Written by Terry Oldfield & Mike Oldfield
Appears on: Journey Into Space
A great piece, with a very aboriginal/native flavour. Terry plays the Bansuri flute, keyboards and sings, with Mike on guitar. As the first track, it sets up the journey into space by starting us firmly on the Earth, away from civilization.

"Flight Of The Eagle" 5:55
Written by Terry Oldfield & Mike Oldfield
Appears on: Journey Into Space
Terry's notes in the album provide a glimpse into, of all things, their short-lived days in the band **Barefoot**, where he says they had a song that started and ended in a very similar way as this (and he quickly points out that this is not that song). This track starts with a guitar strum and Terry singing, joined by Mike's playing, after the opening verse the song picks up with some chanting and the song is an uptempo instrumental creating the image of flight for the sheer love of it. The end features another verse over Mike's guitar again.

"Dancer In The Void" 6:22
Written by Terry Oldfield & Mike Oldfield
Appears on: Journey Into Space
Terry on Bansuri flute, keyboards and vocals again, with Mike on guitar. As with the other two pieces, this is relaxation music, chill out if you will, but much more organic than the computer-based work as hear on *Tr3s Lunas* and *Light + Shade*, so if you're looking for that side of Mike in his projects, seek this album out. The rest of the album is excellent, as well.

Note: Some sources list the release date as September 24.

-Date Unknown-
Mike Oldfield works on remastering and remixing his albums *Five Miles Out* and *Crises*, as his home studio, Nassau, The Bahamas. He also continues collaboratively remixing his work with York and writing and recording his forthcoming "rock album."

-November 9-
The *Amarok* newsletter notes that **Mike Oldfield** is currently working on his new "rock album," with plans to include different male and female guest vocalists.

Tubular Beats

2013

-January 11-
earMusic, a division of Edel Records, releases the music video for "Guilty (Mike Oldfield & York Remix)" on YouTube.

"Guilty (Mike Oldfield & York Video Remix)" 3:34
Written by Mike Oldfield
Appears on: N/A
This remix is pretty different from the mix on the album, with the elements of Mike's original much more upfront. It repeats samples and breaks down parts in a nice, compact version.

-February 1-
Mike Oldfield releases his collaboration remix album with York, *Tubular Beats*, on Edel Records, though the front sleeve doesn't list York at all, despite being a project they shared. Track listing as follows:

"Let There Be Light (York Remix)" - does not feature **Mike**.
"Far Above The Clouds (York Remix)" - does not feature **Mike**.
"Ommadawn (Mike Oldfield & York Remix)"
"Guilty (Mike Oldfield & York Remix)"
"Tubular Bells (Mike Oldfield & York Remix)"
"To France (York & Steve Brian Radio Mix)" – does not feature **Mike**.
"North Star (Mike Oldfield & York Remix)"
"Moonlight Shadow (York & Steve Brian Radio Mix)" – does not feature **Mike**.
"Guilty (Mike Oldfield & York Electrofunkremix)"
"Tubular Bells 2 (Mike Oldfield & York Remix)"
"Never Too Far" – new song, co-written by **Oldfield**, Stenzel and singer Tarja Turunen.

-February 18-
Kevin Ayers dies in his sleep, Montolieu, France. Ayers hired **Mike Oldfield** as bass player (and later guitarist) for **The Whole World**. **Mike** appears on Ayers' albums *Shooting At The Moon*, *Whatevershebringwesing*, *The Confessions Of Dr. Dream And Other Stories*, *Still Life With Guitar* and the live album *June 1, 1974*, as well as various non-album recordings, such as "Stars" and "Lady Rachel." Ayers recorded two versions of "Flying Start," one for **Oldfield**'s album *Islands* and one for his own album *Falling Up*. Ayers rented the house in Tottenham and lent **Mike** his tape recorder so that **Mike** could record the demos that became *Tubular Bells* while he lived there.

-Date Unknown-
Ear Music releases a promo CD single of the *Tubular Beats* remix tracks "To France" and "Moonlight Shadow" in Germany. It is credited to 'Mike Oldfield,' however those specific tracks do not feature material or production by **Mike Oldfield**.

Germany CD single (0208638EREP):
"To France (York & Steve Brian Radio Mix)" – does not feature **Mike**.
"Moonlight Shadow (York & Steve Brian Radio Mix)" – does not feature **Mike**.

-Date Unknown-
Fanny and **Mike Oldfield** separate.

-April 20-
Virgin Records issues a Record Store Day exclusive re-issue of *Mike Oldfield's Single* (though with a different track listing) in the UK and Europe.

Mike Oldfield's Single (2013 Record Store Day Edition)
UK 7" single (VS.101X):
"Tubular Bells (Opening Theme)"
"In Dulci Jubilo"

Mike Oldfield's Single (2013 Record Store Day Edition)
Europe 7" single (0602537540525):
"Tubular Bells (Opening Theme)"
"In Dulci Jubilo"

-April 22-
Spectrum Records releases the **Mike Oldfield** compilation *Moonlight Shadow - The Collection* in the UK on CD (SPEC2134). Track listing as follows:

"Tubular Bells (Part One) (Two Sides Excerpt)"
"Ommadawn (Part One) (Elements Excerpt)"
"In Dulci Jubilo"
"First Excursion"
"Diana (2011 Stereo Mix)"
"Platinum (Part One): Airborne (Moonlight Shadow Edit)"
"Guilty (2011 'Slow' Version)"
"Blue Peter" – a cover of the 1958 TV show theme.
"Sheba"
"Mount Teidi"
"Moonlight Shadow"
"Good News"
"Amarok ('Fast Riff Intro' & 'Intro')"
"Slipstream"
"Sunset"
"Aurora (Moonlight Shadow Edit)"

> "Platinum (Part One): Airborne (Moonlight Shadow Edit)" 5:04
> Written by Mike Oldfield
> Appears on: Moonlight Shadow – The Collection
> This edit fades out at the end, before "Platinum" starts.
>
> "Aurora (Moonlight Shadow Edit)" 3:44
> Written by Mike Oldfield
> Appears on: Moonlight Shadow – The Collection
> This edit also fades out nicely at the end.

Note: Some sources list the release date as April 30.

-May-
Ben Wiseman and Mark Powell mix the Cologne, December 6, 1982, concert and the Wembley Arena, July 22, 1983, concert at Audio Archiving Company, London, England.

-Summer-
Mike Oldfield completes his demos for his *Rocks* album (the working title for *Man On The Rocks*) at his home studio, Nassau, The Bahamas. John Robinson previously recorded his drum parts at Steak House Studios, Los Angeles, California, US. Since the start of the project he has recorded the following:

"Sailing (Demo)" 4:14
Written by Mike Oldfield
Appears on: Man On The Rocks (Super Deluxe Edition)
As Mike decided to release the demos for the album on the Super Deluxe Edition, fans get to hear the album as it was as a work in progress. Before Luke Spiller came in and before the backing track were re-done by his session group, Mike did all the parts (except for drums) himself, including singing. His vocals are immediately familiar to fans, who heard him singing like this last on *Heaven's Open*. This version of the track is a bit rougher and with a slightly more basic backing track. The acoustic guitar part from this demo is retained for the final album version.

"Moonshine (Demo)" 5:25
Written by Mike Oldfield
Appears on: Man On The Rocks (Super Deluxe Edition)
The familiar "Song Of The Boat Men" melody is there, but you may also spot a bit of "The Time Has Come" musical phrase just before the chorus, less obvious in the album version. The backing track is simpler, too, with acoustic guitar and recorder and a feeling more like a jaunty folk drinking song you'd hear down at the pub. The ending of the track just sees Mike stop playing, much like the end of "Rite Of Man." Mike says in a promo video for the album that the original title for the song was "Whiskey In The Wind," but it didn't work, so he changed it to "Moonshine." He doesn't say if that was before or after "The Song Of The Boat Men," but he was apparently inspired by a previous boat trip where one of his band members brought out a flask to warm everyone up.

"Man On The Rocks (Demo)" 5:40
Written by Mike Oldfield
Appears on: Man On The Rocks (Super Deluxe Edition)
Somehow, coming from Mike, this version has an earnestness and reflective quality, different from the more polished album version. Perhaps because it's a very personal song and one can't help but wonder if the direct inspiration is the recent break-up with his wife Fanny. Maybe I'm reading too much into it. Mike says the song is about different kinds of addiction.

"Minutes (Demo)" 4:28
Written by Mike Oldfield
Appears on: Man On The Rocks (Super Deluxe Edition)
This demo starts with the drum track counting in before the acoustic guitar, which is the other way around on the album. Like the other demos, this also features a rougher temporary backing track.

"Dreaming In The Wind (Demo)" 5:27
Written by Mike Oldfield
Appears on: Man On The Rocks (Super Deluxe Edition)
John Robinson's drum parts here were retained for the album version. In fact, some of the other backing track elements sound similar to the finished version, so may have been retained from this. There's less production on this, fewer little bits of instrumentation, giving it a bit lighter feel. Mike says this was second track he wrote for the album, when he didn't yet know the musical direction the album would take.

"Nuclear (Demo)" 4:54
Written by Mike Oldfield
Appears on: Man On The Rocks (Super Deluxe Edition)
Not far off from the finished version, all the ideas and textures are present. The guitar here is subtly less grinding and distorted.

"Chariots (Demo)" 3:54
Written by Mike Oldfield
Appears on: Man On The Rocks (Super Deluxe Edition)

The vocals come in almost immediately, as opposed to after the lengthier intro heard on the album, adding to the runtime of the finished version. This demo is heavier, without the rhythm guitar prominence of the later recording. Mike draws parallels between this and "Shadow On The Wall" when discussing it in a promo video.

> "Following The Angels (Demo)" 6:24
> Written by Mike Oldfield
> Appears on: Man On The Rocks (Super Deluxe Edition)
> Similar to the album version, though a different recording, this demonstrates the basic arrangement Mike started out with, before experimenting with the heavier version of heard in the "Alternate Mix." Ultimately, he went with the lighter production. Mike says this song came about as a way to express his feelings having performed at the Olympic Opening Ceremonies.

> "I Give Myself Away (Demo) 5:08
> Written by William McDowell (arr. Oldfield)
> Appears on: Man On The Rocks (Super Deluxe Edition)
> Mike says he wasn't planning on putting this on the album until Steve Lipson convinced him to. This is a cover of the Christian Rock song by William McDowell (noted as "gospel" rather than "Christian Rock" in articles and promotional material. Hmm, three guesses as to why...). Mike's version, though, changes some lyrics and the context shifts completely. Instead of the singer giving himself to God, Mike's version, here and on the album, has the singer lamenting that giving himself to his lover is what leads to his ultimate unhappiness. There's also the play on words, that the singer gives himself away, as in always reveals himself emotionally (and the music tells us what gets revealed is maybe something pathetic and sad underneath). As for this demo, it has a heavier backing track, lacking the subtly of the album version.

It's from these demos that Luke Spiller first works on his vocals for the tracks, having been brought onto the project prior to the June sessions.

-June-
Mike Oldfield records the backing tracks for his next album (*Man On The Rocks* sessions). The sessions take place via Skype, with **Oldfield** at his home studio, Nassau, The Bahamas, and the session musicians in Studio D, Village Studios, Los Angeles, California, US. Steve Lipson co-produces these sessions with **Mike** and plays electric and acoustic guitar. The session musicians include John Robinson, Leland, Sklar, Matt Rollings, and Michael Thompson.

> "Castaway (Demo)" 6:24
> Written by Mike Oldfield
> Appears on: Man On The Rocks (Super Deluxe Edition)
> Apart from a few minor mixing differences, this is Mike singing to the same backing track that Luke Spiller sing on for the album, indicating that this recording was made after the June sessions. This version fades out earlier, too. Mike says this song came from when, early in the process of making the album, he looked at his childhood and the traumas related to it.

> "Irene (Demo)" 3:59
> Written by Mike Oldfield
> Appears on: Man On The Rocks (Super Deluxe Edition)
> Like "Castaway," this is Mike singing to the same backing track as heard on the album.

-July-
Luke Spiller records his finished vocals for the *Rocks* album, via Skype. He and **Mike** don't actually meet face to face until they later shoot the video for "Sailing." A homemade video from The Village Studios, Los Angeles, California, US, shows the session musicians listening to playback of a mix of "Moonshine," with Spiller's vocal, dated July 1, 2013, indicating Luke's sessions were in tandem with the LA sessions.

-September 2 & 9-
Mike Oldfield releases *Five Miles Out* (2013 Remastered Edition) and *Crises* (2013 Remastered Edition) in the UK, Europe and North America.

Five Miles Out (2013 Remastered Edition)

LP: *Five Miles Out* (2013 Remaster) (274 044-1)
"Taurus II"
"Family Man"
"Orabidoo"
"Mount Teidi"
"Five Miles Out"

LP: *Five Miles Out* (2013 Remaster) 180 gram Yellow vinyl (374 044-2)

CD: *Five Miles Out* (2013 Remastered Edition) ((274 043-8)
"Taurus II"
"Family Man"
"Orabidoo"
"Mount Teidi"
"Five Miles Out"
"Waldberg (The Peak)" The Mike Oldfield Group
"Five Miles Out (Demo)"

Five Miles Out (2013 Remaster) Deluxe Edition (2xCD + DVD) (374 043-7)
CD 1: *Five Miles Out* (2013 Remastered Edition)
"Taurus II"
"Family Man"
"Orabidoo"
"Mount Teidi"
"Five Miles Out"
"Waldberg (The Peak)" The Mike Oldfield Group
"Five Miles Out (Demo)"

CD 2: *Live In Cologne - 6 December 1982 - Five Miles Out Tour* The Mike Oldfield Group

DVD: *Five Miles Out* 5.1 Digital Surround Sound Mix
 "Taurus II" 5.1 Digital Surround Sound Mix
"Family Man" 5.1 Digital Surround Sound Mix
"Orabidoo" 5.1 Digital Surround Sound Mix
"Mount Teidi" 5.1 Digital Surround Sound Mix
"Five Miles Out" 5.1 Digital Surround Sound Mix
"Five Miles Out" Promotional Video
"Five Miles Out" 6:55 Special - The Mike Oldfield Group
"Mistake" 6:55 Special - The Mike Oldfield Group

> "Family Man" 5.1 Digital Surround Sound Mix
> Written by Oldfield, Cross, Fenn, Frye, Reilly and Pert
> Appears on: Five Miles Out (2013 Deluxe Edition)
> For the 5.1 mix, the track seems to run too slow and various elements are substantially remixed. Yes, a 5.1 mix normally lets you hear the piece in a much different way, but this version actually alters the song a good deal more. In addition to the odd speed, things like the "plink, plink" sounds are completely absent.

Crises (2013 Remastered Edition)

LP: *Crises* – 2013 Remaster 180 gram (374 044-9)
"Crises"
"Moonlight Shadow"
"In High Places" Mike Oldfield Featuring Jon Anderson
"Foreign Affair"
"Taurus 3"
"Shadow On The Wall" Mike Oldfield And Roger Chapman

LP: *Crises* – 2013 Remaster (374 045-1) Green 180 gram vinyl (500 Limited Edition copies)

CD: *Crises* (2013 Remastered Edition) (364 044-5)
"Crises"
"Moonlight Shadow"
"In High Places" Mike Oldfield Featuring Jon Anderson
"Foreign Affair"
"Taurus 3"
"Shadow On The Wall" Mike Oldfield And Roger Chapman
"Moonlight Shadow (2013 Unplugged Mix)"
"Shadow On The Wall (2013 Unplugged Mix)"
"Mistake" The Mike Oldfield Group
"Crime Of Passion (Extended Version)"
"Jungle Gardenia"
"Moonlight Shadow (Extended Version)"
"Shadow On The Wall (12" Version)" Mike Oldfield And Roger Chapman

Crises (2013 Remastered Edition) Deluxe Edition (2xCD) (374 044-7)
CD 1: *Crises* (2013 Remastered Edition)
CD 2: *Highlights from Wembley Arena 22 July 1983* – this is the second half of the concert (see below)

Crises (2013 Remastered Edition) 30th Anniversary Boxed Set (3xCD+2xDVD) (374044-8)
CD 1: *Crises* (2013 Remastered Edition)
CD 2: *Live at Wembley Arena 22 July 1983* – the first half of the concert
CD 3: *Live at Wembley Arena 22 July 1983* – the same as the *Highlights* CD, the second half of the concert.

DVD 1: *Crises At Wembley* (Excerpts of the 22 July 1983 concert)
"Crises"
"Tubular Bells (Part One)"
"Moonlight Shadow" Promotional Video
"Shadow On The Wall" Promotional Video – Mike Oldfield And Roger Chapman
"Crime Of Passion" Promotional Video
"Moonlight Shadow" *Top Of The Pops*

DVD 2: *Crises* 5.1 Digital Surround Sound Mix
"Crises" 5.1 Digital Surround Sound Mix
"Moonlight Shadow" 5.1 Digital Surround Sound Mix
"In High Places" 5.1 Digital Surround Sound Mix - Mike Oldfield Featuring Jon Anderson
"Foreign Affair" 5.1 Digital Surround Sound Mix
"Taurus 3" 5.1 Digital Surround Sound Mix
"Shadow On The Wall" 5.1 Digital Surround Sound Mix – Mike Oldfield And Roger Chapman

> "Moonlight Shadow (2013 Unplugged Mix)" 3:36
> Written by Mike Oldfield
> Appears on: Crises (2013 Remastered, Deluxe & 30th Anniversary Editions)

Pretty much as described, this mix strips out most of the electric guitars, bass and drums, leaving the track to be mostly Maggie Reilly and Mike's acoustic guitar. The electric guitars do come in for the solo and remain until the end. Reilly's vocals recur over the entire guitar solo (which is a bit distracting) and the song ends not in a fade out, but at full volume, which is pretty neat.

"Shadow On The Wall (2013 Unplugged Mix)" 3:23
Written by Mike Oldfield
Appears on: Crises (2013 Remastered, Deluxe & 30th Anniversary Editions)
Like "Moonlight Shadow," this almost entirely stripped down, removing the drums, bass and electric guitar. Some synths survive low in the mix under the verses. The layers of acoustic guitar backing parts are fantastic, giving the song an almost folk sound. The backing vocals at the end also sound great, which come from the "12" Version."

Crises 5.1 Digital Surround Sound Mix
Written by Mike Oldfield ("In High Places" Oldfield & Anderson, "Foreign Affair" Oldfield & Reilly)
Appears on: Crises (30th Anniversary Boxed Set)
Previously, the 5.1 mixes of the album re-issues, starting with Tubular Bells in 2009, were very faithful the original albums, not making a lot of changes. Crises would prove different. The 5.1 mix alters each of the tracks to varying degrees, now offering us a different version of the album.
For example:
"Crises" has more noticeable extra drum and percussion parts throughout.
"Moonlight Shadow" features the intro from the "Extended Version," the vocals parts over the guitar solo and it ends at full volume, no fade out.
"In High Places" doesn't start with Jon Anderson's solo vocals, but are now accompanied by the full backing track.
"Foreign Affair" has additional backing vocals and an accordian part at the end.
"Taurus 3" starts with an extended drum intro over the synths and the sudden finish is followed by a reprise of those same synth.
"Shadow On The Wall" is based on the "12" Version," rather than the album version, so the we get the extended ending and second guitar solo.

-Autumn-
Mike Oldfield completes work on his album *Man On The Rocks,* at his home studio, Nassau, The Bahamas. Sessions took place there and at The Village, Los Angeles, California, US, and at Battery Studios, London, England. Stephen Lipson co-produced the album with **Oldfield** and played acoustic and electric guitar. Luke Spiller (of The Struts) records lead vocals.

"Sailing (Alternate Mix)" 4:45
Written by Mike Oldfield
Appears on: Man On The Rocks (Super Deluxe Edition)
This mix isn't too far from the album version, featuring a bit more prominent guitars throughout, making for a slightly heavier version of the track.

"Dreaming In The Wind (Alternate Mix)" 5:25
Written by Mike Oldfield
Appears on: Man On The Rocks (Super Deluxe Edition)
This mix also isn't that far from the album version, with the electric guitar being a bit more present in the mix.

"Following The Angels (Alternate Mix)" 7:04
Written by Mike Oldfield
Appears on: Man On The Rocks (Super Deluxe Edition)
This mix is a much more heavily produced one compared to the album version. The backing track has more power, giving a more rock than acoustic feel.

"I Give Myself Away (Alternate Mix) 5:11
Written by William McDowell (arr. Oldfield)
Appears on: Man On The Rocks (Super Deluxe Edition)
Like "Following The Angels," this mix has heavier production on it, with a more dominant backing track and double-tracked vocals for more power.

-October 11-
Virgin EMI issues a press release about the forthcoming new **Mike Oldfield** album, *Man On The Rocks*, scheduled for release January 27, 2014 (it would later be pushed back to March 3rd, 2014).

-November 3-
Mike Oldfield does an interview, broadcast on this date, on Stuart Maconie's *Freak Zone* discussing his career and *Man On The Rocks*.

Man On The Rocks

2014

-Early 2014-
Fanny and **Mike Oldfield** are granted a divorce.

-February 7-
Mike Oldfield releases the music video for his forthcoming single "Sailing" on iTunes.

>"Sailing (Radio Edit)" 3:34
>Written by Mike Oldfield
>Appears on: UK CDr Promo single; UK Digital single
>This edit cuts the song down by removing some of the material throughout. It doesn't hurt the song at all.

-February 8-
Mike Oldfield releases the music video for his forthcoming single "Sailing" on YouTube.

-February 18-
Mike Oldfield releases the music videos for his song "Man On The Rocks (Acoustic Version)" on YouTube.

>"Man On The Rocks (Acoustic Version)" 4:40
>Written by Mike Oldfield
>Appears on: YouTube; Man On The Rocks digital single
>This video features a new mix of the song, with only Spiller's vocals and Oldfield's acoustic guitar. It works really well. The track is also edited down, removing sections where the electric guitar dominated.

-February 26-
An "Unplugged" version of "Chariots," complete with video featuring **Mike Oldfield** and Luke Spiller (similar to the "Man On The Rocks [Acoustic Version])," is uploaded onto YouTube, interestingly not via an official record company or artist account.

>"Chariots (Unplugged Version)" 3:15
>Written by Mike Oldfield
>Appears on: N/A
>It's possible this was viral leak (or an official posting somewhere that was quickly removed, but not before someone copied it and posted it themselves), as the video is similar to the "Man On The Rocks (Acoustic Version)," likely shot on the same day. The mix of the song features only Luke's vocal and Mike's acoustic guitar and it's quite good.

-March 3-
Mike Oldfield releases his album *Man On The Rocks* in the UK and Europe on Virgin EMI. Several Editions are released. Track listing as follows:

UK & Europe *Man On The Rocks* 2xLP (376 069-8)
UK & Europe *Man On The Rocks* 2xLP (376 069-9) Blue vinyl

LP 1:
Side 1:
"Sailing"
"Moonshine"
Side 2:
"Man On The Rocks"
"Castaway"
"Minutes"

LP 2:
Side 1:
"Dreaming In The Wind"
"Nuclear"
"Chariots"
Side 2:
"Following The Angels"
"Irene"
"I Give Myself Away" – a cover of the 2009 song by William McDowell.

UK & Europe *Man On The Rocks* CD (376 069-5)
CD: *Man On The Rocks*
"Sailing"
"Moonshine"
"Man On The Rocks"
"Castaway"
"Minutes"
"Dreaming In The Wind"
"Nuclear"
"Chariots"
"Following The Angels"
"Irene"
"I Give Myself Away" – a cover of the 2009 song by William McDowell.

UK & Europe *Man On The Rocks* 2xCD Deluxe Edition (376 069-6)
CD 1: *Man On The Rocks*

CD 2: *Instrumental Versions*
"Sailing (Instrumental)"
"Moonshine (Instrumental)"
"Man On The Rocks (Instrumental)"
"Castaway (Instrumental)"
"Minutes (Instrumental)"
"Dreaming In The Wind (Instrumental)"
"Nuclear (Instrumental)"
"Chariots (Instrumental)"
"Following The Angels (Instrumental)"
"Irene (Instrumental)"
"I Give Myself Away (Instrumental)" – a cover of the 2009 song by William McDowell.

UK & Europe *Man On The Rocks* 3xCD Super Deluxe Edition (376 933-8)
CD 1: *Man On The Rocks*
CD 2: *Instrumental Versions*

CD 3: *Demos & Alternate Versions*
"Sailing (Demo)"
"Moonshine (Demo)"
"Man On The Rocks (Demo)"
"Castaway (Demo)"
"Minutes (Demo)"
"Dreaming In The Wind (Demo)"
"Nuclear (Demo)"
"Chariots (Demo)"
"Following The Angels (Demo)"
"Irene (Demo)"
"I Give Myself Away (Demo)" – a cover of the 2009 song by William McDowell.
"Sailing (Alternate Mix)"
"Dreaming In The Wind (Alternate Mix)"
"Follow The Angels (Alternate Mix)"
"I Give Myself Away (Alternate Mix)" – a cover of the 2009 song by William McDowell.

    "Sailing (Instrumental)" 4:46
    Written by Mike Oldfield
    Appears on: Man On The Rocks (Super Deluxe Edition)
    This is the complete backing track for the song.

    "Moonshine (Instrumental)" 5:46
    Written by Mike Oldfield
    Appears on: Man On The Rocks (Super Deluxe Edition)
    This is the complete backing track for the song, or looking at it another way, a different version of "The Song Of The Boat Men."

    "Man On The Rocks (Instrumental)" 6:11
    Written by Mike Oldfield
    Appears on: Man On The Rocks (Super Deluxe Edition)
    This is the complete backing track for the song.

    "Castaway (Instrumental)" 6:37
    Written by Mike Oldfield
    Appears on: Man On The Rocks (Super Deluxe Edition)
    This is the complete backing track for the song.

    "Minutes (Instrumental)" 4:51
    Written by Mike Oldfield
    Appears on: Man On The Rocks (Super Deluxe Edition)
    This is the complete backing track for the song.

    "Dreaming In The Wind (Instrumental)" 5:33
    Written by Mike Oldfield
    Appears on: Man On The Rocks (Super Deluxe Edition)
    This is the complete backing track for the song.

    "Nuclear (Instrumental)" 5:03
    Written by Mike Oldfield
    Appears on: Man On The Rocks (Super Deluxe Edition); 7" single Record Store Day Picture disc
    This is the complete backing track for the song.

> "Chariots (Instrumental)" 4:26
> Written by Mike Oldfield
> Appears on: Man On The Rocks (Super Deluxe Edition)
> This is the complete backing track for the song.
>
> "Following The Angels (Instrumental)" 7:06
> Written by Mike Oldfield
> Appears on: Man On The Rocks (Super Deluxe Edition)
> This is the complete backing track for the song.
>
> "Irene (Instrumental)" 3:58
> Written by Mike Oldfield
> Appears on: Man On The Rocks (Super Deluxe Edition)
> This is the complete backing track for the song.
>
> "I Give Myself Away (Instrumental)" 5:08
> Written by William McDowell (arr. Oldfield)
> Appears on: Man On The Rocks (Super Deluxe Edition)
> This is the complete backing track for the song.

Mike Oldfield also releases on Virgin EMI Records a promo CDr single of "Sailing" in the UK.

UK 1-track CDr single promo:
"Sailing (Radio Edit)"

-March 7-
Mike Oldfield releases the music video for his new song "Man On The Rocks (Electric Version)" on YouTube. This is the same version as on the album, but is a different video from the "Acoustic Version."

-March 15-
In an article published on this date in the *Huffington Post*, **Mike Oldfield** expresses the idea of doing a prequel to *Tubular Bells*, a look back to a time before synthesizers.

-March 17-
In an article published on this date on hmv.com, **Mike Oldfield** again expresses the idea of doing a prequel to *Tubular Bells*.

-May 5-
Virgin EMI Records releases **Mike Oldfield**'s "Moonshine" promo CDr single in the UK.

UK 1-track CDr single promo:
"Moonshine (Radio Edit)"

> "Moonshine (Radio Edit)" 3:26
> Written by Mike Oldfield
> Appears on: UK CDr Promo single; UK Digital single
> Like with "Man On The Rocks" from the UK Digial single, it is both an edit and a remix.

-May 20-
Mike Oldfield issues a thank you to his fans for their birthday wishes of May 15th and says he's currently working on a radio edit for the next single from *Man On The Rocks*.

-August 4-
Mike Oldfield releases his "Man On The Rocks" digital single in the UK.

UK digital single:
"Man On The Rocks (Radio Edit)"
"Moonshine (Radio Edit)"
"Sailing (Radio Edit)"
Video: "Man On The Rocks (Acoustic Version)"

    "Man On The Rocks (Radio Edit)" 3:48
    Written by Mike Oldfield
    Appears on: UK Digital single
    This version is both an edit and a remix of the track.

-October-
Warner Music releases the following **Mike Oldfield** albums on 180 vinyl LP in the UK and Europe.

2014 *Tubular Bells III* LP (2564623317)
2014 *Voyager* LP (2564623319)

-October 20 & 21-
Warner Music releases an 8xCD boxed set of **Mike Oldfield**'s post-Virgin albums titled *The Studio Albums: 1992 - 2003* in Europe.

The Studio Albums: 1992 - 2003 8xCD (825646233298)
CD 1: *Tubular Bells II*
CD 2: *The Songs Of Distant Earth*
CD 3: *Voyager*
CD 4: *Tubular Bells III*
CD 5: *Guitars*
CD 6: *The Millennium Bell*

CD 7: *Tr3s Lunas* The Studio Albums Boxed Set Edition
"Misty"
"No Man's Land"
"Return To The Origin"
"Landfall"
"Viper"
"Turtle Island"
"To Be Free"
"Fire Fly"
"Tr3s Lunas"
"Daydream"
"Thou Art In Heaven"
"Sirius"
"No Man's Land (Reprise)"

CD 8: *Tubular Bells 2003*

-Date Unknown
Mike Oldfield begins work on remastering his album *Discovery* and his Original Film Soundtrack album *The Killing Fields*. Work takes place at his home in Nassau, The Bahamas, and at The Audio Archiving Company, London, England.

Zombies

2015

-April 27-
Warner Music releases the following **Mike Oldfield** albums on 180 vinyl LP in the UK and Europe.

2014 *The Songs Of Distant Earth* LP (2564623321)
2014 *Tubular Bells II* LP (2564623323)

Also released is the 2xCD *The Best Of: 1992 - 2003* in the UK and Europe. Track listing as follows:

CD 1:
"Sentinel (Single Restructure)"
"Tattoo (Edit)"
"The Bell (MC Viv Stanshall)"
"Hibernaculum (Single Version)"
"Let There Be Light (Single Version)"
"The Voyager"
"Women Of Ireland (Lurker Edit)"
"Man In The Rain"
"Far Above The Clouds (Timewriter's Radio Edit)"
"Cochise"
"Out Of Mind"
"Pacha Mama"
"Sunlight Shining Through Cloud"
"Amber Light"
"To Be Free (Radio Edit)"
"Though Art In Heaven (Radio Edit)"
"Tubular Bells 2003: Introduction (Radio Edit)"
"Tubular Bells 2003: The Sailor's Hornpipe"

CD 2: *Rarities & Mixes*
"Early Stages"
"Silent Night"
"The Bell (MC Billy Connolly)"
"The Spectral Army"
"The Song Of The Boat Men"
"Indian Lake"
"Mike's Reel"
"Sentinel (Orbular Bells Mix)" Mike Oldfield vs The ORB
"Let There Be Light (BT's Pure Luminescence Remix)"
"Women Of Ireland (System 7 12" Mix)"
"Far Above The Clouds (Jam & Spoon Mix)"
"To Be Free (Soultronik Mix-tical Mix)"
"Thou Art In Heaven (Pumpin' Dolls v Mighty Mike Radio Edit)"

-May 17-
Dougal Oldfield, son of **Mike Oldfield** and Sally Cooper, dies suddenly of natural causes, while at work, Soho, London, England.

-July 10-
Universal Music Group releases the **Mike Oldfield** collection *Lo Mejor De... Mike Oldfield* CD (0602547430779) in Spain. Track listing as follows:

"Moonlight Shadow"
"Crystal Gazing"
"Magic Touch (Original Mix)"
"Foreign Affair"
"Family Man"
"Live Punkaddidle" The Mike Oldfield Group
"Aurora (Live At The Guggenheim 2008 Bilbao)"
"Harbinger"
"Mount Teidi"
"Ommadawn (Part One) (Elements Excerpt)"
"Tubular Bells (Now The Original Theme From 'The Exorcist' - Version 1)"
"Sheba"
"Arrival" - a cover of the 1976 ABBA instrumental.
'Étude'
"Angelique"
"Portsmouth"

-Date Unknown-
Mike Oldfield finishes work on remastering his album *Discovery* and his Original Film Soundtrack album *The Killing Fields*. He also assembles *The 1984 Suite* as part of this collective project.

-October 16-
Gonzo Media Group releases a CD+DVD edition of *The Space Movie* Original Soundtrack in UK, featuring the **Mike Oldfield** excerpts heard in the film.

The Space Movie Original Soundtrack CD+DVD (TPCD192)
CD: *The Space Movie* soundtrack
"The Space Movie"

DVD: *The Space Movie* (Directors Cut)

> "The Space Movie" 1:18:22
> Written by N/A
> A licensed release of the soundtrack and movie, this set doesn't do Oldfield fans any favours. Unlike a standard movie soundtrack album, which often includes the full recordings of the tracks featured in the film, this is literally a dump of the film's audio onto CD, without even an attempt to separate the excerpts. Don't be tempted to seek this out. Someday we may get a proper release of "A Spell For Creation," the only piece of music on the soundtrack not to have been released or leaked, but you won't find it here. *The Orchestral Hergest Ridge* isn't hard to find online, so you can assemble this soundtrack almost entirely on your own if it means that much to you.

-October 20-
Jean-Michel Jarre hosts a live Facebook Q&A on this date. **Mike Oldfield** observes the discussion and notes Jarre's answer to a fan's question about the possibility of Jarre working with **Oldfield**. Jarre says that **Oldfield** is "too acoustic" for Jarre's work. **Mike** later reports that this statement directs his attention to focusing on acoustic material for his next album.

-October 30-
In conjunction with the announcement of the forthcoming re-issues of his albums *Discovery* and *The Killing Fields*, **Mike Oldfield** posts on Vevo.com and YouTube a Halloween Special video for the track "Zombies."

"Zombies" 3:46
Written by Mike Oldfield
Appears on: Digital single; Discovery (2016 Remaster) Deluxe Edition, The 1984 Suite LP
Here we have the remixed backing track for "Poison Arrows" with slightly altered lyrics, with "Somebody's out to get you" replaced with "Zombies are out to get you" (same with the "...break you" line). But that's not the really odd bit. Mike has the new vocals performed with computer software (like on the 2011 *Incantations* re-issue and the "Diana – Desiderata" track). This version might take some getting used to.

-October 31-
Mike Oldfield releases "Zombies" as a digital single on Amazon (and possibly other online outlets).

1-track digital single:
"Zombies"

-December-
Mike Oldfield begins working on his next album, in Nassau, The Bahamas (*Return To Ommadawn* sessions). He records that album entirely by himself, with no guest artists involved (however he does use some samples of *Ommadawn* and *Amarok*). The sessions last until November 2016.

The 1984 Suite

2016

-January 14-
Alan Rickman dies of pancreatic cancer in London, England. Rickman, a celebrated actor of stage and screen, was MC on "The Bell" for *Tubular Bells II*, credited as "A Strolling Player."

-January 29-
Mike Oldfield releases his album *Discovery* (2016 Remaster), his Original Film Soundtrack album *The Killing Fields* (2016 Remaster) and *The 1984 Suite* in the UK and Europe in various formats.

Discovery (2016 Remaster)
Note: the spine and back cover list the title as *Discovery And The Lake*.

LP: *Discovery* (2016 Remaster) (474 777-3)
"To France"
"Poison Arrows"
"Crystal Gazing"
"Tricks Of The Light"
"Discovery"
"Talk About Your Life"
"Saved By A Bell"
"The Lake"

CD: *Discovery* (2016 Remaster) (474 657-8)
"To France"
"Poison Arrows"
"Crystal Gazing"
"Tricks Of The Light"
"Discovery"
"Talk About Your Life"
"Saved By A Bell"
"The Lake"
Bonus Tracks
"To France (Extended Version)"
"In The Pool"
"Bones"
"Afghan"
"Tricks Of The Light (Instrumental)"

Discovery (2016 Remaster) Deluxe Edition (2xCD+DVD) (474 657-9)
CD 1: *Discovery* (2016 Remaster)

CD 2: *The 1984 Suite*
"To France (The 1984 Suite)"
"The Lake (The 1984 Suite)"
"The Killing Fields (The 1984 Suite)"
"Étude (The 1984 Suite)"
"The Royal Mile"
"Zombies"
"Discovery (The 1984 Suite)"

DVD: *The 1984 Suite* (5.1 Mix)
"To France (The 1984 Suite)" 5.1 Mix
"The Lake (The 1984 Suite)" 5.1 Mix
"The Killing Fields (The 1984 Suite)" 5.1 Mix
"Étude (The 1984 Suite)" 5.1 Mix
"The Royal Mile" 5.1 Mix
"Zombies" 5.1 Mix
"Discovery (The 1984 Suite)" 5.1 Mix
Music Video "To France"
Music Video "Étude"
Music Video "Tricks Of The Light"

Europe *The 1984 Suite* LP (474 779-1)
Side 1: *The 1984 Suite* Part 1
"To France (The 1984 Suite)"
"The Lake (The 1984 Suite)"
"The Killing Fields (The 1984 Suite)"

Side 2: *The 1984 Suite* Part 2
"Étude (The 1984 Suite)"
"The Royal Mile"
"Zombies"
"Discovery (The 1984 Suite)"

The 1984 Suite
Written by Mike Oldfield ("Étude" by Francisco Tárrega [arr. Oldfield])
Appears on: Discovery (2016 Remaster) Deluxe Edition; The 1984 Suite LP
Rather than remix either or both *Discovery* and *The Killing Fields* into 5.1 surround sound editions, Mike decided to create a suite of material culled from the 1984 sessions of both albums. Both a stereo and 5.1 mix of this suite were created and included on the 2016 *Discovery* Deluxe Edition and by itself on a standalone vinyl release, which is pretty cool.
"To France" is a subtly different mix here than is heard on the original *Discovery* album, with the acoustic guitar having more presence and the synth and drum parts pulled back a little, so the entire track sounds less densely packed. It retains the album outro, which now segues into "The Late."
"The Lake" has been re-mixed and extended, now featuring two longer sections (the up-tempo portion starting around 2:21 and the finale).
"The Killing Fields" as heard here is actually a new mix of "The Boy's Burial / Pran Sees The Red Cross." Apart from sounding cleaner overall, there don't appear to be any significant changes to the original track.
"Étude" now features an added acoustic guitar backing and strangely sounds like a mono mix, with all the instruments crammed into the center on the stereo version. It's still a beautiful piece and the acoustic guitar works well, but the lack of stereo sonic range doesn't help the piece.
"The Royal Mile," the re-discovered track, is "Afghan" with a previously unheard extended intro, some different mixing here and there, and a slightly extended outro. Like with "Étude," it lacks the breadth of stereo heard in the standard B-side version.
"Zombies" sounds identical to the original 2015 digital single release.
"Discovery" is both remixed and is a minor edit, removing some of the intro.

The Killing Fields Original Film Soundtrack (2016 Remaster)

LP: *The Killing Fields* Original Film Soundtrack (2016 Remaster) (474 777-1)
"Pran's Theme"
"Requiem For A City"
"Evacuation"
"Pran's Theme 2"
"Capture"
"Execution"
"Bad News"
"Pran's Departure"
"Worksite"
"The Year Zero" David Bedford
"Blood Sucking"
"The Year Zero 2" David Bedford
"Pran's Escape / The Killing Fields"
"The Trek"
"The Boy's Burial / Pran Sees The Red Cross"
"Good News"
"Étude"

CD: *The Killing Fields* Original Film Soundtrack (2016 Remaster) (474 658-6)
"Pran's Theme"
"Requiem For A City"
"Evacuation"
"Pran's Theme 2"
"Capture"
"Execution"
"Bad News"
"Pran's Departure"
"Worksite"
"The Year Zero" David Bedford
"Blood Sucking"
"The Year Zero 2" David Bedford
"Pran's Escape / The Killing Fields"
"The Trek"
"The Boy's Burial / Pran Sees The Red Cross"
"Good News"
"Étude"
Bonus Tracks:
"Evacuation (Single Edit)"
"Étude (Single Edit)"

-February 4-
Mike Oldfield announces his intention for his new album to be released in August 2016 and that it will include a 5.1 surround sound mix (*Return To Ommadawn* sessions).

-February 12-
Mike Oldfield releases his album *Discovery* (2016 Deluxe Edition), his Original Film Soundtrack album *The Killing Fields* (2016 Remastered Edition) and *The 1984 Suite* in North America in various formats.

-April 9
Mike Oldfield posts on his Facebook Group about the following:
"Return To Ommadawn Pt. II" – **Mike** notes that he has reached "the end of Part 2" and that he's happy with most of it. He also notes that he still has to polish it.

"Return To Ommadawn Pt. I" – **Mike** says he also has to polish Part 1 and that he hopes to have everything done by mid-May.

-April 16-
Virgin EMI Records releases **Mike Oldfield**'s "Nuclear" single as part of Record Store Day in the UK and Europe, in support of its appearance in the video game *Metal Gear Solid V: The Phantom Pain*.

UK & Europe 7" single (476 323-0) Record Store Day Picture disc:
"Nuclear"
"Nuclear (Instrumental)"

-April 21-
Mike Oldfield posts on his Facebook Group a breakdown of his forthcoming album (*Return To Ommadawn* sessions), as follows:

INTRO
Spanish Tune Acoustic
Mandolins 1
Spanish Tune 2
Mandolins 2
High Bridge 1
Spanish Tune 3
High Bridge 2
Bodhrans
Fast Tune 1
Fast Tune Bridge 1
Fast Tune 2
Fast Tune Bridge 2
Fast Tune Boogie 1
Fast Tune Break
Grand Tune 1
Victory V 1
Victory V 2
Victory V 3
Reef Intro
REEF 1
BASS SOLO
HeavyFUZZ
FUZZ TUNE 2
AFRICA 2
Big WhistleTune
BWT END
END TUNE
CLIMAX ENDING
JIG
JIG 2

WhistleInt
Tune 1
EthnicFlute 1
2 Spanish
Glock 1 Riff
Glok 2 Eloc
Glok 3 Mandolins
EthnicFlute 2
Tune 1 *2GT
Not Happy
BIG Tune
Soft Tune
Bolero
Bolero Blues
Glock 3 Blues Guitar
WhistleMIX
Africa 1
CHANT 1
AF PIANO
AF QUIET
AF ACOUSTICS
AF BASS
AF GIBSON SOLO
CODA

Note: Though the order of the two parts isn't indicated in the post (they are simply two screen shots), it would appear in retrospect that Part II is noted first, followed by Part I.

-Date Unknown-
Rhino Records releases the 5xCD set of **Mike Oldfield** albums titled *Original Album Series* in the UK.

Original Album Series 5xCD boxed set (0190295911034)
CD 1: *Tubular Bells II*
CD 2: *The Songs Of Distant Earth*
CD 3: *Voyager*

CD 4: *Tubular Bells III*
CD 5: *Tubular Bells 2003*

-August 11-
Dr. Raymond Henry Oldfield, father of Terry, Sally and **Mike Oldfield**, dies in Germany.

-August 29-
Music On Vinyl releases **Mike Oldfield**'s album *The Millennium Bell* on 180 gram vinyl LP (MOVLP1695) in the UK and Europe.

-September 19-
Music On Vinyl releases **Mike Oldfield**'s album *Guitars* on 180 gram vinyl LP (MOVLP1694) in the UK and Europe.

-September 28-
Hurricane Matthew forms, a Category 5 Atlantic hurricane. **Mike Oldfield**'s home in Nassau, The Bahamas, is in the eventual path of the hurricane, during which he takes shelter.

-October 10-
Hurricane Matthew dissipates, leaving **Mike Oldfield** with limited internet service via his old satellite dish.

-November-
Mike Oldfield completes work on his album *Return To Ommadawn* at his home in Nassau, The Bahamas. When it comes time to deliver the album to Virgin EMI, his only option is via his satellite dish. The process of transferring the finished recording takes 15 hours.

-November 25-
Virgin Records re-issues **Mike Oldfield**'s album *Tubular Bells* in Europe on 180 gram vinyl 2xLP as part of their Back To Black series. This edition is mastered by Miles Showell at Abbey Roads Studios, London, England, using half-speed mastering.

Tubular Bells 180 gram vinyl 2xLP Back To Black Edition (0600753695036)
LP 1: *Tubular Bells* 180 gram vinyl (1973 Original Mix Remastered)
"Tubular Bells (Part One)" - 2009 Remaster
"Tubular Bells (Part Two)" - 2009 Remaster

LP 2: *Tubular Bells* 180 gram vinyl (2009 Stereo Mix)"
"Tubular Bells (Part One - 2009 Stereo Mix)"
"Tubular Bells (Part Two - 2009 Stereo Mix)"

Note: the labels on each LP are reversed, so each incorrectly lists the wrong mix.

-December 2-
Universal Records issues the following **Mike Oldfield** releases on LP in Europe.

2016 *Exposed* 2xLP (570 580-0)

2016 *Collaborations* LP (570 580-9)
"The Phaeacian Games" David Bedford
"An Extract from 'Star's End'" David Bedford
"The Rio Grande (Boxed Version)" David Bedford
"First Excursion"
"Argiers"
"Portsmouth"
"In Dulci Jubilo"

"Speak (Tho' You Only Say Farewell)" – a version 1926 Ray Morello & Horatio Nicholls song.

Note: This is the same *Collaborations* collection previously featured as part of the 1976 *Boxed* set. The LP is cut from the original master by Sean Magee at Abbey Road Studios, London, England.

-December 6-
In a promo interview posted to YouTube by On The Record UMG, **Mike Oldfield** discusses his career, *Return To Ommadawn* and his desire to record a fourth *Tubular Bells* album.

Return To Ommadawn

2017

-January 6-
In a New Year's message, **Mike Oldfield** says the plan for *Tubular Bells IV* is to have multitrack mixing via a "Super Advanced" music player, as well as a virtual reality component, in addition to high definition audio.

-January 23-
In an article published on this date in *The Quietus*, **Mike Oldfield** discusses *Return To Ommadawn* and says he is currently working on *Tubular Bells IV*.
"Tubular Bells IV: Introduction" – **Mike** says he has written the "introduction" music for the new album by this point.

-January 20-
Mike Oldfield releases his album *Return To Ommadawn* on Virgin EMI Records in Europe on CD, CD+DVD and LP.

Europe *Return To Ommadawn* CD (CDV 3166)
"Return To Ommadawn Pt. I"
"Return To Ommadawn Pt. II"

Europe *Return To Ommadawn* CD+DVD (CDVX3166)
CD: *Return To Ommadawn*
DVD: *Return To Ommadawn* DTS 5.1 Mix

Europe *Return To Ommadawn* LP (V 3166)
"Return To Ommadawn Pt. I"
"Return To Ommadawn Pt. II"

Note: Based on the earlier posted breakdown of the two parts, it would appear the final album aligns with the tracks as follows:

"Return To Ommadawn Pt. I"
00:00 - WhistleInt
01:20 - Tune 1
01:43 - EthnicFlute 1
01:58 - 2 Spanish
02:43 - Glock 1 Riff
03:14 - Glok 2 Eloc
03:44 - Glok 3 Mandolins
05:00 - EthnicFlute 2
05:15 - Tune 1 *2GT
05:30 - Not Happy
06:33 - BIG Tune
08:15 - Soft Tune
10:03 - Bolero
11:01 - Bolero Blues
11:52 - Glock 3 Blues Guitar
12:22 - WhistleMIX
12:52 - Africa 1
13:09 - CHANT 1
14:12 - AF PIANO
14:44 - AF QUIET
14:53 - AF ACOUSTICS

15:53 - AF BASS
16:09 - AF GIBSON SOLO
18:40 - CODA

"Return To Ommadawn Pt. II"
00:00 - INTRO
01:30 - Spanish Tune Acoustic
02:14 - Mandolins 1
02:43 - Spanish Tune 2
03:13 - Mandolins 2
03:29 - High Bridge 1
03:44 - Spanish Tune 3
04:14 - High Bridge 2
05:16 - Bodhrans
05:25 - Fast Tune 1
05:42 - Fast Tune Bridge 1
05:50 - Fast Tune 2
06:08 - Fast Tune Bridge 2
06:25 - Fast Tune Boogie 1
07:00 - Fast Tune Break
07:08 - Grand Tune 1
07:43 - Victory V 1
08:33 - Victory V 2
09:40 - Victory V 3
10:13 - Reef Intro
10:45 - REEF 1
11:32 - BASS SOLO
12:03 - HeavyFUZZ
13:03 - FUZZ TUNE 2
15:10 - AFRICA 2
16:09 - Big WhistleTune
16:17 - BWT END
16:27 - END TUNE
17:07 - CLIMAX ENDING
17:54 - JIG
18:54 - JIG 2

-February 14-
In an article published on this date in *Louder*, **Mike Oldfield** discusses *Return To Ommadawn* and says he is currently working on *Tubular Bells IV*.

-February 20-
In an article published on this date in *Tribune 242*, **Mike Oldfield** discusses his *Tubular Bells IV* project, noting he plans for it to include something like a multimedia component.

-February 22-
Wasabi Records / Transatlantic Records re-issues **The Sallyangie**'s album *Children Of The Sun* as a 2xCD Mini-LP reproduction set in Japan (WSBAC-0044). Track listing as follows:

CD 1:
"Strangers"
"Lady Mary"
"Children Of The Sun"
"A Lover For All Seasons"
"River Song"
"Banquet On The Water"
"Balloons"
"Midsummer Night's Happening"
"Love In Ice Crystals"

"Changing Colours"
"Chameleon"
"Milk Bottle"
"Murder Of The Children Of San Francisco"
"Strangers (Reprise)"

CD 2:
"Twilight"
"Song Of The Healer"
"Two Ships" – a cover of the 1968 Maria Dallas song.
"Colour Of The World"
"Children Of The Sun (Minus Intro)"

Also issued by Wasabi Records / Transatlantic Records in Japan is a 3" CD promo single of "Children Of The Sun" with purchase the 2xCD Mini-LP reproduction set at Disk Union Tokyo and on their online store.

3" CD single (WSBPROMO 017) promo:
"Children Of The Sun"

-June 9-
Mike Oldfield releases online (via Amazon and Spotify) *Mike Oldfield's Stream*.

Mike Oldfield's Stream
Digital single:
"Theme From Return To Ommadawn Pt. 1"
"Theme From Return To Ommadawn Pt. 2"

> "Theme From Return To Ommadawn Pt. 1" 4:10
> Written by Mike Oldfield
> Appears on: Mike Oldfield's Stream
> This track is made up of different segments of parts I and II of *Return To Ommadawn*, re-ordered and re-sequenced to make an overall excellent sampler of the album. Unlike previous edits of albums, like the "Now The Original Theme From 'The Exorcist'" re-edits, the two created for the stream release are cohesive and flow very well, standing on their own rather than sounding disjointed.
>
> "Theme From Return To Ommadawn Pt. 2" 4:25
> Written by Mike Oldfield
> Appears on: Mike Oldfield's Stream
> Like with "Return To Ommadawn Pt. I," this track is also made up of pieces from both parts of *Return To Ommadawn*, starting with the opening of part I and end with the finale of part II.

-Date Unknown-
Spotify uploads to their music streaming service **Mike Oldfield**'s album *Tubular Bells III*, track listing as follows:

Tubular Bells III Spotify Edition
"The Source Of Secrets"
"The Watchful Eye"
"Jewel In The Crown (Spotify Album Version)"
"Outcast"
"Serpent Dream"
"The Inner Child"
"Man In The Rain" Mike Oldfield Featuring Cara
"The Top Of The Morning"

"Moonwatch"
"Secrets"
"Far Above The Clouds"

> "Jewel In The Crown (Spotify Album Version)" 5:51
> Written by Mike Oldfield
> Appears on: Tubular Bells III (Spotify Edition)
> This version seems to have gone unnoticed by many. Rather than getting cut off at the 5:45 mark as heard on the standard album, this version continues on for a few more seconds, with the music fading out and more thunder rolling in. "Outcast" comes in as the thunder gets very quiet. It's not a major change, but it adds a lot of atmosphere and keeps the storm motif going on the album. I haven't seen this version on any other release so far, so maybe Spotify was sent the wrong master copy for their files.

Note: I'm not at all certain when this version first appeared on Spotify (or when it may disappear, as sometimes happens when licensing agreements run their course), because that information isn't available from the service, so I'm noting it here for lack of a better place.

AFTERWORD

Like with the first edition, which concluded partway into 2014, this updated Chronology draws to a close mid-2017. Mike at this time has reported that he is working on a fourth *Tubular Bells* project, and with the media promotion of *Return To Ommadawn* finished, things grow quiet for the next year. Mike has remained active with his Facebook group, but news about his recording work trickles to a halt. This is to be expected in his semi-retirement in The Bahamas, where he can work at his leisure in relative isolation.

So, like before, this book is as up-to-date as it can be, given the information available.

Patrick Lemieux, May 2018

My drama teacher and later good friend, John Sheridan, introduced me to Mike Oldfield's music in high school. We were setting up some audio gear and to test it we needed some music. This was the early '90s and he had a box of cassette tapes, things he'd transferred from his records. I looked at the selection and saw one labelled *Tubular Bells*. I said something like, "How about this?"

"*Tubular Bells?* Okay, but you may not like it."

A fair enough warning, but as it turned out I did like it!

This was also the era where many people were getting rid of their records and 45s and replacing them with CDs. Yard sales and flea markets in and around my hometown of Bowmanville almost always had a box or two of records, a dollar each, maybe even 50 cents; a price just right for a teenage with no paying job (I was too busy working plays at both my high school and local Drama Workshop). My parents, happy I was doing something productive with my nights and weekends, would spot me a few dollars every once in a while for fun and no small part of that money went to picking up these old records. It also helped that I wasn't an angst-ridden teen (well, not too much) so a lot of the Nirvana-era Grunge and Alternative didn't appeal to me. Working with adults in the Workshop, whose tastes were of the Classic Rock persuasion, I actually heard more of Zeppelin and The Who on average than I did of Pearl Jam. So, here were all of these records: Rush, Meat Loaf, Springsteen, T. Rex, Queen and of course Mike Oldfield. There was no internet to just download everything. I found *Tubular Bells* and *Ommadawn* after that fateful day when I first heard Oldfield. I transferred them to tape and took them everywhere, keeping them in regular rotation in my collection. Later, I found *Five Miles Out* and *Crises*, then *QE2* (man, how different are those albums from the earlier ones, huh? That was mind-blowing!).

Anyhow, in a lot of ways I've been writing this book in my mind ever since those heady days of first delving into Mike's work and each time a new album came out after that it was exciting. I watched Mike on TV during the Olympic Opening Ceremonies, wondering how many young viewers would now do as I did, seek out the man's work and hopefully be pleasantly surprised at what they find.

And for me, it's still going on. When I started actually researching this book, I found myself going down paths still new to me, like much of his work with Kevin Ayers And The Whole World and his many guest appearances. Some I'd heard about but never listened to before, while other things I didn't even know existed.

That's really why I wrote this book, because the adventure of discovering all his work, side projects and guest appearances needed a map. There's a good amount of information online now, but it's still in pieces. His autobiography and various other biographies focus on the story of the man himself, but the collective back catalogue of his work is still so vast and far-reaching. I wanted to put all that information and my own observations of it all into one place, as Adam and I had done with *The Queen Chronology*.

So, I hope you found this book detailed, informative and maybe even entertaining.

Patrick Lemieux, April 2014

Acknowledgements

I'd like to thank the following people for their support in the writing of this book:

Mom and Dad, for everything.
Tim, Mel, Emmet, Jill, Dave, Jack, Josephine, Mark & Liv, for always being there.
Tom Blake, my old friend.
Michael, Elyn and Willow, for hot meals and hang-outs in the man cave.
Adam Unger, someday we'll actually meet face to face.
Heidi Loney, for continued support and lunch meet-ups.

Also, York, for answering my questions.
Ron Betman & Richard Bogg for their expertise.
Yannick Dély, for his feedback and sharing some of his research.

And of course, thank you to Mike Oldfield for years of great music!

About The Author

Patrick Lemieux is a Canadian artist and writer who makes his home in Toronto, Ontario. He has exhibited his artwork in galleries and venues throughout North America. In addition writing Chronologies about Mike Oldfield, Rush, David Bowie, Barenaked Ladies and Queen (co-authored with Adam Unger), he has penned two novels, *The Prisoner Of Orchard Bend* and *The Murder Ballad Of Orchard Bend*, with the third book of the series forthcoming. You can follow him on Twitter @MadTheDJ and on Instagram @patricklemieuxartist

Bibliography:

Mike Oldfield, *Changeling: The Autobiography* (London, *Virgin Books Ltd*, 2007)
Chris Dewey (Editor), *Dark Star: The Official Mike Oldfield Magazine* (Issue 24 – May 2003)
Richard Newman, *The Making Of Mike Oldfield's Tubular Bells* (Cambridgeshire, *Music Maker Books*, 1993)
Mark Powell, *Tubular Bells 2009 liner notes* (United States, *Mercury Records Ltd*, 2009)
Mark Powell, *Walking The Hergest Ridge* (United States, *Mercury Records Ltd*, 2010)
Mark Powell, *Ommadawn 2010 liner notes* (United States, *Mercury Records Ltd*, 2010)
Mark Powell, *Incantations 2011 liner notes* (United States, *Mercury Records Ltd*, 2011)
Mark Powell, *Platinum 2012 liner notes* (United States, *Mercury Records Ltd*, 2012)
Mark Powell, *QE2 2012 liner notes* (United States, *Mercury Records Ltd*, 2012)
Mark Powell, *Five Miles Out 2013 liner notes* (United States, *Mercury Records Ltd*, 2013)
Mark Powell, *Crises 2013 liner notes* (United States, *Mercury Records Ltd*, 2013)
Mark Powell, *Discovery 2016 liner notes* (United States, *Mercury Records Ltd*, 2016)
Mark Powell, *The Killing Fields 2016 liner notes* (United States, *Mercury Records Ltd*, 2016)
Martin Kietly, *SAHB: The Tale Of The Sensational Alex Harvey Band* (England, *Neil Wilson Publishing*, 2004)
Michael Palin, *Diaries 1969-1979: The Python Years* (London, *Phoenix, Orion Books Ltd*, 2006)
Mark Jones, *The Virgin Discography: The 1970s* (Bristol, *The Record Press*, 2015)

Websites:
http://mikeoldfieldofficial.com The Official Mike Oldfield Site
http://tubular.net Tubular.Net – Open Mike Oldfield Website
http://www.argiers.com Argiers (Yes! Mike Oldfield) (webmaster Fèlix Marcader)
http://www.mikeoldfield.org Dark Star – The Mike Oldfield Magazine
http://calyx.perso.neuf.fr/bands/chrono/ayers.html Kevin Ayers Concerts - Calyx: The Canterbury Website
http://www.discogs.com Discogs
http://peel.wikia.com The John Peel Wiki
http://www.bbc.co.uk BBC Official Website
http://britishrockmemorabilia.blogspot.ca/2011/06/sensational-alex-harvey-band.html
                                                                    David Miller's Rock Scrapbook
http://www.45cat.com 45Cat
http://amarok.ommadawn.net Amarok – The Original Mike Oldfield Mailing List
http://www.dbennett.karoo.net Yet Another Mike Oldfield Web Site (webmaster David Bennett)
http://www.mike-oldfield.es Mike-Oldfield.es
http://www.mikeoldfield.it/ Mike Oldfield Fan Club Italiano (webmaster Roberto Tosi)
http://www.infernus.jawnet.pl/rare_footage_1970_-_2011_6_x_dvd-r-1.html Mike Oldfield Collection
http://www.philspalding.com Phil Spalding: Music & Mayhem

Articles:
http://www.backgroundmagazine.nl/CDreviews/SallyangieChildrenSun.html
http://www.soundonsound.com/sos/apr13/articles/classic-tracks-0413.htm

Copyright © 2018, Patrick Lemieux

Also From
Across The Board Books™
www.acrosstheboardbooks.ca

THE DAVID BOWIE CHRONOLOGY
VOLUME 1 1947 - 1974
By Patrick Lemieux

205 Pages
Non-Fiction
$25.99 US

From the time he left school to pursue a career in music, David Bowie was always working. After years of struggling with bands, releasing singles and a debut album, all of which failed to chart, success first came with "Space Oddity" in 1969. The 1972 album The Rise And Fall Of Ziggy Stardust And The Spiders From Mars made David Bowie a household name. This Chronology covers every aspect of David Bowie's recording career. It looks at his singles, albums and rarities. Demos, alternate versions, remixes and edits, side projects and his work with other artists such as Mott The Hoople and Lou Reed are all explored. The information is presented date by date in chronological order, accompanied by detailed descriptions of each song version, guest appearance, edit, non-album track and alternate version. The book also covers his tours and live appearances.

THE QUEEN CHRONOLOGY
SECOND EDITION
By Patrick Lemieux & Adam Unger

266 Pages
Non-Fiction
$27.99 US

The Queen Chronology is a comprehensive account of the studio recording and release history of Freddie Mercury, Brian May, John Deacon and Roger Taylor, who joined forces in 1971 as the classic line-up of the rock band Queen.

Years of extensive research have gone into the creation of the Chronology which covers the very beginnings of the band members' careers, their earliest songwriting efforts and recording sessions through the recording and releasing of Queen's 15 original studio albums with their classic line-up, to the present-day solo careers of Brian May and Roger Taylor.

THE BARENAKED LADIES CHRONOLOGY
By Patrick Lemieux

214 Pages
Non-Fiction
$24.99 US

Ed Robertson, Steven Page, Jim Creeggan, Andy Creeggan, Tyler Stewart and Kevin Hearn are the past and present members of a band which continues to captivate audience the world over after more than 25 years.

This Chronology covers every aspect of the band's recording careers both as Barenaked Ladies and beyond. It looks at the band's indie releases, studio and live albums, singles and collections. In 1991, the band released The Yellow Tape, the first indie demo release to go platinum in Canada. This was followed by a string of hits from their albums, which include *Gordon*, *Rock Spectacle* and *Stunt*.

THE RUSH CHRONOLOGY
By Patrick Lemieux

272 Pages
Non-Fiction
$27.99 US

The Rush Chronology is a comprehensive look at the recording and release history of Geddy Lee, Alex Lifeson, Neil Peart and John Rutsey, the past and present members of the Canadian rock band whose uncompromising career has spanned more than 40 years. This Chronology covers every aspect of the band members' recording careers. It looks at the band's singles, studio and live albums, rarities and collections. Pre-release live versions and works-in-progress, remixes and edits, side projects, solo albums and their many guest appearances on other artists' works are all explored. The information is presented date by date in chronological order, accompanied by detailed descriptions of each song version, guest appearance, the edits, remixes and works in progress. The book covers as well Rush's tours and live appearances. It's all here, in The Rush Chronology!

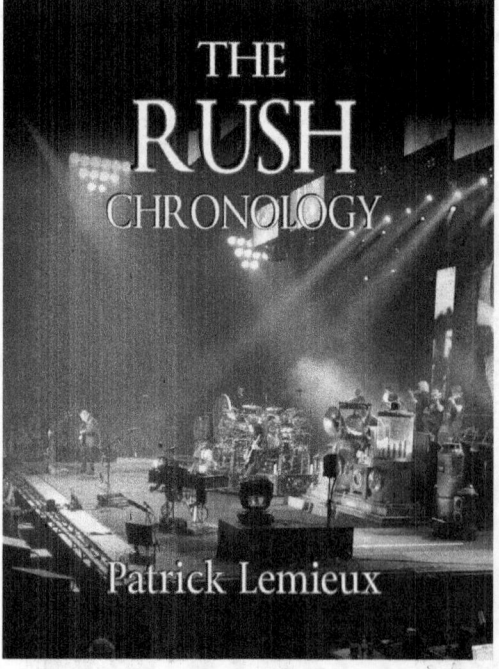

REVENGE OF THE DARK WITCH OF OZ
The Illustrated Screenplay
By Patrick Lemieux

115 Pages
Fiction
$19.99 US

Dorothy Gale finds herself trapped in the mysterious land of Oz and her presence threatens to re-ignite a war between magic and machines. The secret to getting home lies in the lost City of Emerald Light.

Revenge Of The Dark Witch Of Oz is a science fiction/fantasy adaptation of L. Frank Baum's The Wonderful Wizard Of Oz. The tale is told in an illustrated screenplay format, complete with paintings, detailed images, sketches and storyboards.

Play Of Light: The Art Of Patrick Lemieux
By Patrick Lemieux

100 Pages
Full Colour
Non-Fiction
$39.99 US

Journey through the theatre-inspired and story-driven work of Canadian artist and illustrator Patrick Lemieux. It is an exploration backstage, of the fantastical and of reality-based pieces, collected here for the first time, complete with notes, photos, sketches and paintings in full colour documenting his process. Experience the play of light!

THE PRISONER OF ORCHARD BEND

By Patrick Lemieux

240 Pages
Fiction
$19.99 US

In Orchard Bend, there is a gruesome discovery.

It threatens to reveal a secret lost in the history of the small town. There is one person, however, who would prefer such questions remain unanswered and buried in the past.

Who was Emery Dale?

Where did she come from?

What happened to her?

THE MURDER BALLAD OF ORCHARD BEND

By Patrick Lemieux

268 Pages
Fiction
$19.99 US

In this sequel to The Prisoner of Orchard Bend, a killer lurks in the shadows of a small town.

Two women, lost and separated by decades, must fight to survive as darkness closes in around each of them.

The past never really goes away.

Death is sometimes just the beginning.

www.ingramcontent.com/pod-product-compliance
Lightning Source LLC
Chambersburg PA
CBHW060246240426
43673CB00047B/1882